A Jonathan Edwards Reader

A Jonathan Edwards Reader

Edited by
John E. Smith, Harry S. Stout,
and Kenneth P. Minkema

Yale University Press
New Haven and London

Funds for editing *The Works of Jonathan Edwards* have been provided by
The Pew Charitable Trusts, Lilly Endowment, Inc., The Andrew W. Mellon
Foundation, and the Henry Luce Foundation, Inc.

First published as a Yale Nota Bene book in 2003.
Hardcover edition first published by Yale University Press in 1995.

For information about this and other Yale University Press publications,
please contact:

U.S. office	sales.press@yale.edu
Europe office	sales@yaleup.co.uk

Printed in the United States of America

Library of Congress Control Number: 2002114372

ISBN 978-0-300-09838-9 (pbk.)

A catalogue record for this book is available from the British Library.

Contents

Letters

Editors' Introduction

Jonathan Edwards (1703–58) is colonial America's greatest theologian and philosopher. During his life, he served as a teacher, pastor, revivalist, missionary, and college president, in the process establishing himself as one of the most influential churchmen in the Anglo-American religious world. Beyond his impact on his own times, his work and life continue to impress and enrich generations of students, who find in his writings keys to the past and their own present.

Edwards stands as the towering religious figure of an age when religion predominated. The Revolution of 1776 was not yet on the horizon at the time of his death in 1758, though the democratic and individualist ethos that would characterize it was in its birth throes. Edwards' world was to a great extent the one made by the Puritans. From them he inherited the supreme challenge of reconciling all of life and learning to the dictates of God's law as contained in Scripture and in nature. Yet, like all geniuses, he did not merely accept unquestioningly truths from the past. In the course of a career spanning four decades, he reshaped and refashioned a seventeenth-century Puritan worldview into something that was entirely different; something that, by enlightened eighteenth-century standards, was "modern" and uniquely his own.

In a Puritan culture not given to secular pursuits or belles lettres, theology necessarily stood as the artistic and intellectual means through which the culture's highest ideas were expressed. In his classic biography, *Jonathan Edwards* (1949), Perry Miller likened Edwards to an American Milton, whose medium was theology as surely as blank verse was Milton's. In the same heroic vein, but with a different model in mind, H. Richard Niebuhr dubbed Edwards "America's Augustine." Both were correct. Like Milton, Edwards sought a renewal in English-speaking religion that would do justice to the Reformation, which the German-speaking Martin Luther and his Protestant heirs had caused. And, as Augustine sought to reconcile piety with the highest forms of secular learning in the Latin world of logic and rhetoric, so Edwards sought to reconcile piety with the new scientific and philosophical age demarcated by Newton and Locke. However, neither the term "artist" nor "theologian," when taken alone, can capture the full measure of the man; it is only in the intersection of the two that we can begin to take in the extent of his achievements.

Like all creative geniuses, Edwards borrowed from much of the best of his time and place without being beholden to any. As Edwards' disciple Samuel Hopkins said of his mentor, "he called no man Father."[1] Besides the Reformers and Puritans, Edwards read widely in the great luminaries of the age, including Descartes, Newton, Locke, Malebranche, and Berkeley. From all these domains of knowledge he picked and borrowed, until, at a remarkably early age, he fashioned his own synthesis: an "Edwardsean" worldview whose conceptual and metaphorical pillars upheld traditional doctrines in compelling new ways.

Nothing short of the full Edwardsean corpus will finally do justice to the range and depth of Edwards' piety and erudition. To take one or two specimens as somehow representative of the whole is to risk caricature. Regrettably, countless schoolchildren have encountered Edwards only in a reprinting of *Sinners in the Hands of an Angry God* in their high school anthologies. That sermon, Perry Miller once quipped, did more to vilify Edwards' reputation than all of his critics combined. In order to appreciate fully Edwards' power and artistry, each individual composition must be viewed as an exquisitely fashioned jewel in a larger, albeit incomplete, crown. There is a massive coherence to Edwards that no single selection or essay can fully comprehend, and that only the whole can fully reveal.

To say that only the complete Edwards will do justice to his essential genius is to say quite a bit. Edwards was one of the most prolific of American authors before 1800. And unlike authors who did publish more, such as Cotton Mather, much of Edwards' work lay at the cutting edge of knowledge, inaccessible to earlier times. Numerous as his publications are, they stand alongside an equally prodigious cache of unpublished notebooks, sermons, personal writings, and letters, many of which have never been systematically studied or even transcribed. Only now, at the

---

1. Hopkins, *The Life and Character of the Late Reverend Mr. Jonathan Edwards* (Boston, 1765), p. 41.

dawn of the twenty-first century, is an all-encompassing edition of Edwards' published and unpublished writings nearing completion in the Yale edition of *The Works of Jonathan Edwards*, begun in 1953. Unlike earlier editions, virtually half of the Yale edition will feature manuscript sources never before published. When complete, it will unveil for the first time the full extent of Edwards' fecund mind.

Because the edition is not yet complete, and because it spans too many volumes to be useful in classroom applications, the members of the Edwards edition, together with Yale University Press, decided to issue a new and comprehensive selection of Edwards' public and private writings that would represent something of the breadth and depth of the larger corpus under our direction. The timing seems appropriate for two reasons. First, for all of his recognized importance, comprehensive selections of Edwards' works are rare. The finest early twentieth-century edition, by Clarence H. Faust and Thomas H. Johnson (1935), is out of print—not to mention outdated—so that there is virtually nothing available to guide the serious student into the labyrinth of Edwards studies. Second, it is only now that the Edwards edition is far enough into the corpus of Edwards' writings to gain a sense of what is truly representative in the voluminous notebooks, sermons, and letters stored chiefly in Yale's Beinecke Rare Book and Manuscript Library, but also in Andover Newton Theological School's Trask Library and in scattered archives throughout the world.

Considerable care has gone into the selection of documents for this volume. An initial questionnaire soliciting suggestions for an Edwards anthology was sent out from the editorial offices to teachers and scholars in the United States, Britain, Canada, and Australia. The response level was exceptionally high, as was the enthusiasm for a new anthology. When asked for particular suggestions, these respondents returned to the previously printed classics that rightly established Edwards' international reputation in his own lifetime and afterward. Foremost on their list were such standards as "The Mind," *Faithful Narrative*, *Religious Affections*, *Freedom of the Will*, and *The Nature of True Virtue*.

Although the teachers confirmed the enduring interest in Edwards the philosopher and the theologian, they were for the most part not aware of the subterranean Edwards, whose unpublished notes, sermons, and letters survived in abundance. This more private and personal Edwards was by no means a secret skeptic or cryptic agnostic, as some earlier biographers implied. But he was a *human* Edwards, whose humanity shone through in everything from quibbling over salary to home remedies for ailing children. For that more personal Edwards to be represented in the anthology, the edition's executive committee turned to associate editors and research editors, who had been working through these manuscripts, to make selections. As well, the committee asked editors of earlier volumes to select materials they had edited. Thus to a significant extent this anthology is a collaborative effort, going much beyond the three editors responsible for putting the volume together. The result is a volume brief enough for classroom use, but inclusive enough to reflect substantially the *whole* Edwards, public and personal. Such a view can never substitute for the whole, but it can, and in our view does, faithfully characterize the full outline of his remarkable life.

In presenting these selections to the reader, we have divided them into two major sections dealing, respectively, with Edwards' public, printed oeuvre and the sermons and treatises on which it rested, and his personal life as revealed in autobiographical writings, correspondence, and family papers.

The Public Edwards

The public Edwards represented in these selections follows an essentially chronological sequence. Edwards was born in East Windsor, Connecticut, on October 5, 1703, the only son of the Reverend Timothy Edwards and Esther Stoddard Edwards, daughter of the Reverend Solomon Stoddard, the magisterial "pope" of Northampton, Massachusetts. Edwards' parents invested all their hopes and energies for family fame in Jonathan, rigorously training him for a life in the clergy. A precocious lad, he entered Yale College in 1716 already possessed of an inquiring mind that knew no boundaries, scientific or literary. Along with his prodigious mind came a burning desire to be widely recognized as an "instrument" in the cause of his Christ.

Our first selections introduce Edwards the student. Graduating from Yale College in 1720, he went on to obtain a master's degree and then, during 1722 and 1723, his first pulpit, in a Presbyterian church in New York City. After a brief pastorate at Bolton, Connecticut, Edwards in 1724 assumed a two-year post as a tutor at Yale. These years were incredibly fruitful for him. In the essays from this period the reader will gain an appreciation of the profundity of his scientific and philosophical inquiry, as well as of the larger theological universe in which that inquiry always took place. In the "Spider Letter," written in 1723, we see Edwards the fledgling scientist astutely observant of the ways of a specie of flying spider, "resolving if possible to find out the mysteries of these their amazing works." Gleefully pursuing his experiment and, in the process, flexing the considerable powers of his developing mind, Edwards declares, "I discovered one wonder after another till I have been so happy as very frequently to see their whole manner of working." We see as well the metaphysical Edwards, discerning in the mysterious outfitting of the spider for flight an object lesson in "the wisdom of the Creator." Throughout his life Edwards retained this image of the spider, featuring it in his infamous *Sinners* sermon and wherever else the self-destructive paths of humans were imagined and portrayed.

For the more empirically minded students of the eighteenth century, natural science was to be pursued for its own sake. Edwards the student, however, encountered in plants or animals, physics or optics, the face of God. The twentieth-century literary scholar Vernon Parrington regretted the "anachronism" of Edwards and mourned the loss of a potentially great scientist to religion.[2] But Parrington missed the point. The young Edwards' explorations of the natural, material world were, from the start, merely entry points to a larger, invisible world. In his notes toward the treatises "Of Being" and "The Mind," not published until after his death, Edwards displayed the brilliant philosophical arguments that would fix his reputation. Like the great Irish philosopher George Berkeley, Ed-

2. Vernon Parrington, *Main Currents of the American Mind* (3 vols. New York, Harcourt, Brace, 1927; rep. 1930), *1*, 152–63.

wards here defines spirit as true substance and existence as a divine emanation from the mind of God. But unlike Berkeley, Edwards resists a
thoroughgoing doubt of the "external world," insisting that "things are
where they seem to be." At the other extreme, in opposition to Descartes,
Hobbes, and others who posited the separate autonomous existence of
matter, Edwards insisted on the priority of God's consciousness upholding all. So vast was Edwards' sense of divine sovereignty, that if God's
consciousness ceased even for a moment, the universe itself would cease to
be. By thus mediating between Berkeley on the one hand and Locke,
Descartes, and Hobbes on the other, the young Edwards hoped to rescue
Christianity from the deadweight of rationalism and the paralyzing iner-
tia of skepticism.

The selections from "Of Being" and "The Mind" are remarkable not
only for displaying the young Edwards' depth of learning, but also for
their permanence in his thought. Like Augustine and Calvin, Edwards hit
on fundamental insights at a preternaturally early age and never repudi-
ated them. Instead he complicated, extended, and applied these first
principles for the remainder of his life and ministry.

Many selections reveal Edwards to be deeply concerned with and disturbed by the reality of sin, but in "Beauty of the World," we see another
side: his preoccupation with beauty, excellence, and the goodness of creation. In this essay, written in 1725, we see an ecstatic view of the material
world and nature that reflects the mystical side of Edwards. In nature,
physics, and mathematics Edwards perceives a beauty whose essence lay
in the way it "shadowed forth" the divine Creator. All reality, he concludes, is but the "shadows of being," really an analogy to the divine truth
and being of God. All of created reality is permeated with clues to divine
truths, if we can but remove the scales from our eyes and see them. This,
too, is a theme that the adult Edwards could not abandon, and that would
issue in "Images of Divine Things." Representative entries from this
notebook, begun only three years after "Beauty of the World," illustrate
Edwards' theory of typology, which was the biblical discipline of detect-
ing parallels between Old Testament persons and events (types) and their
New Testament counterparts or fulfillments (anti-types). Edwards, how-

ever, expanded typology beyond the confines of Scripture into nature, history, and human experience, thereby anticipating the Transcendentalists of nineteenth-century New England.

In the notes on "The Mind," Edwards moved beyond strictly philosophical reflections in ontology and epistemology to a consideration of aesthetics and the structure of beauty. To illustrate (simple) "equality" and (complex) "proportion," Edwards relied on mathematics and the relationship between shapes and numbers. Equality, harmony, ratio, and proportion all implied relationship, which relationship proved to be the key both to nature and to grace. Edwards believed that the same tendency of the human mind to order things in certain ways so that they appear more in relation to each other was inherited from the Creator, and expressed the same inclination of godly souls to their Maker. Thus the similarity of the saints to Christ defined their excellency, and the contrariness of sinners to Christ their deformity. From philosophy and aesthetics Edwards journeyed to the farthest reaches of theology, using his reciprocal insights to explore the most hidden and central of Christian doctrines, the Trinity. Like a composer of music building toward a crescendo, Edwards moves from nature and grace to the Deity itself in a remarkable speculation on the innermost meaning of the Trinity. No harmony is possible with only one, and no proportion is possible with only two; only with three are both harmony and proportion possible and, indeed, perfectly embodied in the triune God.

Beginning in his youth, and continuing regularly until the year of his death, Edwards kept a series of topically organized notebooks that have no equal in the Puritan era. For comparability one must look ahead to the philosophical and literary journals of Ralph Waldo Emerson. In both cases, the documents served as the storehouse of genius from which all the polished orations and essays would flow. In the case of Edwards' notebooks, or "Miscellanies," understanding the exact nature of the interconnections between notebook and treatise has been hampered by the inability to date the various entries. Only in the past generation, through the Herculean efforts of "Miscellanies" editor Thomas A. Schafer, has a chronology been established by means of sophisticated ink, paper, and content analysis.[3] This, in turn, has paved the way for dating many other of Edwards' manuscripts.

Topics in the "Miscellanies" run the gamut of Edwards' philosophical and theological interests, but in choosing entries for the anthology, the editors have sought subjects not reflected in other selections. Several entries on the "end of creation" (nos. f, gg, kk, 3, 106) represent Edwards' lifelong struggle with the time-honored theological issue of whether the triune God created the universe for the happiness of "intelligent creatures" or for God's own glory. In these entries, as in the posthumously published dissertation *The End for Which God Created the World* (1765), Edwards characteristically hits upon his own solution to this problem. Our ultimate happiness is not in ourselves but in God and religious devotion to God, and therefore "religion is the very business, the noble business of intelligent beings." In this way, our happiness and God's glory become one and the same. Thus for Edwards "the pleasure of religion" (no. x) is far above the pleasures of "worldly enjoyments" because of its divine object. In a related vein is no. 314, in which Edwards connects God's bestowing of free grace and his "propensity . . . to communicate goodness." But there is also a dark, and to many modern readers a harsh, side to this story. In no. 279, Edwards describes the miserable fate of those who are not the subjects of grace. The sight of the damned in hell will excite not pity but rather love, joy, and happiness in the saints and angels.

Edwards' notebook entries provide an index not only to his own thought but also to the assumptions and attitudes of his day. "Miscellanies" no. 350 argues the necessity of divine revelation, or the recorded Word of God. Humankind, Edwards believes, could never survive by relying on its own reason and experience; history shows that those places without benefit of revelation were sunk in "gross darkness and brutal stupidity." In "Miscellanies" no. 37, he likens faith to marriage and reveals in this comparison insights into the gender roles that then defined the institution of marriage. Similarly, in no. 241, Edwards compares the New Birth, or regeneration, to "the vivification of the fetus in the womb" in that

3. See the Editor's Introduction to *The Works of Jonathan Edwards, 13, The Miscellanies, Entry Nos. a–500,* ed. Thomas A. Schafer (New Haven, Yale Univ. Press, 1994).

both are "exceeding gradual." It is only at a certain unknown moment after conception that "an immortal spirit begins to exist . . . by God's appointment." No. 40 indicates the position of authority that was accorded to ministers in the hierarchical, deferential society in which Edwards lived. But he reveals his own ambitious nature when he anticipates rising above the influence of "other ministers": "If it was plain to all the world of Christians that I was under the infallible guidance of Christ," he muses, "then I should have power in all the world."

Beginning during his student days and accelerating rapidly in his early pastorate, Edwards complemented his study of nature and philosophy with an even more rigorous study of Scripture and revelation.[4] One central concern, which has preoccupied many Christian interpreters, was the book of Revelation and its prophecies of the end times. In a selection from his "Notes on the Apocalypse," begun in 1722 at roughly the same time he began "The Mind," Edwards identifies the destruction of "Babylon" or the "Antichrist" with the defeat of the Roman Catholic Church. Here as elsewhere we see ways in which Edwards was very much a product of his time. Enmities between Catholics and Protestants wrought by the Reformation enveloped Europe and the New World, and Edwards, like his Protestant peers, did not hesitate to identify the papacy with the greatest enemies of the "true" church. The selection given here is notable for the stridency of its language, the undisguised hatred for the Catholic Church, and the anticipation of its demise. Specifically, Edwards interprets the prophecies of Revelation to apply to the "drying up or diminishing" of the "temporal supplies" of the "Church of Rome" through the decline of its main sources of revenue, Spain and France. Later, when war with France would erupt in the American colonies, Edwards would not hesitate to locate that war—and the cause of British America—as a central chapter in the coming of the millennium.

One of Edwards' most influential works, and the one that propelled him to the international fame that he deliberately sought from an early age, was the *Faithful Narrative of the Surprising Work of God* (1737), an

4. See the Editor's Introduction to *The Works of Jonathan Edwards, 5, Apocalyptic Writings*, ed. Stephen J. Stein (New Haven, Yale Univ. Press, 1977).

account of the awakening that occurred in Northampton under his ministry in 1734 and 1735. This document, which combined Edwards' skills as a
scientific observer with his abilities as a religious psychologist, provided
an empirical model for other ministers throughout the New World and
was translated into many languages for use among European revivalists.
In the excerpted version presented here, Edwards starts by sketching the
history of the town, its ministers, and the beginnings of the awakening
among the youth in late 1733. "Presently upon this," Edwards writes, "a
great and earnest concern about the great things of religion and the eternal
world became universal in all parts of the town, and among persons of all
degrees and all ages; the noise amongst the dry bones waxed louder and
louder." Edwards himself estimates that "more than 300 souls were savingly brought home to Christ." Next, he enters into a lengthy and detailed
exploration of the subjects of conversion, noting that "here there is a vast
variety, perhaps as manifold as the subjects of the operation; but yet in
many things there is a great analogy." Moving from the general to the
specific, Edwards then provides case studies of actual converts; the account given here is that of Abigail Hutchinson.

In contrast to the optimism and hope of the *Narrative* as a whole,
Edwards must end on a somber note. Several individuals, swept away by
emotional fervor, became despondent; one person, Edwards' own uncle,
Joseph Hawley, put "an end to his own life, by cutting his throat." Though
Edwards included this postscript to warn his fellow revivalists against the
danger of "melancholy," it forecast the disillusionment that Edwards
would experience. Gradually he came to see that precious few of the
supposed "converts" persisted in their newfound convictions, a fact that
would lead him to reconsider the nature of conversion and that would
result finally in his masterly commentaries on the revivals, especially
Religious Affections.

The central vehicle for revivalism was pulpit oratory, and for virtually
his entire adult life Edwards was first and foremost a preacher. The
efflorescence of scientific, philosophical, and, later, psychological rumina-
tion took place within a context of weekly preaching on the Word. Few of
these sermons were published in Edwards' lifetime or since, but as ser-

mons editor Wilson H. Kimnach has convincingly demonstrated,[5] they undergirded almost all of his philosophical work and lent that work much of its urgency. Ultimately, Edwards' ideas, visions, and insights were applied to the central task of converting hardened sinners in the pews from love of self and self-righteousness to disinterested love of God and divine righteousness.

So vast is Edwards' surviving unpublished sermon corpus (more than 1,200 manuscript sermons) that a separate sermon anthology is presently in preparation. For this general anthology we have chosen and grouped together, irrespective of chronology, three selections notable for their historical impact and for their skillful composition and language. These sermons present Edwards' depiction of the human problem—its sinful condition—and of God's solution on both the individual and cosmic levels.

If *Sinners in the Hands of an Angry God* distorts the larger issue when taken alone, it clearly belongs in any representation of Edwards' work for the sheer power of its imagery. Who can resist trembling before the frightening image of sinners dangled by a vengeful God like loathsome spiders over the flames, or of treading on a paper-thin, rotting canvas, not knowing at what moment you might plunge into the abyss and face a just and judging God? The words echo through time in their haunting description of the plight of the damned. In his measured cadence, Edwards says: "The wrath of God burns against them, their damnation don't slumber, the pit is prepared, the fire is made ready, the furnace is now hot, ready to receive them, the flames do now rage and glow. The glittering sword is whet, and held over them, and the pit hath opened her mouth under them."

Beyond the imagery, the focus on sin is important as a counter to humankind's optimistic excesses. It was the sense of sin, however dark and hideous, that drew such eminent twentieth-century neo-orthodox scholars as the brothers Reinhold Niebuhr and H. Richard Niebuhr to

5. See the Editor's Introduction to *The Works of Jonathan Edwards, 10, Sermons and Discourses, 1720–1723*, ed. Wilson H. Kimnach (New Haven, Yale Univ. Press, 1992).

Edwards. Speaking in Stockbridge, Massachusetts, at a commemoration in 1958 of the bicentennial of Edwards' death, H. Richard Niebuhr recognized how, in the horrific aftermath of World War II, "we have changed our minds about the truth of many things Edwards said. No, rather, our minds have been changed by what has happened to us in our history. We have seen evil somewhat as he saw it, not because we desired to see it, but because it thrust itself upon us."[6] It was this same sense that drew self-confessed "atheists" like Perry Miller to a lifelong fascination with Edwards. In the foreword to his biography, Miller confessed:

> [Edwards] repays study because, while he speaks from a primitive religious conception which often seems hopelessly out of touch with even his own day, yet at the same time he speaks from an insight into science and psychology so much ahead of his time that our own can hardly be said to have caught up with him. Though he had followers, he was not the sort of artist who really can found a "school." He is unique, an aboriginal and monolithic power, with nothing of that humanity which opens every heart to Franklin; but he is a reminder that, although our civilization has chosen to wander in the more genial meadows to which Franklin beckoned it, there come periods, either through disaster or through self-knowledge, when applied science and Benjamin Franklin's *The Way of Wealth* seem not a sufficient philosophy of national life.[7]

As important as *Sinners* is, however, it cannot stand alone. Enveloping it is a cosmic optimism so inclusive that it binds individuals and planets into a universe of ultimate judgment and redemption. Even in *Sinners*, the reader discovers that all is not lost. The pessimism of sin and an angry God is overcome by the comforting hope of salvation through a triumphant, loving Savior. Whenever Edwards preached terror, it was part of a larger campaign to turn sinners from their disastrous path and to the rightful object of their affections, Jesus Christ. In *A Divine and Supernatural Light*, published in 1734, the other half of Edwards the preacher is

6. H. Richard Niebuhr, "The Anachronism of Jonathan Edwards," unpub. transcript (courtesy of Richard R. Niebuhr), p. 15.

7. Perry Miller, *Jonathan Edwards* (New York, Sloan, 1949), p. xii.

revealed: the one preoccupied with the dazzling vision of God's love and grace made manifest on the cross, and supernaturally conferred to the souls of humankind by a "new sense" and an "indwelling principle" that makes all things new.

If *A Divine and Supernatural Light* shows the divine solution to the human predicament on an individual level, the next sermon registers Edwards' broader vision of salvation. In the sermons from *A History of the Work of Redemption* (preached as a lengthy series of sermons in 1739 but published posthumously), Edwards takes the plan of salvation to a cosmic level, showing the trinitarian genius of redemption in the covenantal interworkings of the three persons of the Trinity.[8] God's righteousness, Edwards states, consists in God's everlasting "faithfulness in fulfilling his covenant promises to his church, or his faithfulness towards his church and people in bestowing the benefits of the covenant of grace upon them." That trinitarian genius, and the plan of redemption from which it grows, separated all of human creation into the elect and the reprobate and, by extension, organized all of human history from Adam's original sin to a final state in which history is subsumed in eternity.

Edwards and his Northampton church also participated in the famous revival during the early 1740s, popularly known as the Great Awakening. Though *Religious Affections* appeared too late to have any influence on the revivals themselves—two years before its publication in 1746, Edwards declared the awakenings "dead"—it still stands as the most penetrating interpretation that exists concerning the *special* work of the divine Spirit in New England during Edwards' time. Here Edwards argued against both the excesses and aberrations in the revivals as well as the intellectualist opponents of "heart religion." Affections are essential to religion, he thought, but they must be tested. For that purpose, he proposed a set of twelve "signs" whereby true piety can be distinguished from false.

The work is divided into three parts: the first sets forth the nature of affections and shows their central importance for religion; the second has to do with what Edwards called "negative" signs or factors present in the

---

8. See *The Works of Jonathan Edwards, 9, A History of the Work of Redemption,* ed. John F. Wilson (New Haven, Yale Univ. Press, 1989).

experiences of the revivals which he regarded as unreliable criteria for judging whether affections are gracious or not; and the third part describes the positive signs distinctive of the holy affections, marks of the indwelling of the Holy Spirit in the person having true Christian faith. "Affections" is Edwards' word for the biblical "fruits of the Spirit"—love, faith, joy, hope, gratitude—and he was at pains to describe them accurately and, in so doing, to distinguish them from *passions*, which he saw as violent, as overpowering the mind so as to leave it "less in its own command." The soul, according to Edwards, has two faculties. One is the ability to perceive and judge the natures of things and is called "understanding." The other faculty is the capacity to pass beyond the spectator's neutral stance and be inclined to accept or reject, like or dislike, what we perceive. This faculty he calls "will" when overt action is involved, and "heart" when the inclination is in the mind, as, for example, the perception of the beauty of holiness. Affections are, for him, the "more vigorous and sensible exercises" of this second faculty.

We see here one result of Edwards' having studied John Locke's *Essay Concerning Human Understanding*, in which a distinction was drawn between having "a merely notional understanding" about something and having "a sense of" the object of attention. Thus, in one of Edwards' favorite examples, one can have a notional understanding that honey is sweet, but only those who have tasted the honey can have a sense of what that sweetness means. Important as correct doctrine was for Edwards, if it remains purely notional and is unaccompanied by affections, it is futile.

One must guard against supposing that there is an opposition between understanding and affections, the "head" and the "heart," because—and this is Edwards' original contribution—gracious affections are "raised" *only* when the person has a "spiritual understanding" of the true nature of that to which she or he is responding. A proper love to God, the most basic of all affections, must be rooted in the person's perception of the supreme amiability, holiness, and beauty that God alone possesses. For Edwards, that is having a "sense of" divine love.

Part II of *Religious Affections* concerns certain features of the revivals which Edwards took to be unreliable criteria for judging the graciousness of affections. He aimed to "test the spirits," or to separate the tares from the wheat, and he was fully aware of the excesses and corruptions in many revival experiences. Thus it is no sure sign that affections are genuine because they are raised very high, or have effects on the body (such as groaning, weeping, or writhing), or come with texts of Scripture remarkably brought to mind, or follow each other in a *certain order*—for example, that joys and comforts come after convictions of conscience. Edwards from his earliest days was intensely critical of the "morphology of conversion." That term, coined by Edmund S. Morgan to describe the Puritan sense of discrete stages on the road to salvation,[9] fits neither Edwards' experience nor his theology. He repeatedly denied that such an idea is to be found in the Bible. The importance of the entire discussion in Part II is that Edwards was defusing the arguments advanced by the opponents of the revivals—he admitted the existence of aberrations and then claimed that they are unreliable criteria. How astute he was in this regard is seen in the fact that Charles Chauncy, a senior minister in Boston and the most powerful critic of revivalism, cited against it most of the features that Edwards described as spurious and irrelevant criteria for judgment.

Part III speaks for itself as Edwards' portrait of the visible saints, the persons who show throughout an entire course of life the signs of gracious affections—love to God, to Christ, and to neighbors. In considering these signs, the reader will do well to bear in mind two essential points: first, that the signs were meant for self-examination, that is, no one was to use them to judge the sincerity of another; and second, that a special priority is given to the last sign—the evidence of *holy practice* as a public manifestation of the state of heart—of which Edwards was fond of saying, "'Tis a great deal easier to get 'em to talk like saints than to get 'em to act like saints."

As Northampton's pastor, Edwards was responsible for maintaining church discipline as a means of promoting Christian behavior among his flock. His efforts to be the community's moral regulator led, in 1744, to the famous Bad Book Case, brought on when a group of young men, many of them the children of influential parents, were caught reading illustrated

9. Edmund S. Morgan, *Visible Saints: The History of a Puritan Idea* (New York, New York Univ. Press, 1963).

books on midwifery for prurient reasons and using them to taunt young women in Northampton. Angered by their behavior, Edwards initiated disciplinary hearings against the youths. Unfortunately, in his zeal he failed to discriminate between the innocent and the guilty, thus incurring the anger of a number of implicated families and other influential members of the community, who already chafed under his pronouncements against materialism and pride. During the hearings that followed, Edwards drew up a collection of testimonies against the chief culprits, Oliver Warner and Timothy and Simeon Root, as well as a subsequent document describing the young men's irreverent behavior on the day that the disciplinary council was meeting. Both documents are printed here. The second contains especially earthy, derogatory, and anti-authoritarian comments ("I won't worship a wig") and demonstrates Edwards' waning influence on his Northampton parishioners, even as his international reputation was growing. Among the most alienated were those same young people who in the revivals several years earlier had constituted the bulk of the converted. Such a development only deepened Edwards' disillusionment about the effects of the revivals in Northampton and further drove a wedge between him and his congregation.

Edwards' disputes with his congregation did not end with the Bad Book Case. Instead, they escalated steadily through the 1740s, compounded, in Edwards' view, by irreligious members brought into the church under Stoddard's open admission policies, which Edwards had followed with increasing reluctance. In response to both doctrinal and practical exigencies, Edwards sought to impose stiffer requirements that would restrict access to church membership and the sacraments. This proposal departed radically from Stoddard and served as a cause around which Edwards' enemies could rally. In 1748, Edwards refused to admit an applicant without "a profession of the things wherein godliness consists," and the battle was met. In response to a request from the church, Edwards published *An Humble Inquiry*, both defending his innovations and criticizing his grandfather's views of visible sainthood. But the issue could never be resolved; pastor and congregation had become too estranged. On June 22, 1750, a council of ministers and delegates from nine churches recommended immediate separation of Edwards from his congregation.

Over the protests of a loyal minority, the church acted on the council's recommendation, and on July 2, 1750, Edwards preached his *Farewell Sermon*. The irony of Jonathan Edwards, the internationally revered theologian, being summarily dismissed by his own congregation offers compelling testimony to the power of the pew in Congregational New England and to the changes that were occurring in colonial American society.

From Northampton, Edwards settled in Stockbridge, Massachusetts, as pastor of the local church and missionary to Mahican and Mohawk Indians. His ministry to the Indians was sincere and far more serious than most earlier historians have conceded, but in practical terms it also allowed much more time for extended reflection and composition on issues of faith that were first confronted in his "Miscellanies" and sermons. Between 1754 and his death in 1758, he would write and publish the major treatises on which his philosophical reputation would be confirmed for ages to come.

In approaching Edwards' later doctrinal treatises—*Freedom of the Will* (1754), *Original Sin* (1758), and *The Nature of True Virtue* (1765)—the reader should bear in mind two important features of these works. The first is that they are tightly constructed discourses weaving together philosophical analysis and argument on the one side and biblical evidence and experience on the other. Selecting from them has its hazards, but we have sought to preserve the integrity of Edwards' arguments and to limit the biblical examples when their point has become sufficiently clear. The second feature of these works is their involvement in theological and philosophical controversies and the polemical tone set by Edwards' pointed attacks on the writings of particular opponents. The issues, for the most part, concern anti-Calvinist arguments as well as Edwards' attempts to refute them, most notably in *Freedom of the Will* and *Original Sin*, but present to a degree in *True Virtue*, where he raises critical questions about the "moral sense" advocated by Scottish philosopher Francis Hutcheson, by which Hutcheson meant a tendency rooted in human nature issuing in benevolence to humankind. As might be expected, Edwards was not persuaded by this optimistic view, but he was even more opposed to the idea that true virtue can have for its central object the public or humankind with no reference to God whatever. In all cases,

Edwards' own views emerge both through his positive statements and through the criticism of the beliefs held by his opponents.

Since the reader is presented with selected portions of all these works, it will be helpful to have in each case an indication of the main topics discussed and the organization of the work as a whole.

Freedom of the Will was published in 1754 and represents Edwards' comprehensive attempt to refute Arminianism, a position named after the Dutch theologian Jacobus Arminius (1560–1609). Since the term "Arminianism" was often used quite broadly to denote a number of doctrines that stood opposed to Calvinism, let us take note of the theses posed by Arminius which were the direct object of Edwards' attack. Chief among them are that God's sovereignty and human freedom are not incompatible, that Christ's death secured universal atonement for all sinners and was not limited simply to the elect, and that a regenerated person can freely choose what is right. For Edwards, such teachings represented all that was wrong with the "fashionable" schemes of divinity that were then on the rise, for they compromised the absolute sovereignty of God and the need for Christ's incarnation and sacrifice. As such, they were to be opposed at all costs.

Freedom of the Will is divided into four parts. The first deals with terminology, the nature and determination of the will, the meaning of necessity, impossibility, and contingency, the distinction between natural and moral necessity, and the nature of moral agency and liberty. The second is a consideration of whether there is or ever could be a freedom of self-determination, which the Arminians regard as essential for the assigning of praise or blame. The third is an analysis, in relation to the arguments of his opponents, of divine agency as it concerns human beings and the world. In a conclusion, Edwards seeks to anticipate the reception the work will receive. It is interesting to note, with respect to the basic argument of the work, that Edwards began by saying, in agreement with Locke, that to consider the freedom of the "will" is an issue badly posed, because the essential question is the freedom of the *person* or the self as a whole. Edwards nevertheless changed the emphasis largely because the Arminian position was focused on the freedom of the will and thus suited his purposes very well.

In order to sharpen his discussion, Edwards attacked the expressed views of three writers, very different in character from each other, but generally recognized as upholders of anti-Calvinist doctrines: Thomas Chubb (1679–1746), Daniel Whitby (1638–1726), and Isaac Watts (1674–1748). Chubb, a sometime chandler's aide and glove maker, became quite well known through his writings on theological and philosophical subjects. Though a Christian and a churchgoer, Chubb was an avowed Deist who had criticized trinitarianism and stoutly maintained a belief in free will—the object of Edwards' attack. Whitby was a clergyman in the Church of England who enjoyed early notoriety through his tracts attacking the Church of Rome, but later wrote an influential treatise on five theological points with a ten-line title that Edwards shortened to *The Discourse on the Five Points*. The majority of Edwards' references to this *Discourse* are to Point IV, "The Liberty of the Will in a State of Trial and Probation." Isaac Watts, a dissenter in Edwards' own tradition, is best known for the many familiar hymns he wrote, but he was also the author of several theological works. Edwards never refers to Watts by name, but only as "the author of an Essay on the Freedom of Will in God and the Creatures."

Although *Freedom of the Will* is a long, subtle, and demanding work, Edwards very helpfully singled out in his conclusion the central contention that lay behind it. "The decision," he wrote, "of most of the points in controversy between Calvinists and Arminians, depends on the determination of this grand article concerning *the freedom of the will, requisite to moral agency.*" He believed that if he could show the falsity of the idea of a self-determining will, he would have succeeded in undermining the entire position. His reason for so believing was that he saw *all* the Arminians' errors as stemming from a denial of the sovereignty of God. They allowed *secondary* causes that operated in the creation apart from the divine will. The refusal of the Arminians to acknowledge the total corruption of the human creature, their rejection of efficacious and irresistible grace, their claim that the ascription of praise and blame requires the freedom of self-determination, and their consequent belief that true virtue cannot be wrought in the heart by the power of another—that is, God—all depend on their doctrine of the self-determining will. Hence, although the story is long in the telling, Edwards believed that the destruction of this idea of freedom accomplishes at one stroke the destruction of Arminianism.

Basic to Edwards' view is the distinction between *natural* and *moral* necessity. The former has to do with the necessary cause-and-effect relation between things (for example, things fall downward if unsupported), and the latter concerns the necessary connection between moral causes—strength of inclinations or motives—and consequent behavior. For Edwards, the necessity is the same in both cases; the difference is found in the nature of the terms. His main contention against the Arminians is that there is no such incompatability as they claim between moral necessity and freedom, since freedom means "liberty" or the opportunity to do as one pleases in the absence of any hindrance. Edwards is, of course, assuming that this is the meaning of liberty in "common speech," and he takes advantage at this point of the ambiguity previously noted about whether the issue is the freedom of the *person* or the freedom of the *will* to insist on the former, declaring that liberty belongs to the person and *not* to the will. Accordingly, he can claim that the notion of a self-determining *will* is incoherent because it is supposed to be independent of any prior conditions, and this leads to an infinite regress: before any free act, there must be another free act and so on, and in order to stop the regress, there must be a first act that is not free. But if this is so, no subsequent act can be free. Here we have the basic contention of the entire treatise, and for Edwards it was enough to overcome the Arminian position.

Original Sin was published in 1758 after Edwards' death in that same year. It is announced on the title page that the work is a "Reply to the Objections and Arguings of Dr. John Taylor, in His Book, Intitled 'The Scripture Doctrine of Original Sin.'" Rev. John Taylor of Norwich was a sometime Presbyterian and a Hebrew scholar of note. In his discussion of the doctrine of original sin he put great emphasis on the "Scriptural" basis for his view, and this was no doubt an added incentive for Edwards, since he set great store by his own knowledge of the Bible and his skill in exegesis. Edwards concentrated on this work because it was a widely recognized presentation of the anti-Calvinist position; it also provided him with arguments he could cite without having to construe an Arminian position of his own. Curiously enough, however, Edwards says in his

Preface that his discussion is "intended not merely" as a reply to any particular book written against the doctrine, but is a "general defense" of the doctrine itself. In view of the "not merely," we can only suppose that the book was meant to serve both ends.

Original Sin is another four-part treatise. Part I is a consideration of the evidence for the human propensity to wickedness, gathered through observation and experience, together with the testimony of Scripture. Part II is given over to Edwards' thoughts on particular texts of Scripture—notably the first three chapters of Genesis and other Old Testament books, and passages from the Gospel of John and chapters 3, 5, and 7 in Romans—which to Edwards' mind prove the doctrine of original sin. Part III has to do with the connection between redemption by Christ and original sin. Edwards ends in his usual manner in Part Four, by answering anticipated objections. The brief conclusion gives Edwards an opportunity to take note of certain "artful methods" used by his opponents for the purpose of prejudicing readers against the doctrine he was defending.

The doctrine of original sin, for Edwards, encompasses two basic ideas that are so closely connected that proving one at the same time establishes the other. The first is the "*innate sinful depravity of the heart*," and the second is the *imputation* of Adam's first sin to his posterity, which now stands under divine judgment. With respect to the first idea, it is important to notice that Edwards put great emphasis on the fact of tendency or disposition, sometimes called "propensity," by which he meant the detection of what is constant and general in the world of nature and the behavior of human beings. Such a tendency, he claimed, becomes more evident when the same effect continues to manifest itself throughout a great variety of circumstances and is not thwarted by opposing factors. In his view, all experience confirms the tendency of the human creature toward evil, and in calling it "innate" he meant that we are to consider this tendency without the *interposition of divine grace* which served to mitigate its consequences. Moreover, he argued, God's intervention, which is admitted by all parties to the debate, would not have been necessary were it not for our evil disposition.

The emphasis on tendency is one of Edwards' original contributions to the discussion. His point is that there is far more evil in the world than can be explained by considering sinful acts one at a time. The tendency, the disposition of the heart, to sin points to *sin* as a prevalent condition in the world as distinct from *sins* or particular acts of misconduct. "A notion of a stated tendency or fixed propensity," Edwards writes, "is not obtained by observing only a single event." And in assigning this tendency to the human creature, Edwards was denying the view that the propensity toward evil is not in human nature but must be put down to the general constitution of the world.

The imputation of Adam's sin to his posterity, what it means and, especially, whether it means that God is unjust, is an old theological problem. Edwards' proposed resolution of it is both original and brilliant. The central idea is actually a philosophical one and concerns Edwards' contention that there are real *kinds* in the world—including human*kind* —as over against the main thesis of Nominalism that only individuals exist and that kinds are merely human-made conveniences if not actually fictions. Edwards' primary point is that God always dealt with Adam not as an isolated individual but as *one* with his posterity. The one who deals with the root of the tree also deals with the *individual* branches, "as if they had been existing in their root." Here Edwards is applying to the relation between Adam and his posterity the same argument he had used previously in connection with the identity of the individual. Locke had assumed that the presence of the "same consciousness" is essential to identity; Edwards does not deny that, but insists that it is insufficient, since the *continuation* of the same consciousness is dependent on a law of nature established by God. Since, however, no such law operates independently of divine agency, personal identity becomes a matter of God's *continuous* creation. For Edwards, the same holds true of Adam and his posterity; God has constituted *humankind* as one and Adam as one with humankind. Thus, in Edwards' view, God does not treat individuals *one at a time*, but deals with *humankind as a whole*, which runs directly counter to Taylor's claim that Adam and his posterity are entirely distinct agents. Taylor's concern was for *personal* sin, hence he regarded it as unjust that each individual should have to bear the guilt and shame of the sin of Adam or indeed of any other individual. Edwards rejected this individualistic approach and insisted instead that it is not unheard of for people to be

ashamed of things done by others "whom they are nearly concerned in."
Thus we see how important it was for Edwards to defend the reality of
humankind: "all are made of one blood, to dwell on all the face of the
earth."

The Nature of True Virtue was not published until 1765, seven years after
Edwards' death. *True Virtue* is one of two "dissertations," the other being
Concerning the End for Which God Created the World, which Edwards
meant to go together. As Paul Ramsey has pointed out, "one is the mirror
image of the other" in that the "'end' for which God created the world
must be the 'end' of a truly virtuous and holy life."[10] In *True Virtue,*
Edwards sought to develop the meaning of the pure benevolence that
characterizes Christian morality and at the same time to show that common morality based on natural principles, important as it is, still falls short
of Christian charity. That Edwards was aware of the moral philosophy
being written in Britain at the time is shown by his references to key
authors, including the earl of Shaftesbury, Francis Hutcheson, William
Wollaston, and David Hume. These thinkers based their moral philosophy on the idea of a "moral sense" essentially rooted in human nature;
Shaftesbury is often credited with having been the first to use the expression. Edwards' involvement with the doctrines of these thinkers is an
extremely complex affair, and their influence upon him has been the
subject of controversy. He was critical of these authors, but he was also
appreciative of their work in helping to define the "common morality"
that he regarded as of great importance in the divine economy.

It is essential to understand the double-barreled character of Edwards'
approach in *True Virtue.* On the one hand, he was presenting true virtue
and common morality—secondary beauty, self-love, conscience, and
friendly affection—together for a comparison aimed at showing not only
that the former is superior to the latter but also why people tend to
mistake one for the other (for example, they have similarities in nature and
tendency). On the other hand, Edwards was seeking to show the important role played by common morality both in individual life and in society;

10. *The Works of Jonathan Edwards, 8, Ethical Writings,* ed. Paul Ramsey (New Haven, Yale Univ.
Press, 1989), p. 5.

hence he emphasized the power of natural principles, including pity, gratitude, and parental affection, to restrain vice and curtail acts of wickedness. Edwards, in short, was contending that the human situation would be much worse than it actually is if it were not for the force of these natural virtues.

It is, moreover, to the greater glory of God that this morality, which is surpassed by Christian charity, should be no mean thing. Edwards argued time and again that the beauty and truth of what is based on spiritual principles becomes even more evident when it transcends what is based on natural principles developed to the highest degree. In this case, common morality, *even when it is advanced to the utmost*—what Ramsey calls the "splendor of common morality"—still falls short of true virtue. Even so, it makes the glory of Christian charity shine forth more clearly.

True Virtue consists of eight chapters, in which the following topics are discussed: the nature of true virtue as an unqualified love to God; the relation of that virtue to God and the creatures; the secondary beauty inherent in natural principles; the influence of self-love on our love to others; natural conscience and the moral sense; particular natural instincts bearing resemblances to virtue; the reasons why these instincts, though not of the nature of true virtue, have been mistaken for it; and finally, the respects in which moral good is founded in sentiment and how far it is founded in the reason and nature of things. The unity of *True Virtue* exists in the one basic principle governing the entire discussion, a principle provided by the nature of true virtue itself. Stated generally, it is that true virtue must be found in a *first* benevolence that has "none prior to it," and such a benevolence or virtuous love arises only when the object of that love is God or what Edwards calls "Being, simply considered." Love to *particular beings* because of their virtue or beauty cannot of itself be the basis of true virtue, since their virtue and beauty *presuppose* a pure benevolence. Hence Edwards' thesis: "True virtue primarily consists . . . in a propensity or union of heart . . . to Being in general," or to God. To put the point another way (Edwards in fact puts it in several ways), we may say that love to any being other than God cannot be the basis of that pure benevolence which is the essence of true virtue. Invoking a formula he had expressed in earlier writings, Edwards speaks of the "consent" of beings to Being, where "consent" includes benevolence and union of heart in a harmony or general beauty that is beautiful in itself.

It would be a mistake to suppose that for Edwards there is no virtue whatever in a love that is not pure benevolence, since love to the neighbor and a concern for the good of others are offshoots of our love to Being. There is, he says, a *secondary* object of virtuous benevolence, and a secondary beauty, based on the presence of true virtue in the object. When we see in our neighbor a benevolence that is like to our own general benevolence, our hearts are drawn to that person in love and concern; we can, however, perceive the beauty of general benevolence in the other person only if we have it ourselves.

Secondary beauty forms the basis of common morality, which includes self-love, conscience, and kindly affections. The importance of secondary beauty stems primarily from the fact that it is an image of divine beauty—regularity, order, symmetry, harmony, and proportion—and is the source of other virtues. Secondary beauty is found in inanimate things such as the sides of a regular polygon or the figures on a piece of brocade. As an analogue of God's handiwork, it is God's way of making those of a truly virtuous temper more vividly aware of divine love. Secondary beauty provides the basis for other virtues, such as order in society, wisdom in uniting thought and action to some purpose, and justice in accordance with just deserts.

The theory of a "moral sense" set forth by the British moral philosophers is too complex to be discussed here. We can, however, note his estimate of the idea. While Edwards did not flatly deny the reality of a moral sense, by which its proponents meant a sense of good that is distinct from advantage and interest and even from a perception of beauty and harmony, he nevertheless had at least three reservations. First, he did not think it necessary to appeal to such a sense, since he believed that he had shown how natural affections all derive from self-love. Second, he was doubtful, and for very obvious reasons, about the idea that there is implanted in human nature a natural benevolence to others—a favorite idea of the Enlightenment thinkers. Third, he saw that the moral-sense thinkers identified true virtue solely with *public benevolence,* the idea that developed later in Utilitarianism as the "greatest happiness for the greatest number." In Edwards' view, this outlook left God entirely out of the picture. Needless to say, that is a consequence Edwards could not countenance.

The Personal Edwards

For many Edwards scholars whose interests lie in the history of ideas, the "real" Edwards is the intellectual Edwards, the Edwards of the treatises and the published sermons. But a generation of social historians has taught us not to lose sight of the personal, the domestic, and the episodic in historical analysis, for these too supply invaluable insights into people and the periods in which they lived. This is certainly the case with Edwards, who left not only his learned compositions, but a battery of personal writings that illustrate his humanity and the mores of the age in which he lived.

The extraordinarily ambitious Edwards, determined to make his way in the world of ideas, is not someone readily apparent in the published treatises, but very much alive in camera. That Edwards strove from an early age for temporal as well as spiritual success is seen in a list of memoranda he drew up on the cover of one his notebooks. His visions of literary glory come through in such characteristic statements as the following: "Before I venture to publish in London, to make some experiment in my own country; to play at small games first, that I may gain some experience in writing."[11] The sample entries from his "Diary" reproduced here show a young man intent on self-improvement, certainly before the world, but more important, before God. Here we see the ups and downs of his spiritual life—with entries beginning "dull," "decayed," and "reviving"—in reaction to his circumstances. Like his equally ambitious contemporary, Benjamin Franklin, Edwards early drew up a list of "Resolutions," here reprinted in full. Intended to curb his "appetites" and refine what he perceived as undesirable aspects of his personality, the "Resolutions" offers an invaluable glimpse into Edwards' self-identity and

---

11. "Cover-Leaf Memoranda to 'Natural Philosophy,'" in *The Works of Jonathan Edwards, 6, Scientific and Philosophical Writings*, ed. Wallace E. Anderson (New Haven, Yale Univ. Press, 1980), p. 194.

his sense of duty. These rules number seventy in all, a figure far in excess of the young Franklin's thirteen, and illustrate the profound differences in temperament as well as philosophy that separated these two "representative men."

Edwards' determination to live by rule and to discipline his life did not come at the expense of his emotions and a healthy marriage, which produced eleven children. While still an undergraduate at Yale College, the young Edwards first spotted the even younger Sarah Pierpont and identified her as his life's dream. The two would marry in 1727, and Edwards' infatuation with her would never abate. In the "Apostrophe to Sarah Pierpont," supposedly written by Edwards when he was twenty years old and she thirteen, he reveals his beguilement with her person and her piety. The hymn can easily be misunderstood as simply a love poem; in fact, it is much more than that. It is a psychological examination of Pierpont that left him both enraptured with her person and jealous of her spirituality, as he would be throughout their marriage. If the public Edwards was primarily a philosopher, a theologian, and a preacher, the personal Edwards was a psychologist, forever examining his own and others' souls for the same spiritual clues he sought in science and philosophy.

Edwards' relationship with his wife is evident even in his so-called theoretical writings. In "Miscellanies" nos. 189 and 198, written when Edwards was courting Sarah Pierpont in 1724, we see how his relationship with her is essential for our understanding of the beauty and almost sexual intimacy that he used to characterize the saint's relationship to Christ. Toppling modern-day assumptions about Puritan prudery, Edwards celebrates sexual attraction: "How greatly are we inclined to the other sex!" Even more, attraction to "fellow creatures" does not get in the way of our love to God, "but only refines and purifies it." Yet, unlike the love of humans, who soon run out of ways to express their affection for each other, union with God "will become more close, and communion more intimate" in the life hereafter.

Fueled in part by his intimate relationship with Sarah Pierpont, who always served as his model of true piety, and in part by his own incessant curiosity about the psychological makeup of the self, Edwards subjected his own soul to painstaking analysis and in 1739 or 1740 penned a "Personal Narrative" intended to summarize that analysis. On one level—the level of spiritual autobiography—the "Personal Narrative" bears all the earmarks of the classic Puritan conversion narrative and its obsessive concern with the salvation of the soul. But on closer examination, it is clear that Edwards in private departs from the traditional form that he publicly condemned in *Religious Affections*. In particular, the preoccupation with correct sequence and order in conversion is largely abandoned by Edwards in favor of an all-consuming submission to divine sovereignty and the freedom of God to effect and affect salvation according to God's own mysterious purposes. This exploration of the self, together with his observations of Sarah Pierpont, furnished Edwards with many of the empirical insights he would express more generally and abstractly in his printed works.

A family of thirteen required money as well as love and ideals, and Edwards *was* a good provider. The personal Edwards cared deeply about his creaturely comforts and his salary. From private writings and correspondence, it is clear that he was not indifferent to his social status and guarded his gentlemanly prerogatives jealously. Those prerogatives included slaves. Like many other mid-eighteenth-century New England gentry, Edwards possessed domestic slaves, including one whose name comes down to us as simply Venus. The Receipt for Slave Venus is included in this section as a reminder of Edwards' place in time. Edwards himself never evidenced any sense of contradiction between his own disinterested ethic of freedom and the fact of slavery, though it is significant that many of his devoted disciples, including most notably his son Jonathan Edwards, Jr., and Samuel Hopkins, became early leaders in the moral crusade to end slavery.

Throughout his life Edwards was a tireless letter writer. Most of the surviving letters date from the Stockbridge period late in his life. With few exceptions, Edwards never prepared letters for publication, and so they remain as invaluable records of the daily preoccupations of the man. In the representative letters collected by George S. Claghorn and printed here, we encounter an Edwards who is far from lost in an ivory tower.

Rather, he is a person very much engaged in the lives of the people around him, including his congregants, family, and admiring students.

In the letter to his father, Timothy Edwards, written while still in college, Edwards provides a glimpse into eighteenth-century college life outside the classroom, as well as his own self-satisfaction at being "perfectly free" of the "janglings" and illicit activities of the other disobedient students, such as night-walking, card playing, and excessive drinking. This sense of self would persist throughout his life and would be an important determinative source of both his achievements and his failings.

If Edwards was the theologian of the revivals, he was not its quintessential preacher. That honor belongs to the Anglican itinerant George Whitefield, whose transatlantic revivals were without precedent and, quite possibly, without successor. Whitefield and Edwards long knew of each other by reputation, though the two were never close friends or even working associates. Nevertheless, Edwards recognized talent and sincerity when he saw them, and so invited Whitefield to visit Northampton. In his letter of invitation to Whitefield, printed in this volume, Edwards writes, "I apprehend, from what I have heard, that you are one that has the blessing of heaven attending you wherever you go." Edwards wished that blessing to come on his town, his own house, and himself. Here we see both the enthusiasm for souls and the apocalyptic expectation that Whitefield's revivals generated, even in so careful an observer as Edwards.

In the *Religious Affections*, Edwards went to great pains to limit the emotions in the revivals and the aberrant behavior that could ensue from those emotions. As pastor, he confronted individual cases of this among both the laity and the clergy. He had to discipline the fiery James Davenport for his excesses, which culminated in New London in 1743, as well as other lay itinerants who took it upon themselves to exhort as though they were ordained ministers. Later American denominations would be built on the principle of lay exhorting and an uneducated clergy, but this carried no weight with Edwards. In his letter of 1742 to Moses Lyman, former member of his Northampton congregation and later a deacon at Goshen, Connecticut, Edwards reproved him for "exhorting a public congregation," thereby underscoring the limits of his support for the revival and his

traditional sense of the high and separate calling of the professional ministry. "If God had not seen it necessary that such things should have certain
limits and bounds," Edwards points out, "he never would have appointed
a certain particular order of men to that work and office." Here again the
reader sees an Edwards who believes very much in the traditional social
hierarchy of eighteenth-century Anglo-America and who is loath to see
the radical theological implications of his support for revivals issue in
correspondingly radical social applications.

In the eighteenth century, before there were seminaries for education in
the professional ministry, pastors were trained in homes of more experienced clergymen whom they admired. These domestic "schools of the
prophets" existed throughout New England. One of the largest was at
Northampton, where students from throughout the region came to study
with Edwards. Of these "Edwardsean" or "New Divinity" ministers, as
they came to be known, the closest to Edwards was Joseph Bellamy, who
later became the pastor of Bethlehem, Connecticut. In the letter to Bellamy printed here, we see how business and scholarship naturally com-
mingled in Edwards' mind, bringing together an impending sale of sheep
with recommendations for theological books and meditations on the
Arminian controversy threatening to rend the New England clergy.

Much of the honor for organizing a family of thirteen plus assorted
seminarians belonged to Sarah Pierpont. While her piety may have been
Edwards' exemplum for his psychological ruminations, her social skills
were equally acknowledged as binding in the Edwards home. In the letter
to Sarah Edwards included in this volume, we see Edwards' recognition of
her ultimate authority in household affairs—an acknowledgment that in
part reflects general gender divisions of labor in eighteenth-century
America (and beyond)—as well as her own peculiar genius for organization. With his wife attending a sick friend in Boston and a number of their
own children ill, Edwards can only lament to her, "We have been without
you almost as long as we know how to be."

Edwards' concern for family extended beyond Sarah Edwards to his
children, many of whom lived to become remarkable adults. In his letter
to one of his daughters, Esther Edwards Burr (married to the Reverend
Aaron Burr, president of the College of New Jersey), we see Edwards

revealed as a caring father and spiritual counselor. The letter begins with inquiries into her health and the spiritual lessons to be learned from illness. Ever the pastor, Edwards puts these spiritual lessons first, for they are clearly the most important message in the letter. "Therefore I would advise, if it pleases God to restore you, to let upon no happiness here . . . and never expect to find this world anything better than a wilderness." But the parent concludes with advice for healing his daughter's body with a rattlesnake potion, including a lengthy postscript with an herb, spice, and wine recipe.

As a writer, Edwards developed a close working friendship with the Reverend Thomas Foxcroft of Boston, who served as his literary agent. In the letter to Foxcroft published in this volume, Edwards reveals his editorial side, urging changes in the *Humble Inquiry* as it moves to press. He also uses the opportunity to discuss, with unusual frankness, his controversy with his Northampton congregation, knowing that the result will be his dismissal. Throughout there is a sense of destiny. In one revealing, melodramatic statement, he confides: "I seem as it were to be casting myself off from a precipice; and have no other way, but to go on, as it were blindfold, i.e. shutting my eyes to everything else but the evidences of the mind and will of God, and the path of duty."

If there is one area of Edwards' life that has been consistently overlooked and understated by contemporaries and scholars alike, it is his role as Indian missionary and advocate for Indian affairs. Indeed, Edwards had an interest in missions long before coming to Stockbridge in 1751, as evidenced by his role in the founding of the Stockbridge mission in the 1730s and by his publication of *The Life of David Brainerd* (1749), the journal of the famous evangelist to the Indians. In the lengthy letter (excerpted here) to Boston clergyman and Commissioner of Indian Affairs Thomas Prince, Edwards reflects his deep concern for the Mahicans and Mohawks under his ministry, who were "heartily sick" of the exploitation of Indian boys by schoolmaster Captain Martin Kellogg and the inability of the province to fulfill its treaty. This time Edwards would not fail. Stuck in the middle between disgruntled Indians and complacent commissioners, Edwards worked energetically to persuade the Indians not to leave the mission. Despite the external threat of war and the internal threat from English settlers who wished to get rid of him (midway through the letter it becomes obvious that Edwards is writing to clear himself of charges made by certain "enemies"), Edwards proved himself an effective administrator of the mission and advocate of Indian rights.

In 1757, Edwards was asked to be president of the College of New Jersey as successor to his recently deceased son-in-law, Aaron Burr. In the final letter Edwards responds to the invitation, listing several objections to his assuming the position, including his poor health and a "constitution in many respects peculiar unhappy, attended with flaccid solids, vapid, sizy and scarce fluids, and a low tide of spirits." He also points to his many projects and his large family. But he then goes on to accept, provided certain conditions are met, including a release from extended teaching duties and the liberty to pursue his own writing projects, including, most important, the uncompleted opus entitled *A History of the Work of Redemption.* Like a modern-day academician, Edwards succeeded in driving his bargain. He assumed the office in January 1758. As a safeguard against the smallpox epidemic then prevailing in the Princeton area, Edwards, ever the student of the new science, agreed to be inoculated. Unfortunately, the serum was infected, and Edwards died on March 22.

In the years and centuries since his death, Edwards continues to inspire, convict, enrage, and beguile as no other American Puritan. It is the hope of the editors that through these selections the reader will begin to get a sense of why Edwards continues to fascinate and, with that sense, develop a curiosity to embark on a lifelong journey engaging the full corpus of writings that time has not displaced.

Editing the Texts

The text of Jonathan Edwards is reproduced here as he wrote it in manuscript; or, if he published it himself, as it was printed in the first edition; or as found in the earliest posthumous edition. With the exception of dated letters, dates of the selections are provided in parentheses after the titles. In order to present this text to modern readers, several technical adjustments have been made, including the regularization of spelling, punctuation, and capitalization. Lacunae caused by manuscript damage as well as by Edwards' omissions are filled by insertions in square brackets, and ellipsis dots indicate points at which passages were intentionally left out by the editors. Textual intervention to regularize Edwards' citation of Scripture includes the correction of erroneous citation, the regularizing of citation form, and the completion of quotations that Edwards' textual markings indicate should be completed.[12]

Acknowledgments

Many of the selections were based on suggestions made by the editors of *The Works of Jonathan Edwards*, including Thomas A. Schafer, Stephen J. Stein, John F. Wilson, David D. Hall, and Wilson H. Kimnach. George S. Claghorn kindly provided transcriptions of several letters. Ava Chamberlain was instrumental in every step of textual selection and preparation. Margaret McComish assisted in typing and proofreading. Special thanks go to Judith Calvert, Editions and Series Editor of Yale University Press, for encouraging the edition to produce this volume. Finally, we would be remiss if we did not acknowledge Marjorie Wynne, former librarian at the Sterling and Beinecke libraries at Yale University, who did so much for the edition during its "lean" years. The publication of this volume, as well as the edition as a whole, is made possible through the generous support of The Pew Charitable Trusts, Lilly Endowment, Inc., The Andrew W. Mellon Foundation, and The Henry Luce Foundation, Inc.

This volume represents not only many years of labor by the editors of the *Works of Jonathan Edwards* but also the cooperation of many libraries that possess Edwards' manuscripts. "Beauty of the World," "Images of Divine Things," "Notes on the Apocalypse," the Receipt for Slave Venus, and the letters to Moses Lyman, Joseph Bellamy, Sarah Edwards, and Thomas Foxcroft are published courtesy of the Beinecke Rare Book and Manuscript Library, Yale University. "Of Being," the Apostrophe to Sarah Pierpont, the documents relating to the Bad Book Case, and the

12. For a complete statement of editorial policies, see *Works*, *10*, xi–xv.

letter to Timothy Edwards are printed with permission from the Franklin Trask Library, Andover Newton Theological School, Newton Center, Massachusetts, which, as the repository of the most significant collection of Edwards manuscripts beside that at the Beinecke Library, has gener-ously contributed to this edition since its inception. In addition, the Spider Letter is printed with permission from the New-York Historical Society; Edwards' letter to George Whitefield, from the Methodist Archives and Research Center, Manchester, England; the letter to Esther Edwards Burr, from the Boston Public Library, Boston, Massachusetts; and the letter to Thomas Prince, from the Massachusetts Historical Society, Boston, Massachusetts. We also acknowledge Richard R. Niebuhr's permission to quote from H. Richard Niebuhr's unpublished sermon, "The Anachronism of Jonathan Edwards."

Chronology of Edwards' Life

Further Reading

Cherry, Conrad. *The Theology of Jonathan Edwards: A Reappraisal.* Garden City, N.Y., Doubleday, 1966; rep. Bloomington, Indiana University Press, 1990.

Daniel, Stephen H. *The Philosophy of Jonathan Edwards: A Study in Divine Semiotics.* Bloomington, Indiana University Press, 1994.

Delattre, Roland A. *Beauty and Sensibility in the Thought of Jonathan Edwards.* New Haven, Yale University Press, 1968.

Fiering, Norman. *Jonathan Edwards's Moral Thought and Its British Context.* Chapel Hill, University of North Carolina Press, 1981.

Guelzo, Allan C. *Edwards on the Will: A Century of American Theological Debate.* Middletown, Conn., Wesleyan University Press, 1989.

Hatch, Nathan O., and Harry S. Stout, eds. *Jonathan Edwards and the American Experience.* New York, Oxford University Press, 1988.

Jenson, Robert. *America's Theologian: A Recommendation of Jonathan Edwards.* New York, Oxford University Press, 1988.

Kuklick, Bruce. *Churchmen and Philosophers: From Jonathan Edwards to John Dewey.* New Haven, Yale University Press, 1985.

Lee, Sang H. *The Philosophical Theology of Jonathan Edwards.* Princeton, Princeton University Press, 1988.

Lesser, M. X. *Jonathan Edwards: A Reference Guide.* Boston, G. K. Hall, 1981.

Lowance, Mason I., Jr. *The Language of Canaan: Metaphor and Symbol in New England from the Puritans to the Transcendentalists.* Cambridge, Harvard University Press, 1980.

McDermott, Gerald R. *One Holy and Happy Society: The Public Theology of Jonathan Edwards.* University Park, Pennsylvania State University Press, 1992.

Miller, Perry. *Jonathan Edwards.* New York, Sloane, 1949; rep. Amherst, University of Massachusetts Press, 1981.

Murray, Iain H. *Jonathan Edwards: A New Biography.* Carlisle, Pa., Banner of Truth, 1987.

Oberg, Barbara B., and Harry S. Stout, eds. *Benjamin Franklin, Jonathan Edwards, and the Representation of American Culture.* New York, Oxford University Press, 1993.

Smith, John E. *Jonathan Edwards: Puritan, Preacher, Philosopher.* Notre Dame, Ind., University of Notre Dame Press, 1992.

Tracy, Patricia. *Jonathan Edwards, Pastor: Religion and Society in Eighteenth-Century Northampton.* New York, Hill and Wang, 1980.

Winslow, Ola E. *Jonathan Edwards, 1703–1758.* New York, Macmillan, 1941.

A Jonathan Edwards Reader

The Spider Letter

Windsor, Oct. 31, 1723

Sir;[1]

In the postscript of your letter to my father you manifest a willingness to receive anything else that he has observed in nature worthy of remark; that which is the subject of the following lines by him was thought to be such: he has laid it upon me to write the account, I having had advantage to make more full observations. If you think, sir, that they are not worthy the taking notice of, with greatness and goodness overlook and conceal. They are some things that I have happily seen of the wondrous and curious works of the spider. Although everything pertaining to this insect is admirable, yet there are some phenomena relating to them more particularly wonderful.

Everybody that is used to the country knows of their marching in the air from one tree to another, sometimes at the distance of five or six rods, though they are wholly destitute of wings: nor can one go out in a dewy morning at the latter end of August and beginning of September but he shall see multitudes of webs reaching from one tree and shrub to another; which webs are commonly thought to be made in the night because they appear only in the morning by reason of the dew that hangs on them, whereas they never work in the night, they love to lie still when the air is dark and moist; but these webs may be seen well enough in the daytime by an observing eye, by their reflection of the sunbeams; especially late in the afternoon may those webs that are between the eye, and that part of the horizon that is under the sun, be seen very plainly, being advantageously posited to reflect the rays, and the spiders themselves may be very often seen traveling in the air from one stage to another amongst the trees in a very unaccountable manner. But, sir, I have often seen that which is yet

---

1. The letter was almost certainly addressed to Judge Paul Dudley, Fellow of the Royal Society of London and Associate Justice of the Superior Court of Massachusetts. Edwards apparently hoped to have his letter published in the Royal Society's *Philosophical Transactions*.

more astonishing. In a very calm serene day in the forementioned time of year, standing at some distance between the end of an house or some other opaque body, so as just to hide the disk of the sun and keep off his dazzling rays, and looking along close by the side of it, I have seen vast multitudes of little shining webs and glistening strings, brightly reflecting the sunbeams, and some of them of a great length, and at such a height that one would think that they were tacked to the vault of the heavens, and would be burnt like tow in the sun, making a very pleasing as well as surprising appearance. It is wonderful at what a distance these webs may plainly be seen in such a position to the sunbeams, which are so fine that they cannot be seen in another position, though held near to the eye; some that are at a great distance appear (it cannot be otherwise) several thousands of times as big as they ought: They doubtless appear under as great an angle as a body of a foot diameter ought to do at such a distance; so greatly doth coruscation increase the apparent bigness of bodies at a distance, as is observed in the fixed stars. But that which is most astonishing is that very often there appears at the end of these webs, spiders sailing in the air with them, doubtless with abundance of pleasure, though not with so much as I have beheld them and showed them to others. And since I have seen these things I have been very conversant with spiders. Resolving if possible to find out the mysteries of these their amazing works, and pursuing my observations, I discovered one wonder after another till I have been so happy as very frequently to see their whole manner of working; which is thus:

When a spider would go from one tree or branch to another, or would recreate himself by sailing or floating in the air, he first lets himself down a little way from the twig he stands on by a web, as [in] Fig. 1; and then taking hold of it by his forefeet as in Fig. 2, and then separates or loosens the part of the web *cd* from the part *bc* by which he hangs; which part of the web *cd,* being thus loosened, will by the motion of the air be carried out towards *e,* which will by the sufferance of the spider be drawn [out] of his tail with infinite ease by the moving air, to what length the spider pleases, as [in] Fig. 3: And if the further end of the web *de,* as it is running out and moving to and fro, happens to catch by a shrub or the branch of a tree, the spider immediately feels it and fixes the hither end of it, *d,* to the web *bc,*

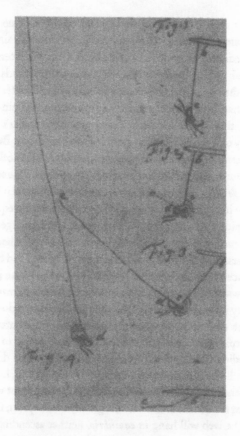

and goes over as by a bridge by the web *de*. Every particular of this, sir, my eyes have innumerable times made me sure of, saving that I never could distinctly see how they separated the part of the web *cd* (Fig. 2) from the part *bc*, whether it be done by biting of it off or how, because so small a piece of so fine a web is altogether imperceptible amongst the spider's legs, and because the spider is so very quick and dexterous in doing of it all. But I have seen that it is done, though I have not seen how they do it. For this, sir, I can see: that the web *bc* (Fig. 3) is separated, and not joined to the spider's tail, while the web *de* is drawing out.

Now, sir, it is certain that these webs, when they first come from the spider, are so rare a substance that they are lighter than the air, because they will immediately ascend in a calm air, and never descend except driven by a wind: and 'tis as certain that what swims and ascends in the air is lighter than the air, as that what ascends and swims in water is lighter than that: So that if we should suppose any such time wherein the air is perfectly calm, this web is so easily drawn out of the spider's tail, that barely the levity of it is sufficient to carry it out to any length. But at least its levity, or ascending inclination, together with so much motion as the air is never without, will well suffice for this. Wherefore, if it be so that the end of the web *de* (Fig. 3) catches by no tree nor other body till it be drawn out so long that its levity shall be so great as to be more than equal to the gravity of the spider, or so that the web and the spider taken together shall be lighter than such a quantity of air as takes up equal space, then according to the universally acknowledged laws of nature the web and the spider together will ascend and not descend in the air. As when a man [is] at the bottom of the water, if he has hold of a piece of timber so great that the wood's tendency upwards is greater than the man's tendency downwards, he together with the wood will ascend to the surface of the water. Therefore, when the spider perceives that the web *de* is long enough to bear him up by its ascending force (which force the spider feels by its drawing of him towards *e*), he lets go his hold of the web *bc* (Fig. 4) and, holding by the web *de*, ascends and floats in the air with it. If there be not web more than enough just to equal with its levity the gravity of the spider, the spider together with the web will hang *in equilibrio*, neither ascending nor descending, otherwise than as the air moves; but if there be so much web that its ascending tendency, or rather the buoying force of the air upon it, shall be greater than the descending tendency of the spider, they will ascend till the air is so thin, till they together are just of an equal weight with so much air. But if the web be so short as not to counterpoise the weight of the spider, the web and spider will fall till they come to the ground.

And this very way, sir, I have multitudes of times seen spiders mount away into the air with a vast train of this silver web before them from a stick in mine hand; for if the spider be disturbed upon the stick by shaking of [it] he will presently in this manner leave it. Their way of working may very distinctly be seen if they are held up in the sun, in a calm day, against a dark door or anything that is black.

And this, sir, is the way of spiders' working. This is the way of their going from one thing to another at a distance, and this is the way of their flying in the air. And although I can say I am certain of it, I don't desire that the truth of it should be received upon my word, though I could bring others to testify to it to whom I have shown it, and who have looked on with admiration: But everyone's eyes who will take the pains to observe will make them equally sure of it; only those who would make experiment must take notice that it is not every sort of spider that is a flying spider, for those spiders that keep in houses are a quite different sort, as also those that keep in the ground, and those [that] keep in swamps upon the ground amongst the bogs, and those that keep in hollow trees and rotten logs; but those spiders that keep on branches of trees and shrubs are the flying spiders. They delight most in walnut trees, and are that sort of spiders that make those curious, network, polygonal webs that are so frequently to be seen in the latter end of the year. There are more of this sort of spider by far than of any other.

Corollary 1. Hence the wisdom of the Creator in providing of the spider with that wonderful liquor with which their bottle tail is filled, that may so easily be drawn out so exceeding fine, and being in this way exposed to the air will so immediately convert to a dry substance that shall be so very rare as to be lighter than the air, and will so excellently serve to all their purposes.

Corol. 2. Hence the exuberant goodness of the Creator, who hath not only provided for all the necessities, but also for the pleasure and recreation of all sorts of creatures, even the insects.

But yet, sir, I am assured that the chief end of this faculty that is given them is not their recreation but their destruction, because their destruction is unavoidably the constant effect of it; and we find nothing that is the continual effect of nature but what is the end of the means by which it is brought to pass: but it is impossible but that the greatest part of the spiders upon the land should every year be swept into the ocean. For these spiders never fly except the weather be fair and the atmosphere dry, but the atmosphere is never clear and dry, neither in this nor any other continent, only when the wind blows from the midland parts, and consequently towards the sea; as here in New England, the fair weather is only when the wind is westerly, the land being on that side and the ocean on the easterly. I scarcely ever have seen any of these spiders flying but when they have been hastening directly towards the sea. And the time of their flying being so long, even from about the middle of August, every sunshiny day till about the end of October (though their chief time, as was observed before, is the latter end of August and beginning of September). And they, never flying from the sea but always towards it, must get there at last. And it seems unreasonable to think that they have sense to stop themselves when they come near the sea, for then we should [see] hundreds of times more spiders on the seashore than anywhere else. When they are once carried over the water their webs grow damp and moist and lose their levity and their wings fail them, and let them down into the water.

The same also holds true of other sorts of flying insects, for at those times that I have viewed the spiders with their webs in the air there has also appeared vast multitudes of flies at a great height, and all flying the same way with the spiders and webs, direct to the ocean. And even such as butterflies, millers, and moths, which keep in the grass at this time of year, I have seen vastly higher than the tops of the highest trees, all going the same way. These I have seen towards evening, right overhead, and without a screen to defend my eye from the sunbeams, which I used to think were seeking a warmer climate. The reason of their flying at that time of year I take to be because the ground and trees and grass, the places of their residence in summer, begin to be chill and uncomfortable. Therefore when the sun shines pretty warm they leave them, and mount up into the air and expand their wings to the sun, and flying for nothing but their own ease and comfort, they suffer themselves to go that way that they can go with the greatest ease, and so where the wind pleases: and it being warmth they fly for, they never fly against the wind nor sidewise to it, they find it cold and laborious; they therefore seem to use their wings but just so much as to bear them up, and suffer themselves to go with the wind. So that it must necessarily be that almost all aerial insects, and spiders which live upon them and are made up of them, are at the end of the year swept away into the sea and buried in the ocean, and leave nothing behind them but their eggs for a new stock the next year.

Corol. 1. Hence [there] is reason to admire at the wisdom of the Creator, and to be convinced that it is exercised about such little things in this wonderful contrivance of annually carrying off and burying the corruption and nauseousness of the air, of which flying insects are little collections, in the bottom of the ocean where it will do no harm; and especially the strange way of bringing this about in spiders, which are collections of these collections, their food being flying insects, flies being the poison of the air, and spiders are the poison of flies collected together. And what great inconveniences should we labor under if it were not so, for spiders and flies are such exceedingly multiplying creatures, that if they only slept or lay benumbed in winter, and were raised again in the spring, which is commonly thought, it would not be many years before we should be plagued with as vast numbers as Egypt was. And if they died ultimately in winter, they by the renewed heat of the sun would presently again be dissipated into the nauseous vapors of which they are made up, and so would be of no use or benefit in that in which now they are so very serviceable and which is the chief end of their creation.

Corol. 2. The wisdom of the Creator is also admirable in so nicely and mathematically adjusting their plastic nature, that notwithstanding their destruction by this means and the multitudes that are eaten by birds, that they do not decrease and so by little and little come to nothing; and in so adjusting their destruction to their multiplication they do neither increase, but taking one year with another, there is always an equal number of them.

These, sir, are the observations I have had opportunity to make on the wonders that are to be seen in the most despicable of animals. Although these things appear for the main very certain to me, yet, sir, I submit it all to your better judgment, and deeper insight. I humbly beg to be pardoned for running the venture, though an utter stranger, of troubling you with so prolix an account of that which I am altogether uncertain whether you will esteem worthy of the time and pains of reading. Pardon me if I thought it might at least give you occasion to make better observations on these

wondrous animals, that should be worthy of communicating to the
learned world, from whose glistening webs so much of the wisdom of the
Creator shines.

                              Pardon, sir, your most obedient humble servant,
                              Jonathan Edwards

Of Being (1721)

That there should absolutely be nothing at all is utterly impossible. The mind can never, let it stretch its conceptions ever so much, bring itself to conceive of a state of perfect nothing. It puts the mind into mere convulsion and confusion to endeavor to think of such a state, and it contradicts the very nature of the soul to think that it should be; and it is the greatest contradiction, and the aggregate of all contradictions, to say that there should not be. 'Tis true we can't so distinctly show the contradiction by words, because we cannot talk about it without speaking horrid nonsense and contradicting ourselves at every word, and because "nothing" is that whereby we distinctly show other particular contradictions. But here we are run up to our first principle, and have no other to explain the nothingness or not being of nothing by. Indeed, we can mean nothing else by "nothing" but a state of absolute contradiction. And if any man thinks that he can think well enough how there should be nothing, I'll engage that what he means by "nothing" is as much something as anything that ever [he] thought of in his life; and I believe that if he knew what nothing was it would be intuitively evident to him that it could not be. So that we see it is necessary some being should eternally be. And 'tis a more palpable contradiction still to say that there must be being somewhere, and not otherwhere; for the words "absolute nothing" and "where" contradict each other. And besides, it gives as great a shock to the mind to think of pure nothing in any one place, as it does to think of it in all; and it is self-evident that there can be nothing in one place as well as in another, and so if there can be in one, there can be in all. So that we see this necessary, eternal being must be infinite and omnipresent.

(Place this as a lemma where it suits best, and let it be more fully demonstr[ated]:) This infinite and omnipresent being cannot be solid. Let us see how contradictory it is to say that an infinite being is solid; for solidity surely is nothing but resistance to other solidities.

Space is this necessary, eternal, infinite and omnipresent being. We find that we can with ease conceive how all other beings should not be. We can remove them out of our minds, and place some other in the room of them; but space is the very thing that we can never remove and conceive of its not being. If a man would imagine space anywhere to be divided, so as there should be nothing between the divided parts, there remains space between notwithstanding, and so the man contradicts himself. And it is self-evident, I believe, to every man, that space is necessary, eternal, infinite and omnipresent. But I had as good speak plain: I have already said as much as that space is God. And it is indeed clear to me, that all the space there is not proper to body, all the space there is without the bounds of the creation, all the space there was before the creation, is God himself. And nobody would in the least stick at it, if it were not because of the gross conceptions that we have of space.

And how doth it grate upon the mind, to think that something should be from all eternity, and nothing all the while be conscious of it. Let us suppose, to illustrate it, that the world had a being from all eternity, and had many great changes and wonderful revolutions, and all the while nothing knew; there was no knowledge in the universe of any such thing. How is it possible to bring the mind to imagine? Yea, it is really impossible it should be, that anything should be, and nothing know it. Then you'll say, if it be so, it is because nothing has any existence anywhere else but in consciousness. No, certainly nowhere else, but either in created or uncreated consciousness.

Supposing there were another universe only of bodies, created at a great distance from this, created in excellent order and harmonious motions, and a beautiful variety; and there was no created intelligence in it, nothing but senseless bodies. Nothing but God knew anything of it. I demand in what respect this world has a being, but only in the divine consciousness. Certainly in no respect. There would be figures and magnitudes, and motions and proportions—but where? Where else, but in the Almighty's knowledge. How is it possible there should? Then you'll say: For the same reason, in a room close shut up, that nobody sees nor hears nothing in it, there is nothing any other way than in God's knowledge. I answer: Created beings are conscious of the effects of what is in the room; for perhaps there is not one leaf of a tree, nor spire of grass, but what has effects all over the universe, and will have to the end of eternity. But any otherwise, there is nothing in a room shut up, but only in God's consciousness. How can anything be there any other way? This will appear to be truly so to anyone that thinks of it with the whole united strength of his mind. Let us suppose for illustration this impossibility, that all the spirits in the universe to be for a time deprived of their consciousness, and God's consciousness at the same time to be intermitted. I say, the universe for that time would cease to be, of itself; and not only, as we speak, because the Almighty could not attend to uphold the world, but because God knew nothing of it. 'Tis our foolish imagination that will not suffer us to see. We fancy there may be figures and magnitudes, relations and properties, without anyone's knowing of it. But it is our imagination hurts us. We don't know what figures and properties are.

Our imagination makes us fancy we see shapes and colors and magnitudes though nobody is there to behold it. But to help our imagination let us thus state the case: Let us suppose the world deprived of every ray of light, so that there should not be the least glimmering of light in the universe. Now all will own that in such a case, the universe would be immediately really deprived of all its colors. One part of the universe is no more red, or blue, or green, or yellow, or black, or white, or light, or dark, or transparent or opaque than another. There would be no visible distinction between the world and the rest of the incomprehensible void—yea, there would be no difference in these respects between the world and the infinite void. That is, any part of that void would really be as light and as dark, as white and as black, as red and green, as blue and as brown, as transparent and as opaque as any part of the universe. Or, as there would be in such case no difference between the world and nothing in these respects, so there would be no difference between one part of the world and another. All, in these respects, is alike confounded with and indistinguishable from infinite emptiness.

At the same time, also let us suppose the universe to be altogether deprived of motion, and all parts of it to be at perfect rest (the former supposition is indeed included in this, but we distinguish them for better clearness). Then the universe would not differ from the void in this respect; there will be no more motion in one than the other. Then also solidity would cease. All that we mean or can be meant by solidity is resistance—resistance to touch, the resistance of some parts of space. This is all the knowledge we get of solidity by our senses, and, I am sure, all that we can get any other way. . . . But there can be no resistance if there is no motion. One body cannot resist another when there is perfect rest amongst them. But you'll say, though there is not actually resistance, yet there is potential existence, that is, such and such parts of space would resist upon occasion. But this is all I would have: that there is no solidity now; not but that God would cause there to be on occasion. And if there is no solidity, there is no extension, for extension is the extendedness of the solidity. Then all figure and magnitude and proportion immediately ceases.

Put both these suppositions together, that is, deprive the world of light and motion, and the case would stand thus with the world: There would be neither white nor black, neither blue nor brown, bright nor shaded, pellucid nor opaque; no noise or sound, neither heat nor cold, neither fluid nor wet nor dry, hard nor soft, nor solidity, nor extension, nor figure, nor magnitude, nor proportion; nor body, nor spirit. What then is become of the universe? Certainly, it exists nowhere but in the divine mind. . . . So that we see that a world without motion can exist nowhere else but in the mind, either infinite or finite.

Corollary 1. It follows from hence, that those beings which have knowledge and consciousness are the only proper and real and substantial beings, inasmuch as the being of other things is only by these. From hence we may see the gross mistake of those who think material things the most substantial beings, and spirits more like a shadow; whereas spirits only are properly substance.

A state of absolute nothing is a state of absolute contradiction. Absolute nothing is the aggregate of all the absurd contradictions in the world, a state wherein there is neither body, nor spirit, nor space: neither empty space nor full space, neither little nor great, narrow nor broad, neither infinitely great space nor finite space, nor a mathematical point; neither up nor down, neither north nor south (I don't mean as it is with respect to the body of the earth or some other great body, but no contrary points nor positions nor directions); no such thing as either here or there, this way and that way, or only one way. When we go about to form an idea of perfect nothing we must shut out all these things. We must shut out of our minds both space that has something in it, and space that has nothing in it. We must not allow ourselves to think of the least part of space, never so small, nor must we suffer our thoughts to take sanctuary in a mathematical point. When we go to expel body out of our thoughts, we must be sure not to leave empty space in the room of it; and when we go to expel emptiness from our thoughts we must not think to squeeze it out by anything close, hard and solid, but we must think of the same that the sleeping rocks dream of; and not till then shall we get a complete idea of nothing.

A state of nothing is a state wherein every proposition in Euclid is not true, nor any of those self-evident maxims by which they are demonstrated; and all other eternal truths are neither true nor false.

When we go to inquire whether or no there can be absolutely nothing we speak nonsense. In inquiring, the stating of the question is nonsense, because we make a disjunction where there is none. "Either being or absolute nothing" is no disjunction, no more than whether a triangle is a triangle or not a triangle. There is no other way, but only for there to be existence; there is no such thing as absolute nothing. There is such a thing as nothing with respect to this ink and paper. There is such a thing as nothing with respect to you and me. There is such a thing as nothing with respect to this globe of earth, and with respect to this created universe. There is another way besides these things having existence. But there is no such thing as nothing with respect to entity or being, absolutely considered. And we don't know what we say, if we say we think it possible in itself that there should not be entity.

Beauty of the World (1725)

The beauty of the world consists wholly of sweet mutual consents, either within itself, or with the Supreme Being. As to the corporeal world, though there are many other sorts of consents, yet the sweetest and most charming beauty of it is its resemblance of spiritual beauties. The reason is that spiritual beauties are infinitely the greatest, and bodies being but the shadows of beings, they must be so much the more charming as they shadow forth spiritual beauties. This beauty is peculiar to natural things, it surpassing the art of man.

Thus there is the resemblance of a decent trust, dependence and acknowledgment in the planets continually moving round the sun, receiving his influences by which they are made happy, bright and beautiful, a decent attendance in the secondary planets, an image of majesty, power, glory and beneficence in the sun in the midst of all; and so in terrestrial things. . . .

'Tis very probable that that wonderful suitableness of green for the grass and plants, the blue of the sky, the white of the clouds, the colors of flowers, consists in a complicated proportion that these colors make one with another, either in the magnitude of the rays, the number of vibrations that are caused in the optic nerve, or some other way. So there is a great suitableness between the objects of different senses, as between sounds, colors, and smells—as between the colors of the woods and flowers, and the smell, and the singing of birds—which 'tis probable consist in a certain proportion of the vibrations that are made in the different organs. So there are innumerable other agreeablenesses of motions, figures, etc.: the gentle motions of trees, of lily, etc., as it is agreeable to other things that represent calmness, gentleness and benevolence, etc. The fields and woods seem to rejoice, and how joyful do the birds seem to be in it. How much a resemblance is there of every grace in the fields covered with plants and flowers, when the sun shines serenely and undisturbedly upon them. How a resemblance, I say, of every grace and beautiful disposition of mind; of an inferior towards a superior cause, preserver, benevolent benefactor, and a fountain of happiness.

How great a resemblance of a holy and virtuous soul in a calm serene day. What an infinite number of such-like beauties is there in that one thing, the light; and how complicated an harmony and proportion is it probable belongs to it.

There are beauties that are more palpable and explicable, and there are hidden and secret beauties. The former pleases and we can tell why: we can explain and particularly point forth agreements that render the thing pleasing. Such are all artificial regularities: we can tell wherein the regularity lies that affects us. The latter sort are those beauties that delight us and we can't tell why. Thus we find ourselves pleased in beholding the color of the violets, but we know not what secret regularity or harmony it is that creates that pleasure in our minds. These hidden beauties are commonly by far the greatest, because the more complex a beauty is, the more hidden is it. In this latter sort consists principally the beauty of the world; and very much in light and colors. Thus, mere light is pleasing to the mind. If it be to the degree of effulgence, 'tis very sensible, and mankind have agreed in it: they all represent glory and extraordinary beauty by brightness. The reason of it is either that light, or our organ of seeing, is so contrived that an harmonious motion is excited in the animal spirits and propagated to the brain. That mixture of all sorts of rays, which we call white, is a proportionate mixture that is harmonious (as Sir Isaac Newton has shown) to each particular simple color and contains in it some harmony or other that is delightful. And each sort of rays play a distinct tune to the soul, besides those lovely mixtures that are found in nature— those beauties, how lovely, in the green of the face of the earth, in all manner of colors in flowers, the color of the skies, and lovely tinctures of the morning and evening.

Corollary. Hence the reason why almost all men, and those that seem to be very miserable, love life: because they cannot bear to lose the sight of such a beautiful and lovely world—the ideas, that every moment whilst we live have a beauty that we take not distinct notice of, but bring a pleasure that, when we come to the trial, we had rather live in much pain and misery than lose. . . .

Images of Divine Things (1728)

7. That the things of the world are ordered [and] designed to shadow forth spiritual things, appears by the Apostle's arguing spiritual things from them. I Cor. 15:36, "Thou fool, that which thou sowest is not quickened, except it die." If the sowing of seed and its springing were not designedly ordered to have an agreeableness to the resurrection, there could be no sort of argument in that which the Apostle alleges; either to argue the resurrection itself or the manner of it, either its certainty, or probability, or possibility. See how the Apostle's argument is thus founded (Heb. 9:16–17) about the validity of a testament.

8. Again, it is apparent and allowed that there is a great and remarkable analogy in God's works. There is a wonderful resemblance in the effects which God produces, and consentaneity in his manner of working in one thing and another, throughout all nature. It is very observable in the visible world. Therefore 'tis allowed that God does purposely make and order one thing to be in an agreeableness and harmony with another. And if so, why should not we suppose that he makes the inferior in imitation of the superior, the material of the spiritual, on purpose to have a resemblance and shadow of them? We see that even in the material world God makes one part of it strangely to agree with another; and why is it not reasonable to suppose he makes the whole as a shadow of the spiritual world? . . .

27. The waves and billows of the sea in a storm and the dire cataracts there are of rivers have a representation of the terrible wrath of God, and amazing misery of [them] that endure it. Misery is often compared to waters in the Scripture—a being overwhelmed in waters. God's wrath is compared to waves and billows (Ps. 88:7, Ps. 42:7). Job 27:20, "Terrors take hold as waters." Hos. 5:10, "I will pour out my wrath upon them like water." In Ps. 42:7, God's wrath is expressly compared to cataracts of

water: "Deep calleth unto deep at the noise of thy waterspouts." And the same is represented in hail and stormy winds, black clouds and thunder, etc.

29. When we travail up an hill 'tis against our natural tendency and inclination, which perpetually is to descend; and therefore we can't go on ascending without labor and difficulty. But there arises a pleasant prospect to pay us for our labor as we ascend, and as we continue our labor in ascending, still the pleasantness of the prospect grows. Just so is a man paid for his labor and self-denial in a Christian course. . . .

35. The silkworm is a remarkable type of Christ, which, when it dies, yields us that of which we make such glorious clothing. Christ became a worm for our sakes, and by his death finished that righteousness with which believers are clothed, and thereby procured that we should be clothed with robes of glory. . . . See II Sam. 5:23–24 and Ps. 84:6; the valley of mulberry trees.

61. Ravens that with delight feed on carrion seem to be remarkable types of devils who with delight prey upon the souls of the dead. A dead, filthy, rotten carcass is a lively image of the soul of a wicked man that is spiritually and exceeding filthy and abominable. Their spiritual corruption is of a far more loathsome savor than the stench of a putrefying carcass. Such souls the devil delights in; they are his proper food. Again, dead carcasses are types of the departed souls of the dead, and are so used (Is. 66:24). Ravens don't prey on the bodies of animals till they are dead; so the devil has not the souls of wicked men delivered into his tormenting hands and devouring jaws till they are dead. Again, the body in such circumstances, being dead and in loathsome putrefaction, is a lively image of a soul in the dismal state it is in under eternal death. . . .

Ravens are birds of the air that are expressly used by Christ as types of the devil in the parable of the sower and the seed [Matt. 13:3–8]. The devil is "the prince of the power of the air," as he is called [Eph. 2:2]; devils are spirits of the air. The raven by its blackness represents the prince of darkness. Sin and sorrow and death are all in Scripture represented by darkness or the color black; but the devil is the father of sin, a most foul and wicked spirit, and the prince of death and misery.

63. In the manner in which birds and squirrels that are charmed by serpents go into their mouths and are destroyed by them, is a lively representation of the manner in which sinners under the gospel are very often charmed and destroyed by the devil. The animal that is charmed by the serpent seems to be in great exercise and fear, screams and makes ado, but yet don't flee away. It comes nearer to the serpent, and then seems to have its distress increased and goes a little back again, but then comes still nearer than ever, and then appears as if greatly affrighted and runs or flies back again a little way, but yet don't flee quite away, and soon comes a little nearer and a little nearer with seeming fear and distress that drives 'em a little back between whiles, until at length they come so [near] that the serpent can lay hold of them: and so they become their prey.

Just thus, oftentimes sinners under the gospel are bewitched by their lusts. They have considerable fears of destruction and remorse of conscience that makes 'em hang back, and they have a great deal of exercise between while, and some partial reformations, but yet they don't flee away. They won't wholly forsake their beloved lusts, but return to 'em again; and so whatever warnings they have, and whatever checks of conscience that may exercise 'em and make [them] go back a little and stand off for a while, yet they will keep their beloved sin in sight, and won't utterly break off from it and forsake [it], but will return to it again and again, and go a little further and a little further, until Satan remedilessly makes a prey of them. But if anyone comes and kills the serpent, the animal immediately escapes. So the way in which poor souls are delivered from the snare of the devil is by Christ's coming and bruising the serpent's head.

108. Bread-corn is much used in Scripture to represent the saints. The wicked are represented by the clusters of the vine, but the godly by bread-corn. They are called Christ's wheat, that he will gather into his barn and into his garner, and we are all said to be that one bread. Now this is remarkable of wheat and other bread-corn: that it is sown and grows

before winter, and then is as it were killed, and long lies dead in the winter season, and then revives in the spring and grows much taller than before, and comes to perfection and brings forth fruit; which is a lively image of the resurrection of saints—as well as the grain's being first buried in the earth and dying there before it comes up—and that often comes to pass, concerning the saints in this life, that is livelily represented by it. After their conversion they have a falling away, and long continue in a cold and dead carnal state, and then revive again and grow much taller than before, and never fail again till they bring fruit to perfection. 'Tis also a lively image of what comes to pass with respect to the Christian church, which after it was planted by the apostles and flourished a while, then fell under a wintry season, a low and very suffering state, for a long while, and so continues till about the time of the destruction of Antichrist, and then revives and grows and comes to a glorious degree of prosperity and fruitfulness, which is what is called in Scripture "the first resurrection" [Rev. 20:5–6]. Therefore 'tis said of Israel, Hos. 14:7, "They shall revive as the corn." The reviving of the church after a low state and a time of trouble is compared to the reviving of corn from under the earth in the spring in Is. 37:30–31.

109. The inside of the body of man is full of filthiness, contains his bowels that are full of dung, which represents the corruption and filthiness that the heart of man is naturally full of. . . .

118. IMAGES OF DIVINE THINGS. It is with many of these images as it was with the sacrifices of old. They are often repeated, whereas the antitype is continual and never comes to pass but once. Thus sleep is an image of death that is repeated every night. So the morning is the image of the resurrection. So the spring of the year is the image of the resurrection, which is repeated every year. And so of many other things that might be mentioned. They are repeated often, but the antitype is but once. The shadows are often repeated to show two things: viz. that the thing shadowed is not yet fulfilled; and second, to signify the great importance of the antitype, that we need to be so renewedly and continually put in mind of it.

156. The Book of Scripture is the interpreter of the book of nature two ways: viz. by declaring to us those spiritual mysteries that are indeed signified or typified in the constitution of the natural world; and secondly, in actually making application of the signs and types in the book of nature as representations of those spiritual mysteries in many instances.

158. The way in which most of the things we use are serviceable to us and answer their end is in their being strained, or hard-pressed, or violently agitated. Thus the way in which the bow answers its end is in hard straining of it to shoot the arrow and do the execution; the bow that won't bear straining is good for nothing. So it is with a staff that a man walks with: it answers its end in being hard-pressed. So it is with many of the members of our bodies, our teeth, our feet, etc.; and so with most of the utensils of life, an ax, a saw, a flail, a rope, a chain, etc. They are useful and answer their end by some violent straining, pressure, agitation, collision or impulsion, and they that are so weak not to bear the trial of such usage are good for nothing.

Here is a lively representation of the way in which true and sincere saints (which are often in Scripture represented as God's instruments or utensils) answer God's end, and serve and glorify him in it: by enduring temptation, going through hard labor, suffering, or self-denial or such service or strains hard upon nature and self. Hypocrites are like a broken tooth, a foot out of joint, a broken staff, a deceitful bow, which fail when pressed or strained.

171. Concerning the blossoming and ripening of fruits and other things of that nature. The first puttings forth of the tree in order to fruit make a great show and are pleasant to the eye, but the fruit then is very small and tender. Afterwards, when there is less show, the fruit is increased. So it often is at first conversion: there are flowing affections, passionate joys, that are the flower that soon falls off, etc. The fruit when young is very tender, easily hurt with frost, or heat, or vermin, or anything that touches it. So it is with young converts. Cant. 2:15, "Take us the foxes the little foxes, that spoil the vines: for our vines have tender grapes."

Fruit on the tree or in the field is not in its fixed and ultimate state, or the state where it properly answers its end, but in a state wholly subordinate and preparatory to another. So it is with the saints. The fruit, while it stands in the field, or hangs on the tree till fully ripe and the time of gathering comes, is in a progressive state, growing in perfection. So it is with grace in the saints.

Many kinds of fruit have a great deal of bitterness and sourness while green, and much that is crude and unwholesome, which as it ripens becomes sweeter, the juices purer, the crude parts are removed. The burning heat of the summer sun purges away that which is crude, sour and unwholesome, and refines the fruit and ripens it, and fits it more for use; which burning heat withers and destroys those fruits that han't substance in them.

So young converts have a remaining sourness and bitterness. They have a great mixture in their experiences and religious exercises, but as they ripen for heaven they are more purified. Their experiences become purer, their tempers are more mollified and sweetened with meekness and Christian love; and this by afflictions, persecutions and occasions of great self-denial, or in one word, by the cross of Christ. Whereas these trials bring hypocrites to nothing.

Green fruit hangs fast to the tree, but when it is ripe it is loose and easily picked. Wheat, while it is green in the field, sucks and draws for nourishment from the ground, but when it is ripe, it draws no more. So a saint, when ripe for heaven, is weaned from the world.

212. The immense magnificence of the visible world, its inconceivable vastness, the incomprehensible height of the heavens, etc. is but a type of the infinite magnificence, height and glory of God's work in the spiritual world: the most incomprehensible expression of his power, wisdom, holiness and love, in what is wrought and brought to pass in that world; and in the exceeding greatness of the moral and natural good, the light, knowledge, holiness and happiness which shall be communicated to it. And therefore to that magnificence of the world, height of heaven, those things are often compared in such expressions, "Thy mercy is great above the heavens, thy truth reacheth [unto the clouds]"; "Thou hast set thy glory above the heavens," etc. . . .

The Mind (1723)

[1]. EXCELLENCY. There has nothing been more without a definition than excellency, although it be what we are more concerned with than anything else whatsoever. Yea, we are concerned with nothing else. But what is this excellency? Wherein is one thing excellent and another evil, one beautiful and another deformed? Some have said that all excellency is harmony, symmetry or proportion; but they have not yet explained it. We would know why proportion is more excellent than disproportion, that is, why proportion is pleasant to the mind and disproportion unpleasant. Proportion is a thing that may be explained yet further. It is an equality, or likeness of ratios; so that it is the equality that makes the proportion. Excellency therefore seems to consist in equality. Thus, if there be two perfect equal circles or globes together, there is something more of beauty than if they were of unequal, disproportionate magnitudes. And if two parallel lines be drawn, the beauty is greater than if they were obliquely inclined without proportion, because there is equality of distance. And if, betwixt two parallel lines, two equal circles be placed, each at the same distance from each parallel line, as in Fig. 1, the beauty is greater than if they stood at irregular distances from the parallel lines. If they stand each in a perpendicular line going from the parallel lines (Fig. 2), it is requisite that they should each stand at an equal distance from the perpendicular line next to them; otherwise there is no beauty. If there be three of these circles between two parallel lines, and near to a perpendicular line run between them (Fig. 3), the most beautiful form, perhaps, that they could be placed in, is in an equilateral triangle with the cross line, because there are the most equalities: the distance of the two next to the cross line is equal from that, and also equal from the parallel lines. The distance of the third from each parallel is equal, and its distance from each of the other two circles is equal, and is also equal to their distance from one another, and likewise equal to their distance from each end of the cross line. There are two equilateral triangles, one made by the three circles, and the other

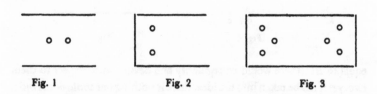

Fig. 1   Fig. 2   Fig. 3

made by the cross line and two of the sides of the first protracted till they meet that line. And if there be another like it on the opposite side, to correspond with it, and it be taken altogether, the beauty is still greater where the distances from the lines in the one are equal to the distances in the other; also the two next to the cross lines are at equal distances from the other two. Or, if you go crosswise from corner to corner, the two cross lines are also parallel, so that all parts are at an equal distance; and innumerable other equalities might be found.

This simple equality, without proportion, is the lowest kind of regularity, and may be called simple beauty; all other beauties and excellencies may be resolved into it. Proportion is complex beauty. Thus, if we suppose that there are two points, A [and] B, placed at two inches' distance, and the next, C, one inch farther (Fig. 4), it is requisite, in order to regularity and beauty, if there be another, D, that it should be at half an inch distance (otherwise there is no regularity, and the last, D, would stand out of its proper place), because now the relation that the space CD bears to BC is equal to the relation that BC bears to AB, so that BCD is exactly similar to ABC. 'Tis evident this is a more complicated excellency than that which consisted in equality, because the terms of the relation are here complex, and before were simple. When there are three points set in a right line, it is requisite, in order to regularity, that they should be set at an equal distance, as ABC (Fig. 5), where AB is similar to BC, or the relation of C to B is the same as of B to A. But in the other are three terms necessary in each of the parts between which is the relation (BCD is as ABC), so that here more simple beauties are omitted, and yet there is a general complex beauty. That is, BC is not as AB, nor is CD as BC; but yet BCD is as ABC. It is requisite that the consent or regularity of CD to BC be omitted, for the sake of the harmony of the whole. For although, if CD was perfectly

Fig. 4   Fig. 5

equal to *BC,* there would be regularity and beauty with respect to them two, yet if *AB* be taken into the idea, there is nothing but confusion. And it might be requisite, if these stood with others, even to omit this proposition for the sake of one more complex still. Thus, if they stood with other points, where *B* stood at four inches' distance from *A, C* at two from *B,* and *D* at six from *C* [Fig. 6], the place where *D* must stand in (if *A, B, C, D* were alone, viz., one inch from *C*) must be so as to be made proportionate with the other points beneath. So that although *A, B, C, D* are not proportioned, but are confusion among themselves, yet taken with the whole they are proportioned and beautiful.

All beauty consists in similarness, or identity of relation. In identity of relation consists all likeness, and all identity between two consists in identity of relation. Thus, when the distance between two is exactly equal, their distance is their relation one to another; the distance is the same, the bodies are two, wherefore this is their correspondency and beauty. So bodies exactly of the same figure: the bodies are two, the relation between the parts of the extremities is the same, and this is their agreement with them. But if there are two bodies of different shapes, having no similarness of relation between the parts of the extremities, this, considered by itself, is a deformity, because being disagrees with being; which must undoubtedly be disagreeable to perceiving being, because what disagrees with being must necessarily be disagreeable to being in general, to everything that partakes of entity, and of course to perceiving being. And what agrees with being must be agreeable to being in general, and therefore to

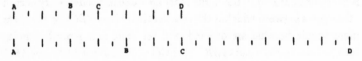

Fig. 6

perceiving being. But agreeableness of perceiving being is pleasure, and disagreeableness is pain. Disagreement or contrariety to being is evidently an approach to nothing, or a degree of nothing, which is nothing else but disagreement or contrariety of being, and the greatest and only evil; and entity is the greatest and only good. And by how much more perfect entity is, that is, without mixture of nothing, by so much the more excellency. Two beings can agree one with another in nothing else but relation; because otherwise the notion of their twoness (duality) is destroyed and they become one.

And so in every case, what is called correspondency, symmetry, regularity and the like, may be resolved into equalities; though the equalities in a beauty in any degree complicated are so numerous that it would be a most tedious piece of work to enumerate them. There are millions of these equalities. Of these consist the beautiful shape of flowers, the beauty of the body of man and of the bodies of other animals. That sort of beauty which is called "natural," as of vines, plants, trees, etc., consists of a very complicated harmony; and all the natural motions and tendencies and figures of bodies in the universe are done according to proportion, and therein is their beauty. Particular disproportions sometimes greatly add to the general beauty, and must necessarily be, in order to a more universal proportion—so much equality, so much beauty—though it may be noted that the quantity of equality is not to be measured only by the number, but the intenseness, according to the quantity of being. As bodies are shadows of being, so their proportions are shadows of proportion.

The pleasures of the senses, where harmony is not the object of judgment, are the result of equality. Thus in music, not only in the proportion which the several notes of a tune bear one among another, but in merely two notes, there is harmony; whereas it is impossible there should be proportion between only two terms. But the proportion is in the particular vibrations of the air which strike on the ear. And so in the pleasantness of light, colors, tastes, smells and touch: all arise from proportion of motion. The organs are so contrived that, upon the touch of such and such particles, there shall be a regular and harmonious motion of the animal spirits.

Spiritual harmonies are of vastly larger extent; i.e. the proportions are vastly oftener redoubled, and respect more beings, and require a vastly larger view to comprehend them, as some simple notes do more affect one who has not a comprehensive understanding of music.

The reason why equality thus pleases the mind, and inequality is unpleasing, is because disproportion, or inconsistency, is contrary to being. For being, if we examine narrowly, is nothing else but proportion. When one being is inconsistent with another being, then being is contradicted. But contradiction to being is intolerable to perceiving being, and the consent to being most pleasing.

Excellency consists in the similarness of one being to another—not merely equality and proportion, but any kind of similarness. Thus similarness of direction: supposing many globes moving in right lines, it is more beautiful that they should move all the same way and according to the same direction, than if they moved disorderly, one one way and another another. This is an universal definition of excellency: The consent of being to being, or being's consent to entity. The more the consent is, and the more extensive, the greater is the excellency.

How exceedingly apt are we, when we are sitting still and accidentally casting our eye upon some marks or spots in the floor or wall, to be ranging of them into regular parcels and figures; and if we see a mark out of its place, to be placing of it right by our imagination—and this even while we are meditating on something else. So we may catch ourselves at observing the rules of harmony and regularity in the careless motions of our heads or feet, and when playing with our hands or walking about the room.

Pleasedness in perceiving being always arises, either from a perception of consent to being in general, or of consent to that being that perceives. As we have shown, that agreeableness to entity must be agreeable to perceiving entity. It is as evident that it is necessary that agreeableness to that being must be pleasing to it, if it perceives it; so that pleasedness does not always arise from a perception of excellency in general; but the greater a being is, and the more it has of entity, the more will consent to being in general please it. But God is proper entity itself, and these two therefore in him become the same; for so far as a thing consents to being in general, so far it consents to him. And the more perfect created spirits are, the nearer do they come to their creator in this regard.

That which is often called self-love is exceedingly improperly called love. For they do not only say that one loves himself when he sees something amiable in himself, the view of which begets delight; but merely an inclination to pleasure and averseness to pain they call self-love: so that the devils and other damned spirits love themselves, not because they see anything in themselves which they imagine to be lovely, but merely because they do not incline to pain, but to pleasure; or merely because they are capable of pain or pleasure, for pain and pleasure include an inclination to agreeableness and an aversion to disagreeableness. Now how improper is it to say, that one loves himself because what is agreeable to him is agreeable to him, and what is disagreeable to him is disagreeable to him, which mere entity supposes. So that this that they call self-love is no affection, but only the entity of the thing, or his being what he is.

One alone, without any reference to any more, cannot be excellent; for in such a case there can be no manner of relation no way, and therefore, no such thing as consent. Indeed, what we call "one" may be excellent, because of a consent of parts, or some consent of those in that being that are distinguished into a plurality some way or other. But in a being that is absolutely without any plurality there cannot be excellency, for there can be no such thing as consent or agreement.

One of the highest excellencies is love. As nothing else has a proper being but spirits, and as bodies are but the shadow of being, therefore, the consent of bodies to one another, and the harmony that is among them, is but the shadow of excellency. The highest excellency, therefore, must be the consent of spirits one to another. But the consent of spirits consists half in their mutual love one to another, and the sweet harmony between the various parts of the universe is only an image of mutual love. But yet a lower kind of love may be odious, because it hinders or is contrary to a higher and more general. Even a lower proportion is often a deformity, because it is contrary to a more general proportion.

Corollary 1. If so much of the beauty and excellency of spirits consists in love, then the deformity of evil spirits consists as much in hatred and malice.

Corol. 2. The more any doctrine or institution brings to light of the spiritual world, the more will it urge to love and charity.

Happiness, strictly, consists in the perception of these three things: of the consent of being to its own being; of its own consent to being; and of being's consent to being.

[2]. PLACE OF MINDS. Our common way of conceiving of what is spiritual is very gross and shadowy and corporeal, with dimensions and figure, etc.; though it be supposed to be very clear, so that we can see through it. If we would get a right notion of what is spiritual, we must think of thought or inclination or delight. How large is that thing in the mind which they call thought? Is love square or round? Is the surface of hatred rough or smooth? Is joy an inch, or a foot in diameter? These are spiritual things. And why should we then form such a ridiculous idea of spirits, as to think them so long, so thick, or so wide; or to think there is a necessity of their being square or round or some other certain figure?

Therefore spirits cannot be in place in such a sense, that all within the given limits shall be where the spirit is, and all without such a circumscription where he is not; but in this sense only, that all created spirits have clearer and more strongly impressed ideas of things in one place than in another, or can produce effects here and not there; and as this place alters, so spirits move. In spirits united to bodies, the spirit more strongly perceives things where the body is, and can there immediately produce effects, and in this sense the soul can be said to be in the same place where the body is; and this law is that we call the union between soul and body. So the soul may be said to be in the brain, because ideas that come by the body immediately ensue only on alterations that are made there, and the soul most immediately produces effects nowhere else.

No doubt that all finite spirits, united to bodies or not, are thus in place; that is, that they perceive or passively receive ideas only or chiefly of created things that are in some particular place at a given time. At least a finite spirit cannot thus be in all places at a time equally. And doubtless the change of the place where they perceive most strongly, and produce effects immediately, is regular and successive; which is the motion of spirits.

[34]. When we say that the world, i.e., the material universe, exists nowhere but in the mind, we have got to such a degree of strictness and abstraction that we must be exceedingly careful that we do not confound and lose ourselves by misapprehension. That is impossible, that it should be meant that all the world is contained in the narrow compass of a few inches of space, in little ideas in the place of the brain; for that would be a contradiction. For we are to remember that the human body and the brain itself exist only mentally, in the same sense that other things do. And so that which we call place is an idea too. Therefore things are truly in those places, for what we mean when we say so is only that this mode of our idea of place appertains to such an idea. We would not, therefore, be understood to deny that things are where they seem to be, for the principles we lay down, if they are narrowly looked into, do not infer that. Nor will it be found that they at all make void natural philosophy, or the science of the causes or reasons of corporeal changes; for to find out the reasons of things in natural philosophy is only to find out the proportion of God's acting. And the case is the same, as to such proportions, whether we suppose the world only mental in our sense, or no.

Though we suppose that the existence of the whole material universe is absolutely dependent on idea, yet we may speak in the old way, and as properly and truly as ever: God in the beginning created such a certain number atoms, of such a determinate bulk and figure, which they yet maintain and always will; and gave them such a motion, of such a direction, and of such a degree of velocity; from whence arise all the natural changes in the universe forever in a continued series. Yet perhaps all this does not exist anywhere perfectly but in the divine mind. But then, if it be inquired what exists in the divine mind, and how these things exist there, I answer: there is his determination, his care and his design that ideas shall be united forever, just so and in such a manner as is agreeable to such a series. For instance, all the ideas that ever were or ever shall be to all eternity, in any created mind, are answerable to the existence of such a peculiar atom in the beginning of the creation, of such a determinate figure and size, and have such a motion given it. That is, they are all such as infinite wisdom sees would follow, according to the series of nature, from such an atom so moved. That is, all ideal changes of creatures are just so, as if just such a particular atom had actually all along existed even in some finite mind, and never had been out of that mind, and had in that mind caused these effects which are exactly according to nature, that is, according to the nature of other matter that is actually perceived by the mind. God supposes its existence; that is, he causes all changes to arise as if all these things had actually existed in such a series in some created mind, and as if created minds had comprehended all things perfectly. And although created minds do not, yet the divine mind doth, and he orders all things according to his mind, and his ideas.

And these hidden things do not only exist in the divine idea, but in a sense in created idea, for that exists in created idea which necessarily supposes it. If a ball of lead were supposed to be let fall from the clouds and no eye saw it till it got within ten rods of the ground, and then its motion and celerity was perfectly discerned in its exact proportion, if it were not for the imperfection and slowness of our minds, the perfect idea of the rest of the motion would immediately and of itself arise in the mind, as well as that which is there. So, were our thoughts comprehensive and perfect enough, our view of the present state of the world would excite in us a perfect idea of all past changes. And we need not perplex our minds with a thousand questions and doubts that will seem to arise, as to what purpose is this way of exciting ideas, and what advantage is there in observing such a series. I answer: it is just all one as to any benefit or advantage, any end that we can suppose was proposed by the Creator, as if the material universe were existent in the same manner as is vulgarly thought. For the corporeal world is to no advantage but to the spiritual, and it is exactly the same advantage this way as the other; for it is all one as to anything excited in the mind.

[61]. SUBSTANCE. It is intuitively certain that if solidity be removed from body, nothing is left but empty space. Now in all things whatsoever,

that which cannot be removed without removing the whole thing, that thing which is removed is the thing itself; except it be mere circumstance and manner of existence, such as time and place, which are in the general necessary because it implies a contradiction to existence itself to suppose that it exists at no time and in no place. And therefore, in order to remove time and place in the general, we must remove the thing itself; so, if we remove figure and bulk and texture in the general, which may be reduced to that necessary circumstance of place.

If, therefore, it implies a contradiction to suppose that body, or anything appertaining to body beside space, exists when solidity is removed, it must be either because body is nothing but solidity and space, or else that solidity is such a mere circumstance and relation of existence which the thing cannot be without, because whatever exists must exist in some circumstances or other, as at some time or some place. But we know and everyone perceives it to be a contradiction to suppose that body or matter exists without solidity; for all the notion we have of empty space is space without solidity, and all the notion we have of full space is space resisting.

The reason is plain: for if it implies a contradiction to suppose solidity absent and the thing existing, it must be because solidity is that thing, and so it is a contradiction to say the thing is absent from itself; or because it is such a mode or circumstance or relation of the existence as it is a contradiction to suppose existence at all without it, such as time and place, to which both figure and texture are reduced. For nothing can be conceived of so necessarily in an existence, that it is a contradiction to suppose it without it, but the existence itself, and those general circumstances or relations of existence which the very supposition of existence itself implies.

Again, solidity or impenetrability is as much action or the immediate result of action as gravity. Gravity by all will be confessed to be immediately from some active influence. Being a continual tendency in bodies to move, and being that which will set them in motion though before at perfect rest, it must be the effect of something acting on that body. And it is as clear and evident that action is as requisite to stop a body that is already in motion, as in order to set bodies a-moving that are at perfect rest. Now we see continually that there is a stopping of all motion at the limits of such and such parts of space, only this stoppage is modified and diversified according to certain laws. For we get the idea and apprehension of solidity only and entirely from the observation we make of that ceasing of motion, at the limits of some parts of space, that already is, and that beginning of motion that till now was not, according to a certain constant manner.

And why is it not every whit as reasonable that we should attribute this action or effect to the influence of some agent, as that other action or effect which we call gravity, which is likewise derived from our observation of the beginning and ceasing of motion according to a certain method? In either case there is nothing observed but the beginning, increasing, directing, diminishing and ceasing of motion. And why is it not as reasonable to seek a reason beside that general one, that it is something—which is no reason at all? I say, why is it not as reasonable to seek a reason or cause of these actions as well in one as in the other case? We do not think it sufficient to say it is the nature of the unknown substance in the one case; and why should we think it a sufficient explication of the same actions or effects in the other? By substance, I suppose it is confessed, we mean only "something," because of abstract substance we have no idea that is more particular than only existence in general. Now why is it not as reasonable, when we see something suspended in the air, set to move with violence towards the earth, to rest in attributing of it to the nature of the something that is there, as when we see that motion, when it comes to such limits, all on a sudden cease? For this is all that we observe in falling bodies. Their falling is the action we call gravity; their stopping upon the surface of the earth the action whence we gain the idea of solidity. It was before agreed on all hands that there is something there that supports that resistance. It must be granted now that that something is a being that acts there, as much as that being that causes bodies to descend towards the center. Here is something in these parts of space that of itself produces effects, without previously being acted upon. For that being that lays an arrest on bodies in motion, and immediately stops them when they come to such limits and bounds, certainly does as much as that being that sets a body in motion that before was at rest. Now this being, acting altogether of itself, producing new effects that are perfectly arbitrary, and that are no way necessary of themselves, must be intelligent and voluntary. There is no reason in the nature of the thing itself why a body, when set in motion, should stop at such limits more than at any other. It must therefore be some arbitrary, active and voluntary being that determines it. If there were but one body in the universe that always in time past had been at rest, and should now without any alteration be set in motion, we might certainly conclude that some voluntary being set it in motion, because it can certainly be demonstrated that it can be for no other reason; so, with just the same reason, in the same manner we may conclude, if the body had hitherto been in motion and is at a certain point of space now stopped. And would it not be every whit as reasonable to conclude it must be from such an agent, as if in certain portions of space we observed bodies to be attracted a certain way, and so at once to be set into motion, or accelerated in motion? And it is not at all the less remarkable because we receive the ideas of light and colors from those spaces, for we know that light and colors are not there, and are made entirely by such a resistance, together with attraction, that is antecedent to these qualities, and would be a necessary effect of a mere resistance of space without other substance.

The whole of what we any way observe whereby we get the idea of solidity or solid body are certain parts of space from whence we receive the ideas of light and colors, and certain sensations by the sense of feeling. And we observe that the places whence we receive these sensations are not constantly the same, but are successively different, and this light and colors are communicated from one part of space to another. And we observe that these parts of space, from whence we receive these sensations, resist and stop other bodies, which we observe communicated successively through the parts of space adjacent, and that those that there were before at rest, or existing constantly in one and the same part of space, after this exist successively in different parts of space. And these observations are according to certain stated rules. I appeal to anyone that takes notice and asks himself, whether this be not all that ever he experienced in the world whereby he got these ideas, and that this is all that we have or can have any idea of, in relation to bodies. All that we observe of solidity is that certain parts of space, from whence we receive the ideas of light and colors and a few other sensations, do likewise resist anything coming within them. It therefore follows that if we suppose there be anything else than what we thus observe, it is but only by way of inference.

I know that it is nothing but the imagination will oppose me in this. I will therefore endeavor to help the imagination thus. Suppose that we received none of the sensible qualities of light, colors, etc. from the resisting parts of space (we will suppose it possible for resistance to be without them), and they were to appearance clear and pure, and all that we could possibly observe was only and merely resistance; we simply observed that motion was resisted and stopped here and there, in particular parts of infinite space. Should we not then think it less unreasonable to suppose that such effects should be produced by some agent present in those parts of space, though invisible? If we, when walking upon the face of the earth, were stopped at certain limits and could not possibly enter into such a part of space, nor make any body enter into it, and we could observe no other difference, no way nor at any time, between that and other parts of clear space; should we not be ready to say: What is it stops us? What is it hinders all entrance into that place?

The reason why it is so exceedingly natural to men to suppose that there is some latent substance, or something that is altogether hid, that upholds the properties of bodies, is because all see at first sight that the properties of bodies are such as need some cause that shall every moment have influence to their continuance, as well as a cause of their first existence. All therefore agree that there is something that is there, and upholds these properties; and it is most true, there undoubtedly is. But men are wont to content themselves in saying merely that it is something; but that "something" is he by whom all things consist.

Miscellanies (1722)

f. SPIRITUAL HAPPINESS. As we have shown and demonstrated, that, contrary to the opinion of Hobbes (that nothing is substance but matter), that no matter is substance but only God, who is a spirit, and that other spirits are more substantial than matter: so also it is true, that no happiness is solid and substantial but spiritual happiness; although it may seem that sensual pleasures are most real, and spiritual only imaginary, as it seems as if sensible matter were only real, and spiritual substance only imaginary.

x. PLEASANTNESS OF RELIGION. It is no argument against the pleasantness of religion, that it has no tendency to raise laughter, and rather [tends] to remove [it]. For that pleasure which raises laughter is never great—everyone knows this by his own experience—and besides, it is flashy, external, and not lasting. The greater sort of temporal pleasures don't raise laughter, as the joy of the sight and enjoyment of most dear friends, but only raises a smile, without any of that shaking laughter, which always arises from a mixture of pleasure and sorrow and never from pure pleasure, because it always arises from something that is ridiculous. Now a thing that is ridiculous is a mixture of what is painful with what is pleasant; for a thing is never ridiculous, except there be something in it that is deformed and contrary to beautiful, and therefore disagreeable to the soul. But that pleasure which is raised from the apprehension of something purely agreeable never causes laughter. The pleasure of religion raises one clear above laughter, and rather tends to make the face to shine than screw it into a grimace; though when it is at its height it begets a sweet, inexpressibly joyful smile, as we know only a smile is begotten by the great pleasure of dear friends' society. The reason why the pleasures of religion be not always attended with such a smile, is because we have so many sins and have so much offended God; and almost all our religious thoughts are unavoidably attended with repentance and a sense of our own misery. It is the pleasure of repentance alone that don't tend to a smile.

The reason why religious thoughts will cause one to sigh sometimes, is not from the melancholiness of religion, but because religious thoughts are of such an high, internal and spiritual nature as very much abstracts the soul from the body, and so the operations of the body are deadened; when arises a sigh to renew it, as a sigh will arise from weakness of body, whether by sickness or labor, whether one is melancholy or no. 'Tis this abstraction of the soul, in its height, leaves the body even dead; and then the soul is in a trance.

gg. RELIGION. 'Tis most certain that God did not create the world for nothing. 'Tis most certain that if there were not intelligent beings in the world, all the world would be without any end at all. For senseless matter, in whatever excellent order it is placed, would be useless if there were no intelligent beings at all, neither God nor others; for what would it be good for? So certainly, senseless matter would be altogether useless, if there was no intelligent being but God, for God could neither receive good himself nor communicate good. What would this vast universe of matter, placed in such excellent order and governed by such excellent rules, be good for, if there was no intelligence that could know anything of it? Wherefore it necessarily follows that intelligent beings are the end of the creation, that their end must be to behold and admire the doings of God, and magnify him for them, and to contemplate his glories in them.

Wherefore religion must be the end of the creation, the great end, the very end. If it were not for this, all those vast bodies we see ordered with so excellent skill, so according to the nicest rules of proportion, according to such laws of gravity and motion, would be all vanity, or good for nothing and to no purpose at all. For religion is the very business, the noble business of intelligent beings, and for this end God has placed us on this earth. If it were not for men, this world would be altogether in vain, with all the curious workmanship of it and accoutrements about it.

It follows from this that we must be immortal. The world had as good have been without us, as for us to be a few minutes and then be annihilated—if we are now to own God's works to his glory, and only glorify him a few minutes, and then be annihilated, and it shall after that be all one to eternity as if we never had been, and be in vain after we are dead that we have been once; and then, after the earth shall be destroyed, it shall be for the future entirely in vain that either the earth or mankind have ever been. The same argument seems to be used, Is. 45:17-18. . . .

kk. RELIGION. *Corollary* on the former on this subject [no. gg]. Since the world would be altogether good for nothing without intelligent beings, so intelligent beings would be altogether good for nothing except to contemplate the Creator. Hence we learn that devotion, and not mutual love, charity, justice, beneficence, etc. is the highest end of man, and devotion is his principal business. For all justice, beneficence, etc. are good for nothing without it, are to no purpose at all. For those duties are only for the advancement of the *great* business, to assist mutually each other to it.

3. HAPPINESS IS THE END OF THE CREATION, as appears by this, because the creation had as good not be, as not rejoice in its being. For certainly it was the goodness of the Creator that moved him to create; and how can we conceive of another end proposed by goodness, than that he might delight in seeing the creatures he made rejoice in that being that he has given them?

It appears also by this, because the end of the creation is that the creation might glorify him. Now what is glorifying God, but a rejoicing at that glory he has displayed? An understanding of the perfections of God, merely, cannot be the end of the creation; for he had as good not understand it, as see it and not be at all moved with joy at the sight. Neither can the highest end of the creation be the declaring God's glory to others; for the declaring God's glory is good for nothing otherwise than to raise joy in ourselves and others at what is declared.

Wherefore, seeing happiness is the highest end of the creation of the universe, and intelligent beings are that consciousness of the creation that is to be the immediate subject of this happiness, how happy may we conclude will be those intelligent beings that are to be made eternally happy!

37. FAITH. The soul is espoused and married unto Jesus Christ; the believing soul is the bride and spouse of the Son of God. The union between Christ and believers is very often represented to a marriage. This similitude is much insisted on in Scripture—how sweetly is it set forth in the Song of Songs! Now it is by faith that the soul is united unto Christ; faith is this bride's reception of Christ as a bridegroom. Let us, following this similitude that we may illustrate the nature of faith, a little consider what are those affections and motions of heart that are proper and suitable in a spouse toward her bridegroom, what are those conjugal motions of soul which are most agreeable to, and do most harmonize with, that relation that she bears as a spouse.

Now it is easy to everyone to know that when marriage is according to nature and God's designation, when a woman is married to an husband she receives him as a guide, as a protector, a safeguard and defense, a shelter from harms and dangers, a reliever from distresses, a comforter in afflictions, a support in discouragements. God has so designed it, and therefore has made man of a more robust [nature], and strong in body and mind, with more wisdom, strength and courage, fit to protect and defend; but he has made woman weaker, more soft and tender, more fearful, and more affectionate, as a fit object of generous protection and defense. Hence it is, that it is natural in women to look most at valor and fortitude, wisdom, generosity and greatness of soul: these virtues do—or at least ought, according to nature—move most upon the affections of the woman. Hence also it is, that man naturally looks most at a soft and tender disposition of mind, and those virtues and affections which spring from it, such as humility, modesty, purity, chastity. And the affections which he most naturally looks at in her, are a sweet and entire confidence and trust, submission and resignation; for when he receives a woman as wife, he receives her as an object of his guardianship and protection, and therefore looks at those qualifications and dispositions which exert themselves in trust and confidence. Thus it's against nature for a man to love a woman as wife that is rugged, daring and presumptuous, and trusts to herself, and thinks she is able to protect herself and needs none of her husband's defense or guidance. And it is impossible a woman should love a man as an husband, except she can confide in him, and sweetly rest in him as a safeguard.

Thus also, when the believer receives Christ by faith, he receives him as a safeguard and shelter from the wrath of God and eternal torments, and defense from all the harms and dangers which he fears; Is. 32:2, "And a man shall be as an hiding place from the wind, and a covert from the tempest; as rivers of water in a dry place, as the shadow of a great rock in a weary land." Wherefore, the dispositions of soul which Christ looks at in his spouse are a sweet reliance and confidence in him, a humble trust in him as her only rock of defence, whither she may flee. And Christ will not receive those as the objects of his salvation who trust to themselves, their own strength or worthiness, but those alone who entirely rely on him. The reason of this is very natural and easy.

40. MINISTERS. . . . 'Tis a thousand pities that the words "church office" and "power" should so tear the world to pieces, and raise such a fog and dust about apostolic office, power and succession, [and about] popes', bishops' and presbyters' power. It is not such a desperately difficult thing to know what power belongs to each of these; if we will let drop those words, that are without fixed meaning, the light of nature will lead us right along in a plain path.

Without doubt, ministers are to administer the sacraments to Christians, and that they are to administer them only to such as they think Christ would have them administer them. Without doubt, ministers are to teach men what Christ would have them to do, and to teach them who doth these things and who doth them not, that is, who are Christians and who are not; and the people are to hear them as much in this as in other things: and that so far forth as the people are obliged to hear what I teach them, so great is my pastoral, or ministerial, or teaching power. And this is all the difference of power there is amongst ministers, whether apostles or whatever.

Thus if I in a right manner am become the teacher of a people, so far as they ought to hear what I teach them, so much power I have. Thus if they are obliged to hear me only because they themselves have chosen me to

guide them, and therein declared that they thought me sufficiently instructed in the mind of Christ to teach them, and because I have the other
requisites of being their teacher, then I have power as other ministers have
in these days. But if it was plain to them that I was under the infallible
guidance of Christ, then I should have more power. And if it was plain to
all the world of Christians that I was under the infallible guidance of
Christ, and [that] I was sent forth to teach the world the will of Christ,
then I should have power in all the world: I should have power to teach
them what they ought to do, and they would be obliged to hear me; I
should have power to teach them who were Christians and who not, and
in this likewise they would be obliged to hear me.

106. HAPPINESS. We argue very justly, that seeing God has created the
whole world for his own glory, that therefore he will glorify himself
exceeding transcendently; but we have showed that is, he will give his
creatures occasion to glorify him exceedingly: but glorifying of God, as we
have remarked in No. 3, is nothing but rejoicing in the manifestations of
him. Wherefore it may with equal evidence be argued, that man's happiness, i.e. the happiness of the saints, will be very transcendent, as transcendent as the glory of God, seeing it is the same. Again, seeing that God
has created man as the intelligence of the creation, to behold the manifestation of God's excellency—and we have proved that God created all
things only for the happiness of the intelligence of the creation [no. gg],
and we have showed that happiness is the perception and possession of
excellency—therefore, in proportion as God has manifested his excellency, will the intelligence or perception of the world be happy. We
therefore may be without doubt, that man shall be exceeding happy beyond conception.

Again, that the saints will be full of happiness, will have as much
happiness as they can contain (that is, they will have happiness completely
adequate to their capacity), is evident, because happiness is nothing, as we
have showed, but the perception and the possession of excellency. Therefore if they are not full, it must be for want of excellency or the possession
of it. But they can't want excellency to behold in God, he being infinite in

it; neither will they want the means of beholding or perceiving it, as far as their capacity allows; nor will they want possession.

189. LOVE OF CHRIST. We see how great love the human nature is capable of, not only to God but fellow creatures. How greatly are we inclined to the other sex! Nor doth an exalted and fervent love to God hinder this, but only refines and purifies it. God has created the human nature to love fellow creatures, which he wisely has principally turned to the other sex; and the more exalted the nature is, the greater love of that kind that is laudable is it susceptive of; and the purer and better natured, the more is it inclined to it.

Christ has an human nature as well as we, and has an inclination to love those that partake of the human [nature] as well as we. That inclination which in us is turned to the other sex, in him is turned to the church, which is his spouse. He is as much of a purer and better and more benevolent nature than we, whereby he is inclined to a higher degree of love, as he is of a greater capacity, whereby he is capable of a more exalted, ardent and sweet love. Nor is his love to God, in him more than in us (nor half so much), an hindrance or diversion to this love; because his love to God and his love to the saints are an hundred times nearer akin than our love to God and our love to the other sex. Therefore when we feel love to anyone of the other sex, 'tis a good way to think of the love of Christ to an holy and beautiful soul.

198. HAPPINESS. How soon do earthly lovers come to an end of their discoveries of each other's beauty; how soon do they see all that is to be seen! Are they united as near as 'tis possible, and have communion as intimate as possible? how soon do they come to the most endearing expressions of love that 'tis possible to give, so that no new ways can be invented, given or received. And how happy is that love, in which there is an eternal progress in all these things; wherein new beauties are continually discovered, and more and more loveliness, and in which we shall forever increase in beauty ourselves; where we shall be made capable of finding out and giving, and shall receive, more and more endearing ex-

pressions of love forever: our union will become more close, and communion more intimate.

241. REGENERATION. It may be in the new birth as it is in the first birth. The vivification of the fetus in the womb is exceeding gradual; the vital operations of it arise from the most imperfect to the more perfect by an insensible increase, so that there is no determining at what time it first begins to be [a] living creature and to have a rational soul. Yet there is a certain moment that an immortal spirit begins to exist in it by God's appointment; so that if the fetus should be destroyed before that moment, there would be an end to its existence; but if at any time after, there would remain an immortal spirit, that would be translated into another world. I don't see why it may not be sometimes so, though at other times there is doubtless a remarkable and very sensible change made at once when the soul is newborn.

In the new birth there is certainly a very great change made in the soul: so in the first birth there is a very great change when the rational soul is first infused, for the fetus immediately upon it becomes a living creature and a man, that before had no life; yet the sensible change is very gradual. It likewise seems reasonable to me to suppose that the habit of grace in adults is always begun with an act of grace that shall imply faith in it, because a habit can be of no manner of use till there is occasion to exert it; and all habits being only a law that God has fixed, that such actions upon such occasions should be exerted, the first new thing that there can be in the creature must be some actual alteration. So in the first birth it seems to me probable that the beginning of the existence of the soul, whose essence consists in powers and habits, is with some kind of new alteration there, either in motion or sensation.

279. ETERNITY OF HELL TORMENTS. I am convinced that hell torments will be eternal from one great good the wisdom of God proposes by them, which is, by the sight of them to exalt the happiness, the love, and joyful thanksgivings of the angels and men that are saved; which it tends exceedingly to do. I am ready to think that the beholding the sight of the great miseries of those of their species that are damned will double the ardor of their love, and the fullness of the joy of the elect angels and men. It will do it many ways. The sight of the wonderful power, the great and dreadful majesty and authority, and the awful justice and holiness of God manifested in their punishment, will make them prize his favor and love exceedingly the more; and will excite a most exquisite love and thankfulness to him, that he chose them out from the rest to make them thus happy, that God did not make them such vessels of wrath, according to Rom. 9:22–23, "What if God, willing to show his wrath," etc. "and that he might make known the riches of his glory on the vessels of mercy." And then, only a lively sense of the opposite misery makes any happiness and pleasure double what it would be. Seeing therefore that this happiness of the blessed is to be eternal, the misery of the damned will be eternal also.

314. FREE GRACE. This appears to me to be a rational account of God's free grace, and also a certain one. God has in his own nature a propensity to communicate goodness and to make happy; and having created creatures for that end, he has a propensity to communicate happiness to those of them that he in his wisdom chooses, without any consideration of anything that is good of one kind or other to incline him. For he would have an inclination to it though they were considered as nonentities; for he has an absolute inclination to goodness in his own nature, which is the reason even of their being, so that he loves them with a love of benevolence for nothing at all in them, and without being inclined thereto by any of their perfections natural or moral. Now a love free in this sense is a perfection of God, and what rationally obliges our love to him more than any love for anything good in us can do, because 'tis a greater manifestation of a loving and good nature. He therefore wills absolutely, and freely in this sense, all the happiness that he ever confers on the elect; and his wisdom determines the degree of happiness antecedent to any consideration of the degree of goodness in them.

But because God does everything beautifully, he brings about this their happiness which he determined, in an excellent manner; but it would be a grating, dissonant and deformed thing for a sinful creature to be happy in God's love. He therefore gives them holiness, which holiness he really delights in—he has really complacence in them after he has given them beauty, and not before—and so the beauty that he gives, when given, induces God in a certain secondary manner to give them happiness. That is, he wills their happiness antecedently, of himself, and he gives them holiness that he may be induced to confer it; and when it is given by him, then he is induced by another consideration besides his mere propensity to goodness. For there are these two propensities in the divine nature: to communicate goodness absolutely to that which now is nothing, and to communicate goodness to that which is beautiful and holy, and which he has complacence in. He has a propensity to reward holiness, but he gives it on purpose that he may reward it; because he loves the creature, and loves to reward, and therefore gives it something that he may reward.

350. CHRISTIAN RELIGION. . . . Were it not for divine revelation, I am persuaded that there is no one doctrine of that which we call natural religion [but] would, notwithstanding all philosophy and learning, forever be involved in darkness, doubts, endless disputes and dreadful confusion. There are many things, now they are revealed, seem very plain, and as if we could easily arrive at a certainty of them if we never had had a revelation of them. It is one thing to see that a truth is exceeding agreeable to reason, after we have been told it and have had it explained to us, and have been told the reasons of it; and another to find it out, and clearly and certainly to explain it, by mere reason. 'Tis one thing to prove a thing after we are showed how, and another to find it out and prove it of ourselves. . . .

And it would be so also with respect to abundance of moral duties that respect ourselves and one another. Every man would plead for the lawfulness of this or that practice, just as suited his fancy and agreed with his interest and appetites; and there would be room for a great deal of uncertainty and difference of opinion amongst those that were most speculative and impartial. There would be uncertainty, in a multitude of instances, what was just and what unjust: 'twould be very uncertain how far self-interest should govern men, and how far love to our neighbor; how far revenge would be right, and whether or no a man might hate his neighbors, and for what causes; what degree of passion and high-spiritedness and ambition was justifiable and laudable; what acts of venery were lawful and what not; how far we ought to honor and respect and submit to our parents and other superiors; how far it would be lawful to dissemble and deceive. It seems to me there would be infinite confusion in these and such like things, and that there hardly would be any such thing as conscience in the world.

The world has had a great deal of experience of the necessity of a revelation. We may see it in all parts of mankind, in all ages, that have been without a revelation: what gross darkness and brutal stupidity have such places in these matters always been overwhelmed in! and how many, and how great and foolish mistakes, and what endless uncertainties and differences of opinion, have there been amongst the most learned and philosophical! Yet there never was a real trial how it would be with mankind in this respect, without having anything any way from revelation. I believe that most of those parts of natural religion that were held by the heathens before Christ came into the world, were owing to tradition from those of their forefathers that had the light of revelation; and many of these, being exceeding evidently agreeable to reason, were more easily upheld and propagated: and especially because many of their wise men, and men that had influence and rule over them, who saw their rectitude and agreeableness to reason better than others, did as it were renew them from time to time, and used to travel into other countries and gather up remains of truth which they found scattered about in other parts of the world, preserved in the same manner by tradition; and some of them traveled to that part of the world that had divine revelation in their possession, and those things amongst them which appeared most agreeable to their reason, they transplanted to their own country.

Judea was a sort of a light amongst the nations, though they did not know it. The practice and principles of that country had this influence, that it kept the neighboring nations in remembrance of their traditions which they had from their forefathers, that professed the same truths, and so kept them from degenerating so much as otherwise they would have done. The philosophers had the foundation of most of their truth from the ancients or from the Phoenicians, and what they picked up here and there of the relics of revelation.

How came all the heathen nations to agree in that custom of sacrificing? the light of nature did not teach it [to] 'em. Without doubt they had it by tradition; and therefore it need not seem strange, that what of natural religion they had amongst them came the same way. And I suppose, most of the principles of justice and right rules they had of behavior towards themselves and their neighbors, was also by tradition. They were the more easily obtained, partly because they were agreeable to reason, and partly because their rulers saw the necessity of 'em in order to their quiet, strength and prosperity. . . .

We hardly can have a conception how it would be, if there never had been any revelation, for we are bred up in the light of revelation from our very infancy. If there was a nation of philosophers, where all were taught philosophy as soon as they came to be capable of understanding anything, and so were bred up in [it], they would admire at the ignorance and the thoughtlessness of a people that did not meddle with it; they would wonder that they could have so little reflection, and that they should be so ignorant of these and those things that were so plain and easy to them. Knowledge is easy to us that understand by revelation; but we don't know what brutes we should have been, if there never had been any. . . .

416. JUSTIFICATION. When it is said that we are not justified by works, nothing else can be intended but this, viz. that nothing that we do procures reconciliation with God for us and an admittance into his favor, by virtue of the loveliness of it, or by reason of any influence the loveliness of it has to move God's love or favorable respect, or any attracting or uniting influence the excellency and amiableness of it has with him, that should incline him so to abate of his anger or to receive into favor. God don't justify us in this manner, upon the account of any act of ours, whether it be the act of faith or any other act whatsoever, but only upon the account of what the Savior did.

But 'tis something that we do, that renders it in God's account (as the case now stands, there being a Savior) a meet thing, that God should let go his anger and admit us into his favor, as it may render it a meet thing in the sight of God, that we in particular should be looked upon as united to the Savior, and having the merit of what he did and suffered (upon the account of which we are so justified) belonging to us; by reason of its being the primary, and most simple and direct exercise of an uniting, harmony and agreement in the soul with that Savior and his salvation, and the way of it, and the proper act of reception of him, or closing and uniting with him as a Savior. This is quite a different thing from the former.

And thus it is that we are said to be justified by faith alone: that is, we are justified only because our souls close and join with Christ the Savior, his salvation, and the way of it; and not because of the excellency or loveliness of any of our dispositions or actions, that moves God to it. And we are justified by obedience or good works, only as a principle of obedience or a holy disposition is implied in such a harmonizing or joining, and is a secondary expression of the agreement and union between the nature of the soul and the gospel, or as an exercise and fruit and evidence of faith. . . .

471. SPIRIT'S OPERATION. CONVICTION. CONVERSION. Difference between [the] Spirit's operation in converted and unconverted men. The Spirit of God influences and operates upon the minds of both natural and regenerate men; but doubtless there is a great difference, not only in the works he does or the effects he produces, but also in the manner of his operation: for wicked men are sensual and have not the Spirit; those that are none of Christ's have not the Spirit of Christ. And the difference seems to be this: the Holy Ghost influences the godly as dwelling in them as a vital principle, or as a new supernatural principle of life and action. But in unregenerate men, he operates only by assisting natural principles to do the same work which they do of themselves, to a greater degree. As for instance, the Spirit assists natural conscience. The work of natural conscience that it doth of itself, is to give an apprehension of right and wrong, and to suggest to the mind the relation that there is between right or wrong and a retribution. . . . Sin and sensuality, by its stupifying nature, greatly hinders conscience in doing this work; it clogs and lames it, but don't destroy its power so that it shall not be able to do it; but though sin has the dominion in the heart, yet conscience continues to do this work still. But the Spirit of God, when It convinces and awakens a sinner, assists it to do it to a greater degree by Its assistance, frees it in a measure from its clog and hindrance by sin.

But in the sanctifying work of the Holy Ghost, not only remaining principles are assisted to do their work to a greater degree, but those principles are restored that were utterly destroyed by the fall; [so that] the mind habitually exerts those acts that the dominion of sin had made the soul wholly destitute of, as much as a dead body is destitute of vital acts.

And then there is this other difference: the Spirit of God in the souls of his saints exerts its own proper nature; that is to say, it communicates and exerts itself in the soul, in those acts which are its proper, natural and essential acts in itself *ad intra*, or within the Deity from all eternity. The proper nature of the Spirit of God, the act which is its nature and wherein its being consists, is . . . divine love. Therefore the Holy Ghost influences the minds of the godly by living in the godly. The Spirit of God may operate upon a mind and produce effects in it, and yet not communicate itself in its nature in the soul. The Spirit of God operates in the minds of the godly by only being in them, uniting itself to their souls, and living in 'em and acting itself.

But the Spirit of God influences the minds of the ungodly otherwise. Indeed he acts according to his nature in what he does upon them, for he never acts any otherwise. He acts according to his nature in awakening a sinner, in assisting natural conscience, as he opposes that which is so contrary to his nature, viz. sin, by assisting the natural principles of reason and conscience which do oppose it, by making the soul uneasy with it; but he don't exert his proper nature in them and in union with their souls, so that there shall be a communication of his own natural, essential and eternal act. The Spirit of God may act and not, in acting, communicate itself. The Spirit of God, as well as any other person in the Trinity, may act upon inanimate creatures, as we read that the Spirit of God moved upon the face of the waters. So the Holy Ghost may act upon the mind of [a] man many ways, and communicate himself no more than when he acts upon [an] inanimate creature; for instance, he [can] excite thoughts in him, or he can assist his reason and natural understanding, or he can assist other natural principles. He in these things acts as any agent acts upon an external object; but as he acts in holy influences in men's souls, he acts by way of peculiar communication of himself. . . .

Notes on the Apocalypse
(begun 1723)

Tractate on Revelation 16:12 (1737)

*And the sixth angel poured out his vial upon the great river Euphrates, and
the waters thereof, that the way of the kings of the East may be prepared.*

Mr. Lowman,[1] in his late, excellent exposition of the Revelation, has
made it plain beyond all contradiction, that the five first vials are already
poured out, and there remains only the sixth and seventh; so that this 6th
vial upon the river Euphrates, is [the] next thing in the prophecies of the
Revelation that remains to be accomplished. Mr. Lowman also shows
with great evidence, that the fifth vial, the last before this, was poured out
in the time of the Reformation; and he shows that there has ordinarily
been about 200 years distance between one vial and another. But it is now
more than 200 years since the 5th vial begun to be poured out. He supposes the 6th vial will begin to be poured out sometime after the year 1700.
It is therefore the more worth our while, to inquire what manner of events
are signified by this 6th vial, seeing these events are what we have so much
reason to expect a speedy accomplishment of.

And here is one thing, that is not so usually observed concerning this
prophecy, that I think may be laid down for an evident truth, that may
perhaps serve as a key to open the prophecy. And that is, that here is an
allusion to the way wherein old Babylon was destroyed; which was by
drying up the waters of the great river Euphrates which ran through the
city, whereby the way of the kings of the East, the princes of Media and
Persia, was prepared to come in under the walls of the city and destroy it.
That drying up the river Euphrates, was the last thing done by the
besiegers of Babylon before its destruction, as this 6th vial is the last thing

1. Moses Lowman (1680–1752), an English dissenting clergyman who wrote *Paraphrase and Notes on
the Revelation* (London, 1737).

done against the spiritual Babylon, before her total destruction by the 7th vial. I need not strive particularly to show, that the antichristian church is in this book of Revelation everywhere compared to Babylon, and called by the name of Babylon the Great, as the true church is called Jerusalem; because to mention all the places would be very tedious, and because none can be ignorant of it. Seeing therefore these seven vials are vials of wrath, which God pours out on Babylon (as 'tis called in this book), in order to her destruction, as all allow; and the destruction of this Babylon is what the Holy Spirit has here respect to; and this vial is the last before that which actually brings her destruction; and the destruction of old Babylon was by drying up the river Euphrates, to prepare the way for the kings of the East to come in to her destruction—I think it cannot be doubted but that here is an allusion to that event.

The prophecies of the Old Testament do represent old Babylon as being destroyed by the kings of the East. Is. 46:11, "Calling a ravenous bird from the East, the man that executeth my counsel from a far country," speaking of Cyrus. Jer. 27:7, "Many nations and great kings shall serve themselves of her," speaking of the destruction of Babylon. Jer. 51:11, "The Lord hath raised up the spirit of the kings of the Medes; for his device is against Babylon, to destroy it." And vv. 27–28, "Prepare the nations against her, with the kings of the Medes, and the captains thereof, and the rulers thereof, and all the land of his dominion." Media and Persia were both to the eastward of Babylon.

And the prophets also do take notice of God's drying up the river Euphrates, to make way for these enemies of Babylon to come in and destroy her. Is. 44:27–28, "That saith to the deep, Be dry, and I will dry up thy rivers; that saith of Cyrus, He is my servant, and shall perform all my pleasure." And Jer. 51:31–32, "One post shall run to meet another, and one messenger to meet another, to show the king of Babylon that his city is taken at one end, and that the passages are stopped; and the reeds have they burnt with fire, and the men of war were affrighted." And v. 36, "I will dry up her sea, and make her springs dry."

Now therefore, since this is what this prophecy of the 6th vial has a plain reference to, I am humbly of opinion that the right way of going to work, in order to find the true meaning of this prophecy and to discover what that is appertaining to the Romish Church that is to be removed by this vial, answering to the removal of the river Euphrates in the destruction of old Babylon, is to consider what the river Euphrates was to that city, or wherein it served Babylon and was a benefit to it, so that the drying of it up was a great judgment or calamity to it.

The river Euphrates served the city of Babylon two ways. 1. As a supply. 2. As a defense.

1. It served the city as a supply. The river Euphrates was let through the midst of the city by an artificial canal, and ran through the midst of the palace of the king of Babylon for that end: that the city and palace might have the convenience of its waters, and might be plentifully supplied by water from the river; and not for the convenience of navigation, for that was rendered impossible by the wall built over the river at each end of the city. And it was a common thing for cities to be built by rivers and streams of water for the same end. Hence the temporal supplies of any people are very often in Scripture called "waters," as Isaiah 5:13, "Therefore my people are gone into captivity, and their honorable men are famished, and their multitude dried up with thirst," i.e., were deprived of the supplies and supports of life. So Isaiah 41:17, "When the poor and needy seek water, and there is none, and their tongue faileth for thirst, I the Lord will hear them; I, the God of Israel, will not forsake them." Waters are very often in scripture language used to signify both spiritual and temporal supplies, in places innumerable (Prov. 9:17; Is. 33:16, 43:20, 55:1, 58:11; Jer. 2:13, 18, 17:8, 13).

And therefore, one thing intended by the drying up the river Euphrates, when applied to the mystical Babylon or Church of Rome, must be meant a remarkably drying up or diminishing of her temporal supplies, and supports of power, learning and wealth, which may be accomplished by the taking away from the Church of Rome the supplies and help she has had from the principal powers that have hitherto supported her. Mr. Lowman, in his notes on Revelation 8:10 and 16:4, observes that by rivers and fountains of waters in prophecy, is sometimes meant chief cities and countries, that are original seats of empire, fountains of power and dominion. As Joab, when he had taken Rabbah, the chief city of the Ammonites, sends messengers to David, saying, "I have fought against Rabbah, and have taken the city of waters" (II Sam. 12:27). The chief powers of Europe, that have for many ages been the main fountains of the supply and supports of the Church of Rome, are France, Spain and the emperor. This vial, therefore, may probably include the destroying or remarkably weakening and diminishing or taking away from the Church of Rome some or all of these. What has lately befallen the imperial power is well known.[2] And whether this mayn't probably be an effect of this vial beginning to be poured out on the rivers and fountains of the waters of the Church of Rome, I leave to be considered. And who knows what may yet further be in the issue of the present war,[3] with respect to the other two popish powers of France and Spain, as the vial goes on to be poured out. The one of which has, in a remarkable manner, been the fountain of power, policy and learning for the supply and support of the popish cause; the other, the fountain of her wealth.

And as by waters and rivers in scripture language, is meant supplies of any city or kingdom in general, so more especially are they used to signify their wealth and treasures. And the drying up the waters of a city or kingdom, is often used in scripture prophecy for the depriving them of their wealth, as the Scripture explains itself. So Jer. 50:37–38, "A sword is upon her treasures, and they shall be robbed. A drought is upon her waters, and they shall be dried up." So again, Is. 15:6–7, "For the waters of Nimrim shall be desolate; for the hay withereth away, the grass faileth; there is no green thing. Therefore the abundance they have gotten, and that which they have laid up, shall they carry away to the brook of the willows." And Hos. 13:15, "His spring shall become dry, and his fountain shall be dried up; and he shall spoil the treasure of all pleasant vessels."

The wealth, revenue and vast incomes of the Church of Rome, are the waters by which that Babylon has been nourished and supported. These are the waters that the members of the Romish hierarchy thirst after and are continually drinking down with an insatiable appetite. And they are waters that have been for many ages flowing into that spiritual city, like a mighty river, ecclesiastical persons possessing a very great part of the

2. Probably the loss of Silesia to Frederick the Great of Prussia (1712–86) in 1740 during the War of the Austrian Succession.

3. I.e., the War of the Austrian Succession, known in the American theater as King George's War.

wealth of the popish dominions, as this Babylon is represented as vastly rich in this prophecy of Revelation, especially in the 17th and 18th chapters. These are especially the waters that supply the palace of the king of this spiritual Babylon, viz. the Pope, as the river Euphrates of old ran through the midst of the king of Babylon's palace, that part of his palace that was called the old palace being on one side, and the new palace on the other, with communications from one to the other by a bridge over the water, and an arched passage under the water. The revenues of the Pope have been like the waters of a mighty river, coming into his palace from innumerable fountains, and by innumerable branches and lesser streams, coming from many various and distant countries.

Therefore, we may suppose that the drying up of the river Euphrates by the 6th vial, will especially consist in drying up these waters. And agreeable to the significance of this vial, is the popish princes of late making bold with the treasures of the church, in taxing the clergy, as they have often done of late years, which formerly would have been looked on as an unpardonable sacrilege. And also the accounts we some years since had of the kings of Spain and Portugal, withholding great part of the incomes and revenues the Pope used to have from these countries, by strictly forbidding the people to go out of their own dominion for investitures, pardons, indulgences, dispensations and the like.

But the main channel of this great river, seems to be the stream of their wealth from the Spanish West Indies. The silver and gold mines in this country are its main fountain, and indeed have been, for several hundred years, the chief fountain of the treasures of Europe. And if the Protestants that are at this day at war with those principal popish powers, France and Spain, should prevail, so far as to turn the stream of their wealth that flows from hence, away from that church into some other channel, as Cyrus, when he fought against Babylon, diverted the stream of Euphrates from the city [of] Babylon, this will be a great fulfillment of this prophecy.

2. As the river Euphrates served the city [of] Babylon as a supply, so another way it served them was a defense, or an obstacle in the way of its enemies, to hinder their access to it to destroy it. For at each end of the city, it served instead of walls; for the water ran under the walls. And when the waters were gone, the way for her enemies was prepared. There was

nothing to hinder their coming in and destroying the city. And besides, there was a vast moat round the city, of prodigious width and depth, filled with the water of the river, to hinder the access of her besiegers; what moat was left empty when Cyrus had dried up the river, and so his way was prepared.

Therefore, there seems to be good ground for us to suppose, that by drying the river of Euphrates in this prophecy, to make way for her enemies to destroy her, is meant the removal of those things that have been the main defense of the Church or Rome hitherto, and the chief obstacles on the way of the nations embracing the Protestant religion. The waters of rivers were commonly used to defend cities of old. Is. 37:25, "With the soles of my feet have I dried up the rivers of besieged places." Is. 19:4-5, "And the Egyptians will I give over into the hand of a cruel Lord. . . . And the water shall fail from the sea, and the river shall be wasted and dried up; and they shall turn the rivers far away, and the brooks of defense shall be emptied, and dried up."

Now if these things were accomplished that were before mentioned, the Church of Rome would be exceedingly weakened, and her main defense would be gone. If these main kingdoms that are the chief fountains of power, wealth, policy and learning were taken away from the Church of Rome, how exposed and defenseless would she be. If the main channels of her wealth were diverted from her into Protestant countries, how weak and despicable would she become, and how easy a prey to her enemies. And the way would be prepared remarkably for her enemies, called the kings of the East; by which, there is no necessity of understanding any civil powers coming from the eastern parts of the world, but only those powers that are enemies to the Church of Rome, as formerly the kings of the East were enemies to Babylon. For it seems to be a mere allusion to the way of destroying old Babylon.

Another thing that has hitherto been a great defense to the Church of Rome, and a great obstacle on the way of the prevailing of the Protestant religion, are those differences and controversies, sects and errors, among Protestants. These have been great stumbling blocks, and like mountains and rivers have, as it were, made the ground unpassable. And possibly these may be removed to prepare the way of God's people, by God's raising up some in his church, [who] shall in a wonderful manner set forth divine and Christian doctrines in a clear light, and unravel the difficulties that attend them, and defend them with great strength and clearness of reason; and so that voice be fulfilled: "Prepare the way of the Lord. Every valley shall be exalted; every mountain and hill shall be made low" [Is. 40:3–4].

And one thing more I would add, which may greatly prepare the way for the destruction of the Church of Rome; and that is the destruction of the Turkish Empire, and the establishing the true religion of those parts of the world. 'Tis darkness is the defense of the Church of Rome; and if God is pleased to let in light all around them, so that they shall be encompassed with it on every side, it may greatly prepare the way for her destruction. If those two great empires of Russia and Persia (which are kingdoms of the East, with respect to Rome, and one of them the same country that formerly overthrew old Babylon), I say, if those should embrace the true religion (as one of them especially have of late gone far towards it), and should conquer the Turkish Empire, and let in the true religion there, how greatly would it be for the glory of the true church, and the strengthening of the true religion. And how much would it probably stir up the jealousy of the Church of Rome, who doubtless had much rather that the Mahometan religion should remain there as it is, than the Protestant religion let in instead of it. And if Russia and Persia professed the Protestant religion, [the Church of Rome] would esteem the Turks as their defense or barrier on the eastern side, against their encroachments.

Rivers are often a barrier to kingdoms. So the river Jordan was a barrier to Canaan; and therefore, when God brought in his people from the east to destroy the Canaanites under Joshua, Jordan was dried up to prepare their way [Josh. 3:14–17]. So the Rhine has been a defense to France on the eastern side. And the river Euphrates was the bounds of the kingdom of Israel in David's and Solomon's time, and was the boundary that God set to the dominion and possession of his people in the covenant with Abraham, and with the congregation in the wilderness. And therefore, when their territories were overrun by the Assyrians, a people that dwelt on that river, 'tis represented by the prophets, as the waters of the river Euphrates breaking their ancient banks, and coming and overflowing the

land of Israel. Is. 8:7–8, "Now therefore, behold, the Lord bringeth up
upon them the waters of the river, strong and many, even the king of
Assyria and all his glory. And he shall come up over all his channels, and
go over all his banks; and he shall pass through Judah. He shall overflow
and go over. He shall reach even to the neck; and the stretching out of his
wings shall fill the breadth of thy land, O Immanuel." So Euphrates was a
long time the ancient eastern boundary of the Roman Empire. And
therefore, when the Turks (a people that came from about that river)
overran great part of that empire, even to the Adriatic Sea, this was, as it
were, the waters of the river, breaking their ancient bounds and banks, and
overflowing great part of the Roman Empire. And therefore, the destruction of that empire may fitly be compared to the drying up the river
Euphrates.

And this perhaps, may be another thing implied in the pouring out of
that vial, as Lowman makes it exceeding probably that the 4th vial has
respect to several diverse events, and as the seven heads of the beast by the
angel himself is interpreted of two entirely diverse things (Rev. 17), viz. of
seven mountains and seven different forms of government. However, the
whole meaning [of] this prophecy may be summed up in this: that it
signifies the removal of those benefits to the new Babylon, which old
Babylon anciently had by the river Euphrates, viz. its supply and its
defense.

And as Mr. Lowman supposes, that the present time is the time when
we may expect that this vial will be poured out, so I would leave it to be
considered whether everything in divine providence have the appearance
of a beginning of the pouring out of this vial, and don't afford a prospect of
its being speedily, more fully, poured out.

A Faithful Narrative of the Surprising Work of God (1737)

Reverend and Honored Sir,[1]

Having seen your letter to my honored Uncle Williams[2] of Hatfield of July 20 [1736], wherein you inform him of the notice that has been taken of the late wonderful work of God, in this and some other towns in this county; by the Rev. Dr. Watts and Dr. Guyse[3] of London, and the congregation to which the last of these preached on a monthly day of solemn prayer; as also, of your desire to be more perfectly acquainted with it, by some of us on the spot: and having been since informed by my Uncle Williams that you desire me to undertake it; I would now do it in as just and faithful a manner as in me lies.

The people of the county, in general, I suppose, are as sober, and orderly, and good sort of people, as in any part of New England; and I believe they have been preserved the freest by far, of any part of the country, from error and variety of sects and opinions. Our being so far within the land, at a distance from seaports, and in a corner of the country, has doubtless been one reason why we have not been so much corrupted with vice, as most other parts. But without question, the religion and good order of the county, and their purity in doctrine, has, under God, been very much owing to the great abilities and eminent piety of my venerable and honored grandfather Stoddard. I suppose we have been the freest of any part of the land from unhappy divisions and quarrels in our ecclesiastical and religious affairs, till the late lamentable Springfield contention.[4]

---

1. A letter to Benjamin Colman (1673–1747), pastor of the Brattle Street Church in Boston.

2. William Williams (1665–1741) was pastor of Hatfield, Massachusetts, from 1685 until his death. His second wife was Christian Stoddard, sister to Edwards' mother.

3. Isaac Watts (1674–1748) and John Guyse (1680–1761), two eminent English dissenting ministers, instrumental in the publication of the *Faithful Narrative*.

4. A reference to the controversial ordination of Robert Breck (1713–84) in 1734, whose settlement was opposed by the Hampshire County Association of clergymen because of his reputed Arminianism.

We being much separated from other parts of the province, and having comparatively but little intercourse with them, have from the beginning till now, always managed our ecclesiastical affairs within ourselves: 'tis the way in which the county, from its infancy, has gone on, by the practical agreement of all, and the way in which our peace and good order has hitherto been maintained.

The town of Northampton is of about 82 years standing, and has now about 200 families; which mostly dwell more compactly together than any town of such a bigness in these parts of the country; which probably has been an occasion that both our corruptions and reformations have been, from time to time, the more swiftly propagated from one to another through the town. Take the town in general, and so far as I can judge, they are as rational and understanding a people as most I have been acquainted with: many of them have been noted for religion, and particularly have been remarkable for their distinct knowledge in things that relate to heart religion and Christian experience, and their great regards thereto.

I am the third minister that has been settled in the town: the Rev. Mr. Eleazar Mather, who was the first, was ordained in [July 1661 and died] July 1669. He was one whose heart was much in his work, abundant in labors for the good of precious souls; he had the high esteem and great love of his people, and was blessed with no small success. The Rev. Mr. Stoddard, who succeeded him, came first to the town the November after his death, but was not ordained till September 11, 1672, and died February 11, 1728/9. So that he continued in the work of the ministry here, from his first coming to town, near sixty years. And as he was eminent and renowned for his gifts and grace; so he was blessed, from the beginning, with extraordinary success in his ministry in the conversion of many souls. He had five harvests, as he called them: the first was about 57 years ago; the second about 53 years; the third about 40; the fourth about 24; the fifth and last about 18 years ago. Some of these times were much more remarkable than others, and the ingathering of souls more plentiful. Those that were about 53, and 40, and 24 years ago were much greater than either the first or the last: but in each of them, I have heard my grandfather say, the bigger part of the young people in the town seemed to be mainly concerned for their eternal salvation.

After the last of these came a far more degenerate time (at least among the young people), I suppose, than ever before. Mr. Stoddard, indeed, had the comfort before he died, of seeing a time where there were no small appearances of a divine work amongst some, and a considerable ingathering of souls, even after I was settled with him in the ministry, which was about two years before his death; and I have reason to bless God for the great advantage I had by it. In these two years there were near twenty that Mr. Stoddard hoped to be savingly converted; but there was nothing of any general awakening. The greater part seemed to be at that time very insensible of the things of religion, and engaged in other cares and pursuits. Just after my grandfather's death, it seemed to be a time of extraordinary dullness in religion: licentiousness for some years greatly prevailed among the youth of the town; they were many of them very much addicted to night-walking, and frequenting the tavern, and lewd practices, wherein some, by their example exceedingly corrupted others. It was their manner very frequently to get together in conventions of both sexes, for mirth and jollity, which they called frolics; and they would often spend the greater part of the night in them, without regard to any order in the families they belonged to: and indeed family government did too much fail in the town. It was become very customary with many of our young people, to be indecent in their carriage at meeting, which doubtless would not have prevailed to such a degree, had it not been that my grandfather, through his great age (though he retained his powers surprisingly to the last) was not so able to observe them. There had also long prevailed in the town a spirit of contention between two parties, into which they had for many years been divided, by which was maintained a jealousy one of the other, and they were prepared to oppose one another in all public affairs.

But in two or three years after Mr. Stoddard's death, there began to be a sensible amendment of these evils; the young people showed more of a disposition to hearken to counsel, and by degrees left off their frolicking, and grew observably more decent in their attendance on the public worship, and there were more that manifested a religious concern than there used to be.

At the latter end of the year 1733, there appeared a very unusual flexibleness, and yielding to advice, in our young people. It had been too long their manner to make the evening after the Sabbath, and after our public lecture, to be especially the times of their mirth and company-keeping. But a sermon was now preached on the Sabbath before the lecture, to show the evil tendency of the practice, and to persuade them to reform it; and it was urged on heads of families, that it should be a thing agreed upon among them, to govern their families and keep their children at home at these times; and withal it was more privately moved that they should meet together the next day, in their several neighborhoods, to know each other's minds; which was accordingly done, and the motion complied with throughout the town. But parents found little or no occasion for the exercise of government in the case: the young people declared themselves convinced by what they had heard from the pulpit, and were willing of themselves to comply with the counsel that had been given: and it was immediately, and I suppose, almost universally complied with; and there was a thorough reformation of these disorders thenceforward, which has continued ever since.

Presently after this, there began to appear a remarkable religious concern at a little village belonging to the congregation, called Pascommuck, where a few families were settled at about three miles distance from the main body of the town. At this place, a number of persons seemed to be savingly wrought upon. In the April following, anno 1734, there happened a very sudden and awful death of a young man in the bloom of his youth; who being violently seized with a pleurisy and taken immediately very delirious, died in about two days; which (together with what was preached publicly on that occasion) much affected many young people. This was followed with another death of a young married woman, who had been considerably exercised in mind about the salvation of her soul before she was ill, and was in great distress in the beginning of her illness; but seemed to have satisfying evidences of God's saving mercy to her before her death; so that she died very full of comfort, in a most earnest and moving manner warning and counseling others. This seemed much to contribute to the solemnizing of the spirits of many young persons: and there began evidently to appear more of a religious concern on people's minds.

In the fall of that year, I proposed it to the young people, that they should agree among themselves to spend the evenings after lectures in social religion, and to that end divide themselves into several companies to meet in various parts of the town; which was accordingly done, and those meetings have been since continued, and the example imitated by elder people. This was followed with the death of an elderly person, which was attended with many unusual circumstances, by which many were much moved and affected.

About this time, began the great noise that was in this part of the country about Arminianism, which seemed to appear with a very threatening aspect upon the interest of religion here. The friends of vital piety trembled for fear of the issue; but it seemed, contrary to their fear, strongly to be overruled for the promoting of religion. Many who looked on themselves as in a Christless condition, seemed to be awakened by it, with fear that God was about to withdraw from the land, and that we should be given up to heterodoxy and corrupt principles; and that then their opportunity for obtaining salvation would be past; and many who were brought a little to doubt about the truth of the doctrines they had hitherto been taught, seemed to have a kind of a trembling fear with their doubts, lest they should be led into bypaths, to their eternal undoing: and they seemed with much concern and engagedness of mind, to inquire what was indeed the way in which they must come to be accepted with God. There were then some things said publicly on that occasion concerning justification by faith alone.

Although great fault was found with meddling with the controversy in the pulpit, by such a person and at that time, and though it was ridiculed by many elsewhere, yet it proved a word spoken in season here; and was most evidently attended with a very remarkable blessing of heaven to the souls of the people in this town. They received thence a general satisfaction with respect to the main thing in question, which they had been in trembling doubts and concern about; and their minds were engaged the more earnestly to seek that they might come to be accepted of God, and saved in the way of the gospel, which had been made evident to them to be the true and only way. And then it was, in the latter part of December, that the Spirit of God began extraordinarily to set in, and wonderfully to work amongst us; and there were, very suddenly, one after another, five or six persons who were to all appearance savingly converted, and some of them wrought upon in a very remarkable manner. . . .

Presently upon this, a great and earnest concern about the great things of religion and the eternal world became universal in all parts of the town, and among persons of all degrees and all ages; the noise amongst the dry bones waxed louder and louder. All other talk about spiritual and eternal things was soon thrown by; all the conversation in all companies and upon all occasions, was upon these things only, unless so much as was necessary for people, carrying on their ordinary secular business. Other discourse than of the things of religion would scarcely be tolerated in any company. The minds of people were wonderfully taken off from the world; it was treated amongst us as a thing of very little consequence. They seemed to follow their worldly business more as a part of their duty than from any disposition they had to it; the temptation now seemed to lie on that hand, to neglect worldly affairs too much, and to spend too much time in the immediate exercise of religion: which thing was exceedingly misrepresented by reports that were spread in distant parts of the land, as though the people here had wholly thrown by all worldly business, and betook themselves entirely to reading and praying, and such like religious exercises.

But although people did not ordinarily neglect their worldly business; yet there then was the reverse of what commonly is: religion was with all sorts the great concern, and the world was a thing only by the bye. The only thing in their view was to get the kingdom of heaven, and everyone appeared pressing into it. The engagedness of their hearts in this great concern could not be hid; it appeared in their very countenances. It then was a dreadful thing amongst us to lie out of Christ, in danger every day of dropping into hell; and what persons' minds were intent upon was to escape for their lives, and to fly from the wrath to come. All would eagerly lay hold of opportunities for their souls; and were wont very often to meet together in private houses for religious purposes: and such meetings when appointed were wont greatly to be thronged.

There was scarcely a single person in the town, either old or young, that was left unconcerned about the great things of the eternal world. Those that were wont to be the vainest and loosest, and those that had been most disposed to think and speak slightly of vital and experimental religion, were now generally subject to great awakenings. And the work of conversion was carried on in a most astonishing manner, and increased more and more; souls did as it were come by flocks to Jesus Christ. From day to day, for many months together, might be seen evident instances of sinners brought out of darkness into marvellous light, and delivered out of an horrible pit, and from the miry clay, and set upon a rock with a new song of praise to God in their mouths [I Pet. 2:9, Ps. 40:2–3].

This work of God, as it was carried on, and the number of true saints multiplied, soon made a glorious alteration in the town; so that in the spring and summer following, anno 1735, the town seemed to be full of the presence of God: it never was so full of love, nor so full of joy; and yet so full of distress, as it was then. There were remarkable tokens of God's presence in almost every house. It was a time of joy in families on the account of salvation's being brought unto them; parents rejoicing over their children as newborn, and husbands over their wives, and wives over their husbands. The goings of God were then seen in his sanctuary [Ps. 68:24], God's day was a delight, and his tabernacles were amiable [Ps. 84:1]. Our public assemblies were then beautiful; the congregation was alive in God's service, everyone earnestly intent on the public worship, every hearer eager to drink in the words of the minister as they came from his mouth; the assembly in general were, from time to time, in tears while the Word was preached; some weeping with sorrow and distress, others with joy and love, others with pity and concern for the souls of their neighbors.

Our public praises were then greatly enlivened; God was then served in our psalmody, in some measure, in the beauty of holiness [Ps. 96:9]. It has been observable that there has been scarce any part of divine worship, wherein good men amongst us have had grace so drawn forth and their hearts so lifted up in the ways of God, as in singing his praises. Our congregation excelled all that ever I knew in the external part of the duty before, generally carrying regularly and well three parts of music, and the women a part by themselves. But now they were evidently wont to sing with unusual elevation of heart and voice, which made the duty pleasant indeed. . . .

When this work of God first appeared, and was so extraordinarily carried on amongst us in the winter, others round about us seemed not to know what to make of it; and there were many that scoffed at and ridiculed it; and some compared what we called conversion to certain distempers. But it was very observable of many that occasionally came amongst us from abroad, with disregardful hearts, that what they saw here cured them of such a temper of mind: strangers were generally surprised to find things so much beyond what they had heard, and were wont to tell others that the state of the town could not be conceived of by those that had not seen it. The notice that was taken of it by the people that came to town on occasion of the Court, that sat here in the beginning of March, was very observable. And those that came from the neighborhood to our public lectures, were for the most part remarkably affected. Many that came to town, on one occasion or other, had their consciences smitten and awakened, and went home with wounded hearts and with those impressions that never wore off till they had hopefully a saving issue; and those that before had serious thoughts had their awakenings and convictions greatly increased. And there were many instances of persons that came from abroad on visits or on business, that had not been long here before to all appearance they were savingly wrought upon, and partook of that shower of divine blessing that God rained down here, and went home rejoicing; till at length the same work began evidently to appear and prevail in several other towns in the county. . . .

This seems to have been a very extraordinary dispensation of Providence: God has in many respects gone out of, and much beyond his usual and ordinary way. The work in this town and some others about us, has been extraordinary on account of the universality of it, affecting all sorts, sober and vicious, high and low, rich and poor, wise and unwise; it reached the most considerable families and persons, to all appearance, as much as others. In former stirrings of this nature, the bulk of the young people have been greatly affected; but old men and little children have been so now. Many of the last have, of their own accord, formed themselves into religious societies, in different parts of the town. A loose, careless person could scarcely find a companion in the whole neighborhood; and if there was anyone that seemed to remain senseless or unconcerned, it would be spoken of as a strange thing.

This dispensation has also appeared very extraordinary in the numbers of those on whom we have reason to hope it has had a saving effect. We have about six hundred and twenty communicants, which include almost all our adult persons. The church was very large before; but persons never thronged into it as they did in the late extraordinary time. Our sacraments are eight weeks asunder, and I received into our communion about an hundred before one sacrament, and fourscore of them at one time, whose appearance, when they presented themselves together to make an open explicit profession of Christianity, was very affecting to the congregation. I took in near sixty before the next sacrament day; but [it must be noted that] it is not the custom here, as it is in many other churches in this country, to make a credible relation of their inward experiences the ground of admission to the Lord's Supper.

I am far from pretending to be able to determine how many have lately been the subjects of such mercy; but if I may be allowed to declare anything that appears to me probable in a thing of this nature, I hope that more than 300 souls were savingly brought home to Christ in this town in the space of half a year (how many more I don't guess) and about the same number of males as females; which, by what I have heard Mr. Stoddard say, was far from what has been usual in years past, for he observed that in his time, many more women were converted than men. Those of our young people that are on other accounts most likely and considerable, are mostly, as I hope, truly pious and leading persons in the ways of religion. Those that were formerly looser young persons are generally, to all appearances, become true lovers of God and Christ, and spiritual in their dispositions. And I hope that by far the greater part of persons in this town, above sixteen years of age, are such as have the saving knowledge of Jesus Christ; and so by what I heard I suppose it is in some other places, particularly at Sunderland and South Hadley.

This has also appeared to be a very extraordinary dispensation, in that the Spirit of God has so much extended not only his awakening, but regenerating influences, both to elderly persons and also those that are very young. It has been a thing heretofore rarely to be heard of, that any were converted past middle age; but now we have the same ground to think that many such have in this time been savingly changed, as that others have been so in more early years. I suppose there were [converted] upwards of fifty persons in this town above forty years of age; and more than twenty of them above fifty, and about ten of them above sixty, and two of them above seventy years of age.

It has heretofore been looked on as a strange thing, when any have seemed to be savingly wrought upon, and remarkably changed in their childhood; but now, I suppose, near thirty were to appearance so wrought upon between ten and fourteen years of age, and two between nine and ten, and one of about four years of age. . . . There are several families in this town that are all hopefully pious; yea, there are several numerous families in which, I think, we have reason to hope that all the children are truly godly, and most of them lately become so: and there are very few houses in the whole town into which salvation has not lately come, in one or more instances. There are several Negroes, that from what was seen in them then, and what is discernible in them since, appear to have been truly born again in the late remarkable season.

God has also seemed to have gone out of his usual way in the quickness of his work, and the swift progress his Spirit has made in his operations on the hearts of many. 'Tis wonderful that persons should be so suddenly, and yet so greatly, changed: many have been taken from a loose and careless way of living, and seized with strong convictions of their guilt and misery, and in a very little time "old things have passed away, and all things have become new with them" [II Cor. 5:17].

God's work has also appeared very extraordinary in the degrees of the influences of his Spirit, both in the degree of awakening and conviction, and also in the degree of saving light, and love, and joy, that many have experienced. It has also been very extraordinary in the extent of it, and its being so swiftly propagated from town to town. In former times of the pouring out of the Spirit of God on this town, though in some of them it was very remarkable, yet it reached no further than this town; the neighboring towns all around continued unmoved.

The work of God's Spirit seemed to be at its greatest height in this town in the former part of the spring, in March and April; at which time God's work in the conversion of souls was carried on amongst us in so wonderful a manner, that so far as I, by looking back, can judge from the particular acquaintance I have had with souls in this work, it appears to me probable, to have been at the rate at least of four persons in a day, or near thirty in a week, take one with another, for five or six weeks together. When God in so remarkable a manner took the work into his own hands, there was as much done in a day or two as at ordinary times, with all endeavors that men can use, and with such a blessing as we commonly have, is done in a year.

I am very sensible how apt many would be, if they should see the account I have here given, presently to think with themselves that I am very fond of making a great many converts, and of magnifying and aggrandizing the matter; and to think that, for want of judgment, I take every religious pang and enthusiastic conceit for saving conversion; and I don't much wonder if they should be apt to think so: and for this reason I have forborne to publish an account of this great work of God, though I have often been put upon it; but having now as I thought a special call to give an account of it, upon mature consideration I thought it might not be beside my duty to declare this amazing work, as it appeared to me, to be indeed divine, and to conceal no part of the glory of it, leaving it with God to take care of the credit of his own work, and running the venture of any censorious thoughts which might be entertained of me to my disadvantage. But that distant persons may be under as great advantage as may be, to judge for themselves of this matter, I would be a little more large and particular.

I therefore proceed to give an account of the manner of persons being wrought upon: and here there is a vast variety, perhaps as manifold as the subjects of the operation; but yet in many things there is a great analogy in all.

Persons are first awakened with a sense of their miserable condition by nature, the danger they are in of perishing eternally, and that it is of great importance to them that they speedily escape, and get into a better state. Those that before were secure and senseless, are made sensible how much they were in the way to ruin in their former courses. Some are more suddenly seized with convictions; it may be by the news of others' conversion, or something they hear in public, or in private conference, [that] their consciences are suddenly smitten, as if their hearts were pierced through with a dart. Others have awakenings that come upon them more gradually; they begin at first to be something more thoughtful and considerate, so as to come to a conclusion in their minds that 'tis their best and wisest way to delay no longer, but to improve the present opportunity; and have accordingly set themselves seriously to meditate on those things that have the most awakening tendency, on purpose to obtain convictions; and so their awakenings have increased, till a sense of their misery, by God's Spirit setting in therewith, has had fast hold of them. Others that, before this wonderful time, had been something religious and concerned for their salvation, have been awakened in a new manner, and made sensible that their slack and dull way of seeking was never like to attain their purpose, and so have been roused up to a greater violence for the kingdom of heaven.

These awakenings when they have first seized on persons have had two effects: one was, that they have brought them immediately to quit their sinful practices, and the looser sort have been brought to forsake and dread their former vices and extravagancies. When once the Spirit of God began to be so wonderfully poured out in a general way through the town, people had soon done with their old quarrels, backbitings, and intermeddling with other men's matters; the tavern was soon left empty, and persons kept very much at home; none went abroad unless on necessary business, or on some religious account, and every day seemed in many respects like a Sabbath day. And the other effect was, that it put them on earnest application to the means of salvation—reading, prayer, meditation, the ordinances of God's house, and private conference; their cry was "What shall we do to be saved?" The place of resort was now altered; it was no longer the tavern, but the minister's house, that was thronged far more than ever the tavern had been wont to be.

There is a very great variety as to the degree of fear and trouble that persons are exercised with before they obtain any comfortable evidences of pardon and acceptance with God. Some are from the beginning carried on with abundantly more encouragement and hope than others; some have had ten times less trouble of mind than others, in whom yet the issue seems to be the same. Some have had such a sense of the displeasure of God, and the great danger they were in of damnation, that they could not sleep at nights; and many have said that when they have laid down, the thoughts of sleeping in such a condition have been frightful to them, and they have scarcely been free from terror while they have been asleep; and they have awaked with fear, heaviness, and distress still abiding on their spirits. It has been very common that the deep and fixed concern that has been on persons' minds, has had a painful influence on their bodies and given disturbance to animal nature.

The awful apprehensions persons have had of their misery, have for the most part been increasing, the nearer they have approached to deliverance; though they often pass through many changes and alterations in the frame and circumstances of their minds. Sometimes they think themselves wholly senseless, and fear that the Spirit of God has left them, and that they are given up to judicial hardness; yet they appear very deeply exercised about that fear, and are in great earnest to obtain convictions again.

Together with those fears, and that exercise of mind which is rational, and which they have just ground for, they have often suffered many needless distresses of thought, in which Satan probably has a great hand, to entangle them and block up their way; and sometimes the distemper of melancholy has been evidently mixed; of which when it happens the Tempter seems to make great advantage, and puts an unhappy bar in the way of any good effect. One knows not how to deal with such persons, [for] they turn everything that is said to them the wrong way, and most to their own disadvantage: and there is nothing that the devil seems to make so great a handle of, as a melancholy humor, unless it be the real corruption of the heart.

But it has been very remarkable, that there has been far less of this mixture in this time of extraordinary blessing, than there was wont to be in persons under awakenings at other times; for it is evident that many that before had been exceedingly involved in such difficulties, seemed now strangely to be set at liberty. Some persons that had before, for a long time, been exceedingly entangled with peculiar temptations of one sort or other, and unprofitable and hurtful distresses, were soon helped over former stumbling blocks that hindered any progress towards saving good; and convictions have wrought more kindly, and they have been successfully carried on in the way to life. And thus Satan seemed to be restrained, till towards the latter end of this wonderful time, when God's Spirit was about to withdraw. . . .

The corruption of the heart has discovered itself in various exercises, in the time of legal convictions; sometimes it appears in a great struggle, like something roused by an enemy, and Satan the old inhabitant seems to exert himself like a serpent disturbed and enraged. Many in such circumstances have felt a great spirit of envy towards the godly, especially towards those that are thought to have been lately converted, and most of all towards acquaintances and companions, when they are thought to be converted; indeed, some have felt many heart-risings against God, and murmurings at his ways of dealing with mankind, and his dealings with themselves in particular. It has been much insisted on, both in public and private, that persons should have the utmost dread of such envious thoughts, which if allowed tend exceedingly to quench the Spirit of God, if not to provoke him finally to forsake them. And when such a spirit has much prevailed, and persons have not so earnestly strove against it as they ought to have done, it has seemed to be exceedingly to the hindrance of the good of their souls: but in some other instances, where persons have been much terrified at the sight of such wickedness in their hearts, God has brought good to them out of evil; and made it a means of convincing them of their own desperate sinfulness, and bringing them off from all self-confidence.

The drift of the Spirit of God in his legal strivings with persons, has seemed most evidently to be, to make way for, and to bring to, a conviction of their absolute dependence on his sovereign power and grace, and universal necessity of a Mediator, by leading them more and more to a sense of their exceeding wickedness and guiltiness in his sight; the pollution and insufficiency of their own righteousness, that they can in no wise help themselves, and that God would be wholly just and righteous in rejecting them, and all that they do, and in casting them off forever: though there be a vast variety as to the manner and distinctness of persons' convictions of these things.

As they are gradually more and more convinced of the corruption and wickedness of their hearts, they seem to themselves to grow worse and worse, harder and blinder, and more desperately wicked, instead of growing better: they are ready to be discouraged by it, and oftentimes never think themselves so far off from good as when they are nearest. Under the sense which the Spirit of God gives them of their sinfulness, they often think that they differ from all others; their hearts are ready to sink with the thought that they are the worst of all, and that none ever obtained mercy that were so wicked as they.

When awakenings first begin, their consciences are commonly most exercised about their outward vicious course, or other acts of sin; but afterwards, are much more burdened with a sense of heart sins, the dreadful corruption of their nature, their enmity against God, the pride of their hearts, their unbelief, their rejection of Christ, the stubbornness and obstinacy of their wills, and the like. In many, God makes much use of their own experience, in the course of their awakenings and endeavors after saving good, to convince them of their own vile emptiness and universal depravity.

Very often under first awakenings, when they are brought to reflect on the sin of their past lives, and have something of a terrifying sense of God's anger, they set themselves to walk more strictly, and confess their sins, and perform many religious duties, with a secret hope of appeasing God's anger and making up for the sins they have committed. And oftentimes, at first setting out, their affections are moved, and they are full of tears, in their confessions and prayers, which they are ready to make very much of, as though they were some atonement, and had power to move correspondent affections in God too; and hence they are for a while big with expectation of what God will do for them, and conceive that they grow better apace, and shall soon be thoroughly converted. But these affections are but short-lived; they quickly find that they fail, and then they think themselves to be grown worse again; they don't find such a prospect of being soon converted, as they thought: instead of being nearer, they seem to be farther off; their hearts they think are grown harder, and by this means their fears of perishing greatly increase. But though they are disappointed, they renew their attempts again and again; and still as their attempts are multiplied, so are their disappointments; all fails, they see no token of having inclined God's heart to them, they don't see that he hears their prayers at all, as they expected he would; and sometimes there have been great temptations arising hence to leave off seeking, and to yield up the case. But as they are still more terrified with fears of perishing, and their former hopes of prevailing on God to be merciful to them in a great measure fail; sometimes their religious affections have turned into heart-risings against God, because that he won't pity them, and seems to have little regard to their distress and piteous cries, and to all the pains that they take. They think of the mercy that God has shown to others, how soon, and how easily others have obtained comfort, and those too that were worse than they, and have not labored so much as they have done, and sometimes they have had even dreadful blasphemous thoughts in these circumstances.

But when they reflect on these wicked workings of heart against God, if their convictions are continued, and the Spirit of God is not provoked utterly to forsake them, they have more distressing apprehensions of the anger of God towards those whose hearts work after such a sinful manner about him; and it may be have great fears that they have committed the unpardonable sin, or that God will surely never show mercy to them that are such vipers; and are often tempted to leave off in despair. But then perhaps by something they read or hear of the infinite mercy of God and all-sufficiency of Christ for the chief of sinners, they have some encouragement and hope renewed; but think that as yet they are not fit to come to Christ; they are so wicked that Christ will never accept of them: and then it may be they set themselves upon a new course of fruitless endeavors in their own strength to make themselves better, and still meet with new disappointments. They are earnest to inquire what they shall do. They don't know but there is something else to be done, in order to their obtaining converting grace, that they have never done yet. It may be they hope that they are something better than they were; but then the pleasing dream all vanishes again. If they are told that they trust too much to their own strength and righteousness, they go about to strive to bring them-

selves off from it, and it may be, think they have done it, when they only do
the same thing under a new disguise, and still find no appearance of any
good, but all looks as dark as midnight to them. Thus they wander about
from mountain to hill, seeking rest and finding none: when they are beat
out of one refuge they fly to another, till they are as it were debilitated,
broken, and subdued with legal humblings; in which God gives them a
conviction of their own utter helplessness and insufficiency, and discovers
the true remedy. . . .

And whatever minister has a like occasion to deal with souls, in a flock
under such circumstances, as this was in the last year, I can't but think he
will soon find himself under a necessity greatly to insist upon it with them,
that God is under no manner of obligation to show mercy to any natural
man, whose heart is not turned to God: and that a man can challenge
nothing, either in absolute justice or by free promise, from anything he
does before he has believed on Jesus Christ or has true repentance begun
in him. It appears to me, that if I had taught those that came to me under
trouble any other doctrine, I should have taken a most direct course utterly
to have undone them; I should have directly crossed what was plainly
the drift of the Spirit of God in his influences upon them; for if they
had believed what I said, it would either have promoted self-flattery and
carelessness, and so put an end to their awakenings; or cherished and
established their contention and strife with God, concerning his dealings
with them and others, and blocked up their way to that humiliation before
the sovereign disposer of life and death, whereby God is wont to prepare
them for his consolations. And yet those that have been under awakenings
have oftentimes plainly stood in need of being encouraged, by being told
of the infinite and all-sufficient mercy of God in Christ; and that 'tis
God's manner to succeed diligence and to bless his own means, that so
awakenings and encouragements, fear and hope may be duly mixed and
proportioned to preserve their minds in a just medium between the two
extremes of self-flattery and despondence, both which tend to slackness
and negligence, and in the end to security. . . .

In those in whom awakenings seem to have a saving issue, commonly
the first thing that appears after their legal troubles is a conviction of the
justice of God in their condemnation, in a sense of their own exceeding

sinfulness and the vileness of all their performances. In giving account of
this, they expressed themselves very variously: some [said] that they saw
that God was sovereign, and might receive others and reject them; some,
that they were convinced that God might justly bestow mercy on every
person in the town, and on every person in the world, and damn themselves to all eternity; some, that they see that God may justly have no
regard to all the pains they have taken, and all the prayers they have made;
some, that they see that if they should seek and take the utmost pains all
their lives, God might justly cast them into hell at last, because all their
labors, prayers, and tears cannot make an atonement for the least sin, nor
merit any blessing at the hands of God; some have declared themselves to
be in the hands of God, that he can and may dispose of them just as he
pleases; some, that God may glorify himself in their damnation, and they
wonder that God has suffered them to live so long, and has not cast 'em
into hell long ago.

Some are brought to this conviction by a great sense of their sinfulness,
in general, that they are such vile, wicked creatures in heart and life: others
have the sins of their lives in an extraordinary manner set before them,
multitudes of them coming just then fresh to their memory; and being set
before them with their aggravations; some have their minds especially
fixed on some particular wicked practice they have indulged; some are
especially convinced by a sight of the corruption and wickedness of their
hearts; some, from a view they have of the horridness of some particular
exercises of corruption, which they have had in the time of their awakening, whereby the enmity of the heart against God has been manifested;
some are convinced especially by a sense of the sin of unbelief, the opposition of their hearts to the way of salvation by Christ, and their obstinacy in
rejecting him and his grace. . . .

That calm of spirit that some persons have found after their legal
distresses, continues some time before any special and delightful manifestation is made to the soul of the grace of God, as revealed in the gospel;
but very often some comfortable and sweet view of a merciful God, of a
sufficient Redeemer, or of some great and joyful things of the gospel,
immediately follows, or in a very little time: and in some, the first sight of
their just desert of hell, and God's sovereignty with respect to their salva-

tion, and a discovery of all-sufficient grace, are so near that they seem to go as it were together.

These gracious discoveries that are given, whence the first special comforts are derived, are in many respects very various; more frequently Christ is distinctly made the object of the mind, in his all-sufficiency and willingness to save sinners. But some have their thoughts more especially fixed on God, in some of his sweet and glorious attributes manifested in the gospel, and shining forth in the face of Christ. Some view the all-sufficiency of the mercy and grace of God; some chiefly the infinite power of God, and his ability to save them, and to do all things for them; and some look most at the truth and faithfulness of God. In some, the truth and certainty of the gospel in general is the first joyful discovery they have; in others, the certain truth of some particular promises; in some, the grace and sincerity of God in his invitations, very commonly in some particular invitation in the mind, and it now appears real to them that God does indeed invite them. Some are struck with the glory and wonderfulness of the dying love of Christ; and some with the sufficiency and preciousness of his blood, as offered to make an atonement for sin; and others with the value and glory of his obedience and righteousness. In some the excellency and loveliness of Christ chiefly engages their thoughts; in some his divinity, that he is indeed the Son of the living God; and in others, the excellency of the way of salvation by Christ and the suitableness of it to their necessities. . . .

The way that grace seems sometimes first to appear after legal humiliation, is in earnest longings of soul after God and Christ, to know God, to love him, to be humbled before him, to have communion with Christ in his benefits; which longings, as they express them, seem evidently to be of such a nature as can arise from nothing but a sense of the superlative excellency of divine things, with a spiritual taste and relish of 'em, and an esteem of 'em as their highest happiness and best portion. Such longings as I speak of, are commonly attended with firm resolutions to pursue this good forever, together with a hoping, waiting disposition. When persons have begun in such frames, commonly other experiences and discoveries have soon followed, which have yet more clearly manifested a change of heart. . . .

It has more frequently been so amongst us, that when persons have first had the gospel ground of relief for lost sinners discovered to them, and have been entertaining their minds with the sweet prospect, they have thought nothing at that time of their being converted. To see that there is such an all-sufficiency in God, and such plentiful provision made in Christ, after they have been borned down and sunk with a sense of their guilt and fears of wrath, exceedingly refreshes them; the view is joyful to them, as 'tis in its own nature glorious, and gives them quite new and more delightful ideas of God and Christ, and greatly encourages them to seek conversion, and begets in them a strong resolution to give up themselves, and devote their whole lives to God and his Son, and patiently to wait till God shall see fit to make all effectual; and very often they entertain a strong persuasion that he will in his own time do it for them.

There is wrought in them a holy repose of soul in God through Christ, and a secret disposition to fear and love him, and to hope for blessings from him in this way. And yet they have no imagination that they are now converted, it don't so much as come into their minds; and very often the reason is that they don't see that they do accept of this sufficiency of salvation that they behold in Christ, having entertained a wrong notion of acceptance; not being sensible that the obedient and joyful entertainment which their hearts give to this discovery of grace is a real acceptance of it. They know not that the sweet complacence they feel in the mercy and complete salvation of God, as it includes pardon and sanctification, and is held forth to them only through Christ, is a true receiving of this mercy or a plain evidence of their receiving it. They expected I know not what kind of act of soul, and perhaps they had no distinct idea of it themselves.

And indeed it appears very plainly in some of them, that before their own conversion they had very imperfect ideas what conversion was: it is all new and strange, and what there was no clear conception of before. 'Tis most evident, as they themselves acknowledge, that the expressions that were used to describe conversion and the graces of God's Spirit, such as a spiritual sight of Christ, faith in Christ, poverty of spirit, trust in God, resignedness to God, etc., were expressions that did not convey those special and distinct ideas to their minds which they were intended to signify; in some respects no more than the names of colors are to convey the ideas to one that is blind from birth.

This town is a place where there has always been a great deal of talk of conversion and spiritual experiences; and therefore people in general had before formed a notion in their own minds what these things were; but when they come to be the subjects of them themselves, they find themselves much confounded in their notions and overthrown in many of their former conceits. And it has been very observable that persons of the greatest understanding, and that had studied most about things of this nature, have been more confounded than others. Some such persons that have lately been converted, declare that all their former wisdom is brought to nought, and that they appear to have been mere babes who knew nothing. . . .

But to give a clearer idea of the nature and manner of the operations of God's Spirit, in this wonderful effusion of it, I would give an account of . . . an adult person, a young woman whose name was Abigail Hutchinson. I pitch upon her especially because she is now dead, and so it may be more fit to speak freely of her than of living instances: though I am under far greater disadvantages, on other accounts, to give a full and clear narrative of her experiences, than I might of some others; nor can any account be given but what has been retained in the memories of her near friends, and some others, of what they have heard her express in her lifetime.

She was of a rational understanding family: there could be nothing in her education that tended to enthusiasm, but rather to the contrary extreme. 'Tis in no wise the temper of the family to be ostentatious of experiences, and it was far from being her temper. She was before her conversion, to the observation of her neighbors, of a sober and inoffensive conversation; and was a still, quiet, reserved person. She had long been infirm of body, but her infirmity had never been observed at all to incline her to be notional or fanciful, or to occasion anything of religious melancholy. She was under awakenings scarcely a week, before there seemed to be plain evidence of her being savingly converted.

She was first awakened in the winter season, on Monday, by something she heard her brother say of the necessity of being in good earnest in seeking regenerating grace, together with the news of the conversion of the young woman before mentioned, whose conversion so generally affected most of the young people here. This news wrought much upon her, and stirred up a spirit of envy in her towards this young woman, whom she thought very unworthy of being distinguished from others by such a mercy; but withal it engaged her in a firm resolution to do her utmost to obtain the same blessing; and considering with herself what course she could take, she thought that she had not a sufficient knowledge of the principles of religion to render her capable of conversion; whereupon she resolved thoroughly to search the Scriptures; and accordingly immediately began at the beginning of the Bible, intending to read it through. She continued thus till Thursday: and then there was a sudden alteration, by a great increase of her concern, in an extraordinary sense of her own sinfulness, particularly the sinfulness of her nature and wickedness of her heart, which came upon her (as she expressed it) as a flash of lightning, and struck her into an exceeding terror. Upon which she left off reading the Bible in course as she had begun, and turned to the New Testament, to see if she could not find some relief there for her distressed soul.

Her great terror, she said, was that she had sinned against God. Her distress grew more and more for three days; until (as she said) she saw nothing but blackness of darkness before her, and her very flesh trembled for fear of God's wrath: she wondered and was astonished at herself, that she had been so concerned for her body, and had applied so often to physicians to heal that, and had neglected her soul. Her sinfulness appeared with a very awful aspect to her, especially in three things, viz. her original sin, and her sin in murmuring at God's providence, in the weakness and afflictions she had been under, and in want of duty to parents, though others had looked upon her to excel in dutifulness. On Saturday, she was so earnestly engaged in reading the Bible and other books that she continued in it, searching for something to relieve her, till her eyes were so dim that she could not know the letters. Whilst she was thus engaged in reading, prayer, and other religious exercises, she thought of those words of Christ, wherein he warns us not to be as the heathen, that think they shall be heard for their much speaking [Matt. 6:7]; which, she said, led her to see that she had trusted to her own prayers and religious performances, and now she was put to a non-plus, and knew not which way to turn herself, or where to seek relief.

While her mind was in this posture, her heart, she said, seemed to fly to the minister for refuge, hoping that he could give her some relief. She came the same day to her brother, with the countenance of a person in distress, expostulating with him, why he had not told her more of her sinfulness, and earnestly inquiring of him what she should do. She seemed that day to feel in herself an enmity against the Bible, which greatly affrighted her. Her sense of her own exceeding sinfulness continued increasing from Thursday till Monday; and she gave this account of it, that it had been an opinion, which till now she had entertained, that she was not guilty of Adam's sin, nor any way concerned in it, because she was not active in it; but that now she saw she was guilty of that sin, and all over defiled by it; and that the sin which she brought into the world with her, was alone sufficient to condemn her.

On the Sabbath day she was so ill that her friends thought it not best that she should go to public worship, of which she seemed very desirous: but when she went to bed on the Sabbath-day night, she took up a resolution that she would the next morning go to the minister, hoping to find some relief there. As she awaked on Monday morning, a little before day, she wondered within herself at the easiness and calmness she felt in her mind, which was of that kind which she never felt before; as she thought of this, such words as these were in her mind: "The words of the Lord are pure words, health to the soul and marrow to the bones." And then these words came to her mind, "The blood of Christ cleanses [us] from all sin" [I John 1:7]; which were accompanied with a lively sense of the excellency of Christ, and his sufficiency to satisfy for the sins of the whole world. She then thought of that expression, "'tis a pleasant thing for the eyes to behold the sun" [Eccles. 11:7]; which words then seemed to her to be very applicable to Jesus Christ. By these things her mind was led into such contemplations and views of Christ, as filled her exceeding full of joy. She told her brother in the morning that she had seen (i.e. in realizing views by faith) Christ the last night, and that she had really thought that she had not knowledge enough to be converted; "but," says she, "God can make it quite easy!" On Monday she felt all day a constant sweetness in her soul. She had a repetition of the same discoveries of Christ three mornings together, that she had on Monday morning, and much in the same manner at each time, waking a little before day; but brighter and brighter every time. . . .

She had many extraordinary discoveries of the glory of God and Christ; sometimes, in some particular attributes, and sometimes in many. She gave an account that once, as those four words passed through her mind, "wisdom," "justice," "goodness," and "truth," her soul was filled with a sense of the glory of each of these divine attributes, but especially the last; "truth," said she, "sunk the deepest!" And therefore as these words passed, this was repeated, "Truth, truth!" Her mind was so swallowed up with a sense of the glory of God's truth and other perfections, that she said it seemed as though her life was going, and that she saw it was easy with God to take away her life by discoveries of himself. Soon after this she went to a private religious meeting, and her mind was full of a sense and view of the glory of God all the time; and when the exercise was ended, some asked her concerning what she had experienced: and she began to give them an account; but as she was relating it, it revived such a sense of the same things that her strength failed; and they were obliged to take her and lay her upon the bed. Afterwards she was greatly affected, and rejoiced with these words, "Worthy is the Lamb that was slain" [Rev. 5:12]. . . .

Once, when she came to me, she told how that at such and such a time she thought she saw as much of God, and had as much joy and pleasure as was possible in this life, and that yet afterwards God discovered himself yet far more abundantly, and she saw the same things that she had seen before, yet more clearly, and in another, and far more excellent and delightful manner, and was filled with a more exceeding sweetness; she likewise gave me such an account of the sense she once had, from day to day, of the glory of Christ, and of God in his various attributes, that it seemed to me she dwelt for days together in a kind of beatific vision of God; and seemed to have, as I thought, as immediate an intercourse with him as a child with a father: and at the same time, she appeared most remote from any high thought of herself and of her own sufficiency; but was like a little child, and expressed a great desire to be instructed, telling me that she longed very often to come to me for instruction, and wanted to live at my house that I might tell her her duty. . . .

She had a great longings to die, that she might be with Christ; which increased till she thought she did not know how to be patient to wait till God's time should come. But once when she felt those longings, she thought with herself, "If I long to die, why do I go to physicians?" Whence she concluded that her longings for death were not well regulated. After this she often put it to herself, which she should choose, whether to live or to die, to be sick, or to be well; and she found she could not tell, till at last she found herself disposed to say these words: "I am quite willing to live, and quite willing to die; quite willing to be sick, and quite willing to be well; and quite willing for anything that God will bring upon me! And then," said she, "I felt myself perfectly easy, in a full submission to the will of God." She then lamented much that she had been so eager in her longings for death, as it argued want of such a resignation to God as ought to be. She seemed henceforward to continue in this resigned frame till death.

After this her illness increased upon her: and once after she had before spent the greater part of the night in extreme pain, she waked out of a little sleep with these words in her heart and mouth: "I am willing to suffer for Christ's sake, I am willing to spend and be spent for Christ's sake; I am willing to spend my life, even my very life for Christ's sake!" [cf. II Cor. 12:15]. And though she had an extraordinary resignation with respect to life or death, yet the thoughts of dying were exceeding sweet to her. At a time when her brother was reading in Job, concerning worms feeding on the dead body [Job 21:26, 24:20], she appeared with a pleasant smile; and being inquired of about it, she said it was sweet to her to think of her being in such circumstances. At another time, when her brother mentioned to her the danger there seemed to be that the illness she then labored under might be an occasion of her death, it filled her with joy that almost overcame her. At another time, when she met a company following a corpse to the grave, she said it was sweet to her to think that they would in a little time follow her in like manner.

Her illness in the latter part of it was seated much in her throat; and swelling inward, filled up the pipe so that she could swallow nothing but what was perfectly liquid, and but very little of that, and with great and long strugglings and stranglings, that which she took in flying out at her nostrils till she at last could swallow nothing at all. She had a raging appetite to food, so that she told her sister, when talking with her about her circumstances, that the worst bit that she threw to her swine would be sweet to her: but yet when she saw that she could not swallow it, she seemed to be as perfectly contented without it, as if she had no appetite to it. Others were greatly moved to see what she underwent, and were filled with admiration at her unexampled patience. At a time when she was striving in vain to get down a little food, something liquid, and was very much spent with it, she looked up on her sister with a smile, saying, "O Sister, this is for my good!" At another time, when her sister was speaking of what she underwent, she told her that she lived an heaven upon earth for all that. She used sometimes to say to her sister, under her extreme sufferings, "It is good to be so!" Her sister once asked her why she said so. "Why," says she, "because God would have it so: It is best that things should be as God would have 'em: it looks best to me." After her confinement, as they were leading her from the bed to the door, she seemed overcome by the sight of things abroad, as showing forth the glory of the Being that had made them. As she lay on her deathbed, she would often say these words, "God is my friend!" And once looking up on her sister with a smile, said, "O Sister! How good it is! How sweet and comfortable it is to consider, and think of heavenly things!" And [she] used this argument to persuade her sister to be much in such meditations.

She expressed on her deathbed an exceeding longing, both for persons in a natural state, that they might be converted, and for the godly that they might see and know more of God. And when those that looked on themselves as in a Christless state came to see her, she would be greatly moved with compassionate affection. One in particular that seemed to be in great distress about the state of her soul, and had come to see her from time to time, she desired her sister to persuade not to come any more, because the sight of her so wrought on her compassions that it overcame her nature. The same week that she died, when she was in distressing circumstances as to her body, some of the neighbors that came to see her asked if she was willing to die. She replied that she was quite willing either to live or die; she was willing to be in pain; she was willing to be so always as she was then, if that was the will of God. She willed what God willed. They asked her whether she was willing to die that night. She answered,

"Yes, if it be God's will." And [she] seemed to speak all with that perfect composure of spirit, and with such a cheerful and pleasant countenance that it filled them with admiration. . . . She said not long before she died that she used to be afraid how she should grapple with death; but, says she, "God has showed me that he can make it easy in great pain." Several days before she died, she could scarcely say anything but just yes, and no, to questions that were asked her, for she seemed to be dying for three days together; but seemed to continue in an admirable sweet composure of soul, without any interruption, to the last, and died as a person that went to sleep, without any struggling, about noon, on Friday, June 27, 1735.

She had long been infirm, and often had been exercised with great pain; but she died chiefly of famine. It was, doubtless, partly owing to her bodily weakness that her nature was so often overcome, and ready to sink with gracious affection; but yet the truth was, that she had more grace, and greater discoveries of God and Christ, than the present frail state did well consist with. She wanted to be where strong grace might have more liberty, and be without the clog of a weak body; there she longed to be, and there she doubtless now is. She was looked upon amongst us, as a very eminent instance of Christian experience; but this is but a very broken and imperfect account I have given of her; her eminency would much more appear, if her experiences were fully related, as she was wont to express and manifest them, while living. I once read this account to some of her pious neighbors, who were acquainted with her, who said, to this purpose, that the picture fell much short of the life; and particularly that it much failed of duly representing her humility, and that admirable lowliness of heart, that at all times appeared in her. But there are (blessed be God!) many living instances of much the like nature, and in some things no less extraordinary. . . .

In the former part of this great work of God amongst us, till it got to its height, we seemed to be wonderfully smiled upon and blessed in all respects. Satan (as has been already observed) seemed to be unusually restrained: persons that before had been involved in melancholy, seemed to be as it were waked up out of it; and those that had been entangled with extraordinary temptations, seemed wonderfully to be set at liberty; and not only so, but it was the most remarkable time of health, that ever I knew since I have been in the town. We ordinarily have several bills put up every Sabbath, for persons that are sick; but now we had not so much as one for many Sabbaths together. But after this it seemed to be otherwise, when this work of God appeared to be at its greatest height, a poor weak man that belongs to the town, being in great spiritual trouble, was hurried with violent temptations to cut his own throat, and made an attempt; but did not do it effectually. He after this continued a considerable time exceeding overwhelmed with melancholy; but has now of a long time been very greatly delivered, by the light of God's countenance lifted up upon him [Num. 6:26], and has expressed a great sense of his sin in so far yielding to temptation; and there are in him all hopeful evidences of his having been made a subject of saving mercy.

In the latter part of May, it began to be very sensible that the Spirit of God was gradually withdrawing from us, and after this time Satan seemed to be more let loose, and raged in a dreadful manner. The first instance wherein it appeared was a person's putting an end to his own life, by cutting his throat.[5] He was a gentleman of more than common understanding, of strict morals, religious in his behavior, and an useful honorable person in the town; but was of a family that are exceeding prone to the disease of melancholy, and his mother was killed with it. He had, from the beginning of this extraordinary time, been exceedingly concerned about the state of his soul, and there were some things in his experience, that appeared very hopefully; but he durst entertain no hope concerning his own good estate. Towards the latter part of his time, he grew much discouraged, and melancholy grew amain upon him, till he was wholly overpowered by it, and was in great measure past a capacity of receiving advice, or being reasoned with to any purpose. The devil took the advantage, and drove him into despairing thoughts. He was kept awake anights, meditating terror; so that he had scarce any sleep at all, for a long time together. And it was observed at last, that he was scarcely well capable of managing his ordinary business, and was judged delirious by the coroner's inquest. The news of this extraordinarily affected the minds of people here, and struck them as it were with astonishment. After this, multitudes

5. Joseph Hawley, Edwards' uncle by marriage.

in this and other towns seemed to have it strongly suggested to 'em, and pressed upon 'em, to do as this person had done. And many that seemed to be under no melancholy, some pious persons that had no special darkness, or doubts about the goodness of their state, nor were under any special trouble or concern of mind about anything spiritual or temporal, yet had it urged upon 'em, as if somebody had spoke to 'em, "Cut your own throat, now is good opportunity: *now, NOW!*" So that they were obliged to fight with all their might to resist it, and yet no reason suggested to 'em why they should do it.

About the same time, there were two remarkable instances of persons led away with strange enthusiastic delusions: one at Suffield, and another at South Hadley. That which has made the greatest noise in the country was of the man at South Hadley, whose delusion was that he thought himself divinely instructed to direct a poor man in melancholy and despairing circumstances, to say certain words in prayer to God, as recorded in Psalm 116:4, for his own relief. The man is esteemed a pious man: I have, since this error of his, had a particular acquaintance with him; and I believe none would question his piety, that had had such an acquaintance. He gave me a particular account of the manner how he was deluded; which is too long to be here inserted. But in short he was exceedingly rejoiced and elevated with this extraordinary work, so carried on in this part of the country; and was possessed with an opinion that it was the beginning of the glorious times of the church spoken of in Scripture: and had read it as the opinion of some divines, that there would be many in these times that should be endued with extraordinary gifts of the Holy Ghost, and had embraced the notion; though he had at first no apprehensions that any besides ministers would have such gifts. But he since exceedingly laments the dishonor he has done to God, and the wound he has given religion in it, and has lain low before God and man for it.

After these things the instances of conversion were rare here in comparison of what they had before been . . . ; and the Spirit of God not long after this time, appeared very sensibly withdrawing from all parts of the county (though we have heard of its going on in some places of Connecticut, and that it continues to be carried on even to this day). . . . But as to those that have been thought to be converted among us, in this time, they generally seem to be persons that have had an abiding change wrought on them: I have had particular acquaintance with many of them since, and they generally appear to be persons that have a new sense of things, new apprehensions and views of God, of the divine attributes, and Jesus Christ, and the great things of the gospel: they have a new sense of the truth of them, and they affect them in a new manner; though it is very far from being always alike with them, neither can they revive a sense of things when they please. Their hearts are often touched, and sometimes filled, with new sweetnesses and delights; there seems to be an inward ardor and burning of heart that they express, the like to which they never experienced before; sometimes, perhaps, occasioned only by the mention of Christ's name, or some one of the divine perfections: there are new appetites, and a new kind of breathings and paintings of heart, and groanings that cannot be uttered [Rom. 8:26]. There is a new kind of inward labor and struggle of soul towards heaven and holiness. . . . I know of no one young person in the town that has returned to former ways of looseness and extravagancy in any respect; but we still remain a reformed people, and God has evidently made us a new people.

I can't say that there has been no instance of any one person that has carried himself so that others should justly be stumbled concerning his profession; nor am I so vain as to imagine that we han't been mistaken concerning any that we have entertained a good opinion of, or that there are none that pass amongst us for sheep, that are indeed wolves in sheep's clothing; who probably may some time or other discover themselves by their fruits. We are not so pure, but that we have great cause to be humbled and ashamed that we are so impure; nor so religious, but that those that watch for our halting may see things in us whence they may take occasion to reproach us and religion: but in the main, there has been a great and marvellous work of conversion and sanctification among the people here; and they have paid all due respects to those who have been blessed of God to be the instruments of it. Both old and young have shown a forwardness to hearken not only to my counsels, but even to my reproofs from the pulpit.

A great part of the country have not received the most favorable thoughts of this affair; and to this day many retain a jealousy concerning it, and prejudice against it. I have reason to think that the meanness and weakness of the instrument, that has been made use of in this town, has prejudiced many against it; it don't appear to me strange that it should be so: but yet this circumstance of this great work of God is analogous to other circumstances of it. God has so ordered the manner of the work in many respects, as very signally and remarkably to show it to be his own peculiar and immediate work, and to secure the glory of it wholly to his almighty power and sovereign grace. And whatever the circumstances and means have been, and though we are so unworthy, yet so hath it pleased God to work! And we are evidently a people blessed of the Lord! And here, in this corner of the world, God dwells and manifests his glory. . . .

I humbly request of you, reverend sir, your prayers for this county, in its present melancholy circumstances into which it is brought by the Springfield quarrel, which doubtless above all things that have happened, has tended to put a stop to the glorious work here, and to prejudice this country against it, and hinder the propagation of it. I also ask your prayers for this town, and would particularly beg an interest in them for him who is, honored sir, with humble respect,

> Your obedient son and servant,
> Jonathan Edwards.

Northampton, Nov. 6, 1736.

Sermons

Sinners in the Hands of an Angry God (1741)

Deut. 32:35.
Their foot shall slide in due time.

In this verse is threatened the vengeance of God on the wicked unbeliev-
ing Israelites, that were God's visible people, and lived under means of
grace; and that, notwithstanding all God's wonderful works that he had
wrought towards that people, yet remained, as is expressed, v. 28, void of
counsel, having no understanding in them; and that, under all the cultiva-
tions of heaven, brought forth bitter and poisonous fruit; as in the two
verses next preceding the text.

The expression that I have chosen for my text, "Their foot shall slide in
due time," seems to imply the following things, relating to the punishment and destruction that these wicked Israelites were exposed to.

1. That they were *always* exposed to destruction, as one that stands or
walks in slippery places is always exposed to fall. This is implied in the
manner of their destruction's coming upon them, being represented by
their foot's sliding. The same is expressed, Ps. 73:18, "Surely thou didst set
them in slippery places; thou castedst them down into destruction."

2. It implies that they were always exposed to *sudden* unexpected destruction. As he that walks in slippery places is every moment liable to fall;
he can't foresee one moment whether he shall stand or fall the next; and
when he does fall, he falls at once, without warning. Which is also expressed in that, Ps. 73:18–19, "Surely thou didst set them in slippery places;
thou castedst them down into destruction. How are they brought into
desolation as in a moment?"

3. Another thing implied is that they are liable to fall *of themselves*,
without being thrown down by the hand of another. As he that stands or
walks on slippery ground, needs nothing but his own weight to throw him
down.

4. That the reason why they are not fallen already, and don't fall now, is only that God's appointed time is not come. For it is said, that when that due time, or appointed time comes, "their foot shall slide." Then they shall be left to fall as they are inclined by their own weight. God won't hold them up in these slippery places any longer, but will let them go; and then, at that very instant, they shall fall into destruction; as he that stands in such slippery declining ground on the edge of a pit that he can't stand alone, when he is let go he immediately falls and is lost.

The observation from the words that I would now insist upon is this,

[DOCTRINE.]

There is nothing that keeps wicked men, at any one moment, out of hell,
but the mere pleasure of God.

By the mere pleasure of God, I mean his sovereign pleasure, his arbitrary will, restrained by no obligation, hindered by no manner of difficulty, any more than if nothing else but God's mere will had in the least degree, or in any respect whatsoever, any hand in the preservation of wicked men one moment.

The truth of this observation may appear by the following considerations.

I. There is no want of *power* in God to cast wicked men into hell at any moment. Men's hands can't be strong when God rises up: the strongest have no power to resist him, nor can any deliver out of his hands.

He is not only able to cast wicked men into hell, but he can most *easily* do it. Sometimes an earthly prince meets with a great deal of difficulty to subdue a rebel, that has found means to fortify himself, and has made himself strong by the numbers of his followers. But it is not so with God. There is no fortress that is any defense from the power of God. Though hand join in hand, and vast multitudes of God's enemies combine and associate themselves, they are easily broken in pieces: they are as great heaps of light chaff before the whirlwind; or large quantities of dry stubble before devouring flames. We find it easy to tread on and crush a worm that we see crawling on the earth; so 'tis easy for us to cut or singe a slender thread that anything hangs by; thus easy is it for God when he pleases to cast his enemies down to hell. What are we, that we should think to stand before him, at whose rebuke the earth trembles, and before whom the rocks are thrown down?

II. They *deserve* to be cast into hell; so that divine justice never stands in the way, it makes no objection against God's using his power at any moment to destroy them. Yea, on the contrary, justice calls aloud for an infinite punishment of their sins. Divine justice says of the tree that brings forth such grapes of Sodom, "Cut it down, why cumbreth it the ground," Luke 13:7. The sword of divine justice is every moment brandished over their heads, and 'tis nothing but the hand of arbitrary mercy, and God's mere will, that holds it back.

III. They are *already* under a sentence of condemnation to hell. They don't only justly deserve to be cast down thither; but the sentence of the law of God, that eternal and immutable rule of righteousness that God has fixed between him and mankind, is gone out against them, and stands against them; so that they are bound over already to hell. John 3:18, "He that believeth not is condemned already." So that every unconverted man properly belongs to hell; that is his place; from thence he is. John 8:23, "Ye are from beneath." And thither he is bound; 'tis the place that justice, and God's Word, and the sentence of his unchangeable law assigns to him.

IV. They are now the objects of that very *same* anger and wrath of God that is expressed in the torments of hell: and the reason why they don't go down to hell at each moment, is not because God, in whose power they are, is not then very angry with them; as angry as he is with many of those miserable creatures that he is now tormenting in hell, and do there feel and bear the fierceness of his wrath. Yea, God is a great deal more angry with great numbers that are now on earth, yea, doubtless with many that are now in this congregation, that it may be are at ease and quiet, than he is with many of those that are now in the flames of hell.

So that it is not because God is unmindful of their wickedness, and don't resent it, that he don't let loose his hand and cut them off. God is not altogether such an one as themselves, though they may imagine him to be so. The wrath of God burns against them, their damnation don't slumber, the pit is prepared, the fire is made ready, the furnace is now hot, ready to receive them, the flames do now rage and glow. The glittering sword is whet, and held over them, and the pit hath opened her mouth under them.

V. The *devil* stands ready to fall upon them and seize them as his own, at what moment God shall permit him. They belong to him; he has their souls in his possession, and under his dominion. The Scripture represents them as his "goods," Luke 11:21. The devils watch them; they are ever by them, at their right hand; they stand waiting for them, like greedy hungry lions that see their prey, and expect to have it, but are for the present kept back; if God should withdraw his hand, by which they are restrained, they would in one moment fly upon their poor souls. The old serpent is gaping for them; hell opens its mouth wide to receive them; and if God should permit it, they would be hastily swallowed up and lost.

VI. There are in the souls of wicked men those hellish *principles* reigning, that would presently kindle and flame out into hellfire, if it were not for God's restraints. There is laid in the very nature of carnal men a foundation for the torments of hell: there are those corrupt principles, in reigning power in them, and in full possession of them, that are seeds of hellfire. These principles are active and powerful, and exceeding violent in their nature, and if it were not for the restraining hand of God upon them, they would soon break out, they would flame out after the same manner as the same corruptions, the same enmity does in the hearts of damned souls, and would beget the same torments in 'em as they do in them. The souls of the wicked are in Scripture compared to the troubled sea, Is. 57:20. For the present God restrains their wickedness by his mighty power, as he does the raging waves of the troubled sea, saying, "Hitherto shalt thou come, and no further"; but if God should withdraw that restraining power, it would soon carry all afore it. Sin is the ruin and misery of the soul; it is destructive in its nature; and if God should leave it without restraint, there would need nothing else to make the soul perfectly miserable. The corruption of the heart of man is a thing that is immoderate and boundless in its fury; and while wicked men live here, it is like fire pent up by God's restraints, whenas if it were let loose it would set on fire the course of nature; and as the heart is now a sink of sin, so, if sin was not restrained, it would immediately turn the soul into a fiery oven, or a furnace of fire and brimstone.

VII. It is no security to wicked men for one moment, that there are no *visible means of death* at hand. 'Tis no security to a natural man, that he is now in health, and that he don't see which way he should now immediately go out of the world by any accident, and that there is no visible danger in any respect in his circumstances. The manifold and continual experience of the world in all ages, shows that this is no evidence that a man is not on the very brink of eternity, and that the next step won't be into another world. The unseen, unthought of ways and means of persons going suddenly out of the world are innumerable and inconceivable. Unconverted men walk over the pit of hell on a rotten covering, and there are innumerable places in this covering so weak that they won't bear their weight, and these places are not seen. The arrows of death fly unseen at noonday; the sharpest sight can't discern them. God has so many different unsearchable ways of taking wicked men out of the world and sending 'em to hell, that there is nothing to make it appear that God had need to be at the expense of a miracle, or go out of the ordinary course of his providence, to destroy any wicked man, at any moment. All the means that there are of sinners going out of the world, are so in God's hands, and so universally absolutely subject to his power and determination, that it don't depend at all less on the mere will of God, whether sinners shall at any moment go to hell, than if means were never made use of, or at all concerned in the case.

VIII. Natural men's prudence and care to preserve their own lives, or the care of others to preserve them, don't secure 'em a moment. This divine providence and universal experience does also bear testimony to. There is this clear evidence that men's own wisdom is no security to them from death; that if it were otherwise we should see some difference between the wise and politic men of the world, and others, with regard to their liableness to early and unexpected death; but how is it in fact? Eccles. 2:16, "How dieth the wise man? as the fool."

IX. All wicked men's pains and contrivance they use to escape hell, while they continue to reject Christ, and so remain wicked men, don't secure 'em from hell one moment. Almost every natural man that hears of hell, flatters himself that he shall escape it; he depends upon himself for his own security; he flatters himself in what he has done, in what he is now doing, or what he intends to do; everyone lays out matters in his own mind how he shall avoid damnation, and flatters himself that he contrives well for himself, and that his schemes won't fail. They hear indeed that there are but few saved, and that the bigger part of men that have died heretofore are gone to hell; but each one imagines that he lays out matters better for his own escape than others have done: he don't intend to come to that place of torment; he says within himself, that he intends to take care that shall be effectual, and to order matters so for himself as not to fail.

But the foolish children of men do miserably delude themselves in their own schemes, and in their confidence in their own strength and wisdom; they trust to nothing but a shadow. The bigger part of those that heretofore have lived under the same means of grace, and are now dead, are undoubtedly gone to hell: and it was not because they were not as wise as those that are now alive: it was not because they did not lay out matters as well for themselves to secure their own escape. If it were so, that we could come to speak with them, and could inquire of them, one by one, whether they expected when alive, and when they used to hear about hell, ever to be the subjects of that misery, we doubtless should hear one and another reply, "No, I never intended to come here; I had laid out matters otherwise in my mind; I thought I should contrive well for myself; I thought my scheme good; I intended to take effectual care; but it came upon me unexpected; I did not look for it at that time, and in that manner; it came as a thief; death outwitted me; God's wrath was too quick for me. O my cursed foolishness! I was flattering myself, and pleasing myself with vain dreams of what I would do hereafter, and when I was saying peace and safety, then sudden destruction came upon me."

X. God has laid himself under *no obligation* by any promise to keep any natural man out of hell one moment. God certainly has made no promises either of eternal life, or of any deliverance or preservation from eternal death, but what are contained in the covenant of grace, the promises that are given in Christ, in whom all the promises are yea and amen. But surely they have no interest in the promises of the covenant of grace that are not the children of the covenant, and that don't believe in any of the promises of the covenant, and have no interest in the *mediator* of the covenant.

So that whatever some have imagined and pretended about promises made to natural men's earnest seeking and knocking, 'tis plain and manifest that whatever pains a natural man takes in religion, whatever prayers he makes, till he believes in Christ, God is under no manner of obligation to keep him a *moment* from eternal destruction.

So that thus it is, that natural men are held in the hand of God over the pit of hell; they have deserved the fiery pit, and are already sentenced to it; and God is dreadfully provoked, his anger is as great towards them as to those that are actually suffering the executions of the fierceness of his wrath in hell, and they have done nothing in the least to appease or abate that anger, neither is God in the least bound by any promise to hold 'em up one moment; the devil is waiting for them, hell is gaping for them, the flames gather and flash about them, and would fain lay hold on them, and swallow them up; the fire pent up in their own hearts is struggling to break out; and they have no interest in any mediator, there are no means within reach that can be any security to them. In short, they have no refuge, nothing to take hold of, all that preserves them every moment is the mere arbitrary will, and uncovenanted unobliged forbearance of an incensed God.

APPLICATION.

The use may be of *awakening* to unconverted persons in this congregation. This that you have heard is the case of every one of you that are out of Christ. That world of misery, that lake of burning brimstone is extended abroad under you. *There* is the dreadful pit of the glowing flames of the wrath of God; there is hell's wide gaping mouth open; and you have nothing to stand upon, nor anything to take hold of: there is nothing between you and hell but the air; 'tis only the power and mere pleasure of God that holds you up.

You probably are not sensible of this; you find you are kept out of hell, but don't see the hand of God in it, but look at other things, as the good state of your bodily constitution, your care of your own life, and the means you use for your own preservation. But indeed these things are nothing; if

God should withdraw his hand, they would avail no more to keep you from falling, than the thin air to hold up a person that is suspended in it.

Your wickedness makes you as it were heavy as lead, and to tend downwards with great weight and pressure towards hell; and if God should let you go, you would immediately sink and swiftly descend and plunge into the bottomless gulf, and your healthy constitution, and your own care and prudence, and best contrivance, and all your righteousness, would have no more influence to uphold you and keep you out of hell, than a spider's web would have to stop a falling rock. Were it not that so is the sovereign pleasure of God, the earth would not bear you one moment; for you are a burden to it; the creation groans with you; the creature is made subject to the bondage of your corruption, not willingly; the sun don't willingly shine upon you to give you light to serve sin and Satan; the earth don't willingly yield her increase to satisfy your lusts; nor is it willingly a stage for your wickedness to be acted upon; the air don't willingly serve you for breath to maintain the flame of life in your vitals, while you spend your life in the service of God's enemies. God's creatures are good, and were made for men to serve God with, and don't willingly subserve to any other purpose, and groan when they are abused to purposes so directly contrary to their nature and end. And the world would spew you out, were it not for the sovereign hand of him who hath subjected it in hope. There are the black clouds of God's wrath now hanging directly over your heads, full of the dreadful storm, and big with thunder; and were it not for the restraining hand of God it would immediately burst forth upon you. The sovereign pleasure of God for the present stays his rough wind; otherwise it would come with fury, and your destruction would come like a whirlwind, and you would be like the chaff of the summer threshing floor.

The wrath of God is like great waters that are dammed for the present; they increase more and more, and rise higher and higher, till an outlet is given, and the longer the stream is stopped, the more rapid and mighty is its course, when once it is let loose. 'Tis true, that judgment against your evil works has not been executed hitherto; the floods of God's vengeance have been withheld; but your guilt in the meantime is constantly increasing, and you are every day treasuring up more wrath; the waters are continually rising and waxing more and more mighty; and there is nothing but the mere pleasure of God that holds the waters back that are unwilling to be stopped, and press hard to go forward; if God should only withdraw his hand from the floodgate, it would immediately fly open, and the fiery floods of the fierceness and wrath of God would rush forth with inconceivable fury, and would come upon you with omnipotent power; and if your strength were ten thousand times greater than it is, yea ten thousand times greater than the strength of the stoutest, sturdiest devil in hell, it would be nothing to withstand or endure it.

The bow of God's wrath is bent, and the arrow made ready on the string, and justice bends the arrow at your heart, and strains the bow, and it is nothing but the mere pleasure of God, and that of an angry God, without any promise or obligation at all, that keeps the arrow one moment from being made drunk with your blood.

Thus are all you that never passed under a great change of heart, by the mighty power of the Spirit of God upon your souls; all that were never born again, and made new creatures, and raised from being dead in sin, to a state of new, and before altogether unexperienced light and life (however you may have reformed your life in many things, and may have had religious affections, and may keep up a form of religion in your families and closets, and in the house of God, and may be strict in it), you are thus in the hands of an angry God; 'tis nothing but his mere pleasure that keeps you from being this moment swallowed up in everlasting destruction.

However unconvinced you may now be of the truth of what you hear, by and by you will be fully convinced of it. Those that are gone from being in the like circumstances with you, see that it was so with them; for destruction came suddenly upon most of them, when they expected nothing of it, and while they were saying, "Peace and safety": now they see, that those things that they depended on for peace and safety, were nothing but thin air and empty shadows.

The God that holds you over the pit of hell, much as one holds a spider, or some loathsome insect, over the fire, abhors you, and is dreadfully provoked; his wrath towards you burns like fire; he looks upon you as worthy of nothing else, but to be cast into the fire; he is of purer eyes than to bear to have you in his sight; you are ten thousand times so abominable in his eyes as the most hateful venomous serpent is in ours. You have offended him infinitely more than ever a stubborn rebel did his prince: and yet 'tis nothing but his hand that holds you from falling into the fire every moment: 'tis to be ascribed to nothing else, that you did not go to hell the last night; that you was suffered to awake again in this world, after you closed your eyes to sleep: and there is no other reason to be given why you have not dropped into hell since you arose in the morning, but that God's hand has held you up: there is no other reason to be given why you han't gone to hell since you have sat here in the house of God, provoking his pure eyes by your sinful wicked manner of attending his solemn worship: yea, there is nothing else that is to be given as a reason why you don't this very moment drop down into hell.

O sinner! Consider the fearful danger you are in: 'tis a great furnace of wrath, a wide and bottomless pit, full of the fire of wrath, that you are held over in the hand of that God, whose wrath is provoked and incensed as much against you as against many of the damned in hell: you hang by a slender thread, with the flames of divine wrath flashing about it, and ready every moment to singe it, and burn it asunder; and you have no interest in any mediator, and nothing to lay hold of to save yourself, nothing to keep off the flames of wrath, nothing of your own, nothing that you ever have done, nothing that you can do, to induce God to spare you one moment.

And consider here more particularly several things concerning that wrath that you are in such danger of.

First. Whose wrath it is: it is the wrath of the infinite God. If it were only the wrath of man, though it were of the most potent prince, it would be comparatively little to be regarded. The wrath of kings is very much dreaded, especially of absolute monarchs, that have the possessions and lives of their subjects wholly in their power, to be disposed of at their mere will. Prov. 20:2, "The fear of a king is as the roaring of a lion: whoso provoketh him to anger, sinneth against his own soul." The subject that very much enrages an arbitary prince, is liable to suffer the most extreme torments, that human art can invent or human power can inflict. But the greatest earthly potentates, in their greatest majesty and strength, and when clothed in their greatest terrors, are but feeble despicable worms of the dust, in comparison of the great and almighty Creator and King of heaven and earth: it is but little that they can do, when most enraged, and when they have exerted the utmost of their fury. All the kings of the earth before God are as grasshoppers, they are nothing and less than nothing: both their love and their hatred is to be despised. The wrath of the great King of Kings is as much more terrible than theirs, as his majesty is greater. Luke 12:4–5, "And I say unto you my friends, be not afraid of them that kill the body, and after that have no more that they can do: but I will forewarn you whom ye shall fear; fear him, which after he hath killed, hath power to cast into hell; yea I say unto you, fear him."

Second. 'Tis the *fierceness* of his wrath that you are exposed to. We often read of the *fury* of God; as in Is. 59:18, "According to their deeds, accordingly he will repay fury to his adversaries." So Is. 66:15, "For behold, the Lord will come with fire, and with chariots like a whirlwind, to render his anger with fury, and his rebukes with flames of fire." And so in many other places. So we read of God's *fierceness*. Rev. 19:15, there we read of "the winepress of the fierceness and wrath of almighty God." The words are exceeding terrible: if it had only been said, "the wrath of God," the words would have implied that which is infinitely dreadful: but 'tis not only said so, but "the fierceness and wrath of God": the fury of God! the fierceness of Jehovah! Oh how dreadful must that be! Who can utter or conceive what such expressions carry in them! But it is not only said so, but "the fierceness and wrath of *almighty God.*" As though there would be a very great manifestation of his almighty power, in what the fierceness of his wrath should inflict, as though omnipotence should be as it were enraged, and exerted, as men are wont to exert their strength in the fierceness of their wrath. Oh! then what will be the consequence! What will become of the poor worm that shall suffer it! Whose hands can be strong? and whose heart endure? To what a dreadful, inexpressible, inconceivable depth of misery must the poor creature be sunk, who shall be the subject of this!

Consider this, you that are here present, that yet remain in an unregenerate state. That God will execute the fierceness of his anger, implies that he will inflict wrath without any pity: when God beholds the ineffable extremity of your case, and sees your torment to be so vastly disproportioned to your strength, and sees how your poor soul is crushed and sinks down, as it were into an infinite gloom, he will have no compassion upon you, he will not forbear the executions of his wrath, or in the least lighten his hand; there shall be no moderation or mercy, nor will God then at all stay his rough wind; he will have no regard to your welfare, nor be at all careful lest you should suffer too much, in any other sense than only that you shall not suffer beyond what strict justice requires: nothing shall be withheld, because it's so hard for you to bear. Ezek. 8:18, "Therefore will I also deal in fury; mine eye shall not spare, neither will I have pity; and though they cry in mine ears with a loud voice, yet I will not hear them." Now God stands ready to pity you; this is a day of mercy; you may cry now with some encouragement of obtaining mercy: but when once the day of mercy is past, your most lamentable and dolorous cries and shrieks will be in vain; you will be wholly lost and thrown away of God as to any regard to your welfare; God will have no other use to put you to but only to suffer misery; you shall be continued in being to no other end; for you will be a vessel of wrath fitted to destruction; and there will be no other use of this vessel but only to be filled full of wrath: God will be so far from pitying you when you cry to him, that 'tis said he will only laugh and mock, Prov. 1:25–32.

How awful are those words, Is. 63:3, which are the words of the great God, "I will tread them in mine anger, and will trample them in my fury, and their blood shall be sprinkled upon my garments, and I will stain all my raiment." 'Tis perhaps impossible to conceive of words that carry in them greater manifestations of these three things, viz. contempt, and hatred, and fierceness of indignation. If you cry to God to pity you, he will be so far from pitying you in your doleful case, or showing you the least regard or favor, that instead of that he'll only tread you under foot: and though he will know that you can't bear the weight of omnipotence treading upon you, yet he won't regard that, but he will crush you under his feet without mercy; he'll crush out your blood, and make it fly, and it shall be sprinkled on his garments, so as to stain all his raiment. He will not only hate you, but he will have you in the utmost contempt; no place shall be thought fit for you, but under his feet, to be trodden down as the mire of the streets.

Third. The misery you are exposed to is that which God will inflict to that end, that he might show what that wrath of Jehovah is. God hath had it on his heart to show to angels and men, both how excellent his love is, and also how terrible his wrath is. Sometimes earthly kings have a mind to show how terrible *their* wrath is, by the extreme punishments they would execute on those that provoke 'em. Nebuchadnezzar, that mighty and haughty monarch of the Chaldean empire, was willing to show *his* wrath, when enraged with Shadrach, Meshach, and Abednego; and accordingly gave order that the burning fiery furnace should be het seven times hotter than it was before; doubtless it was raised to the utmost degree of fierceness that human art could raise it: but the great God is also willing to show *his wrath*, and magnify his awful majesty and mighty power in the extreme sufferings of his enemies. Rom. 9:22, "What if God, willing to show *his* wrath, and to make his power known, endured with much long-suffering the vessels of wrath fitted to destruction?" And seeing this is his design, and what he has determined, to show how terrible the unmixed, unrestrained wrath, the fury and fierceness of Jehovah is, he will do it to effect. There will be something accomplished and brought to pass, that will be dreadful with a witness. When the great and angry God hath risen up and executed his awful vengeance on the poor sinner; and the wretch is actually suffering the infinite weight and power of his indignation, then will God call upon the whole universe to behold that awful majesty, and mighty power that is to be seen in it. Is. 33:12–14, "And the people shall be as the burning of lime, as thorns cut up shall they be burnt in the fire. Hear ye that are far off what I have done; and ye that are near acknowledge my might. The sinners in Zion are afraid, fearfulness hath surprised the hypocrites. Who among us shall dwell with the devouring fire? who among us shall dwell with everlasting burnings?"

Thus it will be with you that are in an unconverted state, if you continue in it; the infinite might, and majesty and terribleness of the omnipotent God shall be magnified upon you, in the ineffable strength of your torments: you shall be tormented in the presence of the holy angels, and in the presence of the Lamb; and when you shall be in this state of suffering, the glorious inhabitants of heaven shall go forth and look on the awful spectacle, that they may see what the wrath and fierceness of the Almighty is, and when they have seen it, they will fall down and adore that great power and majesty. Is. 66:23–24, "And it shall come to pass, that from one new moon to another, and from one sabbath to another, shall all flesh come to worship before me, saith the Lord; and they shall go forth and look upon the carcasses of the men that have transgressed against me; for their worm shall not die, neither shall their fire be quenched, and they shall be an abhorring unto all flesh."

Fourth. 'Tis *everlasting* wrath. It would be dreadful to suffer this fierceness and wrath of almighty God one moment; but you must suffer it to all eternity: there will be no end to this exquisite horrible misery: when you look forward, you shall see a long forever, a boundless duration before you, which will swallow up your thoughts, and amaze your soul; and you will absolutely despair of ever having any deliverance, any end, any mitigation, any rest at all; you will know certainly that you must wear out long ages, millions of millions of ages, in wrestling and conflicting with this almighty merciless vengeance; and then when you have so done, when so many ages have actually been spent by you in this manner, you will know that all is but a point to what remains. So that your punishment will indeed be infinite. Oh who can express what the state of a soul in such circumstances is! All that we can possibly say about it, gives but a very feeble faint representation of it; 'tis inexpressible and inconceivable: for "who knows the power of God's anger?" [Ps. 90:11].

How dreadful is the state of those that are daily and hourly in danger of this great wrath, and infinite misery! But this is the dismal case of every soul in this congregation, that has not been born again, however moral and strict, sober and religious they may otherwise be. Oh that you would consider it, whether you be young or old. There is reason to think, that there are many in this congregation now hearing this discourse, that will actually be the subjects of this very misery to all eternity. We know not who they are, or in what seats they sit, or what thoughts they now have: it may be they are now at ease, and hear all these things without much disturbance, and are now flattering themselves that they are not the persons, promising themselves that they shall escape. If we knew that there was one person, and but one, in the whole congregation that was to be the subject of this misery, what an awful thing would it be to think of! If we knew who it was, what an awful sight would it be to see such a person! How might all the rest of the congregation lift up a lamentable and bitter cry over him! But alas! instead of one, how many is it likely will remember this discourse in hell? And it would be a wonder if some that are now present, should not be in hell in a very short time, before this year is out. And it would be no wonder if some person that now sits here in some seat of this meetinghouse in health, and quiet and secure, should be there before tomorrow morning. Those of you that finally continue in a natural condition, that shall keep out of hell longest, will be there in a little time! your damnation don't slumber; it will come swiftly, and in all probability very suddenly upon many of you. You have reason to wonder, that you are not already in hell. 'Tis doubtless the case of some that heretofore you have seen and known, that never deserved hell more than you, and that heretofore appeared as likely to have been now alive as you: their case is past all hope; they are crying in extreme misery and perfect despair; but here you are in the land of the living, and in the house of God, and have an opportunity to obtain salvation. What would not those poor damned, hopeless souls give for one day's such opportunity as you now enjoy!

And now you have an extraordinary opportunity, a day wherein Christ has flung the door of mercy wide open, and stands in the door calling and crying with a loud voice to poor sinners; a day wherein many are flocking to him, and pressing into the kingdom of God; many are daily coming from the east, west, north and south; many that were very lately in the same miserable condition that you are in, are in now an happy state, with their hearts filled with love to him that has loved them and washed them from their sins in his own blood, and rejoicing in hope of the glory of God. How awful is it to be left behind at such a day! To see so many others feasting, while you are pining and perishing! To see so many rejoicing and singing for joy of heart, while you have cause to mourn for sorrow of heart, and howl for vexation of spirit! How can you rest one moment in such a condition? Are not your souls as precious as the souls of the people at Suffield,[1] where they are flocking from day to day to Christ?

Are there not many here that have lived *long* in the world, that are not to this day born again, and so are aliens from the commonwealth of Israel, and have done nothing ever since they have lived, but treasure up wrath

---

1. The next neighboring town.—Edwards' note.

against the day of wrath? Oh sirs, your case in an especial manner is extremely dangerous; your guilt and hardness of heart is extremely great. Don't you see how generally persons of your years are passed over and left, in the present remarkable and wonderful dispensation of God's mercy? You had need to consider yourselves, and wake thoroughly out of sleep; you cannot bear the fierceness and wrath of the infinite God.

And you that are *young men*, and *young women*, will you neglect this precious season that you now enjoy, when so many others of your age are renouncing all youthful vanities, and flocking to Christ? You especially have now an extraordinary opportunity; but if you neglect it, it will soon be with you as it is with those persons that spent away all the precious days of youth in sin, and are now come to such a dreadful pass in blindness and hardness.

And you *children* that are unconverted, don't you know that you are going down to hell, to bear the dreadful wrath of that God that is now angry with you every day, and every night? Will you be content to be the children of the devil, when so many other children in the land are converted, and are become the holy and happy children of the King of Kings?

And let everyone that is yet out of Christ, and hanging over the pit of hell, whether they be old men and women, or middle aged, or young people, or little children, now hearken to the loud calls of God's Word and providence. This acceptable year of the Lord, that is a day of such great favor to some, will doubtless be a day of as remarkable vengeance to others. Men's hearts harden, and their guilt increases apace at such a day as this, if they neglect their souls: and never was there so great danger of such persons being given up to hardness of heart, and blindness of mind. God seems now to be hastily gathering in his elect in all parts of the land; and probably the bigger part of adult persons that ever shall be saved, will be brought in now in a little time, and that it will be as it was on that great outpouring of the Spirit upon the Jews in the apostles' days, the election will obtain, and the rest will be blinded. If this should be the case with you, you will eternally curse this day, and will curse the day that ever you was born, to see such a season of the pouring out of God's Spirit; and will wish that you had died and gone to hell before you had seen it. Now undoubtedly it is, as it was in the days of John the Baptist: the ax is in an extraordinary manner laid at the root of the trees, that every tree that brings not forth good fruit, may be hewn down, and cast into the fire.

Therefore let everyone that is out of Christ, now awake and fly from the wrath to come. The wrath of almighty God is now undoubtedly hanging over great part of this congregation: let everyone fly out of Sodom: "Haste and escape for your lives, look not behind you, escape to the mountain, lest you be consumed" [Gen. 19:17].

A Divine and Supernatural Light, Immediately Imparted to the Soul by the Spirit of God, Shown to be Both a Scriptural, and Rational Doctrine (1734)

Matt. 16:17.
And Jesus answered and said unto him, Blessed art thou, Simon Barjona: for flesh and blood hath not revealed it unto thee, but my Father which is in heaven.

Christ says these words to Peter, upon occasion of his professing his faith in him as the Son of God. Our Lord was inquiring of his disciples, who men said that he was; not that he needed to be informed, but only to introduce and give occasion to what follows. They answer, that some said he was John the Baptist, and some Elias, and others Jeremias or one of the prophets. When they had thus given an account, who others said he was, Christ asks them, who they said he was. Simon Peter, whom we find always zealous and forward, was the first to answer; he readily replied to the question, "Thou art Christ, the Son of the living God" [v. 16].

Upon this occasion Christ says as he does *to* him and *of* him in the text: in which we may observe,

1. That Peter is pronounced blessed on this account. "Blessed art thou"—"Thou art an happy man, that thou art not ignorant of this, that I am Christ, the Son of the living God. Thou art distinguishingly happy. Others are blinded, and have dark and deluded apprehensions, as you have now given an account, some thinking that I am Elias, and some that I am Jeremias, and some one thing, and some another; but none of them

thinking right, all of them misled. Happy art thou, that art so distinguished as to know the truth in this matter."

2. The evidence of this his happiness declared; viz. that God, and he only, had revealed it to him. This is an evidence of his being blessed,

(1) First, as it shows how peculiarly favored he was of God, above others, q.d. "How highly favored art thou, that others that are wise and great men, the Scribes, Pharisees, and rulers, and the nation in general, are left in darkness, to follow their own misguided apprehensions, and that thou shouldst be singled out, as it were by name, that my heavenly Father should thus set his love on thee, Simon Barjona. This argues thee blessed, that thou shouldst thus be the object of God's distinguishing love."

(2) Secondly, it evidences his blessedness also, as it intimates that this knowledge is above any that flesh and blood can reveal. "This is such knowledge as my Father which [is] in heaven only can give: it is too high and excellent to be communicated by such means as other knowledge is. Thou art blessed, that thou knowest that which God alone can teach thee."

The original of this knowledge is here declared; both negatively and positively. Positively, as God is here declared the author of it. Negatively, as 'tis declared that flesh and blood had not revealed it. God is the author of all knowledge and understanding whatsoever: he is the author of the knowledge, that is obtained by human learning: he is the author of all moral prudence, and of the knowledge and skill that men have in their secular business. Thus it is said of all in Israel that were wise-hearted, and skilled in embroidering, that God had filled them with the spirit of wisdom (Ex. 28:3).

God is the author of such knowledge; but yet not so but that flesh and blood reveals it. Mortal men are capable of imparting the knowledge of human arts and sciences, and skill in temporal affairs. God is the author of such knowledge by those means: flesh and blood is made use of by God as the mediate or second cause of it; he conveys it by the power and influence of natural means. But this spiritual knowledge, spoken of in the text, is what God is the author of, and none else: he reveals it, and flesh and blood reveals it not. He imparts this knowledge immediately, not making use of any intermediate natural causes, as he does in other knowledge.

What had passed in the preceding discourse, naturally occasioned Christ to observe this; because the disciples had been telling, how others did not know him, but were generally mistaken about him, and divided and confounded in their opinions of him: but Peter had declared his assured faith that he was the Son of God. Now it was natural to observe, how it was not flesh and blood, that had revealed it to him, but God; for if this knowledge were dependent on natural causes or means, how came it to pass that they, a company of poor fishermen, illiterate men, and persons of low education, attained to the knowledge of the truth; while the Scribes and Pharisees, men of vastly higher advantages, and greater knowledge and sagacity in other matters, remained in ignorance? This could be owing only to the gracious distinguishing influence and revelation of the Spirit of God. Hence, what I would make the subject of my present discourse from these words, is this:

DOCTRINE.

There is such a thing, as a spiritual and divine light, immediately imparted to the soul by God, of a different nature from any that is obtained by natural means.

In what I say on this subject at this time, I would:

I. Show what this divine light is.

II. How it is given immediately by God, and not obtained by natural means.

III. Show the truth of the doctrine.

And then conclude with a brief improvement.

I. I would show what this spiritual and divine light is. And in order to it would show,

First, in a few things what it is not. And here,

1. Those convictions that natural men may have of their sin and misery is not this spiritual and divine light. Men in a natural condition may have convictions of the guilt that lies upon them, and of the anger of God, and their danger of divine vengeance. Such convictions are from light or sensibleness of truth: that some sinners have a greater conviction of their guilt and misery than others, is because some have more light, or more of

an apprehension of truth, than others. And this light and conviction may be from the Sprit of God; the Spirit convinces men of sin: but yet nature is much more concerned in it than in the communication of that spiritual and divine light, that is spoken of in the doctrine; 'tis from the Spirit of God only as assisting natural principles, and not as infusing any new principles. Common grace differs from special, in that it influences only by assisting of nature; and not by imparting grace, or bestowing anything above nature. The light that is obtained, is wholly natural, or of no superior kind to what mere nature attains to; though more of that kind be obtained, than would be obtained if men were left wholly to themselves. Or in other words, common grace only assists the faculties of the soul to do that more fully, which they do by nature; as natural conscience, or reason, will by mere nature make a man sensible of guilt, and will accuse and condemn him when he has done amiss. Conscience is a principle natural to men; and the work that it doth naturally, or of itself, is to give an apprehension of right and wrong; and to suggest to the mind the relation that there is between right and wrong, and a retribution. The Spirit of God, in those convictions which unregenerate men sometimes have, assists conscience to do this work in a further degree, than it would do if they were left to themselves: he helps it against those things that tend to stupify it, and obstruct its exercise. But in the renewing and sanctifying work of the Holy Ghost, those things are wrought in the soul that are above nature, and of which there is nothing of the like kind in the soul by nature; and they are caused to exist in the soul habitually, and according to such a stated constitution or law, that lays such a foundation for exercises in a continued course, as is called a principle of nature. Not only are remaining principles assisted to do their work more freely and fully, but those principles are restored that were utterly destroyed by the fall; and the mind thenceforward habitually exerts those acts that the dominion of sin had made it as wholly destitute of, as a dead body is of vital acts.

The Spirit of God acts in a very different manner in the one case, from what he doth in the other. He may indeed act upon the mind of a natural man; but he acts in the mind of a saint as an indwelling vital principle. He acts upon the mind of an unregenerate person as an extrinsic occasional agent; for in acting upon them he doth not unite himself to them; for notwithstanding all his influences that they may be the subjects of, they are still "sensual, having not the Spirit" (Jude 19). But he unites himself with the mind of a saint, takes him for his temple, actuates and influences him as a new, supernatural principle of life and action. There is this difference; that the Spirit of God, in acting in the soul of a godly man, exerts and communicates himself there in his own proper nature. Holiness is the proper nature of the Spirit of God. The Holy Spirit operates in the minds of the godly, by uniting himself to them, and living in them, and exerting his own nature in the exercise of their faculties. The Spirit of God may act upon a creature, and yet not in acting communicate himself. The Spirit of God may act upon inanimate creatures; as, "The Spirit moved upon the face of the waters" [Gen. 1:2] in the beginning of the creation: so the Spirit of God may act upon the minds of men, many ways, and communicate himself no more than when he acts upon an inanimate creature. For instance, he may excite thoughts in them, may assist their natural reason and understanding, or may assist other natural principles, and this without any union with the soul, but may act, as it were, as upon an external object. But as he acts in his holy influences, and spiritual operations, he acts in a way of peculiar communication of himself; so that the subject is thence denominated *spiritual*.

2. This spiritual and divine light don't consist in any impression made upon the imagination. 'Tis no impression upon the mind, as though one saw anything with the bodily eyes: 'tis no imagination or idea of an outward light or glory, or any beauty of form or countenance, or a visible luster or brightness of any object. The imagination may be strongly impressed with such things; but this is not spiritual light. Indeed when the mind has a lively discovery of spiritual things, and is greatly affected with the power of divine light, it may, and probably very commonly doth, much affect the imagination: so that impressions of an outward beauty or brightness, may accompany those spiritual discoveries. But spiritual light is not that impression upon the imagination, but an exceeding different thing from it. Natural men may have lively impressions on their imaginations; and we can't determine but that the devil, who transforms himself

into an angel of light, may cause imaginations of an outward beauty, or visible glory, and of sounds and speeches, and other such things; but these are things of a vastly inferior nature to spiritual light.

3. This spiritual light is not the suggesting of any new truths, or propositions not contained in the Word of God. This suggesting of new truths or doctrines to the mind, independent of any antecedent revelation of those propositions, either in word or writing, is inspiration; such as the prophets and apostles had, and such as some enthusiasts pretend to. But this spiritual light that I am speaking of, is quite a different thing from inspiration: it reveals no new doctrine, it suggests no new proposition to the mind, it teaches no new thing of God, or Christ, or another world, not taught in the Bible; but only gives a due apprehension of those things that are taught in the Word of God.

4. 'Tis not every affecting view that men have of the things of religion that is this spiritual and divine light. Men by mere principles of nature are capable of being affected with things that have a special relation to religion, as well as other things. A person by mere nature, for instance, may be liable to be affected with the story of Jesus Christ, and the sufferings he underwent, as well as by any other tragical story: he may be the more affected with it from the interest he conceives mankind to have in it: yea, he may be affected with it without believing it; as well as a man may be affected with what he reads in a romance, or sees acted in a stage play. He may be affected with a lively and eloquent description of many pleasant things that attend the state of the blessed in heaven; as well as his imagination be entertained by a romantic description of the pleasantness of fairy land, or the like. And that common belief of the truth of the things of religion, that persons may have from education, or otherwise, may help forward their affection. We read in Scripture of many that were greatly affected with things of a religious nature, who yet are there represented as wholly graceless, and many of them very ill men. A person therefore may have affecting views of the things of religion, and yet be very destitute of spiritual light. Flesh and blood may be the author of this: one man may give another an affecting view of divine things with but common assistance; but God alone can give a spiritual discovery of them.

But I proceed to show,

Secondly, positively, what this spiritual and divine light is.

And it may be thus described: a true sense of the divine excellency of the things revealed in the Word of God, and a conviction of the truth and reality of them, thence arising.

This spiritual light primarily consists in the former of these, viz. a real sense and apprehension of the divine excellency of things revealed in the Word of God. A spiritual and saving conviction of the truth and reality of these things, arises from such a sight of their divine excellency and glory; so that this conviction of their truth is an effect and natural consequence of this sight of their divine glory. There is therefore in this spiritual light,

1. A true sense of the divine and superlative excellency of the things of religion; a real sense of the excellency of God, and Jesus Christ, and of the work of redemption, and the ways and works of God revealed in the gospel. There is a divine and superlative glory in these things; an excellency that is of a vastly higher kind, and more sublime nature, than in other things; a glory greatly distinguishing them from all that is earthly and temporal. He that is spiritually enlightened truly apprehends and sees it, or has a sense of it. He don't merely rationally believe that God is glorious, but he has a sense of the gloriousness of God in his heart. There is not only a rational belief that God is holy, and that holiness is a good thing; but there is a sense of the loveliness of God's holiness. There is not only a speculatively judging that God is gracious, but a sense how amiable God is upon that account; or a sense of the beauty of this divine attribute.

There is a twofold understanding or knowledge of good, that God has made the mind of man capable of. The first, that which is merely speculative or notional: as when a person only speculatively judges, that anything is, which by the agreement of mankind, is called good or excellent, viz. that which is most to general advantage, and between which and a reward there is a suitableness; and the like. And the other is that which consists in the sense of the heart: as when there is a sense of the beauty, amiableness, or sweetness of a thing; so that the heart is sensible of pleasure and delight in the presence of the idea of it. In the former is exercised merely the speculative faculty, or the understanding strictly so-called, or as spoken of in distinction from the will or disposition of the soul. In the latter the will, or inclination, or heart, are mainly concerned.

Thus there is a difference between having an opinion that God is holy and gracious, and having a sense of the loveliness and beauty of that holiness and grace. There is a difference between having a rational judgment that honey is sweet, and having a sense of its sweetness. A man may have the former, that knows not how honey tastes; but a man can't have the latter, unless he has an idea of the taste of honey in his mind. So there is a difference between believing that a person is beautiful, and having a sense of his beauty. The former may be obtained by hearsay, but the latter only by seeing the countenance. There is a wide difference between mere speculative, rational judging anything to be excellent, and having a sense of its sweetness, and beauty. The former rests only in the head, speculation only is concerned in it; but the heart is concerned in the latter. When the heart is sensible of the beauty and amiableness of a thing, it necessarily feels pleasure in the apprehension. It is implied in a person's being heartily sensible of the loveliness of a thing, that the idea of it is sweet and pleasant to his soul; which is a far different thing from having a rational opinion that it is excellent.

2. There arises from this sense of divine excellency of things contained in the Word of God, a conviction of the truth and reality of them: and that either indirectly, or directly.

(1) First, indirectly, and that two ways:

1. As the prejudices that are in the heart, against the truth of divine things, are hereby removed; so that the mind becomes susceptive of the due force of rational arguments for their truth. The mind of man is naturally full of prejudices against the truth of divine things: it is full of enmity against the doctrines of the gospel; which is a disadvantage to those arguments that prove their truth, and causes them to lose their force upon the mind. But when a person has discovered to him the divine excellency of Christian doctrines, this destroys the enmity, removes those prejudices, and sanctifies the reason, and causes it to lie open to the force of arguments for their truth.

Hence was the different effect that Christ's miracles had to convince the disciples, from what they had to convince the Scribes and Pharisees. Not that they had a stronger reason, or had their reason more improved;

but their reason was sanctified, and those blinding prejudices, that the Scribes and Pharisees were under, were removed by the sense they had of the excellency of Christ, and his doctrine.

2. It not only removes the hindrances of reason, but positively helps reason. It makes even the speculative notions the more lively. It engages the attention of the mind, with the more fixedness and intenseness to that kind of objects; which causes it to have a clearer view of them, and enables it more clearly to see their mutual relations, and occasions it to take more notice of them. The ideas themselves that otherwise are dim, and obscure, are by this means impressed with the greater strength, and have a light cast upon them; so that the mind can better judge of them. As he that beholds the objects on the face of the earth, when the light of the sun is cast upon them, is under greater advantage to discern them in their true forms, and mutual relations, than he that sees them in a dim starlight or twilight.

The mind having a sensibleness of the excellency of divine objects, dwells upon them with delight; and the powers of the soul are more awakened, and enlivened to employ themselves in the contemplation of them, and exert themselves more fully and much more to purpose. The beauty and sweetness of the objects draws on the faculties, and draws forth their exercises: so that reason itself is under far greater advantages for its proper and free exercises, and to attain its proper end, free of darkness and delusion. But,

(2) Secondly, a true sense of the divine excellency of the things of God's Word doth more directly and immediately convince of the truth of them; and that because the excellency of these things is so superlative. There is a beauty in them that is so divine and godlike, that is greatly and evidently distinguishing of them from things merely human, or that men are the inventors and authors of; a glory that is so high and great, that when clearly seen, commands assent to their divinity, and reality. When there is an actual and lively discovery of this beauty and excellency, it won't allow of any such thought as that it is an human work, or the fruit of men's invention. This evidence, that they, that are spiritually enlightened, have of the truth of the things of religion, is a kind of intuitive and immediate evidence. They believe the doctrines of God's word to be divine, because

they see divinity in them, i.e. they see a divine, and transcendent, and most evidently distinguishing glory in them; such a glory as, if clearly seen, don't leave room to doubt of their being of God, and not of men.

Such a conviction of the truth of religion as this, arising, these ways, from a sense of the divine excellency of them, is that true spiritual conviction that there is in saving faith. And this original of it, is that by which it is most essentially distinguished from that common assent, which unregenerate men are capable of.

II. I proceed now to the second thing proposed, viz. to show how this light is immediately given by God, and not obtained by natural means. And here,

First. 'Tis not intended that the natural faculties are not made use of in it. The natural faculties are the subject of this light: and they are the subject in such a manner, that they are not merely passive, but active in it; the acts and exercises of man's understanding are concerned and made use of in it. God, in letting in this light into the soul, deals with man according to his nature, or as a rational creature; and makes use of his human faculties. But yet this light is not the less immediately from God for that; though the faculties are made use of, 'tis as the subject and not as the cause; and that acting of the faculties in it, is not the cause, but is either implied in the thing itself (in the light that is imparted), or is the consequence of it. As the use that we make of our eyes in beholding various objects, when the sun arises, is not the cause of the light that discovers those objects to us.

Second. 'Tis not intended that outward means have no concern in this affair. As I have observed already, 'tis not in this affair, as it is in inspiration, where new truths are suggested: for here is by this light only given a due apprehension of the same truths that are revealed in the Word of God; and therefore it is not given without the Word. The gospel is made use of in this affair: this light is the "light of the glorious gospel of Christ" (II Cor. 4:4). The gospel is as a glass, by which this light is conveyed to us. I Cor. 13:12, "Now we see through a glass." But,

Third. When it is said that this light is given immediately by God, and not obtained by natural means, hereby is intended, that 'tis given by God without making use of any means that operate by their own power, or a natural force. God makes use of means; but 'tis not as mediate causes to produce this effect. There are not truly any second causes of it; but it is produced by God immediately. The Word of God is no proper cause of this effect: it don't operate by any natural force in it. The Word of God is only made use of to convey to the mind the subject matter of this saving instruction: and this indeed it doth convey to us by natural force or influence. It conveys to our minds these and those doctrines; it is the cause of the notion of them in our heads, but not of the sense of the divine excellency of them in our hearts. Indeed a person can't have spiritual light without the Word. But that don't argue, that the Word properly causes that light. The mind can't see the excellency of any doctrine, unless that doctrine be first in the mind; but the seeing the excellency of the doctrine may be immediately from the Spirit of God; though the conveying of the doctrine or proposition itself may be by the Word. So that the notions that are the subject matter of this light, are conveyed to the mind by the Word of God; but that due sense of the heart, wherein this light formally consists, is immediately by the Spirit of God. As for instance, that notion that there is a Christ, and that Christ is holy and gracious, is conveyed to the mind by the Word of God: but the sense of the excellency of Christ by reason of that holiness and grace, is nevertheless immediately the work of the Holy Spirit. I come now,

III. [In the third place,] to show the truth of the doctrine; that is, to show that there is such a thing as that spiritual light that has been described, thus immediately let into the mind by God. And here I would show briefly, that this doctrine is both scriptural, and rational.

First, 'tis scriptural. My text is not only full to the purpose, but 'tis a doctrine that the Scripture abounds in. We are there abundantly taught, that the saints differ from the ungodly in this, that they have the knowledge of God, and a sight of God, and of Jesus Christ. I shall mention but few texts of many: I John 3:6, "Whosoever sinneth, hath not seen him, nor known him." III John 1:11, "He that doth good, is of God: but he that doth evil, hath not seen God." John 14:19, "The world seeth me no more; but ye see me." John 17:3, "And this is eternal life, that they might know thee, the only true God, and Jesus Christ whom thou hast sent." This knowledge, or sight of God and Christ, can't be a mere speculative knowledge; because it is spoken of as a seeing and knowing, wherein they differ from the ungodly. And by these scriptures it must not only be a different knowledge in degree and circumstances, and different in its effects; but it must be entirely different in nature and kind.

And this light and knowledge is always spoken of as immediately given of God. Matt. 11:25-27, "At that time Jesus answered and said, I thank thee, O Father, Lord of heaven and earth, because thou hast hid these things from the wise and prudent, and hast revealed them unto babes: even so, Father; for so it seemed good in thy sight. All things are delivered unto me of my Father, and no man knoweth the Son but the Father; neither knoweth any man the Father, save the Son, and he to whomsoever the Son will reveal him." Here this effect is ascribed alone to the arbitrary operation, and gift of God, bestowing this knowledge on whom he will, and distinguishing those with it, that have the least natural advantage or means for knowledge, even babes, when it is denied to the wise and prudent. And the imparting the knowledge of God is here appropriated to the Son of God, as his sole prerogative. And again, II Cor. 4:6, "For God, who commanded the light to shine out of darkness, hath shined in our hearts, to give the light of the knowledge of the glory of God in the face of Jesus Christ." This plainly shows, that there is such a thing as a discovery of the divine superlative glory and excellency of God and Christ; and that peculiar to the saints: and also that 'tis as immediately from God, as light from the sun: and that 'tis the immediate effect of his power and will; for 'tis compared to God's creating the light by his powerful word in the beginning of the creation; and is said to be by the Spirit of the Lord, in the 18th verse of the preceding chapter. God is spoken of as giving the knowledge of Christ in conversion, as of what before was hidden and unseen, in that [place], Gal. 1:15-16, "But when it pleased God, who separated me from my mother's womb, and called me by his grace, to reveal his Son in me." The Scripture also speaks plainly of such a knowledge of the Word of God, as has been described, as the immediate gift of God. Ps. 119:18, "Open thou mine eyes, that I may behold wondrous things out of thy law." What could the Psalmist mean, when he begged of God to open his eyes? was he ever blind? might he not have resort to the law and see every word and sentence in it when he pleased? And what could he mean by those "wondrous things"? was it the wonderful stories of the creation, and deluge, and Israel's passing through the Red Sea, and the like? were not his eyes open to read these strange things when he would? Doubtless by "wondrous things" in God's law, he had respect to those distinguishing and wonderful excellencies, and marvellous manifestations of the divine perfections, and glory, that there was in the commands and doctrines of the Word, and those works and counsels of God that were there revealed. So the Scripture speaks of a knowledge of God's dispensation, and covenant of mercy, and way of grace towards his people, as peculiar to the saints, and given only by God, Ps. 25:14, "The secret of the Lord is with them that fear him; and he will show them his covenant."

And that a true and saving belief of the truth of religion is that which arises from such a discovery, is also what the Scripture teaches. As John 6:40, "And this is the will of him that sent me, that every one that seeth the Son, and believeth on him, may have everlasting life." Where it is plain that a true faith is what arises from a spiritual sight of Christ. And John 17:6–8, "I have manifested thy name unto the men which thou gavest me out of the world . . . Now they have known that all things whatsoever thou hast given me are of thee; for I have given unto them the words which thou gavest me, and they have received them, and have known surely that I came out from thee, and they have believed that thou didst send me." Where Christ's manifesting God's name to the disciples, or giving them the knowledge of God, was that whereby they knew that Christ's doctrine was of God, and that Christ himself was of him, proceeded from him, and was sent by him. Again, John 12:44–46, "Jesus cried, and said, He that believeth on me, believeth not on me, but on him that sent me; and he that seeth me seeth him that sent me. I am come a light into the world, that whosoever believeth on me should not abide in darkness." Their believing in Christ and spiritually seeing him, are spoken of as running parallel.

Christ condemns the Jews, that they did not know that he was the Messiah, and that his doctrine was true, from an inward distinguishing taste and relish of what was divine, in Luke 12:56–57. He having there blamed the Jews, that though they could "discern the face of the sky and of the earth," and signs of the weather, that yet they could not discern those times; or as 'tis expressed in Matthew [16:3], "the signs of those times"; he adds, "Yea, and why even of your own selves judge ye not what is right?" i.e. without extrinsic signs. "Why have ye not that sense of true excellency, whereby ye may distinguish that which is holy and divine? Why have ye not that savor of the things of God, by which you may see the distinguishing glory, and evident divinity of me and my doctrine?"

The apostle Peter mentions it as what gave them (the apostles) good and well-grounded assurance of the truth of the gospel, that they had seen the divine glory of Christ. II Pet. 1:16, "For we have not followed cunningly devised fables, when we made known unto you the power and coming of our Lord Jesus Christ, but were eyewitnesses of his majesty." The Apostle has respect to that visible glory of Christ which they saw in his transfiguration: that glory was so divine, having such an ineffable appearance and semblance of divine holiness, majesty, and grace, that it evidently denoted him to be a divine person. But if a sight of Christ's outward glory might give a rational assurance of his divinity, why may not an apprehension of his spiritual glory do so too? Doubtless Christ's spiritual glory is in itself as distinguishing, and as plainly showing his divinity, as his outward glory; and a great deal more: for his spiritual glory is that wherein his divinity consists; and the outward glory of his transfiguration showed him to be divine, only as it was a remarkable image or representation of that spiritual glory. Doubtless therefore he that has had a clear sight of the spiritual glory of Christ, may say, I have not followed cunningly devised fables, but have been an eyewitness of his majesty, upon as good grounds as the Apostle, when he had respect to the outward glory of Christ, that he had seen. But this brings me to what was proposed next, viz. to show that,

Secondly, this doctrine is rational.

1. 'Tis rational to suppose that there is really such an excellency in divine things, that is so transcendent and exceedingly different from what is in other things, that if it were seen would most evidently distinguish them. We can't rationally doubt but that things that are divine, that appertain to the Supreme Being, are vastly different from things that are human; that there is that God-like, high, and glorious excellency in them, that does most remarkably difference them from the things that are of men; insomuch that if the difference were but seen, it would have a convincing,

satisfying influence upon any one, that they are what they are, viz. divine. What reason can be offered against it? Unless we would argue that God is not remarkably distinguished in glory from men.

If Christ should now appear to anyone as he did on the Mount at his transfiguration; or if he should appear to the world in the glory that he now appears in in heaven, as he will do at the day of judgment; without doubt, the glory and majesty that he would appear in, would be such as would satisfy everyone, that he was a divine person, and that religion was true: and it would be a most reasonable, and well-grounded conviction too. And why may there not be that stamp of divinity, or divine glory on the Word of God, on the scheme and doctrine of the gospel, that may be in like manner distinguishing and as rationally convincing, provided it be but seen? 'Tis rational to suppose, that when God speaks to the world, there should be something in his word or speech vastly different from men's word. Supposing that God never had spoken to the world, but we had notice that he was about to do it; that he was about to reveal himself from heaven, and speak to us immediately himself, in divine speeches or discourses, as it were from his own mouth; or that he should give us a book of his own inditing; after what manner should we expect that he would speak? Would it not be rational to suppose, that his speech would be exceeding different from men's speech, that he should speak like a God; that is, that there should be such an excellency and sublimity in his speech or word, such a stamp of wisdom, holiness, majesty, and other divine perfections, that the word of men, yea of the wisest of men, should appear mean and base in comparison of it? Doubtless it would be thought rational to expect this, and unreasonable to think otherwise. When a wise man speaks in the exercise of his wisdom, there is something in everything he says, that is very distinguishable from the talk of a little child. So, without doubt, and much more, is the speech of God (if there be any such thing as the speech of God), to be distinguished from that of the wisest of men; agreeable to Jer. 23:28–29. God having there been reproving the false prophets that prophesied in his name, and pretended that what they spake was his word, when indeed it was their own word, says, "The prophet that hath a dream, let him tell a dream; and he that hath my word, let him speak my word faithfully. What is the chaff to the wheat? saith the Lord.

Is not my word like as a fire? saith the Lord; and like a hammer that breaketh the rock in pieces?"

2. If there be such a distinguishing excellency in divine things, 'tis rational to suppose that there may be such a thing as seeing it. What should hinder but that it may be seen? 'Tis no argument that there is no such thing as a distinguishing excellency, or that, if there be, that it can't be seen, that some don't see it; though they may be discerning men in temporal matters. It is not rational to suppose, if there be any such excellency in divine things, that wicked men should see it. 'Tis not rational to suppose, that those whose minds are full of spiritual pollution, and under the power of filthy lusts, should have any relish or sense of divine beauty, or excellency; or that their minds should be susceptive of that light that is in its own nature so pure and heavenly. It need not seem at all strange, that sin should so blind the mind, seeing that men's particular natural tempers and dispositions will so much blind them in secular matters; as when men's natural temper is melancholy, jealous, fearful, proud, or the like.

3. 'Tis rational to suppose that this knowledge should be given immediately by God, and not be obtained by natural means. Upon what account should it seem unreasonable, that there should be any immediate communication between God and the creature? 'Tis strange that men should make any matter of difficulty of it. Why should not he that made all things, still have something immediately to do with the things that he has made? Where lies the great difficulty, if we own the being of a God, and that he created all things out of nothing, of allowing some immediate influence of God on the creation still? And if it be reasonable to suppose it with respect to any part of the creation, 'tis especially so with respect to reasonable, intelligent creatures; who are next to God in the gradation of the different orders of beings, and whose business is most immediately with God; who were made on purpose for those exercises that do respect God, and wherein they have nextly to do with God: for reason teaches that man was made to serve and glorify his Creator. And if it be rational to suppose that God immediately communicates himself to man in any affair, it is in this. 'Tis rational to suppose that God would reserve that knowledge and wisdom, that is of such a divine and excellent nature, to be

bestowed immediately by himself, and that it should not be left in the power of second causes. Spiritual wisdom and grace is the highest and most excellent gift that ever God bestows on any creature: in this the highest excellency and perfection of a rational creature consists. 'Tis also immensely the most important of all divine gifts: 'tis that wherein man's happiness consists, and on which his everlasting welfare depends. How rational is it to suppose that God, however he has left meaner goods and lower gifts to second causes, and in some sort in their power, yet should reserve this most excellent, divine, and important of all divine communications, in his own hands, to be bestowed immediately by himself, as a thing too great for second causes to be concerned in? 'Tis rational to suppose that this blessing should be immediately from God; for there is no gift or benefit that is in itself so nearly related to the divine nature, there is nothing the creature receives that is so much of God, of his nature, so much a participation of the Deity: 'tis a kind of emanation of God's beauty, and is related to God as the light is to the sun. 'Tis therefore congruous and fit, that when it is given of God, it should be nextly from himself, and by himself, according to his own sovereign will.

'Tis rational to suppose, that it should be beyond a man's power to obtain this knowledge, and light, by the mere strength of natural reason; for 'tis not a thing that belongs to reason, to see the beauty and loveliness of spiritual things; it is not a speculative thing, but depends on the sense of the heart. Reason indeed is necessary in order to it, as 'tis by reason only that we are become the subjects of the means of it; which means I have already shown to be necessary in order to it, though they have no proper causal influence in the affair. 'Tis by reason, that we become possessed of a notion of those doctrines that are the subject matter of this divine light; and reason may many ways be indirectly, and remotely an advantage to it. And reason has also to do in the acts that are immediately consequent on this discovery: a seeing the truth of religion from hence, is by reason; though it be but by one step, and the inference be immediate. So reason has to do in that accepting of, and trusting in Christ, that is consequent on it. But if we take reason strictly, not for the faculty of mental perception in general, but for ratiocination, or a power of inferring by arguments; I say if we take reason thus, the perceiving of spiritual beauty and excellency no more belongs to reason, than it belongs to the sense of feeling to perceive colors, or to the power of seeing to perceive the sweetness of food. It is out of reason's province to perceive the beauty or loveliness of anything: such a perception don't belong to that faculty. Reason's work is to perceive truth, and not excellency. 'Tis not ratiocination that gives men the perception of the beauty and amiableness of a countenance; though it may be many ways indirectly an advantage to it; yet 'tis no more reason that immediately perceives it, than it is reason that perceives the sweetness of honey: it depends on the sense of the heart. Reason may determine that a countenance is beautiful to others, it may determine that honey is sweet to others; but it will never give me a perception of its sweetness.

[IMPROVEMENT.]

I will conclude with a very brief improvement of what has been said.

I. This doctrine may lead us to reflect on the goodness of God, that has so ordered it, that a saving evidence of the truth of the gospel is such, as is attainable by persons of mean capacities, and advantages, as well as those that are of the greatest parts and learning. If the evidence of the gospel depended only on history, and such reasonings as learned men only are capable of, it would be above the reach of far the greatest part of mankind. But persons, with but an ordinary degree of knowledge, are capable, without a long and subtile train of reasoning, to see the divine excellency of the things of religion: they are capable of being taught by the Spirit of God, as well as learned men. The evidence that is this way obtained, is vastly better and more satisfying, than all that can be obtained by the arguings of those that are most learned, and greatest masters of reason. And babes are as capable of knowing these things, as the wise and prudent; and they are often hid from these, when they are revealed to those. I Cor. 1:26–27, "For ye see your calling, brethren, how that not many wise men after the flesh, not many mighty, not many noble, are called: But God hath chosen the foolish things of the world."

II. This doctrine may well put us upon examining ourselves, whether we have ever had this divine light, that has been described, let into our souls. If there be such a thing indeed, and it ben't only a notion, or whimsy of persons of weak and distempered brains, then doubtless 'tis a thing of great importance, whether we have thus been taught by the Spirit of God; whether the light of the glorious gospel of Christ, who is the image of God, hath shined into us, giving us the light of the knowledge of the glory of God in the face of Jesus Christ; whether we have seen the Son, and believed on him, or have that faith of gospel doctrines which arises from a spiritual sight of Christ.

III. All may hence be exhorted, earnestly to seek this spiritual light. To influence and move to it, the following things may be considered.

First. This is the most excellent and divine wisdom, that any creature is capable of. 'Tis more excellent than any human learning; 'tis far more excellent, than all the knowledge of the greatest philosophers, or states-men. Yea, the least glimpse of the glory of God in the face of Christ doth more exalt and ennoble the soul, than all the knowledge of those that have the greatest speculative understanding in divinity, without grace. This knowledge has the most noble object that is, or can be, viz. the divine glory, and excellency of God, and Christ. The knowledge of these objects is that wherein consists the most excellent knowledge of the angels, yea, of God himself.

Second. This knowledge is that which is above all others sweet and joyful. Men have a great deal of pleasure in human knowledge, in studies of natural things; but this is nothing to that joy which arises from this divine light shining into the soul. This light gives a view of those things that are immensely the most exquisitely beautiful, and capable of delight-ing the eye of the understanding. This spiritual light is the dawning of the light of glory in the heart. There is nothing so powerful as this to support persons in affliction, and to give the mind peace and brightness, in this stormy and dark world.

Third. This light is such as effectually influences the inclination, and changes the nature of the soul. It assimilates the nature to the divine nature, and changes the soul into an image of the same glory that is beheld. II Cor. 3:18, "But we all with open face, beholding as in a glass the glory of the Lord, are changed into the same image, from glory to glory, even as by the Spirit of the Lord." This knowledge will wean from the world, and raise the inclination to heavenly things. It will turn the heart to God as the fountain of good, and to choose him for the only portion. This light, and this only, will bring the soul to a saving close with Christ. It conforms the heart to the gospel, mortifies its enmity and opposition against the scheme of salvation therein revealed: it causes the heart to embrace the joyful tidings, and entirely to adhere to, and acquiesce in the revelation of Christ as our Savior: it causes the whole soul to accord and symphonize with it, admitting it with entire credit and respect, cleaving to it with full inclination and affection. And it effectually disposes the soul to give up itself entirely to Christ.

Fourth. This light, and this only, has its fruit in an universal holiness of life. No merely notional or speculative understanding of the doctrines of religion, will ever bring to this. But this light, as it reaches the bottom of the heart, and changes the nature, so it will effectually dispose to an universal obedience. It shows God's worthiness to be obeyed and served. It draws forth the heart in a sincere love to God, which is the only principle of a true, gracious and universal obedience. And it convinces of the reality of those glorious rewards that God has promised to them that obey him.

A History of the Work of Redemption (1739)

Sermon I

Is. 51:8.
For the moth shall eat them [up] like a garment, and the worm shall eat [them] like wool: but my righteousness shall be [for ever], and my salvation from generation to generation.

The drift of this chapter is to comfort the church under her sufferings and the persecutions of her enemies. And the argument of consolation insisted upon is the constancy and perpetuity of God's mercy and faithfulness towards her, which shall be manifest in the continuance of the fruits of that mercy and faithfulness in continuing to work salvation for her, protecting her against all assaults of her enemies, and carrying her safely through all the changes of the world and finally crowning her with victory and deliverance.

In the text this happiness of the church of God is set forth by comparing it with the contrary fate of his enemies that oppose her, and therein we may observe:

1. How short-lived the power and prosperity of the church's enemies is. "The moth shall eat them up like a garment, and the worm shall eat them like wool," i.e. however great their prosperity is, and how[ever] great their present glory, they shall by [degr]ees consume and vanish away by a secret [cu]rse of God till they come to nothing; and all their power and glory, and so their persecutions, eternally cease and they be finally and irrecoverably ruined, as the finest and most glorious apparel will by time wear away and be consumed by moths and rottenness. We learn who these are that shall thus consume away by the foregoing verse, viz. those that are the enemies of God's people that hate 'em, revile and persecute 'em. "Hearken unto me, [ye that know righteousness, the people in whose heart is my law; fear ye not the reproach of men]."

2. The contrary happy lot and portion of God's church expressed in these words, "my righteousness shall be for ever and my salvation [from generation to generation]." Who are meant as those that shall have the benefit of this we also learn by the preceding verse, viz. they "that know righteousness and the people in whose heart is God's law," or in one word, the church of God. And concerning that happiness of theirs here spoken of we may observe two things: viz. (1) wherein it consists and (2) its continuance.

1. Wherein it consists, viz. in God's righteousness [and] salvation towards them. By God's righteousness here is meant his faithfulness in fulfilling his covenant promises to his church, or his faithfulness towards his church and people in bestowing the benefits of the covenant of grace upon them. Which benefits, though they are bestowed of free and sovereign grace as being altogether undeserved, yet as God has been pleased by the promises of the covenant of grace to bind himself to bestow them, so they are bestowed in the exercise of God's righteousness or justice. And therefore the Apostle says in Heb. 6:10, "God is not unrighteous to forget [your work and labor of love]." So I John 1:9, "If we confess our sins, God is faithful and just to forgive our sins, and cleanse us [from all unrighteousness]."

So the word righteousness is very often used in Scripture for his covenant faithfulness; so 'tis in Neh. 9:8, "Thou hast performed thy words for thou art righteous." And so we are very often to understand righteousness and covenant mercy [to] be the same thing, as Ps. 24:5, "He shall receive the blessing from the Lord and righteousness from the God of [his salvation]," Ps. 36:10, "O continue thy lovingkindness to them that know thee; and thy righteousness to the upright," and Ps. 51:14, "Deliver me from bloodguiltiness, O God, thou God of my salvation; and my tongue shall sing aloud of thy righteousness," and Dan. 9:16, "O Lord, according to thy righteousness, I beseech thee, let thine anger and thy fury be turned away" and so in innumerable other places.

The other word here used is salvation. Of these two, God's righteousness and his salvation, the one is the cause of which the other is the effect. God's righteousness or covenant mercy is the root of which his salvation is the fruit. Both of them relate to the covenant of grace; the one is God's covenant mercy and faithfulness, the other intends that work of God by which this covenant mercy is accomplished in the fruits of it. For salvation is the sum of all those works of God by which the benefits that are by the covenant of grace are procured and bestowed.

2. We may observe its continuance signified here by two expressions: forever and from generation to generation. The latter seems to be exegetical or explanatory of the former. The phrase forever is variously used in Scripture. Sometimes thereby is meant as long as a man lives; so is it said the servant that has his ear bored through with an awl to the door of his master should be his servant forever. Sometimes thereby is meant during the continuance of the Jewish state; so of many of the ceremonial and judicial laws, it is said that they should be statutes forever. Sometimes thereby is meant as long as the world stands or to the end of the generations of men; so it is said Eccles. 1:4, "One generation passeth away and another comes but [the earth abideth for ever]." Sometimes thereby is meant to all eternity; so it is said God is "blessed forevermore," Rom. 1:25, and so it is said John 6:51, he that may "eat of this bread, he shall live forever."

And which of these are to be here understood the next words determine, viz. to the end of the world or to the end of the generations of men.

'Tis said in the next words, "my salvation from generation [to generation]." Indeed the fruits of God's salvation shall remain after this as appears by the sixth verse: ["my salvation shall be for ever, and my righteousness shall not be abolished"]. But the work of salvation itself towards the church shall continue to be wrought till then, till the end of the world. God would go on to accomplish deliverance and salvation for the church from all her enemies, for this is what the prophet is here speaking of, till the end of the world, till her enemies cease to be or to [have] any power to molest the church. And this expression "from generation to generation" may determine us as to the time which God continues to carry on the work of salvation for his church both with respect to the beginning and the end. It is from generation to generation, i.e. throughout all generations beginning with the generations of men on the earth and not ending till these generations end at the end of the world.

And therefore the,

DOCTRINE.

The Work of Redemption is a work that God carries on from the fall of man to the end of the world.

The generations of mankind on the earth did not begin till after the fall. The beginning of the posterity of our first parents was after the fall, for all his posterity by ordinary generation are partakers of the fall and the corruption of nature that followed from it. And these generations by which the human race is propagated shall continue to the end of the world; so these two are the limits of the generations of men on the earth: the fall of man, the beginning, and the end of the world—the Day of Judgment—its end. The same are the limits of the Work of Redemption as to those progressive works of God by which that redemption is brought about and accomplished, though not as to the fruits of it, for they as was said before shall be to all eternity. The work of salvation and the Work of Redemption are the same thing. What is sometimes in Scripture called God's saving his people is in others called his redeeming them; so Christ is called both the Savior and the Redeemer of his people.

First. I would show in what sense the terms of the doctrine are used;

and first I would show how I must be understood in the doctrine by the Work of Redemption, and secondly how I must be understood when I say this work is a work that God carries on from the fall of man.

1. I would show how I would be understood by the Work of Redemption. And here it may be observed that the Work of Redemption is sometimes understood in a more limited sense for the purchase of salvation. For so the word strictly signifies a purchase of deliverance. And if we take the word in this restricted sense, the Work of Redemption was not so long a-doing but it was begun and finished with Christ's humiliation, or it was all wrought while Christ was upon earth. It was begun with Christ's incarnation and carried on through Christ's life and finished with his death, or the time of his remaining under the power of death which ended in his resurrection. And so we say that the day of Christ's resurrection is the day when Christ finished the work of our redemption, i.e. then the purchase was finished and the work itself and all that appertained to it was virtually done and finished but not actually.

But then sometimes the Work of Redemption is taken more largely, including all that God works or accomplishes tending to this end, not only the purchasing of redemption but also all God's works that were properly preparatory to the purchase, or as applying the purchase and accomplishing the success of it. So that the whole dispensation as it includes the preparation and the imputation and application and success of Christ's redemption is here called the Work of Redemption. All that Christ does in this great affair as mediator in any of his offices, either Prophet, Priest or King, either when he was in the world in his human [form], or before or since. And not only what Christ the mediator has done, but also what the Father and the Holy Ghost have done as united or confederated in this design of redeeming sinful men; or in one word, all that is wrought in execution of the eternal covenant of redemption. This is what I called the Work of Redemption in the doctrine, for 'tis all but one work, one design. The various dispensations and works that belong to it are but the several parts of one scheme. 'Tis but one design that is done to which all the offices of Christ do directly tend, and in which all the persons of the Trinity do conspire and all the various dispensations that belong to it are united, as the several wheels in one machine, to answer one end and produce one effect. And,

2. When I say this work is carried on from the fall of man to the end of the world, in order to the full understanding of my meaning in it I would desire two or three things to be observed.

(1) That it is not meant that nothing was done in order to it before the fall of man. There were many things done in order to the Work of Redemption before that. Some things were done before the world was created, yea from all eternity. The persons of the Trinity were as it were confederated in a design and a covenant of redemption, in which covenant the Father appointed the Son and the Son had undertaken their work, and all things to be accomplished in their work were stipulated and agreed. And besides these there were things done at the creation of the world in order to that work before man fell. For the world itself seems to have been created in order to it. The work of creation was in order to God's works of providence. So that if it be inquired which of these two kinds of works is the greatest, the works of creation or God's works of providence, I answer providence because God's works of providence are the end of God's works of creation as the building of an house or the forming an engine or machine is for its use. But God's main work of providence is this great work of God that the doctrine speaks of, as may more fully appear afterwards. The creating heaven was in order to the Work of Redemption; it was to be an habitation for the redeemed and the Redeemer, Matt. 25:34. Angels [were created to be] ministering spirits [to the inhabitants of the] lower world [which is] to be the stage of this wonderful Work [of Redemption]. And therefore [it] might be shown in many respects the state of the lower world is wisely fitted in its formation for such a state of man as he is in since the fall under a possibility of redemption. So that when it is said that the Work of Redemption is carried on [from the fall of man to the end of the world], 'tis not meant that all that ever was done in order to a redemption began after that. Nor—

(2) Is it meant that there were no remaining fruits of this work after the end of the world. The greatest fruits of all are after that. The glory and blessedness that will be the sum of all the fruits will remain to all eternity

after that. The Work of Redemption is not an eternal work, that is, it is not a work always a-doing and never accomplished. But the fruits of this work are eternal fruits. The work has an issue, but in the issue the end will be obtained, which end never will have an end. As things that were in order to this work, as God's electing love and the covenant of redemption never had a beginning, so the fruits of this work that shall be after the end of the work never will have an end. And therefore,

(3) When it is said that this is a work that God is carrying on from the fall of man to the end of the world, what I mean is that those things that belong to this work itself are parts of that scheme, are all this accomplishing. There are things that are in order to it that are before the beginning of it, and fruits of it that are after it is finished. But the work itself is so long a-doing even from the fall of man to the end of the world; it is all this while a-carrying on. It was begun immediately upon the fall and will be continued to the end of the world and then will be finished. The various dispensations of God that are in this space do belong to the same work, tend to the same design, and have all one issue and therefore are all to be reckoned but as several parts of one work, as it were several successive motions of one machine to strike out, in the conclusion one great event.

And here also we must distinguish between the parts of redemption itself and parts of the work by which this redemption is wrought out. There is difference between the parts of the benefits procured and bestowed, and the parts of that work of God by which those benefits were procured and bestowed. As for example, there is difference between the parts of the benefit the children of Israel received consisting in their redemption out of Egypt, and the parts of that work of God by which this was wrought. The redemption of the children of Israel out of Egypt considered as the benefit which they enjoyed consisted of two parts: viz. their deliverance from their former Egyptian bondage and misery, and their being brought into a more happy state as the servants of God and heirs of Canaan. But there are many more things that are parts of that work of God which is called his work of redemption of Israel out of Egypt. To this belong his calling of Moses, his sending him to Pharaoh and all the signs and wonders he wrought in Egypt, and his bringing such terrible judgments on the Egyptians, and many others.

For the work by which God wrought out redemption that we are speaking of, that is carried on from the fall of man to the end of the world, this work is carried on from the fall of man to the end of the world in two respects:

1. With respect to the effect wrought on the souls of the redeemed, which is common to all ages from the fall of man to the end of the world. This effect that I here speak [of] is the application of redemption with respect to the souls of particular persons in converting, justifying, sanctifying and glorifying of them. By these things the souls of particular persons are actually redeemed—do receive the benefit of the Work of Redemption in its effect in their souls. And in this sense the Work of Redemption is carried on in all ages from the fall of man to the end of the world. The work of God in converting souls, opening blind eyes, and unstopping deaf [ears], and raising dead souls to life, and rescuing the miserable captured souls of men out of the hands of Satan, was begun soon after the fall of man, has been carried on in the world ever since to this day, and will be to the end of the world. God has always, ever since the first erecting of the church of the redeemed after the fall, had such a church in the world. Though oftentimes it has been reduced to a very narrow compass and to low circumstances, yet it has never wholly failed.

And as God carries on the work of converting the souls of fallen men through all these ages, so he goes on to justify them, to blot out all their sins and to accept them as righteous in his sight through the righteousness of Christ, and to adopt them and receive them from being the children of Satan to be his own children. So he also goes on to sanctify, or to carry on the work of his grace which he has begun in them, and to comfort them with the consolation of his spirit and to glorify them, to bestow upon them when their bodies die that eternal glory which is the fruit of the purchase of Christ. That is the eighth [chapter] of Romans, v. 30: "Whom he did predestinate [them he also called: and whom he called, them he also justified: and whom he justified, them he also glorified]." I say this is applicable to all ages from the fall of man to the end of the world. The way that the Work of Redemption with respect to these effects of it respecting the souls of the redeemed is carried on from the fall of man to the end of the world is by repeating after continually working the same work over again, though in different persons from age to age. But,

2. The Work of Redemption with respect to the grand design in general as it relates to the universal subject and end of it, is carried on from the fall of man to the end of the world in a different manner, not merely by the repeating and renewing the same effect on the different subjects of it, but by many successive works and dispensations of God, all tending to one great end and effect, all united as the several parts of a scheme, and altogether making up one great work. Like an house or temple that is building, first the workmen are sent forth, then the materials are gathered, then the ground fitted, then the foundation is laid, then the superstructure erected one part after another, till at length the topstone is laid. And all is finished. Now the Work of Redemption in that large sense that has been explained may be compared to such a building that is carrying on from the fall of man to the end of the world. God went about it immediately after the fall of man. Some things were done towards this building then, immediately as may be hereafter shown; and so God has gone as it were getting materials and building ever since, and so will go on to the end of the world. And then the time shall come when the topstone shall be brought forth and all will appear complete and consummate. The glorious structure will then stand forth in its proper perfection.

This work is carried on in the former respect that has been mentioned, viz. the effect on the souls of particular persons that are redeemed by its being an effect that is common to all ages. The work is carried on in this latter respect, viz. as it [has] respect to [the] church of God or the grand design in general. It is carried on not only by that which is common to all ages [but] by successive works wrought in different ages, all parts of one whole or one great scheme whereby one work is brought about by various steps, one step in each age and another in another. And 'tis the carrying on the Work of Redemption chiefly that I shall insist upon, though not excluding the former, for one necessarily supposes the other.

Having thus explained what I mean by the terms of the doctrine I now, that you may the more clearly know [that] the great design and Work of

Redemption is carried on from the fall of man to the end of the world, I say in order to this I now proceed in the,

Second place, to show what is the design of this great work or what things are designed to be done by it. In order to see how a design is carried [to] an end, we must first know what the design is. To know how a workman proceeds and to understand the various steps he takes in order to accomplish a piece of work, we need to be informed what he is about or what the thing is that he intends to accomplish. Otherwise we may stand by and see him do one thing after another and be quite puzzled and in the dark about it, seeing nothing of his scheme and understanding nothing [of] what he means by it. If an architect with a great number of hands were about building some great palace, and one that was a stranger to such things should stand by and see some men digging in the earth, others bringing timbers, others hewing stones and the like, he might reason that there was a great deal done. But if he knew not the design, it would all appear confusion to him. And therefore that the great works and dispensations of God that belong to this great affair of redemption may not appear like confusion to you, I would set before you briefly the main things as designed to be accomplished in this great work, to accomplish which God began to work presently after the fall of man and will continue to the end of the world when the whole work will appear completely finished. And the main things designed to be done by it are these that follow.

1. It is to put all God's enemies under his feet and that the goodness of God should finally appear triumphing over all evil. Soon after the world was created, evil entered into the world in the fall of the angels and man. Presently, after God had made rational creatures, there were enemies rose up against him from among them. And in the fall of man evil entered into this lower world, and God's enemies rose up against him here. Satan rose up against God, endeavoring to frustrate his design in the creation of this lower world, to destroy his workmanship here, and to wrest the government of this lower world out of his hands, and usurp the throne himself, and set up himself as God of this world instead of the God that had made it. And to these ends he introduced sin into the world, had made man God's enemy, he brought guilt on man and brought death into

the world, and brought the most extreme and dreadful misery into the world.

Now one great design of God in the affair of redemption was to reduce and subdue those enemies of God till they should all be put under God's feet, I Cor. 15:25. [He did this in order] that he might disappoint and confound and triumph over Satan, and that he [Satan] might be bruised under Christ's feet, Gen. 3:15, "The seed of the woman shall bruise [thy head]." And "that he might destroy the works of the devil" and confound him in all his purposes, I John 3:8, "For this purpose was the son of God [manifested]," and that he might triumph over sin, overcome the corruption of men, and that his Son might triumph over man's guilt and that infinite demerit there is in sin, and might at last triumph over death. God's thus appearing gloriously above all evil and triumphing over all his enemies was one great thing that God intended by the Work of Redemption. And the work by which this was to be done God immediately went about as soon as man fell, and so goes on till he fully accomplishes it in the end of the world.

2. In doing this God's design was perfectly to restore all the ruins of the fall, so far as concerns the elect part of the world, by his Son. And therefore we read of the restitution of all things, Acts 3:21: "[Jesus Christ] whom the heavens must receive [until the times of restitution of all things]," and "times of refreshing from the presence of the Lord Jesus," Acts 3:19.

Man's soul was ruined by the fall, the image of God was ruined, man's nature corrupted and destroyed, and man became dead in sin. The design was to restore the soul of man in conversion and to restore life to it, and the image of God in conversion and to carry on the restoration in sanctification, and to perfect it in glory. Man's body was ruined by the fall, became subject to death. The world was ruined as to man as effectively as if it were reduced to a chaos again, all heavens and earth were overthrown. But the design was to restore all, as it were to create a new heaven and a new earth, Is. 65:17, "For behold I create [new heavens and a new earth]." The work by which this was to be done was begun immediately after the fall and so is carried on till all is finished at the end when the whole world, heaven and earth, shall be restored. And there shall be, as it were, a "new heaven and a new earth" in a spiritual sense at the end of the world. Thus 'tis represented, Rev. 21 at beginning.

3. Another great design in the affair of redemption was to gather together in one all things in Christ in heaven and on earth, i.e. all elect creatures. . . . [This is] to bring all elect creatures in heaven and earth to an union one to another, in one body under one head, and to unite all together in one body to God the Father. This was begun soon after the fall and is carried on through all ages of the world and finished at the end of the world. And,

4. God designed by this means to complete and perfect the glory of all the elect by Christ. It was a great design of God to advance all the elect to an exceeding pitch of glory, such as eye has not seen. He intended to bring them to perfect excellency and beauty in his image and in holiness which is the proper beauty of spiritual beings, and to advance 'em to a glorious degree of honor and also to an ineffable pitch of pleasure and joy. And thus to glorify the whole church of elect men in soul and body, and unite them by the glory of the elect angels to its highest pitch under one head. Towards this God began to work immediately after the fall [of man] and goes on through all [ages], and it will be perfected at the end of the world.

5. In all this God designed to accomplish the glory of the blessed Trinity in an exceeding degree. God had a design of glorifying himself from eternity, to glorify each person in the Godhead. The end must be considered as first in the order of nature and then the means, and therefore we must conceive that God having proposed this end had then, as it were, the means to choose. And the principal means that he pitched [upon] was this great Work of Redemption that we are speaking [of]. It was his design in this work to glorify his only begotten Son, Jesus Christ, in this great work, and it was his design by the Son to glorify the Father, John 13:31–32 ["Now is the Son of man glorified, and God is glorified in him. If God be glorified in him, God shall also glorify him in himself,"] and John 17:1 ["glorify thy Son, that thy Son also may glorify thee"]. And [also] that the Son should thus be glorified and should glorify the Father by what should

be accomplished by the Spirit to the glory of the Spirit, that the whole Trinity conjunctly and each person singly might be exceedingly glorified. The work that was the appointed means of this was begun immediately after the fall and is carried on and finished at the end of the world when all this intended glory shall be fully accomplished in all things.

A Treatise Concerning Religious Affections (1746)

Author's Preface

There is no question whatsoever, that is of greater importance to mankind, and that it more concerns every individual person to be well resolved in, than this, what are the distinguishing qualifications of those that are in favor with God, and entitled to his eternal rewards? Or, which comes to the same thing, What is the nature of true religion? and wherein do lie the distinguishing notes of that virtue and holiness, that is acceptable in the sight of God. But though it be of such importance, and though we have clear and abundant light in the Word of God to direct us in this matter, yet there is no one point, wherein professing Christians do more differ one from another. It would be endless to reckon up the variety of opinions in this point, that divide the Christian world; making manifest the truth of that of our Savior, "Strait is the gate, and narrow is the way, that leads to life, and few there be that find it."

The consideration of these things has long engaged me to attend to this matter, with the utmost diligence and care, and exactness of search and inquiry, that I have been capable of: it is a subject on which my mind has been peculiarly intent, ever since I first entered on the study of divinity. But as to the success of my inquiries, it must be left to the judgment of the reader of the following treatise.

I am sensible it is much more difficult to judge impartially of that which is the subject of this discourse, in the midst of the dust and smoke of such a state of controversy, as this land is now in, about things of this nature: as it is more difficult to write impartially, so it is more difficult to read impartially. Many will probably be hurt in their spirits, to find so much that appertains to religious affection, here condemned: and perhaps indignation and contempt will be excited in others, by finding so much here justified and approved. And it may be, some will be ready to charge me with inconsistence with myself, in so much approving some things, and so much condemning others; as I have found, this has always been objected to me by some, ever since the beginning of our late controversies about religion. 'Tis a hard thing to be a hearty zealous friend of what has been *good* and glorious, in the late extraordinary appearances, and to rejoice much in it; and at the same time, to see the evil and pernicious tendency of what has been *bad*, and earnestly to oppose that. But yet, I am humbly, but fully persuaded, we shall never be in the way of truth, nor go on in a way acceptable to God, and tending to the advancement of Christ's kingdom, till we do so. . . .

Part I. Concerning the Nature of the Affections, and Their Importance in Religion

I Pet. 1:8.
Whom having not seen, ye love: in whom, though now ye see him not, yet believing, ye rejoice with joy unspeakable, and full of glory.

In these words, the Apostle represents the state of the minds of the Christians he wrote to, under the persecutions they were then the subjects of. These persecutions are what he has respect to, in the two preceding verses, when he speaks of the trial of their faith, and of their being in heaviness through manifold temptations.

Such trials are of threefold benefit to true religion: hereby the truth of it is manifested, and it appears to be indeed true religion: they, above all other things, have a tendency to distinguish between true religion and false, and to cause the difference between them evidently to appear. Hence they are called by the name of trials, in the verse next preceding the text, and in innumerable other places: they try the faith and religion of professors of what sort it is, as apparent gold is tried in the fire, and manifested, whether it be true gold or no. And the faith of true Christians being thus tried and proved to be true, is found to praise, and honor, and glory; as in that preceding verse.

And then, these trials are of further benefit to true religion; they not only manifest the truth of it, but they make its genuine beauty and amiableness remarkably to appear. True virtue never appears so lovely, as when it is most oppressed: and the divine excellency of real Christianity, is never exhibited with such advantage, as when under the greatest trials: then it is that true faith appears much more precious than gold; and upon this account, is found to praise, and honor, and glory.

And again, another benefit that such trials are of to true religion, is, that they purify and increase it. They not only manifest it to be true, but also tend to refine it, and deliver it from those mixtures of that which is false, which encumber and impede it; that nothing may be left but that which is true. They tend to cause the amiableness of true religion to appear to the best advantage, as was before observed; and not only so, but they tend to increase its beauty, by establishing and confirming it, and making it more lively and vigorous, and purifying it from those things that obscured its luster and glory. As gold that is tried in the fire, is purged from its alloy and all remainders of dross, and comes forth more solid and beautiful; so true faith being tried as gold is tried in the fire, becomes more precious; and thus also is found unto praise, and honor, and glory. The Apostle seems to have respect to each of these benefits, that persecutions are of to true religion, in the verse preceding the text.

And in the text, the Apostle observes how true religion operated in the Christians he wrote to, under their persecutions, whereby these benefits of persecution appeared in them; or what manner of operation of *true* religion, in them, it was, whereby their religion, under persecution, was manifested to be true religion, and eminently appeared in the genuine beauty and amiableness of true religion, and also appeared to be increased and purified, and so was like to be found unto praise, and honor, and glory, at the appearing of Jesus Christ. And there were two kinds of operation, or exercise of true religion, in them, under their sufferings, that the Apostle takes notice of in the text, wherein these benefits appeared.

1. *Love to Christ;* "Whom having not seen, ye love." The world was ready to wonder, what strange principle it was, that influenced them to expose themselves to so great sufferings, to forsake the things that were seen, and renounce all that was dear and pleasant, which was the object of sense: they seemed to the men of the world about them, as though they

were beside themselves, and to act as though they hated themselves; there was nothing in their view, that could induce them thus to suffer, and support them under, and carry them through such trials. But although there was nothing that was seen, nothing that the world saw, or that the Christians themselves ever saw with their bodily eyes, that thus influenced and supported 'em; yet they had a supernatural principle of love to something *unseen;* they loved Jesus Christ, for they saw him spiritually, whom the world saw not, and whom they themselves had never seen with bodily eyes.

2. *Joy in Christ.* Though their outward sufferings were very grievous, yet their inward spiritual joys were greater than their sufferings, and these supported them, and enabled them to suffer with cheerfulness.

There are two things which the Apostle takes notice of in the text concerning this joy. (1) The manner in which it rises, the way in which Christ, though unseen, is the foundation of it, viz. by faith; which is the evidence of things not seen; "In whom, though now ye see him not, yet believing, ye rejoice." (2) The nature of this joy; "unspeakable and full of glory." "Unspeakable" in the kind of it; very different from worldly joys, and carnal delights; of a vastly more pure, sublime and heavenly nature, being something supernatural, and truly divine, and so ineffably excellent; the sublimity, and exquisite sweetness of which, there were no words to set forth. Unspeakable also in degree; it pleasing God to give 'em this holy joy, with a liberal hand, and in large measure, in their state of persecution.

Their joy was "full of glory": although the joy was unspeakable, and no words were sufficient to describe it; yet something might be said of it, and no words more fit to represent its excellency, than these, that it was "full of glory"; or, as it is in the original, "glorified joy." In rejoicing with this joy, their minds were filled, as it were, with a glorious brightness, and their natures exalted and perfected: it was a most worthy, noble rejoicing, that did not corrupt and debase the mind, as many carnal joys do; but did greatly beautify and dignify it: it was a prelibation of the joy of heaven, that raised their minds to a degree of heavenly blessedness: it filled their minds with the light of God's glory, and made 'em themselves to shine with some communication of that glory.

Hence the proposition or doctrine, that I would raise from these words is this,

DOCT. True religion, in great part, consists in holy affections.

We see that the Apostle, in observing and remarking the operations and exercises of religion, in the Christians he wrote to, wherein their religion appeared to be true and of the right kind, when it had its greatest trial of what sort it was, being tried by persecution as gold is tried in the fire, and when their religion not only proved true, but was most pure, and cleansed from its dross and mixtures of that which was not true, and when religion appeared in them most in its genuine excellency and native beauty, and was found to praise, and honor, and glory; he singles out the religious affections of love and joy, that were then in exercise in them: these are the exercises of religion he takes notice of, wherein their religion did thus appear true and pure, and in its proper glory.

Here I would, I. Show what is intended by the affections, II. Observe some things which make it evident, that a great part of true religion lies in the affections.

I. It may be inquired, what the affections of the mind are?

I answer, the affections are no other, than the more vigorous and sensible exercises of the inclination and will of the soul.

God has indued the soul with two faculties: one is that by which it is capable of perception and speculation, or by which it discerns and views and judges of things; which is called the understanding. The other faculty is that by which the soul does not merely perceive and view things, but is some way inclined with respect to the things it views or considers; either is inclined to 'em, or is disinclined, and averse from 'em; or is the faculty by which the soul does not behold things, as an indifferent unaffected spectator, but either as liking or disliking, pleased or displeased, approving or rejecting. This faculty is called by various names: it is sometimes called the *inclination:* and, as it has respect to the actions that are determined and governed by it, is called the *will:* and the *mind,* with regard to the exercises of this faculty, is often called the *heart.*

The exercises of this faculty are of two sorts; either those by which the soul is carried out towards the things that are in view, in approving of them, being pleased with them, and inclined to them; or those in which the soul opposes the things that are in view, in disapproving them, and in being displeased with them, averse from them, and rejecting them.

And as the exercises of the inclination and will of the soul are various in their kinds, so they are much more various in their degrees. There are some exercises of pleasedness or displeasedness, inclination or disinclination, wherein the soul is carried but a little beyond a state of perfect indifference. And there are other degrees above this, wherein the approbation or dislike, pleasedness or aversion, are stronger; wherein we may rise higher and higher, till the soul comes to act vigorously and sensibly, and the actings of the soul are with that strength that (through the laws of the union which the Creator has fixed between soul and body) the motion of the blood and animal spirits begins to be sensibly altered; whence oftentimes arises some bodily sensation, especially about the heart and vitals, that are the fountain of the fluids of the body: from whence it comes to pass, that the mind, with regard to the exercises of this faculty, perhaps in all nations and ages, is called the *heart*. And it is to be noted, that they are these more vigorous and sensible exercises of this faculty, that are called the *affections*.

The will, and the affections of the soul, are not two faculties; the affections are not essentially distinct from the will, nor do they differ from the mere actings of the will and inclination of the soul, but only in the liveliness and sensibleness of exercise. . . .

Such seems to be our nature, and such the laws of the union of soul and body, that there never is any case whatsoever, any lively and vigorous exercise of the will or inclination of the soul, without some effect upon the body, in some alteration of the motion of its fluids, and especially of the animal spirits. And on the other hand, from the same laws of the union of soul and body, the constitution of the body, and the motion of its fluids, may promote the exercise of the affections. But yet, it is not the body, but the mind only, that is the proper seat of the affections. The body of man is no more capable of being really the subject of love or hatred, joy or sorrow, fear or hope, than the body of a tree, or than the same body of man is capable of thinking and understanding. As 'tis the soul only that has ideas, so 'tis the soul only that is pleased or displeased with its ideas. As 'tis the soul only that thinks, so 'tis the soul only that loves or hates, rejoices or is grieved at what it thinks of. Nor are these motions of the animal spirits, and fluids of the body, anything properly belonging to the nature of the affections; though they always accompany them, in the present state; but are only effects or concomitants of the affections, that are entirely distinct from the affections themselves, and no way essential to them; so that an unbodied spirit may be as capable of love and hatred, joy or sorrow, hope or fear, or other affections, as one that is united to a body. . . .

II. [The] second thing proposed . . . was to observe some things that render it evident, that true religion, in great part, consists in the affections. And here,

1. What has been said of the nature of the affections, makes this evident, and may be sufficient, without adding anything further, to put this matter out of doubt: for who will deny that true religion consists, in a great measure, in vigorous and lively actings of the inclination and will of the soul, or the fervent exercises of the heart.

That religion which God requires, and will accept, does not consist in weak, dull and lifeless wouldings, raising us but a little above a state of indifference: God, in his Word, greatly insists upon it, that we be in good earnest, fervent in spirit, and our hearts vigorously engaged in religion: "Be ye fervent in spirit, serving the Lord" (Rom. 12:11). . . . 'Tis such a fervent, vigorous engagedness of the heart in religion, that is the fruit of a real circumcision of the heart, or true regeneration, and that has the promises of life; "And the Lord thy God will circumcise thine heart, and the heart of thy seed, to love the Lord thy God, with all thy heart, and with all thy soul, that thou mayest live" (Deut. 30:6).

If we ben't in good earnest in religion, and our wills and inclinations be not strongly exercised, we are nothing. The things of religion are so great, that there can be no suitableness in the exercises of our hearts, to their nature and importance, unless they be lively and powerful. In nothing, is vigor in the actings of our inclinations so requisite, as in religion; and in nothing is lukewarmness so odious. True religion is evermore a powerful

thing; and the power of it appears, in the first place, in the inward exercises
of it in the heart, where is the principal and original seat of it. Hence true
religion is called the power of godliness, in distinction from the external
appearances of it, that are the form of it, "Having a form of godliness, but
denying the power of it" (II Tim. 3:5). The Spirit of God in those that have
sound and solid religion, is a spirit of powerful holy affection; and therefore, God is said to have given them the spirit of power, and of love, and of
a sound mind (II Tim. 1:7). And such, when they received the Spirit of
God, in his sanctifying and saving influences, are said to be baptized with
the Holy Ghost, and with fire; by reason of the power and fervor of those
exercises the Spirit of God excites in their hearts, whereby their hearts,
when grace is in exercise, may be said to burn within them; as is said of the
disciples (Luke 24:32). . . .

And though true grace has various degrees, and there are some that are
but babes in Christ, in whom the exercise of the inclination and will
towards divine and heavenly things, is comparatively weak; yet everyone
that has the power of godliness in his heart, has his inclinations and heart
exercised towards God and divine things, with such strength and vigor,
that these holy exercises do prevail in him above all carnal or natural
affections, and are effectual to overcome them: for every true disciple of
Christ, loves him above father or mother, wife and children, brethren and
sisters, houses and lands; yea, than his own life. From hence it follows, that
wherever true religion is, there are vigorous exercises of the inclination
and will, towards divine objects: but by what was said before, the vigorous,
lively and sensible exercises of the will, are no other than the affections of
the soul.

2. The Author of the human nature has not only given affections to
men, but has made 'em very much the spring of men's actions. As the
affections do not only necessarily belong to the human nature, but are a
very great part of it; so (inasmuch as by regeneration, persons are renewed
in the whole man, and sanctified throughout) holy affections do not only
necessarily belong to true religion, but are a very great part of that. And as
true religion is of a practical nature, and God has so constituted the
human nature, that the affections are very much the spring of men's

actions, this also shows, that true religion must consist very much in the affections.

Such is man's nature, that he is very inactive, any otherwise than he is influenced by some affection, either love or hatred, desire, hope, fear or some other. These affections we see to be the springs that set men agoing, in all the affairs of life, and engage them in all their pursuits: these are the things that put men forward, and carry 'em along, in all their worldly business; and especially are men excited and animated by these, in all affairs, wherein they are earnestly engaged, and which they pursue with vigor. We see the world of mankind to be exceedingly busy and active; and the affections of men are the springs of the motion: take away all love and hatred, all hope and fear, all anger, zeal and affectionate desire, and the world would be, in a great measure, motionless and dead; there would be no such thing as activity amongst mankind, or any earnest pursuit what-soever. 'Tis affection that engages the covetous man, and him that is greedy of worldly profits, in his pursuits; and it is by the affections, that the ambitious man is put forward in his pursuit of worldly glory; and 'tis the affections also that actuate the voluptuous man, in his pursuit of pleasure and sensual delights: the world continues, from age to age, in a continual commotion and agitation, in a pursuit of these things; but take away all affection, and the spring of all this motion would be gone, and the motion itself would cease. And as in worldly things, worldly affections are very much the spring of men's motion and action; so in religious matters, the spring of their actions are very much religious affections: he that has doctrinal knowledge and speculation only, without affection, never is engaged in the business of religion.

3. Nothing is more manifest in fact, than that the things of religion take hold of men's souls, no further than they affect them. There are multitudes that often hear the Word of God, and therein hear of those things that are infinitely great and important, and that most nearly concern them, and all that is heard seems to be wholly ineffectual upon them, and to make no alteration in their disposition or behavior; and the reason is, they are not affected with what they hear. . . . I am bold to assert, that there never was any considerable change wrought in the mind or conversation of any one person, by anything of a religious nature, that ever he read, heard or saw,

that had not his affections moved. Never was a natural man engaged earnestly to seek his salvation: never were any such brought to cry after wisdom, and lift up their voice for understanding, and to wrestle with God in prayer for mercy; and never was one humbled, and brought to the foot of God, from anything that ever he heard or imagined of his own unworthiness and undeservings of God's displeasure; nor was ever one induced to fly for refuge unto Christ, while his heart remained unaffected. Nor was there ever a saint awakened out of a cold, lifeless frame, or recovered from a declining state in religion, and brought back from a lamentable departure from God, without having his heart affected. And in a word, there never was anything considerable brought to pass in the heart or life of any man living, by the things of religion, that had not his heart deeply affected by those things. . . .

Upon the whole, I think it clearly and abundantly evident, that true religion lies very much in the affections. Not that I think these arguments prove, that religion in the hearts of the truly godly, is ever in exact proportion to the degree of affection, and present emotion of the mind. For undoubtedly, there is much affection in the true saints which is not spiritual: their religious affections are often mixed; all is not from grace, but much from nature. And though the affections have not their seat in the body, yet the constitution of the body, may very much contribute to the present emotion of the mind. And the degree of religion is rather to be judged of by the fixedness and strength of the habit that is exercised in affection, whereby holy affection is habitual, than by the degree of the present exercise: and the strength of that habit is not always in proportion to outward effects and manifestations, or inward effects, in the hurry and vehemence, and sudden changes of the course of the thoughts of the mind. But yet it is evident, that religion consists so much in affection, as that without holy affection there is no true religion: and no light in the understanding is good, which don't produce holy affection in the heart; no habit or principle in the heart is good, which has no such exercise; and no external fruit is good, which don't proceed from such exercises. . . . We may hence learn how great their error is, who are for discarding all religious affections, as having nothing solid or substantial in them.

There seems to be too much of a disposition this way, prevailing in this land at this time. Because many who, in the late extraordinary season, appeared to have great religious affections, did not manifest a right temper of mind, and run into many errors, in the time of their affection, and the heat of their zeal; and because the high affections of many seem to be so soon come to nothing, and some who seemed to be mightily raised and swallowed with joy and zeal, for a while, seem to have returned like the dog to his vomit: hence religious affections in general are grown out of credit, with great numbers, as though true religion did not at all consist in them. Thus we easily, and naturally run from one extreme to another. A little while ago we were in the other extreme; there was a prevalent disposition to look upon all high religious affections, as eminent exercises of true grace, without much inquiring into the nature and source of those affections, and the manner in which they arose: if persons did but appear to be indeed very much moved and raised, so as to be full of religious talk, and express themselves with great warmth and earnestness, and to be filled, or to be very full, as the phrases were; it was too much the manner, without further examination, to conclude such persons were full of the Spirit of God, and had eminent experience of his gracious influences. This was the extreme which was prevailing three or four years ago. But of late, instead of esteeming and admiring all religious affections, without distinction, it is a thing much more prevalent, to reject and to discard all without distinction. Herein appears the subtlety of Satan. While he saw that affections were much in vogue, knowing the greater part of the land were not versed in such things, and had not had much experience of great religious affections, to enable them to judge well of 'em, and distinguish between true and false; then he knew he could best play his game, by sowing tares amongst the wheat, and mingling false affections with the works of God's Spirit, he knew this to be a likely way to delude and eternally ruin many souls, and greatly to wound religion in the saints, and entangle them in a dreadful wilderness, and by and by, to bring all religion into disrepute. But now, when the ill consequences of these false affections appear, and 'tis become very apparent, that some of those emotions which made a glaring show, and were by many greatly admired, were in reality nothing; the devil sees it to be for his interest to go another way to work, and to endeavor to his utmost to propagate and establish a persuasion, that all affections and sensible emotions of the mind, in things of religion, are nothing at all to be regarded, but are rather to be avoided, and carefully guarded against, as things of a pernicious tendency. This he knows is the way to bring all religion to a mere lifeless formality, and effectually shut out the power of godliness, and every thing which is spiritual, and to have all true Christianity turned out of doors. For although to true religion, there must indeed be something else besides affection; yet true religion consists so much in the affections, that there can be no true religion without them. He who has no religious affection, is in a state of spiritual death, and is wholly destitute of the powerful, quickening, saving influences of the Spirit of God upon his heart. As there is no true religion, where there is nothing else but affection; so there is no true religion where there is no religious affection. As on the one hand, there must be light in the understanding, as well as an affected fervent heart, where there is heat without light, there can be nothing divine or heavenly in that heart; so on the other hand, where there is a kind of light without heat, a head stored with notions and speculations, with a cold and unaffected heart, there can be nothing divine in that light, that knowledge is no true spiritual knowledge of divine things. If the great things of religion are rightly understood, they will affect the heart. The reason why men are not affected by such infinitely great, important, glorious, and wonderful things, as they often hear and read of, in the Word of God, is undoubtedly because they are blind; if they were not so, it would be impossible, and utterly inconsistent with human nature, that their hearts should be otherwise, than strongly impressed, and greatly moved by such things.

This manner of slighting all religious affections, is the way exceedingly to harden the hearts of men, and to encourage 'em in their stupidity and senselessness, and to keep 'em in a state of spiritual death as long as they live, and bring 'em at last to death eternal. The prevailing prejudice against religious affections at this day, in the land, is apparently of awful effect, to harden the hearts of sinners, and damp the graces of many of the saints, and stunt the life and power of religion, and preclude the effect of ordinances, and hold us down in a state of dullness and apathy, and undoubtedly causes many persons greatly to offend God, in entertaining mean and low thoughts of the extraordinary work he has lately wrought in this land.

And for persons to despise and cry down all religious affections, is the way to shut all religion out of their own hearts, and to make thorough work in ruining their souls.

They who condemn high affections in others, are certainly not likely to have high affections themselves. And let it be considered, that they who have but little religious affection, have certainly but little religion. And they who condemn others for their religious affections, and have none themselves, have no religion.

There are false affections, and there are true. A man's having much affection, don't prove that he has no true religion: but if he has no affection, it proves that he has no true religion. The right way, is not to reject all affections, nor to approve all; but to distinguish between affections, approving some, and rejecting others; separating between the wheat and the chaff, the gold and the dross, the precious and the vile. . . .

Part II. Showing What Are No Certain Signs That Religious Affections Are Truly Gracious or That They Are Not

If anyone, on the reading of what has been just now said, is ready to acquit himself, and say, "I am not one of those who have no religious affections; I am often greatly moved with the consideration of the great things of religion"; let him not content himself with this, that he has religious affections. For (as was observed before) as we ought not to reject and condemn all affections, as though true religion did not at all consist in affection; so on the other hand, we ought not to approve of all, as though everyone that was religiously affected, had true grace, and was therein the subject of the saving influences of the Spirit of God: and that therefore the right way is to distinguish among religious affections, between one sort and another. Therefore let us now endeavor to do this: and in order to it, I would do two things.

I. I would mention some things, which are no signs one way or the other, either that affections are such as true religion consists in, or that they are otherwise; that we may be guarded against judging of affections by false signs.

II. I would observe some things, wherein those affections which are spiritual and gracious, differ from those which are not so, and may be distinguished and known.

First, I would take notice of some things, which are no signs that affections are gracious, or that they are not.

1. 'Tis no sign one way or the other, that religious affections are very great, or raised very high.

Some are ready to condemn all high affections: if persons appear to have their religious affections raised to an extraordinary pitch, they are prejudiced against them, and determine that they are delusions, without further inquiry. But if it be as has been proved, that true religion lies very much in religious affections, then it follows, that if there be a great deal of true religion, there will be great religious affections; if true religion in the hearts of men, be raised to a great height, divine and holy affections will be raised to a great height.

Love is an affection; but will any Christian say, men ought not to love God and Jesus Christ in a high degree? And will any say, we ought not to have a very great hatred of sin, and a very deep sorrow for it? Or that we ought not to exercise a high degree of gratitude to God, for the mercies we receive of him, and the great things he has done for the salvation of fallen men? Or that we should not have very great and strong desires after God and holiness? Is there any who will profess, that his affections in religion are great enough; and will say, "I have no cause to be humbled, that I am no more affected with the things of religion than I am, I have no reason to be ashamed, that I have no greater exercises of love to God, and sorrow for sin, and gratitude for the mercies which I have received"? Who is there that will go and bless God, that he is affected enough with what he has read and heard, of the wonderful love of God to worms and rebels, in giving his only begotten Son to die for them, and of the dying love of Chirst; and will pray that he mayn't be affected with them in any higher degree, because high affections are improper, and very unlovely in Christians, being enthusiastical, and ruinous to true religion? . . .

From these things it certainly appears, that religious affections being in a very high degree, is no evidence that they are not such as have the nature of true religion. Therefore they do greatly err, who condemn persons as enthusiasts, merely because their affections are very high.

And on the other hand, 'tis no evidence that religious affections are of a spiritual and gracious nature, because they are great. 'Tis very manifest by the Holy Scripture, our sure and infallible rule to judge of things of this nature, that there are religious affections which are very high, that are not spiritual and saving. The apostle Paul speaks of affections in the Galatians, which had been exceedingly elevated, and which yet he manifestly speaks of, as fearing that they were vain, and had come to nothing, "Where is the blessedness you spake of? for I bear you record, that if it had been possible, you would have plucked out your own eyes, and have given them to me" (Gal. 4:15). And in the 11th verse he tells them, he was afraid of 'em, lest he had bestowed upon them labor in vain. So the children of Israel were greatly affected with God's mercy to 'em, when they had seen how wonderfully he wrought for them at the Red Sea, where they sang God's praise; though they soon forgat his works. So they were greatly affected again, at Mount Sinai, when they saw the marvelous manifestations God made of himself there; and seemed mightily engaged in their minds, and with great forwardness made answer, when God proposed his holy Covenant to them, saying, "All that the Lord hath spoken will we do, and be obedient." But how soon was there an end to all this mighty forwardness and engagedness of affection? How quickly were they turned aside after other gods, rejoicing and shouting around their golden calf? . . .

2. 'Tis no sign that affections have the nature of true religion, or that they have not, that they have great effects on the body.

All affections whatsoever, have in some respect or degree, an effect on the body. As was observed before, such is our nature, and such are the laws of union of soul and body, that the mind can have no lively or vigorous exercise, without some effect upon the body. So subject is the body to the mind, and so much do its fluids, especially the animal spirits, attend the motions and exercises of the mind, that there can't be so much as an intense thought, without an effect upon them. Yea, 'tis questionable, whether an embodied soul ever so much as thinks one thought, or has any exercise at all, but that there is some corresponding motion or alteration of motion, in some degree, of the fluids, in some part of the body. But universal experience shows, that the exercise of the affections, have in a special manner a tendency, to some sensible effect upon the body. And if this be so, that all affections have some effect on the body, we may then well suppose, the greater those affections be, and the more vigorous their exercise (other circumstances being equal) the greater will be the effect on the body. Hence it is not to be wondered at, that very great and strong exercises of the affections, should have great effects on the body. And therefore, seeing there are very great affections, both common and spiritual; hence it is not to be wondered at, that great effects on the body, should arise from both these kinds of affections. And consequently these effects are not signs, that the affections they arise from, are of one kind or the other.

Great effects on the body certainly are no sure evidences that affections are spiritual; for we see that such effects oftentimes arise from great affections about temporal things, and when religion is no way concerned in them. And if great affections about secular things that are purely natural, may have these effects, I know not by what rule we should determine, that high affections about religious things, which arise in like manner from nature, can't have the like effect.

Nor on the other hand, do I know of any rule any have to determine, that gracious and holy affections, when raised as high as any natural affections, and have equally strong and vigorous exercises, can't have a great effect on the body. No such rule can be drawn from reason: I know of no reason, why a being affected with a view of God's glory should not cause the body to faint, as well as a being affected with a view of Solomon's glory. And no such rule has as yet been produced from the Scripture: none has ever been found in all the late controversies which have been about things of this nature. . . .

3. 'Tis no sign that affections are truly gracious affections, or that they are not, that they cause those who have them, to be fluent, fervent and abundant, in talking of the things of religion. . . .

ns are gracious, or that they are otherwise,
em themselves, or excite 'em of their own
vn strength. . . .

ious affections are truly holy and spiritual, or
hey come with texts of Scripture, remarkably

nly be determined concerning the nature of the
comforts and joys seem to follow awakenings and
nce, in a *certain order.* . . .

Part III. Showing What Are Distinguishing Signs of Truly Gracious and Holy Affections

I come now to the second thing appertaining to the trial of religious affections, which was proposed, viz. to take notice of some things, wherein those affections that are spiritual and gracious, do differ from those that are not so.

But before I proceed directly to the distinguishing characters, I would previously mention some things which I desire may be observed, concerning the marks I shall lay down.

1. That I am far from undertaking to give such signs of gracious affections, as shall be sufficient to enable any certainly to distinguish true affection from false in others; or to determine positively which of their neighbors are true professors, and which are hypocrites. In so doing, I should be guilty of that arrogance which I have been condemning. Though it be plain that Christ has given rules to all Christians, to enable 'em to judge of professors of religion, whom they are concerned with, so far as is necessary for their own safety, and to prevent their being led into a snare by false teachers, and false pretenders to religion; and though it be also beyond doubt, that the Scriptures do abound with rules, which may be very serviceable to ministers, in counseling and conducting souls committed to their care, in things appertaining to their spiritual and eternal

state; yet, 'tis also evident, that it was never God's design to give us any rules, by which we may certainly know, who of our fellow professors are his, and to make a full and clear separation between sheep and goats: but that on the contrary, it was God's design to reserve this to himself, as his prerogative. And therefore no such distinguishing signs as shall enable Christians or ministers to do this, are ever to be expected to the world's end: for no more is ever to be expected from any signs, that are to be found in the Word of God, or gathered from it, than Christ designed them for.

2. No such signs are to be expected, that shall be sufficient to enable those saints certainly to discern their own good estate, who are very low in grace, or are such as have much departed from God, and are fallen into a dead, carnal and unchristian frame. It is not agreeable to God's design (as has been already observed) that such should know their good estate: nor is it desirable that they should; but on the contrary, every way best that they should not; and we have reason to bless God, that he has made no provision that such should certainly know the state that they are in, any other way, than by first coming out of the ill frame and way they are in.

Indeed it is not properly through the defect of the signs given in the Word of God, that every saint living, whether strong or weak, and those who are in a bad frame, as well as others, can't certainly know their good estate by them. For the rules in themselves are certain and infallible, and every saint has, or has had those things in himself, which are sure evidences of grace; for every, even the least act of grace is so. But it is through his defect to whom the signs are given. There is a twofold defect in that saint who is very low in grace, or in an ill frame, which makes it impossible for him to know certainly that he has true grace, by the best signs and rules which can be given him. First, a defect in the object, or the qualification to be viewed and examined. I don't mean an essential defect; because I suppose the person to be a real saint; but a defect in degree: grace being very small, cannot be clearly and certainly discerned and distinguished. . . .

Secondly, there is in such a case a defect in the eye. As the feebleness of grace and prevalence of corruption, obscures the object; so it enfeebles the sight; it darkens the sight as to all spiritual objects, of which grace is one. Sin is like some distempers of the eyes, that make things to appear of different colors from those which properly belong to them, and like many other distempers, that put the mouth out of taste, so as to disenable from distinguishing good and wholesome food from bad, but everything tastes bitter. Men in a corrupt and carnal frame, have their spiritual senses in but poor plight for judging and distinguishing spiritual things.

For these reasons, no signs that can be given, will actually satisfy persons in such a case: let the signs that are given, be never so good and infallible, and clearly laid down, they will not serve them. It is like giving a man rules, how to distinguish visible objects in the dark: the things themselves may be very different, and their difference may be very well and distinctly described to him; yet all is insufficient to enable him to distinguish them, because he is in the dark. And therefore many persons in such a case spend time in a fruitless labor, in poring on past experiences, and examining themselves by signs they hear laid down from the pulpit, or that they read in books; when there is other work for them to do, that is much more expected of them; which, while they neglect, all their self-examinations are like to be in vain, if they should spend never so much time in them. The accursed thing is to be destroyed from their camp, and Achan to be slain; and till this be done they will be in trouble. 'Tis not God's design that men should obtain assurance in any other way, than by mortifying corruption, and increasing in grace, and obtaining the lively exercises of it. And although self-examination be a duty of great use and importance, and by no means to be neglected; yet it is not the principal means, by which the saints do get satisfaction of their good estate. Assurance is not to be obtained so much by self-examination, as by action.

Therefore, though good rules to distinguish true grace from counterfeit . . . may be very useful . . . ; yet I am far from pretending to lay down any such rules . . . to enable all true saints to see their good estate. . . .

Having premised these things, I now proceed directly to take notice of those things in which true religious affections are distinguished from false.

I. Affections that are truly spiritual and gracious, do arise from those influences and operations on the heart, which are *spiritual, supernatural* and *divine*.

I will explain what I mean by these terms, whence will appear their use to distinguish between those affections which are spiritual, and those which are not so.

We find that true saints, or those persons who are sanctified by the Spirit of God, are in the New Testament called spiritual persons. And their being spiritual is spoken of as their peculiar character, and that wherein they are distinguished from those who are not sanctified. This is evident because those who are spiritual are set in opposition to natural men, and carnal men. . . .

And it must be here observed, that although it is with relation to the Spirit of God and his influences, that persons and things are called spiritual; yet not all those persons who are subject to any kind of influence of the Spirit of God, are ordinarily called spiritual in the New Testament. They who have only the common influences of God's Spirit, are not so called, in the places cited above, but only those, who have the special, gracious and saving influences of God's Spirit: as is evident, because it has been already proved, that by spiritual men is meant godly men, in opposition to natural, carnal and unsanctified men. And it is most plain, that the Apostle by spiritually minded, Rom. 8:6, means graciously minded. And though the extraordinary gifts of the Spirit, which natural men might have, are sometimes called spiritual, because they are from the Spirit; yet natural men, whatever gifts of the Spirit they had, were not, in the usual language of the New Testament, called spiritual persons. For it was not by men's having the gifts of the Spirit, but by their having the virtues of the Spirit, that they were called spiritual; as is apparent, by Gal. 6:1: "Brethren, if any man be overtaken in a fault, ye which are spiritual restore such an one in the spirit of meekness." Meekness is one of those virtues which the Apostle had just spoken of, in the verses next preceding, showing what are the fruits of the Spirit. Those qualifications are said to be spiritual in the language of the New Testament, which are truly gracious and holy, and peculiar to the saints. . . .

So that although natural men may be the subjects of many influences of the Spirit of God, as is evident by many Scriptures, as Num. 24:2, I Sam. 10:10 and 11:6 and 16:14; I Cor. 13:1–3; Heb. 6:4–6 and many others; yet they are not in the sense of the Scripture, spiritual persons; either are any of those effects, common gifts, qualities or affections, that are from the influence of the Spirit of God upon them, called spiritual things. The great difference lies in these two things.

1. The Spirit of God is given to the true saints to dwell in them, as his proper lasting abode; and to influence their hearts, as a principle of new nature, or as a divine supernatural spring of life and action. The Scriptures represent the Holy Spirit, not only as moving, and occasionally influencing the saints, but as dwelling in them as his temple, his proper abode, and everlasting dwelling place (I Cor. 3:16; II Cor. 6:16, John 14:16–17). And he is represented as being there so united to the faculties of the soul, that he becomes there a principle or spring of new nature and life.

So the saints are said to live by Christ living in them (Gal. 2:20). Christ by his Spirit not only is in them, but lives in them; and so that they live by his life; so is his Spirit united to them, as a principle of life in them; they don't only drink living water, but this living water becomes a well or fountain of water, in the soul, springing up into spiritual and everlasting life (John 4:14), and thus becomes a principle of life in them; this living water, this Evangelist himself explains to intend the Spirit of God (ch. 7:38–39). The light of the Sun of Righteousness don't only shine upon them, but is so communicated to them that they shine also, and become little images of that Sun which shines upon them; the sap of the true vine is not only conveyed into them, as the sap of a tree may be conveyed into a vessel, but is conveyed as sap is from a tree into one of its living branches, where it becomes a principle of life. The Spirit of God being thus communicated and united to the saints, they are from thence properly denominated from it, and are called spiritual.

On the other hand, though the Spirit of God may many ways influence natural men; yet because it is not thus communicated to them, as an indwelling principle, they don't derive any denomination or character from it; for there being no union it is not their own. The light may shine upon a body that is very dark or black; and though that body be the subject of the light, yet, because the light becomes no principle of light in it, so as to cause the body to shine, hence that body don't properly receive its denomination from it, so as to be called a lightsome body. So the Spirit of God acting upon the soul only, without communicating itself to be an active principle in it, can't denominate it spiritual. A body that continues black, may be said not to have light, though the light shines upon it; so natural men are said not to have the Spirit, Jude 19: "sensual," or natural (as the word is elsewhere rendered) "having not the Spirit."

2. Another reason why the saints and their virtues are called spiritual (which is the principal thing), is that the Spirit of God, dwelling as a vital principle in their souls, there produces those effects wherein he exerts and communicates himself in his own proper nature. Holiness is the nature of the Spirit of God, therefore he is called in Scripture the Holy Ghost. Holiness, which is as it were the beauty and sweetness of the divine nature, is as much the proper nature of the Holy Spirit, as heat is the nature of fire, or sweetness was the nature of that holy anointing oil, which was the principal type of the Holy Ghost in the Mosaic dispensation; yea, I may rather say that holiness is as much the proper nature of the Holy Ghost, as sweetness was the nature of the sweet odor of that ointment. The Spirit of God so dwells in the hearts of the saints, that he there, as a seed or spring of life, exerts and communicates himself, in this his sweet and divine nature, making the soul a partaker of God's beauty and Christ's joy, so that the saint has truly fellowship with the Father, and with his Son Jesus Christ, in thus having the communion or participation of the Holy Ghost. The grace which is in the hearts of the saints, is of the same nature with the divine holiness, as much as 'tis possible for that holiness to be, which is infinitely less in degree; as the brightness that is in a diamond which the sun shines upon, is of the same nature with the brightness of the sun, but only that it is as nothing to it in degree. . . .

Thus not only the manner of the *relation* of the Spirit, who is the operator, to the subject of his operations, is different; as the Spirit operates in the saints, as dwelling in them, as an abiding principle of action, whereas he doth not so operate upon sinners; but the influence and *operation itself* is different, and the effect wrought exceeding different. So that not only the persons are called spiritual, as having the Spirit of God dwelling in them; but those qualifications, affections and experiences that are wrought in them by the Spirit, are also spiritual, and therein differ vastly in their nature and kind from all that a natural man is or can be the subject of, while he remains in a natural state; and also from all that men or devils can be the authors of: 'tis a spiritual work in this high sense; and therefore above all other works is peculiar to the Spirit of God. . . . And the influences of the Spirit of God in this, being thus peculiar to God, and being those wherein God does, in so high a manner, communicate himself, and make the creature partaker of the divine nature (the Spirit of God communicating itself in its own proper nature). This is what I mean by those influences that are divine, when I say that truly gracious affections do arise from those influences that are spiritual and divine.

The true saints only have that which is spiritual; others have nothing which is divine, in the sense that has been spoken of. They not only have not these communications of the Spirit of God in so high a degree as the saints, but have nothing of that nature or kind. For the apostle James tell us, that natural men have not the Spirit; and Christ teaches the necessity of a new birth, or a being born of the Spirit, from this, that he that is born of the flesh, has only flesh, and no spirit (John 3:6). They have not the Spirit of God dwelling in them in any degree; for the Apostle teaches, that all who have the Spirit of God dwelling in them are some of his (Rom. 8:9-11). And an having the Spirit of God is spoken of as a certain sign that persons shall have the eternal inheritance; for 'tis spoken of as the earnest of it (II Cor. 1:22 and 5:5; Eph. 1:14), and an having anything of the Spirit is mentioned as a sure sign of being in Christ, "Hereby know we that we dwell in him, because he hath given us of his Spirit" (I John 4:30). Ungodly men, not only han't so much of the divine nature as the saints, but they are not partakers of it; which implies that they have nothing of it; for a being partaker of the divine nature is spoken of as the peculiar privilege of the true saints (II Pet. 1:4). Ungodly men are not partakers of God's holiness (Heb. 12:10). A natural man has no experience of any of those things that are spiritual: the Apostle teaches us that he is so far from it, that he knows nothing about them, he is a perfect stranger to them, the talk about such things is all foolishness and nonsense to him, he knows not what it means, "The natural man receiveth not the things of the Spirit of God; for they are foolishness to him; neither can he know them; because they are spiritually discerned" (I Cor. 2:14). . . .

From these things it is evident, that those gracious influences which the

saints are subjects of, and the effects of God's Spirit which they experience, are entirely above nature, altogether of a different kind from anything that men find within themselves by nature, or only in the exercise of
natural principles; and are things which no improvement of those qualifications, or principles that are natural, no advancing or exalting them to
higher degrees, and no kind of composition of them, will ever bring men
to; because they not only differ from what is natural, and from everything
that natural men experience, in degree and circumstances; but also in kind;
and are of a nature vastly more excellent. And this is what I mean by
supernatural, when I say, that gracious affections are from those influences
that are supernatural.

From hence it follows, that in those gracious exercises and affections
which are wrought in the minds of the saints, through the saving influences of the Spirit of God, there is a new inward perception or sensation of
their minds, entirely different in its nature and kind, from anything that
ever their minds were the subjects of before they were sanctified. For
doubtless if God by his mighty power produces something that is new, not
only in degree and circumstances, but in its whole nature, and that which
could be produced by no exalting, varying or compounding of what was
there before, or by adding anything of the like kind; I say, if God produces
something thus new in a mind, that is a perceiving, thinking, conscious
thing; then doubtless something entirely new is felt, or perceived, or
thought; or, which is the same thing, there is some new sensation or
perception of the mind, which is entirely of a new sort, and which could be
produced by no exalting, varying or compounding of that kind of perceptions or sensations which the mind had before; or there is what some
metaphysicians call a new simple idea. If grace be, in the sense above
described, an entirely new kind of principle; then the exercises of it are also
entirely a new kind of exercises. And if there be in the soul a new sort of
exercises which it is conscious of, which the soul knew nothing of before,
and which no improvement, composition or management of what it was
before conscious or sensible of, could produce, or anything like it; then it
follows that the mind has an entirely new kind of perception or sensation;
and here is, as it were, a new spiritual sense that the mind has, or a
principle of new kind of perception or spiritual sensation, which is in its

whole nature different from any former kinds of sensation of the mind, as tasting is diverse from any of the other senses; and something is perceived by a true saint, in the exercise of this new sense of mind, in spiritual and divine things, as entirely diverse from anything that is perceived in them, by natural men, as the sweet taste of honey is diverse from the ideas men get of honey by only looking on it, and feeling of it. So that the spiritual perceptions which a sanctified and spiritual person has, are not only diverse from all that natural men have, after the manner that the ideas or perceptions of the same sense may differ one from another, but rather as the ideas and sensations of different senses do differ. Hence the work of the Spirit of God in regeneration is often in Scripture compared to the giving a new sense, giving eyes to see, and ears to hear, unstopping the ears of the deaf, and opening the eyes of them that were born blind, and turning from darkness unto light. And because this spiritual sense is immensely the most noble and excellent, and that without which all other principles of perception, and all our faculties are useless and vain; therefore the giving this new sense, with the blessed fruits and effects of it in the soul, is compared to a raising the dead, and to a new creation.

This new spiritual sense, and the new dispositions that attend it, are no new faculties, but are new principles of nature. I use the word "principles," for want of a word of a more determinate signification. By a principle of nature in this place, I mean that foundation which is laid in nature, either old or new, for any particular manner or kind of exercise of the faculties of the soul; or a natural habit or foundation for action, giving a person ability and disposition to exert the faculties in exercises of such a certain kind; so that to exert the faculties in that kind of exercises, may be said to be his nature. So this new spiritual sense is not a new faculty of understanding, but it is a new foundation laid in the nature of the soul, for a new kind of exercises of the same faculty of understanding. So that new holy disposition of heart that attends this new sense, is not a new faculty of will, but a foundation laid in the nature of the soul, for a new kind of exercises of the same faculty of will.

The Spirit of God, in all his operations upon the minds of natural men, only moves, impresses, assists, improves, or some way acts upon natural principles; but gives no new spiritual principle. Thus when the Spirit of

God gives a natural man visions, as he did Balaam, he only impresses a natural principle, viz. the sense of seeing, immediately exciting ideas of that sense; but he gives no new sense; neither is there anything supernatural, spiritual or divine in it. So if the Spirit of God impresses on a man's imagination, either in a dream, or when he is awake, any outward ideas of any of the senses, either voices, or shapes and colors, 'tis only exciting ideas of the same kind that he has by natural principles and senses. So if God reveals to any natural man, any secret fact; as for instance, something that he shall hereafter see or hear; this is not infusing or exercising any new spiritual principle, or giving the ideas of any new spiritual sense; 'tis only impressing, in an extraordinary manner, the ideas that will hereafter be received by sight and hearing. So in the more ordinary influences of the Spirit of God on the hearts of sinners, he only assists natural principles to do the same work to a greater degree, which they do of themselves by nature. Thus the Spirit of God by his common influences may assist men's natural ingeniosity as he assisted Bezaleel and Aholiab in the curious works of the tabernacle: so he may assist men's natural abilities in political affairs, and improve their courage, and other natural qualifications; as he is said to have put his Spirit on the seventy elders, and on Saul, so as to give him another heart: so God may greatly assist natural men's reason, in their reasoning about secular things, or about the doctrines of religion, and may greatly advance the clearness of their apprehensions and notions of things of religion in many respects, without giving any spiritual sense. So in those awakenings and convictions that natural men may have, God only assists conscience, which is a natural principle, to do that work in a further degree, which it naturally does. . . .

From hence it appears that impressions which some have made on their imagination, or the imaginary ideas which they have of God, or Christ, or heaven, or anything appertaining to religion, have nothing in them that is spiritual, or of the nature of true grace. Though such things may attend what is spiritual, and be mixed with it, yet in themselves they have nothing that is spiritual, nor are they any part of gracious experience. . . .

Many who have had such things have very ignorantly supposed them to be of the nature of spiritual discoveries. They have had lively ideas of some external shape, and beautiful form of countenance; and this they call spiritually seeing Christ. Some have had impressed upon them ideas of a great outward light; and this they call a spiritual discovery of God's or Christ's glory. Some have had ideas of Christ's hanging on the cross, and his blood running from his wounds; and this they call a spiritual sight of Christ crucified, and the way of salvation by his blood. Some have seen him with his arms open ready to embrace them; and this they call a discovery of the sufficiency of Christ's grace and love. Some have had lively ideas of heaven, and of Christ on his throne there, and shining ranks of saints and angels; and this they call seeing heaven opened to them. Some from time to time have had a lively idea of a person of a beautiful countenance smiling upon them; and this they call a spiritual discovery of the love of Christ to their souls, and tasting the love of Christ. . . .

But it is exceeding apparent that such ideas have nothing in them which is spiritual and divine, in the sense wherein it has been demonstrated that all gracious experiences are spiritual and divine. These external ideas are in no wise of such a sort, that they are entirely, and in their whole nature diverse from all that men have by nature, perfectly different from, and vastly above any sensation which 'tis possible a man should have by any natural sense or principle, so that in order to have them, a man must have a new spiritual and divine sense given him, in order to have any sensations of that sort: so far from this, that they are ideas of the same sort which we have by the external senses, that are some of the inferior powers of the humane nature; they are merely ideas of external objects, or ideas of that nature, of the same outward sensitive kind; the same sort of sensations of mind (differing not in degree, but only in circumstances) that we have by those natural principles which are common to us, with the beasts, viz. the five external senses. This is a low, miserable notion of spiritual sense, to suppose that 'tis only a conceiving or imagining that sort of ideas which we have by our animal senses, which senses the beasts have in as great perfection as we; it is, as it were, a turning Christ, or the divine nature in the soul, into a mere animal. . . .

From hence it again clearly appears, that no such things have anything in them that is spiritual, supernatural and divine, in the sense in which it has been proved that all truly gracious experiences have. And though external ideas, through man's make and frame, do ordinarily in some degree attend spiritual experiences, yet these ideas are no part of their spiritual experience, any more than the motion of the blood, and beating of the pulse, that attends experiences, are a part of spiritual experience. And though undoubtedly, through men's infirmity in the present state, and especially through the weak constitution of some persons, gracious affections which are very strong, do excite lively ideas in the imagination; yet 'tis also undoubted, that when persons' affections are founded on imaginations, which is often the case, those affections are merely natural and common, because they are built on a foundation that is not spiritual; and so are entirely different from gracious affections, which, as has been proved, do evermore arise from those operations that are spiritual and divine. . . .

IV. Gracious affections do arise from the mind's being enlightened, rightly and spiritually to understand or apprehend divine things.

Holy affections are not heat without light; but evermore arise from some information of the understanding, or some spiritual instruction that the mind receives, some light or actual knowledge. . . .

XII. Gracious and holy affections have their exercise and fruit in Christian practice. I mean, they have that influence and power upon him who is the subject of 'em, that they cause that a practice, which is universally conformed to, and directed by Christian rules, should be the practice and business of his life.

This implies three things; (1) That his behavior or practice in the world, be universally conformed to, and directed by Christian rules. (2) That he makes a business of such a holy practice above all things; that it be a business which he is chiefly engaged in, and devoted to, and pursues with highest earnestness and diligence: so that he may be said to make this practice of religion eminently his work and business. And (3) That he persists in it to the end of life: so that is may be said, not only to be his business at certain seasons, the business of Sabbath days, or certain extraordinary times, or the business of a month, or a year, or of seven years, or his business under certain circumstances; but the business of his life; it being that business which he perseveres in through all changes, and under all trials, as long as he lives. . . .

The tendency of grace in the heart to holy practice, is very direct, and the connection most natural close and necessary. True grace is not an unactive thing; there is nothing in heaven or earth of a more active nature; for 'tis life itself, and the most active kind of life, even spiritual and divine life. 'Tis no barren thing; there is nothing in the universe that in its nature has a greater tendency to fruit. Godliness in the heart has as direct a relation to practice, as a fountain has to a stream, or as the luminous nature of the sun has to beams sent forth, or as life has to breathing, or the beating of the pulse, or any other vital act; or as a habit or principle of action has to action: for 'tis the very nature and notion of grace, that 'tis a principle of holy action or practice. Regeneration, which is that work of God in which grace is infused, has a direct relation to practice; for 'tis the very end of it, with a view to which the whole work is wrought: all is calculated and framed, in this mighty and manifold change wrought in the soul, so as directly to tend to this end: "For we are his workmanship, created in Christ Jesus, unto good works" (Eph. 2:10). Yea 'tis the very end of the redemption of Christ; "Who gave himself for us, that he might redeem us from all iniquity, and purify unto himself a peculiar people, zealous of good works" (Titus 2:14). "He died for all, that they which live, should not henceforth live unto themselves, but unto him who died, and rose again" (II Cor. 5:15). "How much more shall the blood of Christ, who through the eternal Spirit, offered up himself without spot to God, purge your consciences from dead works, to serve the living God?" (Heb. 9:14). . . .

From what has been said it is manifest, that Christian practice or a holy life is a great and distinguishing sign of true and saving grace. But I may go further, and assert, that it is the chief of all the signs of grace, both as an evidence of the sincerity of professors unto others, and also to their own consciences.

But then it is necessary that this be rightly taken, and that it be well understood and observed, in what sense and manner Christian practice is the greatest sign of grace. Therefore, to set this matter in a clear light, I will endeavor particularly and distinctly to prove, that Christian practice is the *principal sign* by which Christians are to judge, both of their own and others' sincerity of godliness; withal observing some things that are needful to be particularly noted, in order to a right understanding of this matter.

1. I shall consider Christian practice and an holy life, as a manifestation and sign of the sincerity of a professing Christian, to the eye of his neighbors and brethren.

And that this is the chief sign of grace in this respect, is very evident from the Word of God. Christ, who knew best how to give us rules to judge of others, has repeated it and inculcated it, that we should know them by their fruits; "Ye shall know them by their fruits" (Matt. 7:16). . . . So Luke 6:44: "Every tree is known by his own fruit." Christ nowhere says, ye shall know the tree by its leaves or flowers, or ye shall know men by their talk, or ye shall know them by the good story they tell of their experiences, or ye shall know them by the manner and air of their speaking, and emphasis and pathos of expression, or by their speaking feelingly, or by making a very great show by abundance of talk, or by many tears and affectionate expressions, or by the affections ye feel in your hearts towards them: but by their fruits shall ye know them; the tree is known by its fruit; every tree is known by its own fruit. And as this is the evidence that Christ has directed us mainly to look at in others, in judging of them, so it is the evidence that Christ has mainly directed us to give to others, whereby they may judge of us; "Let your light so shine before men, that others seeing your good works, may glorify your Father which is in heaven" (Matt. 5:16). Here Christ directs us to manifest our godliness to others. Godliness is as it were a light that shines in the soul: Christ directs that this light should not only shine within, but that it should shine out before men, that they may see it. But which way shall this be? 'Tis by our good works. Christ don't say, that others hearing your good words, your good story, or your pathetical expressions; but that others seeing your good works, may glorify your Father which is in heaven. Doubtless when Christ gives us a rule how to make our light shine, that others may have evidence of it, his rule is the best that is to be found. And the apostles do mention a Christian practice, as the principal ground of their esteem of persons as true Christians. . . .

Therefore here are two ways of manifesting to our neighbor what is in our hearts; one by what we *say*, and the other by what we *do*. But the Apostle abundantly prefers the latter as the best evidence. Now certainly all accounts we give of ourselves in words, our saying that we have faith, and that we are converted, and telling the manner how we came to have faith, and the steps by which it was wrought, and the discoveries and experiences that accompanied it, are still but manifesting our faith by what we say; 'tis but showing our faith by our words; which the Apostle speaks of as falling vastly short of manifesting of it by what we do, and showing our faith by our works.

And as the Scripture plainly teaches that practice is the best evidence of the sincerity of professing Christians; so reason teaches the same thing. Reason shows that men's deeds are better and more faithful interpreters of their minds, than their words. The common sense of all mankind, through all ages and nations, teaches 'em to judge of men's hearts chiefly by their practice, in other matters: as whether a man be a loyal subject, a true lover, a dutiful child, or a faithful servant. If a man professes a great deal of love and friendship to another, reason teaches all men, that such a profession is not so great an evidence of his being a real and hearty friend, as his appearing a friend in deeds; being faithful and constant to his friend, in prosperity and adversity, ready to lay out himself, and deny himself, and suffer in his personal interest, to do him a kindness. A wise man will trust to such evidences of the sincerity of friendship, further than a thousand earnest professions and solemn declarations, and most affectionate expressions of friendship in words. And there is equal reason why practice should also be looked upon as the best evidence of friendship towards Christ. Reason says the same that Christ said, in John 14:21: "He that hath my commandments, and keepeth them, he it is that loveth me." Thus if we see a man, who in the course of his life, seems to follow and imitate Christ, and greatly to exert and deny himself for the honor of Christ and to promote his kingdom and interest in the world; reason teaches that this is an evidence of love to Christ, more to be depended on, than if a man only says he has love to Christ, and tells of the inward experiences he has had of love to him, what strong love he felt, and how his heart was drawn out in love at such and such a time, when it may be there appears but little imitation of Christ in his behavior, and he seems backward to do any great matter for him, or to put himself out of his way for the promoting of his kingdom, but seems to be apt to excuse himself, whenever he is called to deny himself for Christ. So if a man in declaring his experiences, tells how he found his heart weaned from the world, and saw the vanity of it, so that all looked as nothing to him, at such and such times, and professes that he gives up all to God, and calls heaven and earth to witness to it; but yet in his practice is violent in pursuing the world, and what he gets he keeps close, is exceeding loath to part with much of it to charitable and pious uses, it comes from him almost like his heart's blood. But there is another professing Christian, that says not a great deal, yet in his behavior appears ready at all times to forsake the world, whenever it stands in the way of his duty, and is free to part with it at any time, to promote religion and the good of his fellow creatures; reason teaches that the latter gives far the most credible manifestation of an heart weaned from the world. . . . Persons in a pang of affection may think they have a willingness of heart for great things, to do much and to suffer much, and so may profess it very earnestly and confidently; when really their hearts are far from it. Thus many in their affectionate pangs, have thought themselves willing to be damned eternally for the glory of God. Passing affections easily produce words; and words are cheap; and godliness is more easily feigned in words than in actions. Christian practice is a costly laborious thing. The self-denial that is required of Christians, and the narrowness of the way that leads to life, don't consist in words, but in practice. Hypocrites may much more easily be brought to talk like saints, than to act like saints.

Thus it is plain that Christian practice is the best sign or manifestation of the true godliness of a professing Christian, to the eye of his neighbors. . . .

Secondly, I proceed to show that Christian practice, taken in the sense that has been explained, is the chief of all the evidences of a saving sincerity in religion, to the consciences of the professors of it; much to be preferred to the method of the first convictions, enlightenings and comforts in conversion, or any immanent discoveries or exercises of grace whatsoever, that begin and end in contemplation. The evidence of this appears by the following arguments.

Argument 1. Reason plainly shows that those things which put it to the proof what men will actually cleave to and prefer in their practice, when left to follow their own choice and inclinations, are the proper trial what they do really prefer in their hearts. Sincerity in religion, as has been observed already, consists in setting God highest in the heart, in choosing him before other things, in having a heart to sell all for Christ, etc. But a man's actions are the proper trial what a man's heart prefers. As for instance, when it is so that God and other things come to stand in competition, God is as it were set before a man on one hand, and his worldly interest or pleasure on the other (as it often is so in the course of a man's life), his behavior in such case, in actually cleaving to the one and forsaking the other, is the proper trial which he prefers. Sincerity consists in forsaking all for Christ in heart; but to forsake all for Christ in heart, is the very same thing as to have an heart to forsake all for Christ: but certainly the proper trial whether a man has an heart to forsake all for Christ, is his being actually put to it, the having Christ and other things coming in competition, that he must actually or practically cleave to one and forsake the other. To forsake all for Christ in heart, is the same thing as to have an heart to forsake all for Christ when called to it: but the highest proof to ourselves and others, that we have an heart to forsake all for Christ when called to it, is actually doing it when called to it, or so far as called to it. To follow Christ in heart, is to have an heart to follow him. To deny ourselves in heart for Christ, is the same thing as to have an heart to deny ourselves for him in fact. The main and most proper proof of a man's having an heart to anything, concerning which he is at liberty to follow his own inclinations, and either to do or not to do as he pleases, is his doing of it. When a man is at liberty whether to speak or keep silence, the most proper evidence of his having an heart to speak, is his speaking. When a man is at liberty whether to walk or sit still, the proper proof of his having an heart to walk, is his walking. Godliness consists not in an heart to intend to do the will of God, but in an heart to do it. The children of Israel in the wilderness had the former, of whom we read, "Go thou near, and hear all that the Lord our God shall say; and speak thou unto us all that the Lord our God shall speak unto thee; and we will hear it and do it. And the Lord heard the voice of your words, when ye spake unto me;

and the Lord said unto me, I have heard the voice of the words of this people, which they have spoken unto thee: they have well said all that they have spoken: O that there were such an HEART in them, that they would fear me, and keep all my commandments always, that it might be well with them, and with their children forever" (Deut. 5:27–29). The people manifested that they had a heart to intend to keep God's commandments, and to be very forward in those intentions; but God manifests that this was far from being the thing that he desired, wherein true godliness consists, even an heart actually to keep them. . . .

Arg. 2. As reason shows that those things which occur in the course of life that put it to the proof whether men will prefer God to other things in practice, are the proper trial of the uprightness and sincerity of their hearts; so the same are represented as the proper trial of the sincerity of professors, in the Scripture. There we find that such things are called by that very name, trials or temptations (which I before observed are both words of the same signification). The things that put it to the proof whether men will prefer God to other things in practice, are the difficulties of religion, or those things which occur that make the practice of duty difficult and cross to other principles besides the love of God; because in them, God and other things are both set before men together, for their actual and practical choice; and it comes to this, that we can't hold to both, but one or the other must be forsaken. . . .

Now from all that has been said, I think it to be abundantly manifest, that Christian practice is the most proper evidence of the gracious sincerity of professors, to themselves and others; and the chief of all the marks of grace, the sign of signs, and evidence of evidences, that which seals and crowns all other signs. I had rather have the testimony of my conscience, that I have such a saying of my supreme Judge on my side, as that, "He that hath my commandments and keepeth them, he it is that loveth me" (John 14:21); than the judgment, and fullest approbation, of all the wise, sound and experienced divines, that have lived this thousand years, on the most exact and critical examination of my experiences, as to the manner of my conversion. Not that there are no other good evidences of a state of grace but this. There may be other exercises of grace, besides these efficient exercises, which the saints may have in contemplation, that may be very satisfying to them: but yet this is the chief and most proper evidence. There may be several good evidences that a tree is a fig tree; but the highest and most proper evidence of it, is that it actually bears figs. 'Tis possible that a man may have a good assurance of a state of grace, at his first conversion, before he has had opportunity to gain assurance, by this great evidence I am speaking of. If a man hears that a great treasure is offered him, in a distant place, on condition that he will prize it so much, as to be willing to leave what he possesses at home, and go a journey for it, over the rocks and mountains that are in the way, to the place where it is; 'tis possible the man may be well assured, that he values the treasure to the degree spoken of, as soon as the offer is made him; he may feel a willingness to go for the treasure, within him, beyond all doubt: but yet, this don't hinder but that his actual going for it is the highest and most proper evidence of his being willing, not only to others, but to himself. But then as an evidence to himself, his outward actions, and the motions of his body in his journey, are not considered alone, exclusive of the actions of his mind, and a consciousness within himself, of the thing that moves him, and the end he goes for; otherwise, his bodily motion is no evidence to him, of his prizing the treasure. In such a manner is Christian practice the most proper evidence of a saving value of the pearl of great price, and treasure hid in the field.

The Bad Book Case (1744)

Here Are Included the Testimonies against Oliver Warner, Given in the Spring, in the Year 1744

Rebeccah Strong testifieth that near five years ago the next May, Charles Wright and Timothy Root came into the shop, and [she] found 'em with a book that they were provoked about. Moses Sheldon asked whether we had seen such a book, mentioning the name. She had, at Dr. [Samuel] Mather's, concluding by the pictures that seemed to her to be these parts of a woman's body.

Timothy Root and Simeon [Root] and Moses Sheldon, often talking in a private way about a book, said something about a bible in a laughing way, that she concluded was that. When talking about the book, they talked about women and girls, and turn about and looked upon me, and said, "You had not need to be scared; we know as much about ye as you, and more too." When he (Moses Sheldon) inquired about the book, he asked me if it was not such an one, and I told him it was. "Well," says he, "that was the book that we had here, that you used to look after, and I have read it out." Uncle Moses said Noah Baker had the book, and kept it between his coat and the lining. Sarah Baker found it, and gave it to her mother. Moses Sheldon and those two Roots and Charles Wright. Timothy Root and Charles Wright chiefly used to talk much about such things as I suppose such books relate to.

Rachel Clap. Oliver Warner, Deacon Parsons' son, Medad Lyman wanted Aristotle, intended to find it. Simeon Root noised that he was sorry so that he had not read more. He told what was pictured out in the book. There the child is, lies all pictured out.

John Miller's wife. Delivered by younger sister. Isaac Parsons promises reformation. Never thought of the harm. He would totally and finally have done with it.

Mindwell [Miller]. Moses Sheldon: "I know a great deal more than you can think about the works of nature." Not above two months ago. Turned away and laughed.

Martha Clark. Ebenezer Bartlet: "What if I should say I sat 'till midnight reading one of them books." When he was talking about such books. "Don't you think I would sit up again if I had opportunity?"

Bathsheba [Negro]. At David Burt's, Noah Baker, Timothy Root and Elkanah Burt, reading in a book that they called "the bible" in a laughing way. All read in it. Timothy Root read most. (About the time that Noah Baker was married.) Read it before her [and] Naomi Warner. Laugh. Ready to kiss them, and catch hold of the girls and shook 'em. Timothy Root in particular. Called it "young folks' bible." The book was exceeding unclean to the top of baseness. The book what they read was about women. Samuel Burt's book, they said. It [was] about women's having children.

Had seen the book at Samuel Burt's once before. Timothy Root said at that time at Burt's, after the child is born they burn guts and garbages.

Hannah Clark with her in the street, and Oliver Warner met them. Said, "When will the moon change girls? I believe you can tell. I believe you have circles 'round your eyes. I believe it runs."

Medad Lyman and Oliver Warner knew what the girls was, what nasty creatures they was.

At another time, Oliver Warner and Medad Lyman reading in a base book, nasty book, about womenkind. At Moll Macklin's talk. John Macklin was there; he was worse than others that was there. Thankful Parsons was there. Dorothy Danks was there.

Joanna Clark. Oliver Warner, about a year ago: "When does the moon change girls? Come, I'll look at your [face] and see whether there be a blue circle 'round your eyes." Bathsheba Negro was with her. "I believe it runs."

Ebenezer Pomeroy, last lecture day night, when she groaned, said, "I believe you need the old granny. I have read in a book about that." John Lancton was with him.

Shadrach Bedartha. Oliver Warner asked me if I did not want a book that there had been talk about. I asked him who there be had such a book. He answered, "That is no matter to you." He offered to let me have it; offered it for ten shillings in money. He understood Oliver, and Oliver talked as though he supposed I understood him.

Elizabeth Pomeroy. Found a book in their house up the chimney, on the backside of the chimney on the press. No reason to think it was mother brought it in. The title, "The Midwife Rightly Instructed." Katherine Wright was with her. A new book.

Katherine Wright to the same. See Betty [Pomeroy] took it out. "Midwife Rightly Instructed," etc.

Experience Strong. A year or year and one half [ago], Ebenezer Bartlet at Jonathan Strong's house: "It might be necessary for young men to know such things." He owned that if he had had such a sense as he once had, he should have had no inclination to read such books.

Isaac Searl. Ephraim Wright talked to him and Oliver Warner too, that told him they would not have him tell more than he need, that they would not have him enlarge much upon it. Ephraim Wright told him he need not say a word, if he had not a mind to.

Mary Downing. Two years ago this summer at her mother's. Oliver Warner there. There was reading amongst them in a book. They made sport of what they read in the book. One or two more there; she could not certainly say who they was. They all did so. What they laughed and made sport of was about girls, things concerning girls that it is unclean to speak of. They seemed to boast as if they knew about girls, knew what belonged to girls as well as girls themselves. She took it that the book was about the same things that they talked of. They seemed by their talk to apprehend that they got what they knew about girls out of that book. They run upon the girls at that time, boasting how much they knew about them. Many other times here, talking after the same manner about what he knew about girls. He has talked to me himself about what he knew.

John Lancton, a fortnight ago last Friday, was at the farm where I was and was talking of such things, and he boasted that he had read Aristotle. He talked about his reading that book more than once; talked about the things that was in that book in a most unclean manner a long time. Betty Danks and Moll Waters there. He spoke of the book as a granny book. When I checked him, he laughed. He talked exceeding uncleanly and lasciviously, so that I never heard any fellow go so far. After he was gone, we—the young women that were there—agreed that we never heard any such talk come out of any man's mouth whatsoever. It seemed to me to be almost as bad as tongue could express.

Papers Concerning Young Men's Reading Midwives' Books, Their Contempt of the Church, Etc.

Maj. Pomeroy testified and said that in the time when the affair lately considered in this church concerning the young men's using books written on the business of midwives was first proposed to the church on the sabbath, and the said affair was under consideration, he saw Timothy Root and Simeon Root, diverse times, whispering and laughing together in the open face of the church.

Rachel Clap testifies and says that when the affair lately considered in this church was first proposed to the church, the church being stayed on that occasion, she saw Timothy Root and Simeon Root, whispering and laughing together the bigger part of the time that the church stayed in the meeting house after the congregation was dismissed.

Naomi Strong testifies that at the time forementioned, she saw Timothy Root and Simeon Root whispering and laughing together the biggest part of the time that the church stayed in the meeting house, and had the matter aforesaid under consideration.

Moses Hannam testifies that in the time of the first sitting of the committee of this church, one of the committee, viz. Lieut. Parsons, going out of doors, Simeon Root with some others asked him what the committee were about, and told him that if they did not do something quickly, they would go away, they would not be kept here for nothing; and that when Lieut. Parsons returned into the room where the committee were sitting, he followed him near to the door, and when the door was opened, he stood near the door and spake out in a pretty loud and powerful manner, saying, "What do we here? We won't stay here all day long," or to that purpose.

Col. Stoddard testifies that when the committee of this church, chosen to inquire into the forementioned affair, were first sitting on that business at the house of the pastor of this church, he saw Simeon Root near the door of the room where the committee were sitting, and heard him say in a loud and earnest manner, "What do we hear? We won't stay here all day long."

Capt. Clap, being one of the Committee, testifies that he heard the same thing, and that he spake it in a loud and earnest manner and, as appeared to him, with an air of contempt.

Deac. Pomeroy testified that he heard words to the same purpose, spoken, as he judged, by the same person.

Sarah Edwards, Jr. testifies that she heard the same Simeon Root say, while the committee were sitting, "What are we kept here for all day and hindered from our work? I wonder what is afoot?" And Timothy Root made answer, "Afoot? I desire to know what is afoot in the first place!"

Joseph Lyman and his wife, and Rachel Clap, testified that Timothy Root and Simeon Root came to the tavern that day that the committee of this church sat the first time, and were of a company that called for a mug of flip and drank it. This, as Mrs. Lyman and Rachel Clap said, was, as

near as they could judge, when the sun was about two hours high. Joseph
Lyman says that the company said they came without liberty.

Caleb Sheldon said that he saw Timothy Root and Simeon Root going
that way, and afterwards coming from that way; and that some of them
said they had been to the tavern.

Isaac Searl testifies that when Medad Lyman went in to the committee
to ask leave to go away and get some refreshment, Timothy Root and
Simeon Root put him upon it, and said they would bear him out in it; and
that when Medad came back, he said the committee was very much
displeased.

Sarah Edwards testified that at the time of the first sitting of the
committee of this church, she heard Timothy Root say, "I won't worship a
wig"; and on somebody's making answer that some respect was due to
some persons, he said again, "I won't worship a wig," repeating, "A wig,"
over many times, as appeared, with much of an air of disdain. Timothy
Root implicitly owned before the pastor and brethren that were with him
in the hearing of these things, that he said so, and that therein he had
respect to some of the committee, by saying that the reason he said so was
that he was afraid that the witnesses, when called in, could not exercise
themselves agreeable to themselves, being terrified with the fine clothes of
some of the committee, or to that purpose; although he denied that it was
with any disdain or contempt.

Caleb Sheldon says that Timothy Root, with another, were the first in
moving the young men to play leap frog in the time of the sitting of the
committee.

Moses Hannam testifies that while the committee of this church were
sitting the first time at the pastor's house, Timothy Root moved to others
to go away, and said to 'em, in the presence of a considerable number of
persons, "Come, we'll go away; do you think I'll be kept here for nothing?"

And speaking of the committee, said, "They are nothing but men molded up of a little dirt. I don't care a turd, or I don't care a fart, for any of them."

John Birge testifies and says as follows. At the time of the first sitting of the committee of this church, I, going along in the street on the backside of Mr. Edwards' lot, was surprised to see a considerable number of young men, that I supposed were called to attend the committee, at play in the lot: I there saw and heard one of the young men, whom I knew to be Timothy Root—as well as one could be known by his appearance and voice at such a distance—and heard him say to others, "I will go away, and if you were not devilish cowards, you would have gone away some time ago." And speaking of the committee or church, as I supposed, he said, "If they have any business with me, they may come to me; I ben't obliged to wait any longer on their arses, as I have done." He said thus, or to this purpose: "As to those foul expressions, I have a full remembrance of them."

An Humble Inquiry into the Rules of the Word of God, Concerning the Qualifications Requisite to a Complete Standing and Full Communion in the Visible Christian Church (1749)

Author's Preface

My appearing in this public manner on that side of the question, which is defended in the following sheets, will probably be surprising to many; as 'tis well known, that Mr. Stoddard, so great and eminent a divine, and my venerable predecessor in the pastoral office over the church in Northampton, as well as my own grandfather, publicly and strenuously appeared in opposition to the doctrine here maintained.

However, I hope, it will not be taken amiss, that I think as I do, merely because I herein differ from him, though so much my superior, and one whose name and memory I am under distinguishing obligations, on every account, to treat with great respect and honor. Especially may I justly expect, that it will not be charged on me as a crime, that I don't think in everything just as he did, since none more than he himself asserted this scriptural and Protestant maxim, that we ought to call no man on earth master, or make the authority of the greatest and holiest of mere men the ground of our belief of any doctrine in religion. Certainly we are not obliged to think any man infallible, who himself utterly disclaims infallibility. Very justly Mr. Stoddard observes in his *Appeal to the Learned* (p. 97), "All Protestants agree, that there is no infallibility at Rome; and I know nobody else pretends to any, since the apostles' days." And he insists, in his preface to his sermon on the same subject, that it argues no want of a due respect in us to our forefathers, for us to examine their opinions. . . .

Thus, in these very seasonable and apposite sayings, Mr. Stoddard, though dead, yet speaketh: and here (to apply them to my own case), he tells *me*, that I am not at all blamable, for not taking his principles on trust; that notwithstanding the high character justly belonging to him, I ought not to look on his principles as oracles, as though he could not miss it, as well as Nathan himself in his conjecture about building the house of God; nay, surely that I am, even to be commended, for examining his practice, and judging for myself; that it would ill become me, to do otherwise; that this would be no manifestation of humility, but rather show a baseness of spirit; that if I ben't capable to judge for myself in these matters, I am by no means fit to open the mysteries of the gospel; that if I should believe his principles, because he advanced them, I should be guilty of making him an idol. Also he tells his and my flock, with all others, that it ill becomes them, so to indulge their ease, as to neglect examining of received principles and practices; and that it's fit, mistakes in any particulars be rejected: that if in some things I differ in my judgment from him, it would be very unreasonable, on this account to make a great noise, as though I were bringing in innovations, and departing from the old way; that I may see cause to alter some practices of my grandfather and predecessor, without despising him, without priding myself in my wisdom, without apostasy, without despising the advantages God has given me, without inclination to superstition, and without making disturbance in the church of God; in short, that 'tis beyond him, to find out wherein the iniquity of my so doing lies; and that there is no reason why it should be turned as a reproach upon me. Thus, I think, he sufficiently vindicates my conduct in the present case, and warns all with whom I am concerned, not to be at all displeased with me, or to find the least fault with me, merely because I examine for myself, have a judgment of my own, and am for practicing in some particulars different from him, how positive soever he was that his judgment and practice were right. 'Tis reasonably hoped and expected, that they who have a great regard to his judgment, will impartially regard his judgment, and hearken to his admonition in these things.

I can seriously declare, that an affectation of making a show as if I were something wiser than that excellent person, is exceeding distant from me, and very far from having the least influence in my appearing to oppose, in this way of the press, an opinion which he so earnestly maintained and promoted. Sure I am, I have not affected to vary from his judgment, nor in the least been governed by a spirit of contradiction, neither indulged a cavilling humor, in remarking on any of his arguments or expressions.

I have formerly been of his opinion, which I imbibed from his books, even from my childhood, and have in my proceedings conformed to his practice; though never without some difficulties in my view, which I could not solve: yet, however, a distrust of my own understanding, and deference to the authority of so venerable a man, the seeming strength of some of his arguments, together with the success he had in his ministry, and his great reputation and influence, prevailed for a long time to bear down my scruples. But the difficulties and uneasiness on my mind increasing, as I became more studied in divinity, and as I improved in experience; this brought me to closer diligence and care to search the Scriptures, and more impartially to examine and weigh the arguments of my grandfather, and such other authors as I could get on his side of the question. By which means, after long searching, pondering, viewing and reviewing, I gained satisfaction, became fully settled in the opinion I now maintain, as in the discourse here offered to public view; and dared to proceed no further in a practice and administration inconsistent therewith: which brought me into peculiar circumstances, laying me under an inevitable necessity publicly to declare and maintain the opinion I was thus established in; as also to do it from the press, and so do it at this time without delay. 'Tis far from a pleasing circumstance of this publication, that 'tis against what my honored grandfather strenuously maintained, both from the pulpit and press. I can truly say, on account of this and some other considerations, 'tis what I engage in with the greatest reluctance, that ever I undertook any public service in my life. But the state of things with me is so ordered, by the sovereign disposal of the great Governor of the world, that my doing this appeared to me very necessary and altogether unavoidable. I am conscious, not only is the interest of religion concerned in this affair, but my own reputation, future usefulness, and my very subsistence, all seem to depend on my freely opening and defending myself, as to my principles, and agreeable conduct in my pastoral charge; and on my doing it from the press: in which way alone am I able to state and justify my opinion, to any purpose, before the country (which is full of noise, misrepresentations, and many censures concerning this affair) or even before my own people, as all would be fully sensible, if they knew the exact state of the case.

I have been brought to this necessity in divine providence, by such a situation of affairs and coincidence of circumstances and events, as I choose at present to be silent about; and which it is not needful, nor perhaps expedient for me to publish to the world.

One thing among others that caused me to go about this business with so much backwardness, was the fear of a bad improvement some ill-minded people might be ready, at this day, to make of the doctrine here defended: particularly that wild enthusiastical sort of people, who have of late gone into unjustifiable separations, even renouncing the ministers and churches of the land in general, under pretense of setting up a pure church. 'Tis well known, that I have heretofore publicly remonstrated, both from the pulpit and press, against very many of the notions and practices of this kind of people: and shall be very sorry if what I now offer to the public, should be any occasion of their encouraging or strengthening themselves in those notions and practices of theirs. To prevent which, I would now take occasion to declare, I am still of the same mind concerning them, that I have formerly manifested. I have the same opinion concerning the religion and inward experiences chiefly in vogue among them, as I had when I wrote my *Treatise on Religious Affections*, and when I wrote my observations and reflections on Mr. Brainerd's life.[1] I have no better opinion of their notion of a pure church by means of a spirit of discerning, their censorious outcries against the standing ministers and churches in general, their lay ordinations, their lay preachings, and public exhortings, and administering sacraments; their assuming, self-confident, contentious, uncharitable separating spirit; their going about the country, as sent by the Lord, to make proselytes; with their many other extravagant and wicked ways. My holding the doctrine that is defended in this discourse, is no argument of any change of my opinion concerning them; for when I

---

1. I.e., *An Account of the Life of the Late Reverend Mr. David Brainerd* (1749).

wrote those two books before mentioned, I was of the same mind concerning the qualifications of communicants at the Lord's Table, that I am of now.

However, 'tis not unlikely, that some will still exclaim against my principles, as being of the same pernicious tendency with those of the Separatists: to such I can only by a solemn protestation aver the sincerity of my aims, and the great care I have exercised to avoid whatsoever is erroneous, or might be in any respect mischievous. But as to my success in these my upright aims and endeavors, I must leave it to every reader to judge for himself, after he has carefully perused, and impartially considered the following discourse: which, considering the nature and importance of the subject, I hope, all serious readers will accompany with their earnest prayers to the Father of Lights, for his gracious direction and influence. And to him be glory in the churches by Christ Jesus. Amen.

Jonathan Edwards.

Part I: The Question Stated and Explained

The main question I would consider, and for the negative of which, I would offer some arguments in the following discourse, is this: whether, according to the rules of Christ, any ought to be admitted to the communion and privileges of members of the visible church of Christ in complete standing, but such as are in profession, and in the eye of the church's Christian judgment, godly or gracious persons?

When I speak of members of the visible church of Christ, *in complete standing*, I would be understood of those who are received as the proper immediate subjects of all the external privileges, Christ has appointed for the ordinary members of his church. I say *ordinary members*, in distinction from any peculiar privileges and honors of church officers and rulers. All allow, there are some that are in some respect in the church of God, who are not members in complete standing, in the sense that has been explained: all that acknowledge infant baptism, allow infants, who are proper subjects of baptism, and are baptized, to be in some sort members of the Christian church; yet none suppose them to be members in such standing as to be the proper immediate subjects of all ecclesiastical ordinances and privileges: but that some further qualifications are requisite in order to this, to be obtained, either in a course of nature, or by education, or by divine grace. And some who were baptized in infancy, even after they came to be adult, may yet remain for a season short of such a standing as has been spoken of; being destitute of sufficient knowledge, and perhaps some other qualifications, through the neglect of parents, or their own negligence, or otherwise; or because they carelessly neglect to qualify themselves for ecclesiastical privileges by making a public profession of the Christian faith, or owning the Christian covenant, or forbear to offer themselves as candidates for these privileges; and yet not be cast out of the church, or cease to be in any respect its members: this, I suppose, will also be generally allowed.

One thing mainly intended in the foregoing question is, whether any adult persons but such as are in profession and appearance endowed with Christian grace or piety, ought to be admitted to the Christian sacraments: particularly whether they ought to be admitted to the Lord's Supper; and, if they are such as were not baptized in infancy, ought to be admitted to baptism. Adult persons having those qualifications that oblige others to receive 'em as the proper immediate subjects of the Christian sacraments, is a main thing intended in the question, by being such as ought to be admitted to the communion and privileges of members of the visible church, in complete standing. There are many adult persons that by the allowance of all are in some respect within the church of God, who are not members in good standing, in this respect. There are many, for instance, that have not at present the qualifications proper to recommend 'em to admission to the Lord's Supper: there are many scandalous persons, who are under suspension. The late venerable Mr. Stoddard and many other great divines suppose, that even excommunicated persons are still members of the church of God: and some suppose, the worshippers of Baal in Israel, even those who were bred up such from their infancy, remained still members of the church of God: and very many Protestant divines suppose, that the members of the Church of Rome, though they are brought up and live continually in gross idolatry, and innumerable errors and superstitions that tend utterly to make void the gospel of Christ, still are in the visible church of Christ: yet, I suppose, no orthodox divines would hold these to be properly and regularly qualified for the Lord's Supper. It was therefore requisite, in the question before us, that a distinction should be made between members of the visible church *in general,* and members *in complete standing.*

It was also requisite, that such a distinction should be made in the question, to avoid a lengthening out this discourse exceedingly with needless questions and debates concerning the state of baptized infants; that is, needless as to my present purpose. Though I have no doubts about the doctrine of infant baptism; yet God's manner of dealing with such infants as are regularly dedicated to him in baptism, is a matter liable to great disputes and many controversies, and would require a large dissertation by itself to clear it up; which, as it would extend this discourse beyond all bounds, so it appears not necessary in order to a clear determination of the present question. The revelation of God's Word is much plainer and more express concerning adult persons, that act for themselves in religious matters, than concerning infants. The Scriptures were written for the sake of adult persons, or those that are capable of knowing what is written: 'tis to such the apostles speak in their epistles, and to such only does God speak throughout his Word: and the Scriptures especially speak for the sake of those, and about those to whom they speak. And therefore if the Word of God affords us light enough concerning those spoken of in the question, as I have stated it, clearly to determine the matter with respect to them, we need not wait till we see all doubts and controversies about baptized infants cleared and settled, before we pass a judgment with respect to the point in hand. The denominations, characters and descriptions, which we find given in Scripture to visible Christians, and to the visible church, are principally with an eye to the church of Christ in its adult state and proper standing. If anyone was about to describe that kind of birds called doves, it would be most proper to describe grown doves, and not young ones in the egg or nest, without wings or feathers: so if anyone should describe a palm tree or olive tree by their visible form and appearance, it would be presumed that they described those of these kinds of trees in their mature and proper state; and not as just peeping from the

ground, or as thunderstruck or blown down. And therefore . . . when . . .
I use such-like phrases as "visible saints," "members of the visible church,"
etc. I, for the most part, mean persons that are adult and in good standing.

The question is not, whether Christ has made converting grace or piety
itself the condition or rule of his people's admitting any to the privileges of
members in full communion with them: there is no one qualification of
mind, whatsoever, that Christ has properly made the term of this; not so
much as a common belief that Jesus is the Messiah, or a belief of the being
of a God. 'Tis the credible *profession* and *visibility* of these things, that is
the church's rule in this case. Christian piety or godliness may be a qualification requisite to communion in the Christian sacraments, just in the
same manner as a belief that Jesus is the Messiah, and the Scriptures the
Word of God, are requisite qualifications, and in the same manner as
some kind of repentance is a qualification requisite in one that has been
suspended for being grossly scandalous, in order to his coming again to
the Lord's Supper; and yet godliness itself not be properly the rule of the
church's proceeding, in like manner as such a belief and repentance, as I
have mentioned, are not their rule. 'Tis a visibility to the eye of a Christian
judgment, that is the rule of the church's proceeding in each of these cases.

There are two distinctions must be here observed. As, 1. we must
distinguish between such qualifications as are requisite to give a person a
right to ecclesiastical privileges in *foro ecclesiæ*, or a right to be admitted by
the church to those privileges, and those qualifications that are a proper
and good foundation for a man's own conduct in coming and offering
himself as a candidate for immediate admission to these privileges: there is
a difference between these. Thus, for instance, a *profession* of the belief of a
future state and of revealed religion, and some other things that are
internal and out of sight, and a visibility of these things to the eye of a
Christian judgment, is all, relating to these things, that is requisite to give
a man a right in *foro ecclesiæ*, or before the church; but it is the real existence
of these things that is what lays a proper and good foundation for his
making this profession, and so demanding these privileges. None will
suppose, that he has good and proper ground for such a conduct, who
don't believe [in] another world, nor believe the Bible to be the Word of
God. And then,

2. We must distinguish between that which nextly brings an obligation on a man's conscience to seek admission to a Christian ordinance, and that which is a good foundation for the dictate of an enlightened well-informed conscience, and so is properly a solid foundation of a right in him to act thus. Certainly this distinction does really take place among mankind in innumerable cases. The dictates of men's consciences are what do bring them under a next or most immediate obligation to act: but 'tis that which is a good foundation for such a dictate of an enlightened conscience, that alone is a solid foundation of a right in him so to act. A believing the doctrine of the Trinity *with all the heart*, in some sense (let us suppose a moral sense) is one thing requisite in order to a person's having a solid foundation of a right in him to go and demand baptism in the name of the Trinity: but his best judgment or dictate of his conscience, concerning his believing this doctrine with this sincerity, or with all his heart, may be sufficient to bring an obligation on his conscience. Again, when a delinquent has been convicted of scandal, 'tis repentance in some respect sincere (suppose a moral sincerity) that is the proper foundation of a right in him to offer himself for forgiveness and restoration: but 'tis the dictate of his conscience or his best judgment concerning his sincerity, that is the thing which immediately obliges him to offer himself. 'Tis repentance itself, that is the proper qualification fundamental of his right, and what he can't have a proper right without; for though he may be deceived, and think he has real repentance when he has not, yet he has not properly a right to be deceived; and perhaps deceit in such cases is always owing to something blamable, or the influence of some corrupt principle: but yet his best judgment brings him under obligation. In the same manner, and no otherwise, I suppose that Christian grace itself is a qualification requisite in order to a proper solid ground of a right in a person to come to the Christian sacraments. But of this I may say something more when I come to answer objections.

When I speak, in the question, of being godly or gracious in the eye of a Christian judgment, by "Christian judgment" I intend something further than a kind of mere negative charity, implying that we forbear to censure and condemn a man, because we don't know but that he may be godly, and therefore forbear to proceed on the foot of such a censure or judgment in

our treatment of him: as we would kindly entertain a stranger, not knowing but in so doing we entertain an angel or precious saint of God. But
I mean a positive judgment, founded on some positive appearance, or
visibility, some outward manifestations that ordinarily render the thing
probable. There is a difference between suspending our judgment, or
forbearing to condemn, or having some hope that possibly the thing may
be so, and so hoping the best; and a positive judgment in favor of a person.
For an having some hope, only implies that a man is not in utter despair of
a thing, though his prevailing opinion may be otherwise, or he may
suspend his opinion. Though we can't know a man believes that Jesus is
the Messiah, yet we expect some positive manifestation or visibility of it,
to be a ground of our charitable judgment: so I suppose the case is here.

When I speak of Christian judgment, I mean a judgment wherein men
do properly exercise reason, and have their reason under the due influence
of love and other Christian principles; which don't blind reason, but
regulate its exercises; being not contrary to reason, though they be very
contrary to censoriousness or unreasonable niceness and rigidness.

I say "in the eye of the church's Christian judgment," because 'tis
properly a visibility to the eye of the public charity, and not of a private
judgment, that gives a person a right to be received as a visible saint by the
public. If any are known to be persons of an honest character, and appear
to be of good understanding in the doctrines of Christianity, and particularly those doctrines that teach the grand condition of salvation, and the
nature of true saving religion, and publicly and seriously profess the great
and main things wherein the essence of true religion or godliness consists,
and their conversation is agreeable; this justly recommends 'em to the
good opinion of the public, whatever suspicions and fears any particular
person, either the minister, or some other, may entertain, from what he in
particular has observed, perhaps from the manner of his expressing himself in giving an account of his experiences, or an obscurity in the order
and method of his experiences, etc. The minister, in receiving him to the
communion of the church, is to act as a public officer, and in behalf of the
public society, and not merely for himself, and therefore is to be governed,
in acting, by a proper visibility of godliness in the eye of the public.

'Tis not my design, in holding the negative of the foregoing question, to affirm, that all who are regularly admitted as members of the visible church in complete standing, ought to be believed to be godly or gracious persons, when taken *collectively*, or considered in the gross, by the judgment of any person or society. This may not be, and yet each person taken singly may visibly be a gracious person to the eye of the judgment of Christians in general. These two are not the same thing, but vastly diverse; and the latter may be, and yet not the former. If we should know so much of a thousand persons one after another, and from what we observed in them should have a prevailing opinion concerning each one of them, singly taken, that they were indeed pious, and think the judgment we passed, when we consider each judgment apart, to be right; it won't follow, when we consider the whole company collectively, that we shall have so high an opinion of our own judgment, as to think it probable, there was not one erroneous judgment in the whole thousand. We all have innumerable judgments about one thing or other, concerning religious, moral, secular, and philosophical affairs, concerning past, present and future matters, reports, facts, persons, things, etc. etc. And concerning all the many thousand dictates of judgment that we have, we think 'em every one right, taken singly; for if there was any one that we thought wrong, it would not be our judgment; and yet there is no man, unless he is stupidly foolish, who when he considers all in the gross, will say he thinks that every opinion he is of, concerning all persons and things whatsoever, important and trifling, is right, without the least error. But the more clearly to illustrate this matter, as it relates to visibility, or probable appearances of holiness in professors: supposing it had been found by experience concerning precious stones, that such and such external marks were probable signs of a diamond, and it is made evident, by putting together a great number of experiments, that the probability is as ten to one, and no more nor less; i.e. that, take one time with another, there is one in ten of the stones that have these marks (and no visible signs to the contrary) proves a true diamond, and no more; then it will follow, that when I find a particular stone with these marks, and nothing to the contrary, there is a probability of ten to one, concerning that stone, that it is a diamond; and so concerning each stone that I find with these marks: but if we take ten of these together, 'tis as probable as not, that some one of the ten is spurious;

because, if it were not as likely as not, that one in ten is false, or if taking one ten with another, there were not one in ten that was false, then the probability of those, that have these marks, being true diamonds, would be more than ten to one, contrary to the supposition; because that is what we mean by a probability of ten to one, that they are not false, viz. that take one ten with another there will be one false stone among them, and no more. Hence if we take a hundred such stones together, the probability will be just ten to one, that there is one false among them; and as likely as not that there are ten false ones in the whole hundred: and the probability of the individuals must be much greater than ten to one, even a probability of more than a hundred to one, in order to its making it probable that every one is true. 'Tis an easy mathematical demonstration. Hence the negative of the foregoing question by no means implies a pretense of any scheme, that shall be effectual to keep all hypocrites out of the church, and for the establishing in that sense a pure church.

When it is said, those who are admitted, etc. ought to be by profession "godly" or "gracious" persons, 'tis not meant, they should merely *profess* or *say* that they are converted or are gracious persons, that they *know* so, or *think* so; but that they profess the great things wherein Christian piety consists, viz. a supreme respect to God, faith in Christ, etc. Indeed 'tis necessary, as men would keep a good conscience, that they should think that these things are in them, which they profess to be in them; otherwise they are guilty of the horrid wickedness of willfully making a lying profession. Hence 'tis supposed to be necessary, in order to men's regularly and with a good conscience coming into communion with the church of Christ in the Christian sacraments, that they themselves should suppose the essential things, belonging to Christian piety, to be in them.

It don't belong to the present question, to consider and determine what the nature of Christian piety is, or wherein it consists: this question may be properly determined, and the determination demonstrated, without entering into any controversies about the nature of conversion, etc. Nor does an asserting the negative of the question determine anything how particular the profession of godliness ought to be, but only that the more essential things, which belong to it, ought to be professed. Nor is it determined, but that the public professions made on occasion of persons' admission to the Lord's Supper, in some of our churches, who yet go upon that principle, that persons need not esteem themselves truly gracious in order to a coming conscientiously and properly to the Lord's Supper; I say, 'tis not determined but that some of these professions are sufficient, if those that made them were taught to use the words, and others to understand them, in no other than their proper meaning, and principle and custom had not established a meaning very diverse from it, or perhaps an use of the words without any distinct and clear determinate meaning.

A Careful and Strict Inquiry into the Modern Prevailing Notions of that Freedom of the Will, Which Is Supposed to Be Essential to Moral Agency, Virtue and Vice, Reward and Punishment, Praise and Blame (1754)

Author's Preface

. . . That the difference of the opinions of those, who in their general scheme of divinity agree with these two noted men, Calvin, and Arminius, is a thing there is often occasion to speak of, is what the practice of the latter, itself confesses; who are often, in their discourses and writings, taking notice of the supposed absurd and pernicious opinions of the former sort. . . . Nevertheless, at first I had thoughts of carefully avoiding the use of the appellation "Arminian" in this treatise. But I soon found I should be put to great difficulty by it; and that my discourse would be so encumbered with an often repeated circumlocution, instead of a name, which would express the thing intended, as well and better, that I altered my purpose. And therefore I must ask the excuse of such as are apt to be offended with things of this nature, that I have so freely used the term "Arminian" in the following discourse. I profess it to be without any design, to stigmatize persons of any sort with a name of reproach, or at all to make them appear more odious. If when I had occasion to speak of those divines who are commonly called by this name, I had, instead of styling them Arminians, called them "these men," as Dr. Whitby does Calvinistic divines; it probably would not have been taken any better, or thought to show a better temper, or more good manners. I have done as I would be done by, in this matter. However the term "Calvinist" is in these days, among most, a term of greater reproach than the term "Arminian"; yet I should not take it at all amiss, to be called a Calvinist, for distinction's sake: though I utterly disclaim a dependence on Calvin, or believing the doctrines which I hold, because he believed and taught them; and cannot justly be charged with believing in everything just as he taught. . . .

Part I. Wherein Are Explained and Stated Various Terms and Things Belonging to the Subject of the Ensuing Discourse

Section 1. Concerning the Nature of the Will

It may possibly be thought, that there is no great need of going about to define or describe the "will"; this word being generally as well understood as any other words we can use to explain it: and so perhaps it would be, had not philosophers, metaphysicians and polemic divines brought the matter into obscurity by the things they have said of it. But since it is so, I think it may be of some use, and will tend to the greater clearness in the following discourse, to say a few things concerning it.

And therefore I observe, that the will (without any metaphysical refining) is plainly, that by which the mind chooses anything. The faculty of the will is that faculty or power or principle of mind by which it is capable of choosing: an act of the will is the same as an act of choosing or choice.

If any think 'tis a more perfect definition of the will, to say, that it is that by which the soul either chooses or refuses; I am content with it: though I think that 'tis enough to say, it's that by which the soul chooses: for in every act of will whatsoever, the mind chooses one thing rather than another; it chooses something rather than the contrary, or rather than the want or nonexistence of that thing. So in every act of refusal, the mind chooses the absence of the thing refused; the positive and the negative are set before the mind for its choice, and it chooses the negative; and the mind's making its choice in that case is properly the act of the will: the will's determining between the two is a voluntary determining; but that is the same thing as making a choice. So that whatever names we call the act of the will by—choosing, refusing, approving, disapproving, liking, disliking, embracing, rejecting, determining, directing, commanding, forbidding, inclining or being averse, a being pleased or displeased with—all may be reduced to this of choosing. For the soul to act voluntarily, is evermore to act electively.

Mr. Locke[1] says, "The will signifies nothing but a power or ability to prefer or choose." And in the foregoing page says, "The word 'preferring' seems best to express the act of volition"; but adds, that "it does it not precisely; for (says he) though a man would prefer flying to walking, yet who can say he ever wills it?" But the instance he mentions don't prove that there is anything else in "willing" but merely "preferring": for it should be considered what is the next and immediate object of the will, with respect to a man's walking, or any other external action; which is not his being removed from one place to another; on the earth, or through the air; these are remoter objects of preference; but such or such an immediate exertion of himself. The thing nextly chosen or preferred when a man wills to walk, is not his being removed to such a place where he would be, but such an exertion and motion of his legs and feet, etc. in order to it. And his willing such an alteration in his body in the present moment, is nothing else but his choosing or preferring such an alteration in his body at such a moment, or his liking it better than the forbearance of it. And God has so made and established the human nature, the soul being united to a body in proper state, that the soul preferring or choosing such an immediate exertion or alteration of the body, such an alteration instantaneously follows. There is nothing else in the actings of my mind, that I am conscious of while I walk, but only my preferring or choosing, through successive moments, that there should be such alterations of my external sensations and motions; together with a concurring habitual expectation that it will be so; having ever found by experience, that on such an immediate preference, such sensations and motions do actually instantaneously, and constantly arise. But it is not so in the case of flying: though a man may be said remotely to choose or prefer flying; yet he don't choose or prefer, incline to

1. John Locke (1632–1704), *An Essay Concerning Human Understanding* (London, 1690; 7th ed. 1716), Bk. 2, ch. 21, no. 17.

or desire, under circumstances in view, any immediate exertion of the members of his body in order to it; because he has no expectation that he should obtain the desired end by any such exertion; and he don't prefer or incline to any bodily exertion or effort under this apprehended circumstance, of its being wholly in vain. So that if we carefully distinguish the proper objects of the several acts of the will, it will not appear by this, and suchlike instances, that there is any difference between "volition" and "preference"; or that a man's choosing, liking best, or being best pleased with a thing, are not the same with his willing that thing; as they seem to be according to those general and more natural notions of men, according to which language is formed. Thus an act of the will is commonly expressed by its pleasing a man to do thus or thus; and a man's doing as he wills, and doing as he pleases, are the same thing in common speech. . . . I trust it will be allowed by all, that in every act of will there is an act of choice; that in every volition there is a preference, or a prevailing inclination of the soul, whereby the soul, at that instant, is out of a state of perfect indifference, with respect to the direct object of the volition. So that in every act, or going forth of the will, there is some preponderation of the mind or inclination, one way rather than another; and the soul had rather have or do one thing than another, or than not to have or do that thing; and that there, where there is absolutely no preferring or choosing, but a perfect continuing equilibrium, there is no volition.

Section 2. Concerning the Determination of the Will

By "determining the will," if the phrase be used with any meaning, must be intended, causing that the act of the will or choice should be thus, and not otherwise: and the will is said to be determined, when, in consequence of some action, or influence, its choice is directed to, and fixed upon a particular object. As when we speak of the determination of motion, we mean causing the motion of the body to be such a way, or in such a direction, rather than another. . . .

With respect to that grand inquiry, what determines the will, it would be very tedious and unnecessary at present to enumerate and examine all the various opinions, which have been advanced concerning this matter; nor is it needful that I should enter into a particular disquisition of all points debated in disputes on that question, whether the will always follows the last dictate of the understanding. It is sufficient to my present purpose to say, it is that motive, which, as it stands in the view of the mind, is the strongest, that determines the will.—But it may be necessary that I should a little explain my meaning in this.

By "motive," I mean the whole of that which moves, excites or invites the mind to volition, whether that be one thing singly, or many things conjunctly. Many particular things may concur and unite their strength to induce the mind; and when it is so, all together are as it were one complex motive. And when I speak of the "strongest motive," I have respect to the strength of the whole that operates to induce to a particular act of volition, whether that be the strength of one thing alone, or of many together.

Whatever is a motive, in this sense, must be something that is extant in the view or apprehension of the understanding, or perceiving faculty. Nothing can induce or invite the mind to will or act anything, any further than it is perceived, or is some way or other in the mind's view; for what is wholly unperceived, and perfectly out of the mind's view, can't affect the mind at all. 'Tis most evident, that nothing is in the mind, or reaches it, or takes any hold of it, any otherwise than as it is perceived or thought of.

And I think it must also be allowed by all, that everything that is properly called a motive, excitement or inducement to a perceiving willing agent, has some sort and degree of tendency, or advantage to move or excite the will, previous to the effect, or to the act of the will excited. This previous tendency of the motive is what I call the "strength" of the motive. That motive which has a less degree of previous advantage or tendency to move the will, or that appears less inviting, as it stands in the view of the mind, is what I call a "weaker motive." On the contrary, that which appears most inviting, and has, by what appears concerning it to the understanding or apprehension, the greatest degree of previous tendency to excite and induce the choice, is what I call the "strongest motive." And in this sense, I suppose the will is always determined by the strongest motive.

Things that exist in the view of the mind, have their strength, tendency or advantage to move or excite its will, from many things appertaining to the nature and circumstances of the thing viewed, the nature and circumstances of the mind that views, and the degree and manner of its view; which it would perhaps be hard to make a perfect enumeration of. But so much I think may be determined in general, without room for controversy, that whatever is perceived or apprehended by an intelligent and voluntary agent, which has the nature and influence of a motive to volition or choice, is considered or viewed *as good;* nor has it any tendency to invite or engage the election of the soul in any further degree than it appears such. For to say otherwise, would be to say, that things that appear have a tendency by the appearance they make, to engage the mind to elect them, some other way than by their appearing eligible to it; which is absurd. And therefore it must be true, in some sense, that the will always is as the greatest apparent good is. . . .

When I say, the will is as the greatest apparent good is, or (as I have explained it) that volition has always for its object the thing which appears most agreeable; it must be carefully observed, to avoid confusion and needless objection, that I speak of the direct and immediate object of the act of volition; and not some object that the act of will has not an immediate, but only an indirect and remote respect to. Many acts of volition have some remote relation to an object, that is different from the thing most immediately willed and chosen. Thus, when a drunkard has his liquor before him, and he has to choose whether to drink it; or no; the proper and immediate objects, about which his present volition is conversant, and between which his choice now decides, are his own acts, in drinking the liquor, or letting it alone; and this will certainly be done according to what, in the present view of his mind, taken in the whole of it, is most agreeable to him. If he chooses or wills to drink it, and not to let it alone; then this action, as it stands in the view of his mind, with all that belongs to its appearance there, is more agreeable and pleasing than letting it alone.

But the objects to which this act of volition may relate more remotely, and between which his choice may determine more indirectly, are the present pleasure the man expects by drinking, and the future misery which he judges will be the consequence of it: he may judge that this future misery, when it comes, will be more disagreeable and unpleasant, than refraining from drinking now would be. But these two things are not the proper objects that the act of volition spoken of is nextly conversant about. For the act of will spoken of is concerning present drinking or forbearing to drink. If he wills to drink, then drinking is the proper object of the act of his will; and drinking, on some account or other, now appears most agreeable to him, and suits him best. If he chooses to refrain, then refraining is the immediate object of his will, and is most pleasing to him. If in the choice he makes in the case, he prefers a present pleasure to a future advantage, which he judges will be greater when it comes; then a lesser present pleasure appears more agreeable to him than a greater advantage at a distance. If on the contrary a future advantage is preferred, then that appears most agreeable, and suits him best. And so still the present volition is as the greatest apparent good at present is. . . .

Section 3. Concerning the Meaning of the Terms Necessity, Impossibility, Inability, Etc.; and of Contingence

. . . The word "necessary," as used in common speech, is a relative term; and relates to some supposed opposition made to the existence of the thing spoken of, which is overcome, or proves in vain to hinder or alter it. That is necessary, in the original and proper sense of the word, which is, or will be, notwithstanding all supposable opposition. To say, that a thing is necessary, is the same thing as to say, that it is impossible [it] should not be: but the word "impossible" is manifestly a relative term, and has reference to supposed power exerted to bring a thing to pass, which is insufficient for the effect; as the word "unable" is relative, and has relation to ability or endeavor which is insufficient; and as the word "irresistible" is relative, and has always reference to resistance which is made, or may be made to some force or power tending to an effect, and is insufficient to withstand the power, or hinder the effect. The common notion of necessity and impossibility implies something that frustrates endeavor or desire. . . .

As the word "necessity," in its vulgar and common use, is relative, and has always reference to some supposable insufficient opposition; so when we speak of anything as necessary *to us*, it is with relation to some supposable opposition of our wills, or some voluntary exertion or effort of ours to the contrary. For we don't properly make opposition to an event, any otherwise than as we voluntarily oppose it. Things are said to be what must be, or necessarily are, *as to us*, when they are, or will be, though we desire or endeavor the contrary, or try to prevent or remove their existence: but such opposition of ours always either consists in, or implies opposition of our wills.

'Tis manifest that all suchlike words and phrases, as vulgarly used, are used and accepted in this manner. A thing is said to be necessary, when we can't help it, let us do what we will. So anything is said to be impossible to us, when we would do it, or would have it brought to pass, and endeavor it; or at least may be supposed to desire and seek it; but all our desires and endeavors are, or would be in vain. And that is said to be irresistible, which overcomes all our opposition, resistance, and endeavor to the contrary. And we are to be said unable to do a thing, when our supposable desires and endeavors to do it are insufficient. . . .

It appears from what has been said, that these terms "necessary," "impossible," etc. are often used by philosophers and metaphysicians in a sense quite diverse from their common use and original signification: for they apply them to many cases in which no opposition is supposed or supposable. Thus they use them with respect to God's existence before the creation of the world, when there was no other being but he: so with regard to many of the dispositions and acts of the divine Being, such as his loving himself, his loving righteousness, hating sin, etc. So they apply these terms to many cases of the inclinations and actions of created intelligent beings, angels and men; wherein all opposition of the will is shut out and denied, in the very supposition of the case.

Metaphysical or philosophical necessity is nothing different from their certainty. I speak not now of the certainty of knowledge, but the certainty that is in things themselves, which is the foundation of the certainty of the knowledge of them; or that wherein lies the ground of the infallibility of the proposition which affirms them.

What is sometimes given as the definition of philosophical necessity, namely, that by which a thing cannot but be, or whereby it cannot be otherwise, fails of being a proper explanation of it, on two accounts: first, the words "can" or "cannot" need explanation as much as the word "necessity"; and the former may as well be explained by the latter, as the latter by the former. Thus, if anyone asked us what we mean, when we say, a thing cannot but be, we might explain ourselves by saying, we mean, it must necessarily be so; as well as explain necessity, by saying, it is that by which a thing cannot but be. And secondly, this definition is liable to the forementioned great inconvenience: the words "cannot" or "unable" are properly relative, and have relation to power exerted, or that may be exerted, in order to the thing spoken of; to which, as I have now observed, the word "necessity," as used by philosophers, has no reference.

Philosophical necessity is really nothing else than the full and fixed connection between the things signified by the subject and predicate of a proposition, which affirms something to be true. When there is such a connection, then the thing affirmed in the proposition is necessary, in a philosophical sense; whether any opposition, or contrary effort be supposed, or supposable in the case, or no. When the subject and predicate of the proposition, which affirms the existence of anything, either substance, quality, act or circumstance, have a full and certain connection, then the existence or being of that thing is said to be necessary in a metaphysical sense. And in this sense I use the word "necessity," in the following discourse, when I endeavor to prove that necessity is not inconsistent with liberty. . . .

Section 4. Of the Distinction of Natural and Moral Necessity, and Inability

That necessity which has been explained, consisting in an infallible connection of the things signified by the subject and predicate of a proposition, as intelligent beings are the subjects of it, is distinguished into moral and natural necessity.

I shall not now stand to inquire whether this distinction be a proper and perfect distinction; but shall only explain how these two sorts of necessity are understood, as the terms are sometimes used, and as they are used in the following discourse.

The phrase "moral necessity" is used variously: sometimes 'tis used for a necessity of moral obligation. So we say, a man is under necessity, when he is under bonds of duty and conscience, which he can't be discharged from. So the word "necessity" is often used for great obligation in point of interest. Sometimes by "moral necessity" is meant that apparent connection of things, which is the ground of moral evidence; and so is distinguished from absolute necessity, or that sure connection of things, that is a foundation for infallible certainty. In this sense, "moral necessity" signifies much the same as that high degree of probability, which is ordinarily sufficient to satisfy, and be relied upon by mankind, in their conduct and behavior in the world, as they would consult their own safety and interest, and treat others properly as members of society. And sometimes by "moral necessity" is meant that necessity of connection and consequence, which arises from such *moral causes*, as the strength of inclination, or motives, and the connection which there is in many cases between these, and such certain volitions and actions. And it is in this sense, that I use the phrase, "moral necessity" in the following discourse.

By "natural necessity," as applied to men, I mean such necessity as men are under through the force of natural causes; as distinguished from what are called moral causes, such as habits and dispositions of the heart, and moral motives and inducements. Thus men placed in certain circumstances, are the subjects of particular sensations by necessity: they feel pain when their bodies are wounded; they see the objects presented before them in a clear light, when their eyes are opened: so they assent to the truth of certain propositions, as soon as the terms are understood; as that two and two make four, that black is not white, that two parallel lines can never cross one another: so by a natural necessity men's bodies move downwards, when there is nothing to support them.

But here several things may be noted concerning these two kinds of necessity.

1. Moral necessity may be as absolute, as natural necessity. That is, the effect may be as perfectly connected with its moral cause, as a naturally necessary effect is with its natural cause. Whether the will in every case is necessarily determined by the strongest motive, or whether the will ever makes any resistance to such a motive, or can ever oppose the strongest

present inclination, or not; if that matter should be controverted, yet I suppose none will deny, but that, in some cases, a previous bias and inclination, or the motive presented, may be so powerful, that the act of the will may be certainly and indissolubly connected therewith. When motives or previous bias are very strong, all will allow that there is some difficulty in going against them. And if they were yet stronger, the difficulty would be still greater. And therefore, if more were still added to their strength, to a certain degree, it would make the difficulty so great, that it would be wholly impossible to surmount it; for this plain reason, because whatever power men may be supposed to have to surmount difficulties, yet that power is not infinite; and so goes not beyond certain limits. If a man can surmount ten degrees of difficulty of this kind, with twenty degrees of strength, because the degrees of strength are beyond the degrees of difficulty; yet if the difficulty be increased to thirty, or an hundred, or a thousand degrees, and his strength not also increased, his strength will be wholly insufficient to surmount the difficulty. As therefore it must be allowed, that there may be such a thing as a sure and perfect connection between moral causes and effects; so this only is what I call by the name of "moral necessity."

2. When I use this distinction of moral and natural necessity, I would not be understood to suppose, that if anything comes to pass by the former kind of necessity, the nature of things is not concerned in it, as well as in the latter. I don't mean to determine, that when a moral habit or motive is so strong, that the act of the will infallibly follows, this is not owing to the nature of things. But these are the names that these two kinds of necessity have usually been called by; and they must be distinguished by some names or other; for there is a distinction or difference between them, that is very important in its consequences: which difference does not lie so much in the nature of the connection, as in the two terms connected. The cause with which the effect is connected, is of a particular kind; viz. that which is of a moral nature; either some previous habitual disposition, or some motive exhibited to the understanding. And the effect is also of a particular kind; being likewise of a moral nature; consisting in some inclination or volition of the soul, or voluntary action. . . .

What has been said of natural and moral necessity, may serve to explain what is intended by natural and moral *inability*. We are said to be *naturally* unable to do a thing, when we can't do it if we will, because what is most commonly called nature don't allow of it, or because of some impeding defect or obstacle that is extrinsic to the will; either in the faculty of understanding, constitution of body, or external objects. *Moral* inability consists not in any of these things; but either in the want of inclination; or the strength of a contrary inclination; or the want of sufficient motives in view, to induce and excite the act of the will, or the strength of apparent motives to the contrary. Or both these may be resolved into one; and it may be said in one word, that moral inability consists in the opposition or want of inclination. For when a person is unable to will or choose such a thing, through a defect of motives, or prevalence of contrary motives, 'tis the same thing as his being unable through the want of an inclination, or the prevalence of a contrary inclination, in such circumstances, and under the influence of such views.

To give some instances of this moral inability: A woman of great honor and chastity may have a moral inability to prostitute herself to her slave. A child of great love and duty to his parents, may be unable to be willing to kill his father. A very lascivious man, in case of certain opportunities and temptations, and in the absence of such and such restraints, may be unable to forbear gratifying his lust. A drunkard, under such and such circumstances, may be unable to forbear taking of strong drink. A very malicious man may be unable to exert benevolent acts to an enemy, or to desire his prosperity: yea, some may be so under the power of a vile disposition, that they may be unable to love those who are most worthy of their esteem and affection. A strong habit of virtue and great degree of holiness may cause a moral inability to love wickedness in general, may render a man unable to take complacence in wicked persons or things; or to choose a wicked life, and prefer it to a virtuous life. And on the other hand, a great degree of habitual wickedness may lay a man under an inability to love and choose holiness; and render him utterly unable to love an infinitely holy Being, or to choose and cleave to him as his chief good. . . .

Section 5. Concerning the Notion of Liberty, and of Moral Agency

The plain and obvious meaning of the words "freedom" and "liberty," in common speech, is power, opportunity, or advantage, that anyone has, to do as he pleases. Or in other words, his being free from hindrance or impediment in the way of doing, or conducting in any respect, as he wills. And the contrary to liberty, whatever name we call that by, is a person's being hindered or unable to conduct as he will, or being necessitated to do otherwise.

If this which I have mentioned be the meaning of the word "liberty," in the ordinary use of language; as I trust that none that has ever learned to talk, and is unprejudiced, will deny; then it will follow, that in propriety of speech, neither liberty, nor its contrary, can properly be ascribed to any being or thing, but that which has such a faculty, power or property, as is called "will." For that which is possessed of no such thing as will, can't have any power or opportunity of doing according to its will, nor be necessitated to act contrary to its will, nor be restrained from acting agreeably to it. And therefore to talk of liberty, or the contrary, as belonging to the very will itself, is not to speak good sense; if we judge of sense, and nonsense, by the original and proper signification of words. For the will itself is not an agent that has a will: the power of choosing, itself, has not a power of choosing. That which has the power of volition or choice is the man or the soul, and not the power of volition itself. And he that has the liberty of doing according to his will, is the agent or doer who is possessed of the will; and not the will which he is possessed of. We say with propriety, that a bird let loose has power and liberty to fly; but not that the bird's power of flying has a power and liberty of flying. To be free is the property of an agent, who is possessed of powers and faculties, as much as to be cunning, valiant, bountiful, or zealous. But these qualities are the properties of men or persons; and not the properties of properties.

There are two things that are contrary to this which is called liberty in common speech. One is *constraint*; the same is otherwise called force, compulsion, and coaction; which is a person's being necessitated to do a thing *contrary* to his will. The other is *restraint*; which is his being hindered, and not having power to do *according* to his will. But that which has no will, can't be the subject of these things.—I need say the less on this head, Mr. Locke having set the same thing forth, with so great clearness, in his *Essay on the Human Understanding*.

But one thing more I would observe concerning what is vulgarly called liberty; namely, that power and opportunity for one to do and conduct as he will, or according to his choice, is all that is meant by it; without taking into the meaning of the word, anything of the cause or original of that choice; or at all considering how the person came to have such a volition; whether it was caused by some external motive, or internal habitual bias; whether it was determined by some internal antecedent volition, or whether it happened without a cause; whether it was necessarily connected with something foregoing, or not connected. Let the person come by his volition or choice how he will, yet, if he is able, and there is nothing in the way to hinder his pursuing and executing his will, the man is fully and perfectly free, according to the primary and common notion of freedom.

What has been said may be sufficient to show what is meant by liberty, according to the common notions of mankind, and in the usual and primary acceptation of the word: but the word, as used by Arminians, Pelagians and others, who oppose the Calvinists, has an entirely different signification. These several things belong to their notion of liberty: 1. That it consists in a self-determining power in the will, or a certain sovereignty the will has over itself, and its own acts, whereby it determines its own volitions; so as not to be dependent in its determinations, on any cause without itself, nor determined by anything prior to its own acts. 2. Indifference belongs to liberty in their notion of it, or that the mind, previous to the act of volition be, *in equilibrio*. 3. Contingence is another thing that belongs and is essential to it; not in the common acceptation of the word, as that has been already explained, but as opposed to all necessity, or any fixed and certain connection with some previous ground or reason of its existence. They suppose the essence of liberty so much to consist in these things, that unless the will of man be free in this sense, he has no real freedom, how much soever he may be at liberty to act according to his will. . . .

Part II. Wherein It Is Considered Whether There Is or Can Be Any
Such Sort of Freedom of Will, as That Wherein Arminians Place the
Essence of the Liberty of All Moral Agents; and Whether Any Such
Thing Ever Was or Can Be Conceived Of

Section 1. Showing the Manifest Inconsistence of the Arminian Notion
of Liberty of Will, Consisting in the Will's Self-Determining Power

Having taken notice of those things which may be necessary to be observed, concerning the meaning of the principal terms and phrases made
use of in controversies concerning human liberty, and particularly observed what liberty is, according to the common language, and general
apprehension of mankind, and what it is as understood and maintained by
Arminians; I proceed to consider the Arminian notion of the freedom of
the will, and the supposed necessity of it in order to moral agency, or in
order to anyone's being capable of virtue or vice, and properly the subject
of command or counsel, praise or blame, promises or threatenings, rewards or punishments; or whether that which has been described, as the
thing meant by liberty in common speech, be not sufficient, and the only
liberty, which makes, or can make anyone a moral agent, and so properly
the subject of these things. In this part, I shall consider whether any such
thing be possible or conceivable, as that freedom of will which Arminians
insist on; and shall inquire whether any such sort of liberty be necessary to
moral agency, etc. in the next part.

And first of all, I shall consider the notion of a self-determining power
in the will: wherein, according to the Arminians, does most essentially
consist the will's freedom; and shall particularly inquire, whether it be not
plainly absurd, and a manifest inconsistence, to suppose that the will itself
determines all the free acts of the will.

Here I shall not insist on the great impropriety of such phrases, and
ways of speaking, as "the will's determining itself"; because actions are to
be ascribed to agents, and not properly to the powers of agents; which
improper way of speaking leads to many mistakes, and much confusion, as
Mr. Locke observes. . . . So when we say, valor fights courageously, we
mean, the man who is under the influence of valor fights courageously.
When we say, love seeks the object loved, we mean, the person loving

seeks that object. When we say, the understanding discerns, we mean the soul in the exercise of that faculty. So when it is said, the will decides or determines, the meaning must be, that the person in the exercise of a power of willing and choosing, or the soul acting voluntarily, determines.

Therefore, if the will determines all its own free acts, the soul determines all the free acts of the will in the exercise of a power of willing and choosing; or, which is the same thing, it determines them of choice; it determines its own acts by choosing its own acts. If the will determines the will, then choice orders and determines the choice: and acts of choice are subject to the decision, and follow the conduct of other acts of choice. And therefore if the will determines all its own free acts, then every free act of choice is determined by a preceding act of choice, choosing that act. And if that preceding act of the will or choice be also a free act, then by these principles, in this act too, the will is self-determined; that is, this, in like manner, is an act that the soul voluntarily chooses; or which is the same thing, it is an act determined still by a preceding act of the will, choosing that. And the like may again be observed of the last mentioned act. Which brings us directly to a contradiction: for it supposes an act of the will preceding the first act in the whole train, directing and determining the rest; or a free act of the will, before the first free act of the will. Or else we must come at last to an act of the will, determining the consequent acts, wherein the will is not self-determined, and so is not a free act, in this notion of freedom: but if the first act in the train, determining and fixing the rest, be not free, none of them all can be free; as is manifest at first view, but shall be demonstrated presently.

If the will, which we find governs the members of the body, and determines and commands their motions and actions, does also govern itself, and determine its own motions and acts, it doubtless determines them the same way, even by antecedent volitions. The will determines which way the hands and feet shall move, by an act of volition or choice: and there is no other way of the will's determining, directing or commanding anything at all. Whatsoever the will commands, it commands by an act of the will. And if it has itself under its command, and determines itself in its own actions, it doubtless does it the same way that it determines other things which are under its command. So that if the freedom of the will consists in this, that it has itself and its own actions under its command and direction, and its own volitions are determined by itself, it will follow, that every free volition arises from another antecedent volition, directing and commanding that: and if that *directing* volition be also free, in that also the will is [self-] determined; that is to say, that directing volition is determined by another going before that; and so on, till we come to the first volition in the whole series: and if that first volition be free, and the will self-determined in it, then that is determined by another volition preceding that. Which is a contradiction; because by the supposition, it can have none before it, to direct or determine it, being the first in the train. But if that first volition is not determined by any preceding act of the will, then that act is not determined by the will, and so is not free, in the Arminian notion of freedom, which consists in the will's self-determination. And if that first act of the will, which determines and fixes the subsequent acts, be not free, none of the following acts, which are determined by it, can be free. If we suppose there are five acts in the train, the fifth and last determined by the fourth, and the fourth by the third, the third by the second, and the second by the first; if the first is not determined by the will, and so not free, then none of them are truly determined by the will: that is, that each of them are as they are, and not otherwise, is not first owing to the will, but to the determination of the first in the series, which is not dependent on the will, and is that which the will has no hand in the determination of. And this being that which decides what the rest shall be, and determines their existence; therefore the first determination of their existence is not from the will. The case is just the same, if instead of a chain of five acts of the will, we should suppose a succession of ten, or an hundred, or ten thousand. If the first act be not free, being determined by something out of the will, and this determines the next to be agreeable to itself, and that the next, and so on; they are none of them free, but all originally depend on, and are determined by some cause out of the will: and so all freedom in the case is excluded, and no act of the will can be free, according to this notion of freedom. . . . Thus, this Arminian notion of liberty of the will, consisting in the will's self-determination, is repugnant to itself, and shuts itself wholly out of the world. . . .

Section 3. Whether Any Event Whatsoever, and Volition in Particular, Can Come to Pass without a Cause of Its Existence

Before I enter on any argument on this subject, I would explain how I would be understood, when I use the word "cause" in this discourse: since, for want of a better word, I shall have occasion to use it in a sense which is more extensive, than that in which it is sometimes used. The word is often used in so restrained a sense as to signify only that which has a positive efficiency or influence to produce a thing, or bring it to pass. But there are many things which have no such positive productive influence; which yet are causes in that respect, that they have truly the nature of a ground or reason why some things are, rather than others; or why they are as they are, rather than otherwise. Thus the absence of the sun in the night, is not the cause of the falling of the dew at that time, in the same manner as its beams are the cause of the ascending of the vapors in the daytime; and its withdrawment in the winter, is not in the same manner the cause of the freezing of the waters, as its approach in the spring is the cause of their thawing. But yet the withdrawment or absence of the sun is an antecedent, with which these effects in the night and winter are connected, and on which they depend; and is one thing that belongs to the ground and reason why they come to pass at that time, rather than at other times; though the absence of the sun is nothing positive, nor has any positive influence.

It may be further observed, that when I speak of connection of causes and effects, I have respect to moral causes, as well as those that are called natural in distinction from 'em. Moral causes may be causes in as proper a sense, as any causes whatsoever; may have as real an influence, and may as truly be the ground and reason of an event's coming to pass.

Therefore I sometimes use the word "cause," in this inquiry, to signify any antecedent, either natural or moral, positive or negative, on which an event, either a thing, or the manner and circumstance of a thing, so depends, that it is the ground and reason, either in whole, or in part, why it is, rather than not; or why it is as it is, rather than otherwise; or, in other words, any antecedent with which a consequent event is so connected, that it truly belongs to the reason why the proposition which affirms that event, is true; whether it has any positive influence, or not. And in an agreeableness to this, I sometimes use the word "effect" for the consequence of another thing, which is perhaps rather an occasion than a cause, most properly speaking.

I am the more careful thus to explain my meaning, that I may cut off occasion, from any that might seek occasion to cavil and object against some things which I may say concerning the dependence of all things which come to pass, on some cause, and their connection with their cause.

Having thus explained what I mean by cause, I assert, that nothing ever comes to pass without a cause. What is self-existent must be from eternity, and must be unchangeable: but as to all things that *begin to be*, they are not self-existent, and therefore must have some foundation of their existence without themselves. That whatsoever begins to be, which before was not, must have a cause why it then begins to exist, seems to be the first dictate of the common and natural sense which God hath implanted in the minds of all mankind, and the main foundation of all our reasonings about the existence of things, past, present, or to come. . . .

But if once this grand principle of common sense be given up, that what is not necessary in itself, must have a cause; and we begin to maintain, that things may come into existence, and begin to be, which heretofore have not been, of themselves, without any cause; all our means of ascending in our arguing from the creature to the Creator, and all our evidence of the being of God, is cut off at one blow. In this case, we can't prove that there is a God, either from the being of the world, and the creatures in it, or from the manner of their being, their order, beauty and use. For if things may come into existence without any cause at all, then they doubtless may without any cause answerable to the effect. Our minds do alike naturally suppose and determine both these things; namely, that what begins to be has a cause, and also that it has a cause proportionable and agreeable to the effect. The same principle which leads us to determine, that there cannot be anything coming to pass without a cause, leads us to determine that there cannot be more in the effect than in the cause.

Yea, if once it should be allowed, that things may come to pass without a cause, we should not only have no proof of the being of God, but we should be without evidence of the existence of anything whatsoever, but our own immediately present ideas and consciousness. For we have no way to prove anything else, but by arguing from effects to causes: from the ideas now immediately in view, we argue other things not immediately in view: from sensations now excited in us, we infer the existence of things without us, as the causes of these sensations: and from the existence of these things, we argue other things, which they depend on, as effects on causes. We infer the past existence of ourselves, or anything else, by memory; only as we argue, that the ideas, which are now in our minds, are the consequences of past ideas and sensations. We immediately perceive nothing else but the ideas which are this moment extant in our minds. We perceive or know other things only by means of these, as necessarily connected with others, and dependent on them. But if things may be without causes, all this necessary connection and dependence is dissolved, and so all means of our knowledge is gone. If there be no absurdity or difficulty in supposing one thing to start out of nonexistence, into being, of itself without a cause; then there is no absurdity or difficulty in supposing the same of millions of millions. For nothing, or no difficulty multiplied, still is nothing, or no difficulty: nothing multiplied by nothing don't increase the sum. . . .

So that it is indeed as repugnant to reason, to suppose that an act of the will should come into existence without a cause, as to suppose the human soul, or an angel, or the globe of the earth, or the whole universe, should come into existence without a cause. And if once we allow, that such a sort of effect as a volition may come to pass without a cause, how do we know but that many other sorts of effects may do so too? 'Tis not the particular kind of effect that makes the absurdity of supposing it has being without a cause, but something which is common to all things that ever begin to be, viz. that they are not self-existent, or necessary in the nature of things. . . .

Part III. Wherein Is Inquired, Whether Any Such Liberty of Will as Arminians Hold, Be Necessary to Moral Agency, Virtue and Vice, Praise, and Dispraise, Etc.

Section 1. God's Moral Excellency Necessary, yet Virtuous and Praiseworthy

Having considered the first thing that was proposed to be inquired into, relating to that freedom of will which Arminians maintain; namely, whether any such thing does, ever did, or ever can exist, or be conceived of; I come now to the second thing proposed to be the subject of inquiry, viz. whether any such kind of liberty be requisite to moral agency, virtue and vice, praise and blame, reward and punishment, etc.

I shall begin with some consideration of the virtue and agency of the supreme moral Agent, and fountain of all agency and virtue.

Dr. Whitby,[2] in his *Discourse on the Five Points* (p. 14), says, "If all human actions are necessary, virtue and vice must be empty names; we being capable of nothing that is blameworthy, or deserveth praise; for who can blame a person for doing only what he could not help, or judge that he deserveth praise only for what he could not avoid?" To the like purpose he speaks in places innumerable; especially in his discourse on the freedom of the will; constantly maintaining, that a "freedom not only from coaction, but [from] necessity," is absolutely requisite, in order to actions being either worthy of blame, or deserving of praise. And to this agrees, as is well known, the current doctrine of Arminian writers; who in general hold, that there is no virtue or vice, reward or punishment, nothing to be commended or blamed, without this freedom. And yet Dr. Whitby, p. 300, allows, that God is without this freedom; and Arminians, so far as I have had opportunity to observe, generally acknowledge, that God is necessarily holy, and his will necessarily determined to that which is good.

So that, putting these things together, the infinitely holy God, who always used to be esteemed by God's people, not only virtuous, but a being

2. Daniel Whitby (1638–1726), a minister in the Church of England and Arminian apologist. Edwards refers to his *Discourse Concerning I. The True Import of the Words Election and Reprobation . . . II. The Extent of Christ's Redemption. III. The Grace of God . . . IV. The Liberty of the Will . . . V. The Perseverance or Defectability of the Saints* (London, 1710).

in whom is all possible virtue, and every virtue in the most absolute purity and perfection, and in infinitely greater brightness and amiableness than in any creature; the most perfect pattern of virtue, and the fountain from whom all others' virtue is but as beams from the sun; and who has been supposed to be, on the account of his virtue and holiness, infinitely more worthy to be esteemed, loved, honored, admired, commended, extolled and praised, than any creature; and he who is thus everywhere represented in Scripture; I say, this being, according to this notion of Dr. Whitby, and other Arminians, has no virtue at all; virtue, when ascribed to him, is but "an empty name"; and he is deserving of no commendation or praise; because he is under necessity, he can't avoid being holy and good as he is; therefore no thanks to him for it. It seems, the holiness, justice, faithfulness, etc. of the most High, must not be accounted to be of the nature of that which is virtuous and praiseworthy. They will not deny, that these things in God are good; but then we must understand them, that they are no more virtuous, or of the nature of anything commendable, than the good that is in any other being that is not a moral agent; as the brightness of the sun, and the fertility of the earth are good, but not virtuous, because these properties are necessary to these bodies, and not the fruit of self-determining power. . . .

Section 6. Liberty of Indifference, Not Only Not Necessary to Virtue, but Utterly Inconsistent with It; and All, Either Virtuous or Vicious Habits or Inclinations, Inconsistent with Arminian Notions of Liberty and Moral Agency

To suppose such a freedom of will, as Arminians talk of, to be requisite to virtue and vice, is many ways contrary to common sense.

If indifference belongs to liberty of will, as Arminians suppose, and it be essential to a virtuous action that it be performed in a state of liberty, as they also suppose; it will follow, that it is essential to a virtuous action that it be performed in a state of indifference: and if it be performed in a *state* of indifference, then doubtless it must be performed in the *time* of indifference. And so it will follow, that in order to the virtuousness of an act, the heart must be indifferent in the time of the performance of that act, and the more indifferent and cold the heart is with relation to the act which is performed, so much the better; because the act is performed with so much the greater liberty. But is this agreeable to the light of nature? Is it agreeable to the notions which mankind, in all ages, have of virtue, that it lies in that which is contrary to indifference, even in the tendency and inclination of the heart to virtuous action; and that the stronger the inclination, and so the further from indifference, the more virtuous the *heart*, and so much the more praiseworthy the *act* which proceeds from it?

If we should suppose (contrary to what has been before demonstrated) that there may be an act of will in a state of indifference; for instance, this act, viz. the will's determining to put itself out of a state of indifference, and give itself a preponderation one way, then it would follow, on Arminian principles, that this act or determination of the will is that alone wherein virtue consists, because this only is performed while the mind remains in a state of indifference, and so in a state of liberty: for when once the mind is put out of its equilibrium, it is no longer in such a state; and therefore all the acts which follow afterwards, proceeding from bias, can have the nature neither of virtue or vice. Or if the thing which the will can do, while yet in a state of indifference, and so of liberty, be only to suspend acting, and determine to take the matter into consideration, then this determination is that alone wherein virtue consists, and not proceeding to action after the scale is turned by consideration. So that it will follow from these principles, all that is done after the mind, by any means, is once out of its equilibrium and already possessed by an inclination, and arising from that inclination, has nothing of the nature of virtue or vice, and is worthy of neither blame nor praise. But how plainly contrary is this to the universal sense of mankind, and to the notion they have of sincerely virtuous actions? Which is, that they are actions which proceed from a heart *well disposed* and *inclined;* and the *stronger,* and the more *fixed* and *determined* the good disposition of the heart, the greater the sincerity of virtue, and so the more of the truth and reality of it. But if there be any acts which are done in a state of equilibrium, or spring immediately from perfect indifference and coldness of heart, they cannot arise from any good principle or disposition in the heart; and consequently, according to common sense, have no sincere goodness in 'em, having no virtue of heart in 'em. To have a virtuous heart, is to have a heart that favors virtue, and is friendly to it, and not one perfectly cold and indifferent about it. . . .

On the whole, it appears, that if the notions of Arminians concerning liberty and moral agency be true, it will follow that there is no virtue in any such habits or qualities as humility, meekness, patience, mercy, gratitude, generosity, heavenly-mindedness; nothing at all praiseworthy in loving Christ above father and mother, wife and children, or our own lives; or in delight in holiness, hungering and thirsting after righteousness, love to enemies, universal benevolence to mankind: and on the other hand, there is nothing at all vicious, or worthy of dispraise, in the most sordid, beastly, malignant, devilish dispositions; in being ungrateful, profane, habitually hating God, and things sacred and holy; or in being most treacherous, envious and cruel towards men. For all these things are dispositions and inclinations of the heart. And in short, there is no such thing as any virtuous or vicious *quality of mind;* no such thing as inherent virtue and holiness, or vice and sin: and the stronger those habits or dispositions are, which used to be called virtuous and vicious, the further they are from being so indeed; the more violent men's lusts are, the more fixed their pride, envy, ingratitude and maliciousness, still the further are they from being blameworthy. If there be a man that by his own repeated acts, or by any other means, is come to be of the most hellish disposition, desperately inclined to treat his neighbors with injuriousness, contempt and malignity; the further they should be from any disposition to be angry with him, or in the least to blame him. So on the other hand, if there be a person, who is of a most excellent spirit, strongly inclining him to the most amiable actions, admirably meek, benevolent, etc. so much is he further from anything rewardable or commendable. On which principles, the man Jesus Christ was very far from being praiseworthy for those acts of holiness and kindness which he performed, these propensities being so strong in his heart. And above all, the infinitely holy and gracious God, is infinitely remote from anything commendable, his good inclinations being infinitely strong, and he therefore at the utmost possible distance from being at liberty. And in all cases, the stronger the inclinations of any are to virtue, and the more they love it, the less virtuous they are; and the more they love wickedness, the less vicious. Whether these things are agreeable to Scripture, let every Christian, and every man who has read the Bible, judge: and whether they are agreeable to common sense, let everyone judge, that have human understanding in exercise.

And if we pursue these principles, we shall find that virtue and vice are wholly excluded out of the world; and that there never was, nor ever can be any such thing as one or the other; either in God, angels or men. No propensity, disposition or habit can be virtuous or vicious, as has been shown; because they, so far as they take place, destroy the freedom of the will, the foundation of all moral agency, and exclude all capacity of either virtue or vice. . . .

Part IV. Wherein the Chief Grounds of the Reasoning of Arminians, in Support and Defense of the Forementioned Notions of Liberty, Moral Agency, Etc. and against the Opposite Doctrine, Are Considered

Section 4. It Is Agreeable to Common Sense, and the Natural Notions of Mankind, to Suppose Moral Necessity to Be Consistent with Praise and Blame, Reward and Punishment

Whether the reasons that have been given, why it appears difficult to some persons to reconcile with common sense the praising or blaming, rewarding or punishing those things which are morally necessary, are thought satisfactory, or not; yet it most evidently appears by the following things, that if this matter be rightly understood, setting aside all delusion arising from the impropriety and ambiguity of terms, this is not at all inconsistent with the natural apprehensions of mankind, and that sense of things which is found everywhere in the common people, who are furthest from having their thoughts perverted from their natural channel, by metaphysical and philosophical subtleties; but on the contrary, altogether agreeable *to*, and the very voice and dictate *of* this natural and vulgar sense.

I. This will appear if we consider what the vulgar notion of blameworthiness is. The idea which the common people through all ages and nations have of faultiness, I suppose to be plainly this; a person's being or doing wrong, with his own will and pleasure; containing these two things: 1. His doing wrong, when he does as he pleases. 2. His pleasure's being wrong. Or in other words, perhaps more intelligibly expressing their notion; a person's having his heart wrong, and doing wrong from his heart. And this is the sum total of the matter.

The common people don't ascend up in their reflections and abstractions, to the metaphysical sources, relations and dependences of things, in order to form their notion of faultiness or blameworthiness. They don't wait till they have decided by their refinings, what first determines the will; whether it be determined by something extrinsic, or intrinsic; whether volition determines volition, or whether the understanding determines the will; whether there be any such thing as metaphysicians mean by contingence (if they have any meaning); whether there be a sort of a strange unaccountable sovereignty in the will, in the exercise of which, by its own sovereign acts, it brings to pass all its own sovereign acts. They don't take any part of their notion of fault or blame from the resolution of any such questions. . . .

'Tis true, the common people and children, in their notion of a faulty act or deed of any person, do suppose that it is the person's *own act* and deed. But this is all that belongs to what they understand by a thing's being a person's *own deed* or action; even that it is something done by him of choice. That some exercise or motion should begin of itself, don't belong to their notion of an action, or doing. If so, it would belong to their notion of it, that it is something which is the cause of its own beginning: and that is as much as to say, that it is before it begins to be. Nor is their notion of an action some motion or exercise that begins accidentally, without any cause or reason; for that is contrary to one of the prime dictates of common sense, namely, that everything that begins to be, has some cause or reason why it is.

The common people, in their notion of a faulty or praiseworthy deed or work done by anyone, do suppose that the man does it in the exercise of *liberty*. But then their notion of liberty is only a person's having opportunity of doing as he pleases. They have no notion of liberty consisting in the will's first acting, and so causing its own acts; and determining, and so causing its own determinations; or choosing, and so causing its own choice. Such a notion of liberty is what none have, but those that have darkened their own minds with confused metaphysical speculation, and abstruse and ambiguous terms. If a man is not restrained from acting as his will determines, or constrained to act otherwise; then he has liberty, according to common notions of liberty, without taking into the idea that grand contradiction of all the determinations of a man's free will being the effects of the determinations of his free will. Nor have men commonly any notion of freedom consisting in indifference. For if so, then it would be agreeable to their notion, that the greater indifference men act with, the more freedom they act with; whereas the reverse if true. He that in acting, proceeds with the fullest inclination, does what he does with the greatest freedom, according to common sense. And so far is it from being agreeable to common sense, that such liberty as consists in indifference is requisite to praise or blame, that on the contrary, the dictate of every man's natural sense through the world is, that the further he is from being indifferent in his acting good or evil, and the more he does either with full and strong inclination, the more is he esteemed or abhorred, commended or condemned.

II. If it were inconsistent with the common sense of mankind, that men should be either to be blamed or commended in any volitions they have or fail of, in case of moral necessity or impossibility; then it would surely also be agreeable to the same sense and reason of mankind, that the nearer the case approaches to such a moral necessity or impossibility, either through a strong antecedent moral propensity on the one hand, or a great antecedent opposition and difficulty on the other, the nearer does it approach to a being neither blamable nor commendable; so that acts exerted with such preceding propensity would be worthy of proportionably less praise; and when omitted, the act being attended with such difficulty, the omission would be worthy of the less blame. It is so, as was observed before, with natural necessity and impossibility, propensity and difficulty: as 'tis a plain dictate of the sense of all mankind, that natural necessity and impossibility takes away *all* blame and praise; and therefore, that the nearer the approach is to these through previous propensity or difficulty, so praise and blame are proportionably *diminished.* And if it were as much a dictate of common sense, that moral necessity of doing, or impossibility of avoiding, takes away *all* praise and blame, as that natural necessity or impossibility does this; then, by a perfect parity of reason, it would be as much the dictate of common sense, that an *approach* to moral necessity of doing, or impossibility of avoiding, *diminishes* praise and blame, as that an approach to natural necessity and impossibility does so. 'Tis equally the voice of common sense, that persons are *excusable in part*, in neglecting things difficult against their wills, as that they are *excusable wholly* in neglecting things impossible against their wills. And if it made no difference, whether the impossibility were natural and against the will, or moral, lying in the will, with regard to excusableness; so neither would it make any difference, whether the difficulty, or approach to necessity be natural against the will, or moral, lying in the propensity of the will.

But 'tis apparent, that the reverse of these things is true. If there be an approach to a moral necessity in a man's exertion of good acts of will, they being the exercise of a strong propensity to good, and a very powerful love to virtue; tis so far from being the dictate of common sense, that he is less virtuous, and the less to be esteemed, loved and praised; that 'tis agreeable to the natural notions of all mankind that he is so much the better man, worthy of greater respect, and higher commendation. And the stronger the inclination is, and the nearer it approaches to necessity in that respect, or to impossibility of neglecting the virtuous act, or of doing a vicious one; still the more virtuous, and worthy of higher commendation. And on the other hand, if a man exerts evil acts of mind; as for instance, acts of pride or malice, from a rooted and strong habit or principle of haughtiness and maliciousness, and a violent propensity of heart to such acts; according to the natural sense of all men, he is so far from being the less hateful and blamable on that account, that he is so much the more worthy to be detested and condemned by all that observe him.

Moreover, 'tis manifest that it is no part of the notion which mankind commonly have of a blamable or praiseworthy act of the will, that it is an act which is not determined by an antecedent bias or motive, but by the sovereign power of the will itself; because if so, the greater hand such causes have in determining any acts of the will, so much the less virtuous or vicious would they be accounted; and the less hand, the more virtuous or vicious. Whereas the reverse is true: men don't think a good act to be the less praiseworthy, for the agent's being much determined in it by a good inclination or a good motive; but the more. And if good inclination or motive has but little influence in determining the agent, they don't think his act so much the more virtuous, but the less. And so concerning evil acts, which are determined by evil motives or inclinations. . . .

Some seem to disdain the distinction that we make between *natural* and *moral* necessity, as though it were altogether impertinent in this controversy: "That which is necessary (say they) is necessary; it is that which must be, and can't be prevented. And that which is impossible, is impossible, and can't be done: and therefore none can be to blame for not doing it." And such comparisons are made use of, as the commanding of a man to walk who has lost his legs, and condemning and punishing him for not obeying; inviting and calling upon a man, who is shut up in a strong prison, to come forth, etc. But in these things Arminians are very unreasonable. Let common sense determine whether there be not a great difference between those two cases; the one, that of a man who has offended his prince, and is cast into prison; and after he has lain there a while, the king comes to him, calls him to come forth to him; and tells him that if he will do so, and will fall down before him, and humbly beg his pardon, he shall be forgiven, and set at liberty, and also be greatly enriched, and advanced to honor: the prisoner heartily repents of the folly and wickedness of his offense against his prince, is thoroughly disposed to abase himself, and accept of the king's offer; but is confined by strong walls, with gates of brass, and bars of iron. The other case is, that of a man who is of a very unreasonable spirit, of a haughty, ungrateful, willful disposition; and moreover, has been brought up in traitorous principles; and has his heart possessed with an extreme and inveterate enmity to his lawful sovereign; and for his rebellion is cast into prison, and lies long there, loaden with heavy chains, and in miserable circumstances. At length the compassionate prince comes to the prison, orders his chains to be knocked off, and his prison doors to be set wide open; calls to him, and tells him, if he will come forth to him, and fall down before him, acknowledge that he has treated him unworthily, and ask his forgiveness; he shall be forgiven, set at liberty, and set in a place of great dignity and profit in his court. But he is so stout and stomachful, and full of haughty malignity, that he can't be willing to accept the offer: his rooted strong pride and malice have perfect power over him, and as it were bind him, by binding his heart: the opposition of his heart has the mastery over him, having an influence on his mind far superior to the king's grace and condescension, and to all his kind offers and promises. Now, is it agreeable to common sense, to assert and stand to it, that there is no difference between these two cases, as to any worthiness of blame in the prisoners; because, forsooth, there is a necessity in both, and the required act in each case is impossible? 'Tis true, a man's evil dispositions may be as strong and immovable as the bars of a castle. But who can't see, that when a man, in the latter case, is said to be "unable" to obey the command, the expression is used improperly, and not in the sense it has originally and in common speech? And that it may properly be said to be in the rebel's power to come out of prison, seeing he can easily do it if he pleases; though by reason of his vile temper of heart which is fixed and rooted, 'tis impossible that it should please him? . . .

There is a grand illusion in the pretended demonstration of Arminians from common sense. The main strength of all these demonstrations, lies in that prejudice that arises through the insensible change of the use and meaning of such terms as "liberty," "able," "unable," "necessary," "impossible," "unavoidable," "invincible," "action," etc. from their original and vulgar sense, to a metaphysical sense entirely diverse; and the strong connection of the ideas of blamelessness, etc. with some of these terms, by an habit contracted and established, while these terms were used in their first meaning. This prejudice and delusion is the foundation of all those positions they lay down as maxims, by which most of the scriptures, which they allege in this controversy, are interpreted, and on which all their pompous demonstrations from Scripture and reason depend. From this secret delusion and prejudice they have almost all their advantages: 'tis the strength of their bulwarks, and the edge of their weapons. And this is the main ground of all the right they have to treat their neighbors in so assuming a manner, and to insult others, perhaps as wise and good as themselves, as weak bigots, men that dwell in the dark caves of superstition, perversely set, obstinately shutting their eyes against the noonday light, enemies to common sense, maintaining the first-born of absurdities, etc. But perhaps an impartial consideration of the things which have been observed in the preceding parts of this inquiry, may enable the lovers of truth better to judge, whose doctrine is indeed absurd, abstruse, self-contradictory, and inconsistent with common sense, and many ways repugnant to the universal dictates of the reason of mankind. . . .

The Great Christian Doctrine of Original Sin Defended (1758)

Author's Preface

The following discourse is intended, not merely as an answer to any particular book written against the doctrine of original sin, but as a *general defense* of that great important doctrine. Nevertheless, I have in this defense taken notice of the main things said against this doctrine, by such of the more noted opposers of it, as I have had opportunity to read; particularly those two late writers, Dr. Turnbull, and Dr. Taylor of Norwich; but especially the latter, in what he has published in those two books of his, the first entitled, *The Scripture-Doctrine of Original Sin Proposed to Free and Candid Examination;* the other, his *Key to the Apostolic Writings, with a Paraphrase and Notes on the Epistle to the Romans.*[1] According to my observation, no one book has done so much towards rooting out of these western parts of New England, the principles and scheme of religion maintained by our pious and excellent forefathers, the divines and Christians who first settled this country, and alienating the minds of many from what I think are evidently some of the main doctrines of the gospel, as that which Dr. Taylor has published against the doctrine of original sin. The book has now for many years been spread abroad in the land, without any answer to it, as an antidote; and so has gone on to prevail with little control. . . . The providing one is what I have attempted in the following work; wherein I have closely attended to that piece, in all its parts, and have endeavored that no one thing there said, of any consequence in this controversy, should pass unnoticed, or that anything which has the ap-

---

1. John Taylor (1694–1761), who espoused Arminianism, was pastor of a Presbyterian church in Norwich, England. Edwards used the third edition of *The Scripture-Doctrine of Original Sin* (Belfast, 1746). *The Key to the Apostolic Writings and a Paraphrase with Notes on the Epistle to the Romans* was published in London in 1740. George Turnbull (1698–1748) published *The Principles of Moral Philosophy* in 1740.

pearance of an argument in opposition to this doctrine should be left unanswered. I look on the doctrine as of *great importance;* which everybody will doubtless own it is, if it be true. For, if the case be such indeed, that all mankind are by nature in a state of total ruin, both with respect to the moral evil they are subjects of, and the afflictive evil they are exposed to, the one as the consequence and punishment of the other, then doubtless the great salvation by Christ stands in direct relation to this ruin, as the remedy to the disease; and the whole gospel or doctrine of salvation, must suppose it; and all real belief, or true notion of that gospel, must be built upon it. Therefore, as I think the doctrine is most certainly both true and important, I hope, my attempting a *vindication* of it, will be candidly interpreted, and that what I have done towards its defense, will be impartially considered, by all that will give themselves the trouble to read the ensuing discourse. . . .

Part I. Wherein Are Considered Some Evidences of Original Sin from Facts and Events, as Found by Observation and Experience, Together with Representation and Testimonies of Holy Scripture, and the Confessions and Assertions of Opposers

Chapter I. Evidences of Original Sin from What Appears in Fact of the Sinfulness of Mankind

SECTION I. ALL MANKIND DO CONSTANTLY IN ALL AGES, WITHOUT FAIL IN ANY ONE INSTANCE, RUN INTO THAT MORAL EVIL, WHICH IS IN EFFECT THEIR OWN UTTER AND ETERNAL PERDITION, IN A TOTAL PRIVATION OF GOD'S FAVOR AND SUFFERING OF HIS VENGEANCE AND WRATH

By original sin, as the phrase has been most commonly used by divines, is meant the *innate sinful depravity of the heart.* But yet when the doctrine of original sin is spoken of, it is vulgarly understood in that latitude, as to include not only the depravity of nature, but the *imputation* of Adam's first sin; or in other words, the liableness or exposedness of Adam's posterity, in the divine judgment, to partake of the punishment of that sin. So far as I know, most of those who have held one of these, have maintained the other; and most of those who have opposed one, have opposed the other.

Both are opposed by the author chiefly attended to in the following discourse, in his book against original sin. And it may perhaps appear in our future consideration of the subject, that they are closely connected, and that the arguments which prove the one establish the other, and that there are no more difficulties attending the allowing of one than the other.

I shall in the first place consider this doctrine more especially with regard to the corruption of nature; and as we treat of this, the other will naturally come into consideration in the prosecution of the discourse, as connected with it.

As all moral qualities, all principles, either of virtue or vice, lie in the disposition of the heart, I shall consider whether we have any evidence, that the heart of man is naturally of a corrupt and evil disposition. This is strenuously denied by many late writers, who are enemies to the doctrine of original sin, and particularly by Dr. Taylor. . . .

But for the greater clearness, it may be proper here to premise one consideration, that is of great importance in this controversy, and is very much overlooked by the opposers of the doctrine of original sin in their disputing against it; which is this—

That is to be looked upon as the true tendency of the natural or innate disposition of man's heart, which appears to be its tendency when we consider things as they are in themselves, or in their own nature, without the *interposition of divine grace.* Thus, that state of man's nature, that disposition of the mind, is to be looked upon as evil and pernicious, which, as it is in itself, tends to extremely pernicious consequences, and would certainly end therein, were it not that the free mercy and kindness of God interposes to prevent that issue. It would be very strange, if any should argue that there is no evil tendency in the case, because the mere favor and compassion of the Most High may step in and oppose the tendency, and prevent the sad effect tended to. Particularly, if there be anything in the nature of man, whereby he has an universal, unfailing tendency to that moral evil, which according to the real nature and true demerit of things, as they are in themselves, implies his utter ruin, that must be looked upon as an evil tendency or propensity; however divine grace may interpose, to save him from deserved ruin, and to overrule things to an issue contrary to that which they tend to of themselves. Grace is a sovereign thing, exercised according to the good pleasure of God, bringing good out of evil; the effect of it belongs not to the nature of things themselves, that otherwise have an ill tendency, any more than the remedy belongs to the disease; but is something altogether independent on it, introduced to oppose the natural tendency, and reverse the course of things. But the event that things tend to, according to their own demerit, and according to divine justice, that is the event which they tend to in their own nature; as Dr. Taylor's own words fully imply. "God alone," says he, "can declare whether he will pardon or punish the ungodliness and unrighteousness of mankind, which is in its own nature punishable." Nothing is more precisely according to the truth of things, than divine justice; it weighs things in an even balance; it views and estimates things no otherwise than they are truly in their own nature. Therefore undoubtedly that which implies a tendency to ruin according to the estimate of divine justice, does indeed imply such a tendency in its own nature. . . .

One thing more is to be observed here, viz. that the topic mainly insisted on by the opposers of the doctrine of original sin, is the justice of God; both in their objections against the imputation of Adam's sin, and also against its being so ordered that men should come into the world with a corrupt and ruined nature, without having merited the displeasure of their Creator by any personal fault. But the latter is not repugnant to God's justice, if men can be, and actually are, born into the world with a tendency to sin, and to misery and ruin for their sin, which actually will be the consequence, unless *mere grace* steps in and prevents it. If this be allowed, the argument from *justice* is given up; for it is to suppose that their liableness to misery and ruin comes in a way of justice; otherwise there would be no need of the interposition of divine grace to save 'em. Justice alone would be sufficient security, if exercised, without grace. 'Tis all one in this dispute about what is just and righteous, whether men are born in a miserable state, by a tendency to ruin, which actually follows, and that justly; or whether they are born in such a state as tends to a desert of ruin, which might justly follow, and would actually follow, did not grace prevent. For the controversy is not, what grace will do, but what justice might do. . . .

SECTION 2. IT FOLLOWS FROM THE PROPOSITION PROVED IN THE FOREGOING
SECTION, THAT ALL MANKIND ARE UNDER THE INFLUENCE OF A PREVAILING
EFFECTUAL TENDENCY IN THEIR NATURE, TO THAT SIN AND WICKEDNESS,
WHICH IMPLIES THEIR UTTER AND ETERNAL RUIN

The proposition laid down being proved, the consequence of it remains to
be made out, viz. that the mind of man has a *natural tendency* or propensity
to that event, which has been shown universally and infallibly to take place
(if this ben't sufficiently evident of itself, without proof), and that this is a
corrupt or *depraved* propensity.

I shall here consider the former part of this consequence, namely,
whether such an universal, constant, infallible event is truly a proof of the
being of any tendency or propensity to that event; leaving the evil and
corrupt nature of such propensity to be considered afterwards.

If any shall say, they don't think that its being a thing universal and
infallible in event, that mankind commit some sin, is a proof of a prevailing tendency to sin; because they don't only sin, but also do good, and
perhaps more good than evil: let them remember, that the question at
present is not, how much sin there is a tendency to; but whether there be a
prevailing propensity to that issue, which it is allowed all men do actually
come to, that all fail of keeping the law perfectly, whether there ben't a
tendency to such imperfection of obedience, as always without fail comes
to pass; to that degree of sinfulness, at least, which all fall into; and so to
that utter ruin, which that sinfulness implies and infers. Whether an
effectual propensity to this be worth the name of depravity, because of the
good that may be supposed to balance it, shall be considered by and by. If
it were so, that all mankind, in all nations and ages, were at least one day
in their lives deprived of the use of their reason, and run raving mad; or
that all, even every individual person, once cut their own throats, or put
out their own eyes; it might be an evidence of some tendency in the nature
or natural state of mankind to such an event; though they might exercise
reason many more days than they were distracted, and were kind to and
tender of themselves oftener than they mortally and cruelly wounded
themselves.

To determine whether the unfailing constancy of the above-named event be an evidence of tendency, let it be considered, what can be meant by tendency, but a prevailing liableness or exposedness to such or such an event? Wherein consists the notion of any such thing, but some stated prevalence or preponderation in the nature or state of causes or occasions, that is followed by, and so proved to be effectual to, a stated prevalence or commonness of any particular kind of effect? Or, something in the permanent state of things, concerned in bringing a certain sort of event to pass, which is a foundation for the constancy, or strongly prevailing probability, of such an event? If we mean this by tendency (as I know not what else can be meant by it, but this, or something like this) then it is manifest, that where we see a stated prevalence of any kind of effect or event, there is a tendency to that effect in the nature and state of its causes. A common and steady effect shows, that there is somewhere a preponderation, a prevailing exposedness or liableness in the state of things, to what comes so steadily to pass. The natural dictate of reason shows, that where there is an effect, there is a cause, and a cause sufficient for the effect; because, if it were not sufficient, it would not be effectual: and that therefore, where there is a stated prevalence of the effect, there is a stated prevalence in the cause: a steady effect argues a steady cause. We obtain a notion of such a thing as tendency, no other way than by observation: and we can observe nothing but events: and 'tis the commonness or constancy of events, that gives us a notion of tendency in all cases. Thus we judge of tendencies in the natural world. Thus we judge of the tendencies or propensities of nature in minerals, vegetables, animals, rational and irrational creatures. A notion of a stated tendency or fixed propensity is not obtained by observing only a single event. A stated preponderation in the cause or occasion, is argued only by a stated prevalence of the effect. If a die be once thrown, and it falls on a particular side, we don't argue from hence, that that side is the heaviest; but if it be thrown without skill or care, many thousands or millions of times going, and constantly falls on the same side, we have not the least doubt in our minds, but that there is something of propensity in the case, by superior weight of that side, or in some other respect. How ridiculous would he make himself, who should earnestly dispute against any tendency in the state of things to cold in winter, or heat in the summer; or should stand to it, that although it often happened that water quenched fire, yet there was no tendency in it to such an effect?

In the case we are upon, the human nature, as existing in such an immense diversity of persons and circumstances, and never failing in any one instance, of coming to that issue, viz. that sinfulness which implies extreme misery and eternal ruin, is as the die often cast. For it alters not the case in the least, as to the evidence of tendency, whether the subject of the constant event be an individual, or a nature and kind. Thus, if there be a succession of trees of the same sort, proceeding one from another, from the beginning of the world, growing in all countries, soils and climates, and otherwise in (as it were) an infinite variety of circumstances, all bearing ill fruit; it as much proves the nature and tendency of the kind, as if it were only one individual tree that had remained from the beginning of the world, had often been transplanted into different soils, etc. and had continued to bear only bad fruit. So, if there were a particular family, which, from generation to generation, and through every remove to innumerable different countries and places of abode, all died of a consumption, or all run distracted, or all murdered themselves, it would be as much an evidence of the tendency of something in the nature or constitution of that race, as it would be of the tendency of something in the nature or state of an individual, if some one person had lived all that time, and some remarkable event had often appeared in him, which he been the agent or subject of, from year to year and from age to age, continually and without fail. . . .

SECTION 3. THAT PROPENSITY WHICH HAS BEEN PROVED TO BE IN THE NATURE OF ALL MANKIND, MUST BE A VERY EVIL, DEPRAVED AND PERNICIOUS PROPENSITY; MAKING IT MANIFEST THAT THE SOUL OF MAN, AS IT IS BY NATURE, IS IN A CORRUPT, FALLEN AND RUINED STATE: WHICH IS THE OTHER PART OF THE CONSEQUENCE, DRAWN FROM THE PROPOSITION LAID DOWN IN THE FIRST SECTION

The question to be considered, in order to determine whether man's nature is not depraved and ruined, is not whether he is not inclined to perform as many *good deeds* as *bad ones*, but, which of these two he preponderates to, in the frame of his heart, and state of his nature, a state of innocence and righteousness, and favor with God; or a state of sin, guiltiness and abhorrence in the sight of God. Persevering sinless righteousness, or else the guilt of sin, is the alternative, on the decision of which depends (as is confessed) according to the nature and truth of things, as they are in themselves, and according to the rule of right and perfect justice, man's being approved and accepted of his Maker, and eternally blessed as good; or his being rejected, thrown away and cursed as bad. And therefore the determination of the tendency of man's heart and nature with respect to these terms, is that which is to be looked at, in order to determine whether his nature is good or evil, pure or corrupt, sound or ruined. If such be man's nature, and state of his heart, that he has an infallibly effectual propensity to the latter of those terms; then it is wholly impertinent, to talk of the innocent and kind actions, even of criminals themselves, surpassing their crimes in numbers; and of the prevailing innocence, good nature, industry, felicity and cheerfulness of the greater part of mankind. Let never so many thousands, or millions of acts of honesty, good nature, etc. be supposed; yet, by the supposition, there is an unfailing propensity to such moral evil, as in its dreadful consequences infinitely outweighs all effects or consequences of any supposed good. Surely that tendency, which, in effect, is an infallible tendency to eternal destruction, is an infinitely dreadful and pernicious tendency: and that nature and frame of mind, which implies such a tendency, must be an infinitely dreadful and pernicious frame of mind. It would be much more absurd, to suppose that such a state of nature is good, or not bad, under a notion of men's doing more honest and kind things, than evil ones; than to say, the state of that ship is good, to cross the Atlantic Ocean in, that is such as cannot hold together through the voyage, but will infallibly founder and sink by the way; under a notion that it may probably go great part of the way before it sinks, or that it will proceed and sail above water more hours than it will be sinking: or to pronounce that road a good road to go to such a place, the greater part of which is plain and safe, though some parts of it are dangerous, and certainly fatal to them that travel in it; or to call that a good propensity, which is an inflexible inclination to travel in such a way.

A propensity to that sin which brings God's eternal wrath and curse (which has been proved to belong to the nature of man) is not evil, only as it is calamitous and sorrowful, ending in great *natural evil;* but it is *odious* too, and *detestable;* as, by the supposition, it tends to that *moral evil,* by which the subject becomes odious in the sight of God, and liable, as such, to be condemned, and utterly rejected and cursed by him. This also makes it evident, that the state which it has been proved mankind are in, is a corrupt state in a moral sense, that it is inconsistent with the fulfillment of the law of God, which is the rule of moral rectitude and goodness. That tendency, which is opposite to that which the moral law requires and insists upon, and prone to that which the moral law utterly forbids, and eternally condemns the subject for, is doubtless a corrupt tendency, in a moral sense.

So that this depravity is both odious, and also pernicious, fatal and destructive, in the highest sense, as inevitably tending to that which implies man's eternal ruin; it shows, that man, as he is by nature, is in a deplorable and undone state, in the highest sense. And this proves that men don't come into the world perfectly innocent in the sight of God, and without any just exposedness to his displeasure. For the being by nature in a lost and ruined state, in the highest sense, is not consistent with being by nature in a state of favor with God. . . .

Therefore how absurd must it be for Christians to object, against the depravity of man's nature, a greater number of innocent and kind actions, than of crimes; and to talk of a prevailing innocency, good nature, industry, and cheerfulness of the greater part of mankind? Infinitely more absurd, than it would be to insist, that the domestic of a prince was not a bad servant, because though sometimes he contemned and affronted his master to a great degree, yet he did not spit in his master's face so often as he performed acts of service; or, than it would be to affirm, that his spouse was a good wife to him, because, although she committed adultery, and that with the slaves and scoundrels sometimes, yet she did not do this so often as she did the duties of a wife. These notions would be absurd, because the crimes are too heinous to be atoned for, by many honest actions of the servant or spouse of the prince; there being a vast disproportion between the merit of the one, and the ill-desert of the other: but in no measure so great, nay infinitely less than that between the demerit of our offenses against God and the value of our acts of obedience. . . .

Part IV. Containing Answers to Objections

Chapter II. Concerning that Objection against the Doctrine of Native Corruption, That to Suppose Men Receive Their First Existence in Sin, Is to Make Him Who Is the Author of Their Being, the Author of Their Depravity

One argument against men's being supposed to be born with sinful depravity, which Dr. Taylor greatly insists upon, is, "That this does in effect charge him who is the *Author* of our nature, who formed us in the womb, with being the *author* of a sinful corruption of nature; and that it is highly injurious to the *God* of our nature, whose hands have formed and fashioned us, to believe our nature to be originally corrupted, and that in the worst sense of corruption."

With respect to this, I would observe in the first place, that this writer, in his handling this grand objection, supposes something to belong to the doctrine objected against, as maintained by the divines whom he is opposing, which does not belong to it, nor does follow from it: as particularly, he supposes the doctrine of original sin to imply, that nature must be corrupted by some *positive influence;* "something, by some means or other, *infused* into the human nature; some quality or other, not from the choice of our minds, but like a *taint, tincture,* or *infection,* altering the natural constitution, faculties and dispositions of our souls. That sin and evil dispositions are implanted in the fetus in the womb." Whereas truly our doctrine neither implies nor infers any such thing. In order to account for a sinful corruption of nature, yea, a total native depravity of the heart of man, there is not the least need of supposing any evil quality *infused, implanted,* or *wrought* into the nature of man, by any *positive* cause, or influence whatsoever, either from God, or the creature; or of supposing, that man is conceived and born with a *fountain of evil* in his heart, such as is anything properly positive. I think, a little attention to the nature of things will be sufficient to satisfy any impartial considerate inquirer, that the absence of positive good principles, and so the withholding of a special divine influence to impart and maintain those good principles, leaving the common natural principles of self-love, natural appetite, etc. (which were in man in innocence) leaving these, I say, to themselves, without the government of superior divine principles, will certainly be followed with corruption, yea, the total corruption of the heart, without occasion for any positive influence at all: and that it was thus indeed that corruption of nature came on Adam, immediately on his fall, and comes on all his posterity, as sinning in him and falling with him.

The case with man was plainly this: when God made man at first, he implanted in him two kinds of principles. There was an *inferior* kind, which may be called *natural,* being the principles of mere human nature; such as self-love, with those natural appetites and passions, which belong to the nature of man, in which his love to his own liberty, honor and pleasure, were exercised: these when alone, and left to themselves, are what the Scriptures sometimes call *flesh.* Besides these, there were *superior* principles, that were spiritual, holy and divine, summarily comprehended in divine love; wherein consisted the spiritual image of God, and man's righteousness and true holiness; which are called in Scripture the *divine nature.* These principles may, in some sense, be called *supernatural,* being (however concreated or connate, yet) such as are above those principles that are essentially implied in, or necessarily resulting from, and insepara-bly connected with, *mere human nature;* and being such as immediately depend on man's union and communion with God, or divine communica-tions and influences of God's spirit: which though withdrawn, and man's nature forsaken of these principles, human nature would be human nature still; man's nature as such, being entire without those divine principles, which the Scripture sometimes calls *spirit,* in contradistinction to *flesh.* These superior principles were given to possess the throne, and maintain an absolute dominion in the heart: the other, to be wholly subordinate and subservient. And while things continued thus, all things were in excellent order, peace and beautiful harmony, and in their proper and perfect state. These divine principles thus reigning, were the dignity, life, happiness, and glory of man's nature. When man sinned, and broke God's Covenant, and fell under his curse, these superior principles left his heart: for indeed

God then left him; that communion with God, on which these principles depended, entirely ceased; the Holy Spirit, that divine inhabitant, forsook the house. Because it would have been utterly improper in itself, and inconsistent with the covenant and constitution God had established, that God should still maintain communion with man, and continue, by his friendly, gracious vital influences, to dwell with him and in him, after he was become a rebel, and had incurred God's wrath and curse. Therefore immediately the superior divine principles wholly ceased; so light ceases in a room, when the candle is withdrawn: and thus man was left in a state of darkness, woeful corruption and ruin; nothing but flesh, without spirit. The inferior principles of self-love and natural appetite, which were given only to serve, being alone, and left to themselves, of course became reign- ing principles; having no superior principles to regulate or control them, they became absolute masters of the heart. The immediate consequence of which was a *fatal catastrophe*, a turning of all things upside down, and the succession of a state of the most odious and dreadful confusion. Man did immediately set up himself, and the objects of his private affections and appetites, as supreme; and so they took the place of God. These inferior principles are like fire in an house; which, we say, is a good servant, but a bad master; very useful while kept in its place, but if left to take possession of the whole house, soon brings all to destruction. Man's love to his own honor, separate interest, and private pleasure, which before was wholly subordinate unto love to God and regard to his authority and glory, now dispose and impel man to pursue those objects, without regard to God's honor, or law; because there is no true regard to these divine things left in him. In consequence of which, he seeks those objects as much when against God's honor and law, as when agreeable to 'em. And God still continuing strictly to require supreme regard to himself, and forbidding all gratifications of these inferior passions, but only in perfect subordina- tion to the ends, and agreeableness to the rules and limits, which his holiness, honor and law prescribe, hence immediately arises enmity in the heart, now wholly under the power of self-love; and nothing but war ensues, in a constant course, against God. As, when a subject has once renounced his lawful sovereign, and set up a pretender in his stead, a state of enmity and war against his rightful king necessarily ensues. It were easy to show, how every lust and depraved disposition of man's heart would naturally arise from this *privative* original, if here were room for it. Thus 'tis easy to give an account, how total corruption of heart should follow on man's eating the forbidden fruit, though that was but one act of sin, *without God's putting* any evil into his heart, or *implanting* any bad principle, or *infusing* any corrupt taint, and so becoming the *author* of depravity. Only God's *withdrawing*, as it was highly proper and necessary that he should, from rebel-man, being as it were driven away by his abominable wickedness, and men's *natural* principles being *left to themselves*, this is sufficient to account for his becoming entirely corrupt, and bent on sinning against God. . . .

Chapter III. That Great Objection against the Imputation of Adam's Sin to His Posterity Considered, That Such Imputation Is Unjust and Unreasonable, Inasmuch as Adam and His Posterity Are Not One and the Same. . . .

That we may proceed with the greater clearness in considering the main objections against supposing the guilt of Adam's sin to be imputed to his posterity, I would premise some observations with a view to the right stating of the doctrine of the imputation of Adam's first sin; and then show the *reasonableness* of this doctrine, in opposition to the great clamor raised against it on this head.

I think, it would go far towards directing us to the more clear and distinct conceiving and right stating of this affair, if we steadily bear this in mind; that God, in each step of his proceeding with Adam, in relation to the covenant or constitution established with him, looked on his posterity as being one with him. (The propriety of his looking upon them so, I shall speak to afterwards.) And though he dealt more immediately with Adam, yet it was as the head of the whole body, and the root of the whole tree; and in his proceedings with him, he dealt with all the branches, as if they had been then existing in their root.

From which it will follow, that both guilt, or exposedness to punishment, and also depravity of heart, came upon Adam's posterity just as they came upon him, as much as if he and they had all coexisted, like a tree with many branches; allowing only for the difference necessarily resulting from the place Adam stood in, as head or root of the whole, and being first and most immediately dealt with, and most immediately acting and suffering. Otherwise, it is as if, in every step of proceeding, every alteration in the root had been attended, at the same instant, with the same steps and alterations throughout the whole tree, in each individual branch. I think, this will naturally follow on the supposition of there being a constituted *oneness* or *identity* of Adam and his posterity in this affair. . . .

The depraved disposition of Adam's heart is to be considered two ways. (1) As the first rising of an evil inclination in his heart, exerted in his first act of sin, and the ground of the complete transgression. (2) An evil disposition of heart continuing afterwards, as a confirmed principle, that came by God's forsaking him; which was a *punishment* of his first transgression. This confirmed corruption, by its remaining and continued operation, brought additional guilt on his soul.

And in like manner, depravity of heart is to be considered two ways in Adam's posterity. The first existing of a corrupt disposition in their hearts is not to be looked upon as sin belonging to them, distinct from their participation of Adam's first sin: it is as it were the *extended pollution* of that sin, through the whole tree, by virtue of the constituted union of the branches with the root; or the inherence of the sin of that head of the species in the members, in the consent and concurrence of the hearts of the members with the head in that first act. (Which may be, without God's being the author of sin; about which I have spoken in a former chapter.) But the depravity of nature, remaining an *established principle* in the heart of a child of Adam, and as exhibited in after-operations, is a consequence and punishment of the first apostasy thus participated, and brings new guilt. . . .

The first existence of an evil disposition of heart, amounting to a full consent to Adam's sin, no more infers God's being the author of that evil disposition in the child, than in the father. The first arising or existing of that evil disposition in the heart of Adam, was by God's *permission;* who could have prevented it, if he had pleased, by giving such influences of his spirit, as would have been absolutely effectual to hinder it; which, it is plain in fact, he did withhold: and whatever mystery may be supposed in the affair, yet no Christian will presume to say, it was not in perfect consistence with God's holiness and righteousness, notwithstanding Adam had been guilty of no offense before. So root and branches being one, according to God's wise constitution, the case in fact is, that by virtue of this oneness, answerable changes of effects through all the branches coexist with the changes in the root: consequently an evil disposition exists in the hearts of Adam's posterity, equivalent to that which was exerted in his own heart, when he eat the forbidden fruit. Which God has no hand in, any otherwise, than in *not* exerting such an influence, as might be effectual to prevent it. . . .

But now the grand objection is against the *reasonableness,* of such a constitution, by which Adam and his posterity should be looked upon as one, and dealt with accordingly, in an affair of such infinite consequence; so that if Adam sinned, they must necessarily be made sinners by his disobedience, and come into existence with the same depravity of disposition, and be looked upon and treated as though they were partakers with Adam in his act of sin. I have not room here to rehearse all Dr. Taylor's vehement exclamations against the reasonableness and justice of this. The reader may at his leisure consult his book, and see them in places referred to in the margin. Whatever black colors and frightful representations are employed on this occasion, all may be summed up in this, that Adam and his posterity are *not one,* but entirely *distinct agents.* But with respect to this mighty outcry made against the reasonableness of any such constitution, by which God is supposed to treat Adam and his posterity as one, I would make the following observations.

. . . It signifies nothing, to exclaim against plain fact. Such is the fact, most evident and acknowledged fact, with respect to the state of all mankind, without exception of one individual among all the natural descendants of Adam, as makes it apparent, that God actually deals with Adam and his posterity as one, in the affair of his apostasy, and its infinitely terrible consequences. It has been demonstrated, and shown to be in effect plainly acknowledged, that every individual of mankind comes into the world in such circumstances, as that there is no hope or possibility of any other than their violating God's holy law (if they ever live to act at all, as moral agents), and being thereby justly exposed to eternal ruin. And it is thus by God's ordering and disposing of things. And God either thus

deals with mankind, because he looks upon them as one with their first
father, and so treats them as sinful and guilty by his apostasy; or (which
won't mend the matter) he, without viewing them as at all concerned in
that affair, but as in every respect perfectly innocent, does nevertheless
subject them to this infinitely dreadful calamity. Adam by his sin was
exposed to the calamities and sorrows of this life, to temporal death, and
eternal ruin; as is confessed. And 'tis also in effect confessed, that all his
posterity come into the world in such a state, as that the certain consequence is their being exposed, and justly so, to the sorrows of this life, to
temporal death, and eternal ruin, unless saved by grace. So that we see,
God in fact deals with them together, or as one. If God orders the
consequences of Adam's sin, with regard to his posterity's welfare, even in
those things which are most important, and which do in the highest
degree concern their eternal interest, to be the same with the consequences to Adam himself, then he treats Adam and his posterity as in that
affair one. Hence, however the matter be attended with difficulty, fact
obliges us to get over the difficulty, either by finding out some solution, or
by shutting our mouths, and acknowledging the weakness and scantiness
of our understandings; as we must in innumerable other cases, where
apparent and undeniable fact, in God's works of creation and providence,
is attended with events and circumstances, the manner and reason of
which are difficult to our understandings. . . .

It being thus manifest, that this constitution, by which Adam and his
posterity are dealt with as one, is not unreasonable upon account of its
being injurious and hurtful to the interest of mankind, the only thing
remaining in the objection against such a constitution, is the *impropriety*
of it, as implying *falsehood,* and contradiction to the true nature of things;
as hereby they are viewed and treated as one, who are not one, but wholly
distinct; and no arbitrary constitution can ever make that to be true, which
in itself considered is not true.

The objection, however specious, is really founded on a false hypothesis, and wrong notion of what we call *sameness* or *oneness,* among created
things; and the seeming force of the objection arises from ignorance or
inconsideration of the degree, in which created identity or oneness with

past existence, in general, depends on the sovereign constitution and law of the Supreme Author and Disposer of the universe.

Some things, being most simply considered, are entirely distinct, and very diverse; which yet are so united by the established law of the Creator, in some respects and with regard to some purposes and effects, that by virtue of that establishment it is with them as if they were one. Thus a tree, grown great, and an hundred years old, is one plant with the little sprout, that first came out of the ground, from whence it grew, and has been continued in constant succession; though it's now so exceeding diverse, many thousand times bigger, and of a very different form, and perhaps not one atom the very same: yet God, according to an established law of nature, has in a constant succession communicated to it many of the same qualities, and most important properties, as if it were one. It has been his pleasure, to constitute an union in these respects, and for these purposes, naturally leading us to look upon all as one. So the body of man at forty years of age, is one with the infant body which first came into the world, from whence it grew; though now constituted of different substance, and the greater part of the substance probably changed scores (if not hundreds) of times; and though it be now in so many respects exceeding diverse, yet God, according to the course of nature, which he has been pleased to establish, has caused, that in a certain method it should communicate with that infantile body, in the same life, the same senses, the same features, and many the same qualities, and in union with the same soul; and so, with regard to these purposes, 'tis dealt with by him as one body. . . .

That God does, by his immediate power, *uphold* every created substance in being, will be manifest, if we consider, that their present existence is a *dependent* existence, and therefore is an *effect*, and must have some *cause:* and the cause must be one of these two: either the *antecedent existence* of the same substance, or else the *power of the Creator*. But it can't be the antecedent existence of the same substance. For instance, the existence of the body of the moon at this present moment, can't be the effect of its existence at the last foregoing moment. For not only was what existed the last moment, no active cause, but wholly a passive thing; but this also is to be considered, that no cause can produce effects in a *time* and *place* on which itself is *not*. 'Tis plain, nothing can exert itself, or operate, when and where it is not existing. But the moon's past existence was neither *where* nor *when* its present existence is. In point of time, what is *past* entirely ceases, when *present* existence begins; otherwise it would not be *past*. The past moment is ceased and gone, when the present moment takes place; and does no more coexist with it, than does any other moment that had ceased twenty years ago. Nor could the past existence of the particles of this moving body produce effects in any other place, than where it then was. But its existence at the present moment, in every point of it, is in a different place, from where its existence was at the last preceding moment. From these things, I suppose, it will certainly follow, that the present existence, either of this, or any other created substance, cannot be an effect of its past existence. The existences (so to speak) of an effect, or thing dependent, in different parts of space or duration, though ever so *near* one to another, don't at all coexist one with the other; and therefore are as truly different effects, as if those parts of space and duration were ever so far asunder: and the prior existence can no more be the proper cause of the new existence, in the next moment, or next part of space, than if it had been in an age before, or at a thousand miles distance, without any existence to fill up the intermediate time or space. Therefore the existence of created substances, in each successive moment, must be the effect of the *immediate* agency, will, and power of God.

If any shall say, this reasoning is not good, and shall insist upon it, that there is no need of any immediate divine power, to produce the present existence of created substances, but that their present existence is the same effect or consequence of past existence, according to the nature of things; that the established course of nature is sufficient to continue existence, where existence is once given; I allow it: but then it should be remembered, what nature is, in created things: and what the established course of nature is; that, as has been observed already, it is nothing, separate from the agency of God; and that, as Dr. Taylor says, "God, the Original of all being, is the only cause of all natural effects." A father, according to the course of nature, begets a child; an oak, according to the course of nature, produces an acorn, or a bud; so according to the course of nature, the former existence of the trunk of the tree is followed by its new or present existence. In the one case, and the other, the new effect is consequent on the former, only by the established laws, and settled course of nature; which is allowed to be nothing but the continued immediate efficiency of God, according to a constitution that he has been pleased to establish. Therefore, as our author greatly urges, that the child and the acorn, which come into existence according to the course of nature, in consequence of the prior existence and state of the parent and the oak, are truly *immediately* created or made by God; so must the existence of each created person and thing, at each moment of it, be from the immediate *continued* creation of God. It will certainly follow from these things, that God's *preserving* created things in being is perfectly equivalent to a *continued creation*, or to his creating those things out of nothing at *each moment* of their existence. If the continued existence of created things be wholly dependent on God's preservation, then those things would drop into nothing, upon the ceasing of the present moment, without a new exertion of the divine power to cause them to exist in the following moment. If there be any who own, that God preserves things in being, and yet hold that they would continue in being without any further help from him, after they once have existence; I think, it is hard to know what they mean. To what purpose can it be, to talk of God's preserving things in being, when there is no need of his preserving them? Or to talk of their being dependent on God for continued existence, when they would of themselves continue to exist, without his help, nay, though he should wholly withdraw his sustaining power and influence?

It will follow from what has been observed, that God's upholding created substance, or causing its existence in each successive moment, is altogether equivalent to an *immediate production out of nothing*, at each moment, because its existence at this moment is not merely in part from God, but wholly from him, and not in any part, or degree, from its antecedent existence. For the supposing, that its antecedent existence *concurs* with God in *efficiency*, to produce some part of the effect, is attended with all the very same absurdities, which have been shown to attend the supposition of its producing it wholly. Therefore the antecedent existence is nothing, as to any proper influence or assistance in the affair: and consequently God produces the effect as much from *nothing*, as if there had been nothing *before*. So that this effect differs not at all from the first creation, but only *circumstantially*; as in first creation there had been no such act and effect of God's power before; whereas, his giving existence afterwards, *follows* preceding acts and effects of the same kind, in an established order.

Now, in the next place, let us see how the consequence of these things is to my present purpose. If the existence of created substance, in each successive moment, be wholly the effect of God's immediate power, in that moment, without any dependence on prior existence, as much as the first creation out of nothing, then what exists at this moment, by this power, is a *new effect*; and simply and absolutely considered, not the same with any past existence, though it be like it, and follows it according to a certain established method. And there is no identity or oneness in the case, but what depends on the *arbitrary* constitution of the Creator; who by his wise sovereign establishment so unites these successive new effects, that he *treats them as one*, by communicating to them like properties, relations, and circumstances; and so, leads us to regard and treat them as one. When I call this an arbitrary constitution, I mean, that it is a constitution which depends on nothing but the divine will; which *divine will* depends on nothing but the *divine wisdom*. In this sense, the whole course of nature, with all that belongs to it, all its laws and methods, and constancy and regularity, continuance and proceeding, is an *arbitrary constitution*. In this sense, the continuance of the very being of the world and all its parts, as well as the manner of continued being, depends entirely on an arbitrary constitution: for it don't all *necessarily* follow, that because there was sound, or light, or color, or resistance, or gravity, or thought, or consciousness, or any other dependent thing the last moment, that therefore there shall be the like at the next. All dependent existence whatsoever is in a constant flux, ever passing and returning; renewed every moment, as the colors of bodies are every moment renewed by the light that shines upon them; and all is constantly proceeding from God, as light from the sun. "In him we live, and move, and have our being."

Thus it appears, if we consider matters strictly, there is no such thing as any identity or oneness in created objects, existing at different times, but what depends on *God's sovereign constitution*. And so it appears, that the objection we are upon, made against a supposed divine constitution, whereby Adam and his posterity are viewed and treated as one, in the manner and for the purposes supposed, as if it were not consistent with truth, because no constitution can make those to be one, which are not one; I say, it appears that this objection is built on a false hypothesis: for it appears, that a *divine constitution* is the thing which *makes truth*, in affairs of this nature. The objection supposes, there is a oneness in created beings, whence qualities and relations are derived down from past existence, distinct from, and prior to any oneness that can be supposed to be founded on divine constitution. Which is demonstrably false; and sufficiently appears so from things conceded by the adversaries themselves: and therefore the objection wholly falls to the ground. . . .

The Nature of True Virtue (1765)

Chapter I. Showing Wherein the Essence of True Virtue Consists

Whatever controversies and variety of opinions there are about the nature of virtue, yet all (excepting some skeptics who deny any real difference between virtue and vice) mean by it something *beautiful*, or rather some kind of *beauty* or excellency. 'Tis not *all* beauty that is called virtue; for instance, not the beauty of a building, of a flower, or of the rainbow: but some beauty belonging to beings that have *perception* and *will*. 'Tis not all beauty of *mankind* that is called virtue; for instance, not the external beauty of the countenance, or shape, gracefulness of motion, or harmony of voice: but it is a beauty that has its original seat in the mind. But yet perhaps not *everything* that may be called a beauty of mind is properly called virtue. There is a beauty of understanding and speculation. There is something in the ideas and conceptions of great philosophers and statesmen that may be called beautiful, which is a different thing from what is most commonly meant by virtue. But virtue is the beauty of those qualities and acts of the mind that are of a *moral* nature, i.e. such as are attended with dessert or worthiness of *praise* or *blame*. Things of this sort, it is generally agreed, so far as I know, are not anything belonging merely to speculation; but to the *disposition* and *will*, or (to use a general word, I suppose commonly well understood) to the "heart." Therefore I suppose, I shall not depart from the common opinion when I say that virtue is the beauty of the qualities and exercises of the heart, or those actions which proceed from them. So that when it is inquired, what is the nature of true *virtue*? this is the same as to inquire, what that is which renders any habit, disposition, or exercise of the heart truly *beautiful*?

I use the phrase "true" virtue, and speak of things "truly" beautiful, because I suppose it will generally be allowed that there is a distinction to be made between some things which are truly virtuous, and others which only seem to be virtuous, through a partial and imperfect view of things; that some actions and dispositions appear beautiful, if considered partially and superficially, or with regard to some things belonging to them, and in some of their circumstances and tendencies, which would appear otherwise in a more extensive and comprehensive view, wherein they are seen clearly in their whole nature and the extent of their connections in the universality of things.

There is a general and a particular beauty. By a "particular" beauty I mean that by which a thing appears beautiful when considered only with regard to its connection with, and tendency to some particular things within a limited and, as it were, a private sphere. And a "general" beauty is that by which a thing appears beautiful when viewed most perfectly, comprehensively and universally, with regard to all its tendencies, and its connections with everything it stands related to. The former may be without and against the latter. As a few notes in a tune, taken only by themselves, and in their relation to one another, may be harmonious; which, when considered with respect to all the notes in the tune, or the entire series of sounds they are connected with, may be very discordant and disagreeable. (Of which more afterwards.) *That only*, therefore, is what I mean by true virtue, which is that, belonging to the *heart* of an intelligent being, that is beautiful by a *general* beauty, or beautiful in a comprehensive view as it is in itself, and as related to everything that it stands in connection with. And therefore when we are inquiring concerning the nature of true virtue, viz. wherein this true and general beauty of the heart does most essentially consist, this is my answer to the inquiry—

True virtue most essentially consists in benevolence to Being in general. Or perhaps to speak more accurately, it is that consent, propensity and union of heart to Being in general, that is immediately exercised in a general good will.

The things which were before observed of the nature of true virtue naturally lead us to such a notion of it. If it has its seat in the heart, and is the general goodness and beauty of the disposition and exercise of that, in the most comprehensive view, considered with regard to its universal tendency, and as related to everything that it stands in connection with; what can it consist in, but a consent and good will to Being in general? Beauty does not consist in discord and dissent, but in consent and agreement. And if every intelligent being is some way related to Being in general, and is a part of the universal system of existence; and so stands in connection with the whole; what can its general and true beauty be, but its union and consent with the great whole?

If any such thing can be supposed as an union of heart to some particular being, or number of beings, disposing it to benevolence to a private circle or system of beings, which are but a small part of the whole; not implying a tendency to an union with the great system, and not at all inconsistent with enmity towards Being in general; this I suppose not to be of the nature of true virtue: although it may in some respects be good, and may appear beautiful in a confined and contracted view of things. But of this more afterwards.

It is abundantly plain by the Holy Scriptures, and generally allowed not only by Christian divines but by the more considerable Deists, that virtue most essentially consists in love. And I suppose, it is owned by the most considerable writers to consist in general love of benevolence, or kind affection: though, it seems to me, the meaning of some in this affair is not sufficiently explained; which perhaps occasions some error or confusion in discourses on this subject.

When I say, true virtue consists in love to Being in general, I shall not be likely to be understood, that no one act of the mind or exercise of love is of the nature of true virtue but what has Being in general, or the great system of universal existence, for its *direct* and *immediate* object: so that no exercise of love or kind affection to any one particular being, that is but a small part of this whole, has anything of the nature of true virtue. But, that the nature of true virtue consists in a disposition to benevolence towards Being in general: though, from such a disposition may arise exercises of love to particular beings, as objects are presented and occasions arise. No wonder that he who is of a generally benevolent disposition should be more disposed than another to have his heart moved with benevolent affection to particular persons, whom he is acquainted and conversant with, and from whom arise the greatest and most frequent occasions for exciting his benevolent temper. But my meaning is that no affections towards particular persons, or beings, are of the nature of true virtue but such as arise from a generally benevolent temper, or from that habit or frame of mind, wherein consists a disposition to love Being in general.

And perhaps it is needless for me to give notice to my readers that when I speak of an intelligent being's having a heart united and benevolently disposed to Being in general, I thereby mean *intelligent* Being in general. Not inanimate things, or beings that have no perception or will, which are not properly capable objects of benevolence.

Love is commonly distinguished into love of benevolence and love of complacence. Love of *benevolence* is that affection or propensity of the heart to any being, which causes it to incline to its well-being, or disposes it to desire and take pleasure in its happiness. And if I mistake not, 'tis agreeable to the common opinion that beauty in the object is not always the ground of this propensity: but that there may be such a thing as benevolence, or a disposition to the welfare of those that are not considered as beautiful; unless mere existence be accounted a beauty. And benevolence or goodness in the Divine Being is generally supposed not only to be prior to the beauty of many of its objects, but to their existence: so as to be the ground both of their existence and their beauty, rather than they the foundation of God's benevolence; as 'tis supposed that is God's goodness which moved him to give them both being and beauty. So that if all virtue primarily consists in that affection of heart to being, which is exercised in benevolence, or an inclination to its good, then God's virtue is so extended as to include a propensity not only to being actually existing, and actually beautiful, but to possible being, so as to incline him to give being, beauty and happiness. But not now to insist particularly on this—what I would have observed at present is that it must be allowed, benevolence doth not necessarily presuppose beauty in its object.

What is commonly called love of *complacence* presupposes beauty, for it is no other than delight in beauty; or complacence in the person or being beloved for his beauty.

If virtue be the beauty of an intelligent being, and virtue consists in love, then it is a plain inconsistence to suppose that virtue primarily consists in any love to its object for its beauty; either in a love of complacence, which is delight in a being for his beauty, or in a love of benevolence, that has the beauty of its object for its foundation. For that would be to suppose that the beauty of intelligent beings primarily consists in love to beauty; or, that their virtue first of all consists in their love to virtue. Which is an inconsistence, and going in a circle. Because it makes virtue, or beauty of mind, the foundation or first motive of that love wherein virtue originally consists, or wherein the very first virtue consists; or it supposes the first virtue to be the consequence and effect of virtue. So that virtue is originally the foundation and exciting cause of the very beginning or first being of virtue: which makes the first virtue both the ground and the consequence, both cause and effect of itself. Doubtless virtue primarily consists in something else besides any effect or consequence of virtue. If virtue consists primarily in love to virtue, then virtue, the thing loved, is the love of virtue: so that virtue must consist in the love of the love of virtue. And if it be inquired what that virtue is, which virtue consists in the love of the love of, it must be answered, 'tis the love of virtue. So that there must be the love of the love of the love of virtue, and so on *in infinitum.* For there is no end of going back in a circle. We never come to any beginning or foundation. For 'tis without beginning and hangs on nothing.

Therefore, if the essence of virtue or beauty of mind lies in love, or a disposition to love, it must primarily consist in something *different* both from complacence, which is a delight in beauty, and also from any benevolence that has the beauty of its object for its foundation. Because 'tis absurd to say that virtue is primarily and first of all the consequence of itself. For this makes virtue primarily prior to itself.

Nor can virtue primarily consist in *gratitude*; or one being's benevolence to another for his benevolence to him. Because this implies the same inconsistence. For it supposes a benevolence prior to gratitude that is the cause of gratitude. Therefore the first benevolence, or that benevolence which has none prior to it, can't be gratitude.

Therefore there is room left for no other conclusion than that the primary object of virtuous love is Being, simply considered; or that true virtue primarily consists, not in love to any particular beings, because of their virtue or beauty, nor in gratitude, because they love us; but in a propensity and union of heart to Being simply considered; exciting "absolute Benevolence" (if I may so call it) to Being in general. I say, true virtue "primarily" consists in this. For I am far from asserting that there is no true virtue in any other love than this absolute benevolence. But I would express what appears to me to be the truth on this subject in the following particulars.

The *first* object of a virtuous benevolence is *Being*, simply considered: and if Being, *simply* considered, be its object, then Being *in general* is its object; and the thing it has an ultimate propensity to, is the *highest good* of Being in general. And it will seek the good of every *individual* being unless it be conceived as not consistent with the highest good of Being in general. In which case the good of a particular being, or some beings, may be given up for the sake of the highest good of Being in general. And particularly if there be any being that is looked upon as statedly and irreclaimably opposite and an enemy to Being in general, then consent and adherence to Being in general will induce the truly virtuous heart to forsake that being, and to oppose it.

And further, if Being, simply considered, be the first object of a truly virtuous benevolence, then that Being who has *most* of being, or has the greatest share of existence, other things being equal, so far as such a being is exhibited to our faculties or set in our view, will have the *greatest* share of the propensity and benevolent affection of the heart. I say "other things being equal" especially because there is a *secondary* object of virtuous benevolence, that I shall take notice of presently, which is one thing that must be considered as the ground or motive to a purely virtuous benevolence. Pure benevolence in its *first* exercise is nothing else but being's uniting, consent, or propensity to Being; appearing true and pure by its extending to Being in general, and inclining to the general highest good, and to each being, whose welfare is consistent with the highest general good, in proportion to the degree of *existence*[1]—understand, other things being equal.

1. I say "in proportion to the degree of *existence*" because one being may have more *existence* than another, as he may be *greater* than another. That which is *great* has more existence, and is further from nothing, than that which is *little*. One being may have everything positive belonging to it, or everything which goes to its positive existence (in opposition to defect) in an higher degree than another; or a greater capacity and power, greater understanding, every faculty and every positive quality in an higher degree. An *archangel* must be supposed to have more existence, and to be every way further removed from *nonentity*, than a *worm* or a *flea*.—Edwards' note.

The *second* object of a virtuous propensity of heart is *benevolent* being. A secondary ground of pure benevolence is virtuous benevolence itself in its object. When anyone under the influence of general benevolence sees another being possessed of the like general benevolence, this attaches his heart to him, and draws forth greater love to him, than merely his having existence: because so far as the being beloved has love to Being in general, so far his own being is, as it were, enlarged; extends to, and in some sort comprehends, Being in general: and therefore he that is governed by love to Being in general, must of necessity have complacence in him, and the greater degree of benevolence to him, as it were out of gratitude to him for his love to general existence, that his own heart is extended and united to, and so looks on its interest as its own. 'Tis because his heart is thus united to Being in general, that he looks on a benevolent propensity to Being in general, wherever he sees it, as the beauty of the being in whom it is; an excellency that renders him worthy of esteem, complacence, and the greater good will.

But several things may be noted more particularly concerning this secondary ground of a truly virtuous love.

1. That loving a being on *this ground* necessarily arises from pure benevolence to Being *in general,* and comes to the same thing. For he that has a simple and pure good will to general entity or existence must love that temper in others that agrees and conspires with itself. A spirit of consent to Being must agree with consent to Being. That which truly and sincerely seeks the good of others must approve of, and love, that which joins with him in seeking the good of others.

2. This which has been now mentioned as a secondary ground of virtuous love is the thing wherein true moral or spiritual *beauty* primarily consists. Yea, spiritual beauty consists wholly in this, and the various qualities and exercises of mind which proceed from it, and the external actions which proceed from these internal qualities and exercises. And in these things consist all true *virtue,* viz. in this love of Being, and the qualities and acts which arise from it.

3. As all spiritual beauty lies in these virtuous principles and acts, so 'tis primarily *on this account* that they are beautiful, viz. that they imply *consent* and *union* with Being *in general.* This is the primary and most essential

beauty of everything that can justly be called by the name of virtue, or is any moral excellency in the eye of one that has a perfect view of things. I say "the primary and most essential beauty" because there is a secondary and inferior sort of beauty; which I shall take notice of afterwards.

4. This spiritual beauty, that is but a *secondary* ground of a virtuous benevolence, is the ground not only of benevolence but of *complacence*, and is the *primary* ground of the latter; that is, when the complacence is truly virtuous. Love to us in particular, and kindness received, may be a secondary ground: but this is the primary objective foundation of it.

5. It must be noted, that the *degree* of the *amiableness* or *valuableness* of true virtue, primarily consisting in consent and a benevolent propensity of heart to Being in general, in the eyes of one that is influenced by such a spirit, is not in the *simple* proportion of the degree of benevolent affection seen, but in a proportion *compounded* of the greatness of the benevolent being, or the degree of *being* and the degree of *benevolence*. One that loves Being in general will necessarily value good will to Being in general, wherever he sees it. But if he sees the same benevolence in *two* beings, he will value it *more* in two than in one only. Because it is a greater thing, more favorable to Being in general, to have two beings to favor it than only one of them. For there is more being that favors being: both together having more being than one alone. So, if one being be as great as two, has as much existence as both together, and has the same degree of general benevolence, it is more favorable to Being in general than if there were general benevolence in a being that had but half that share of existence. As a large quantity of gold, with the same degree of preciousness, i.e. with the same excellent quality of matter, is more valuable than a small quantity of the same metal.

6. It is impossible that anyone should truly *relish* this beauty, consisting in general benevolence, who has not that temper himself. I have observed that if any being is possessed of such a temper, he will unavoidably be pleased with the same temper in another. And it may in like manner be demonstrated that 'tis such a spirit, and nothing else, which will relish such a spirit. For if a being, destitute of benevolence, should love benevolence to Being in general, it would prize and seek that which it had no value for. Because to love an inclination to the good of Being in general

would imply a loving and prizing the good of Being in general. For how should one love and value a *disposition* to a thing, or a *tendency to promote* a thing, and for that very reason, because it tends to promote it—when the *thíng* itself is what he is regardless of, and has no value for, nor desires to have promoted?

Chapter II. Showing How That Love Wherein True Virtue Consists Respects the Divine Being and Created Beings

From what has been said, 'tis evident that true virtue must chiefly consist in love to God; the Being of beings, infinitely the greatest and best of beings. This appears, whether we consider the primary or secondary ground of virtuous love. It was observed that the *first* objective ground of that love, wherein true virtue consists, is Being, simply considered: and as a necessary consequence of this, that being who has the most of being, or the greatest share of universal existence, has proportionably the greatest share of virtuous benevolence, so far as such a being is exhibited to the faculties of our minds, other things being equal. But God has infinitely the greatest share of existence, or is infinitely the greatest being. So that all other being, even that of all created things whatsoever, throughout the whole universe, is as nothing in comparison of the Divine Being.

And if we consider the *secondary* ground of love, viz. beauty or moral excellency, the same thing will appear. For as God is infinitely the greatest being, so he is allowed to be infinitely the most beautiful and excellent: and all the beauty to be found throughout the whole creation, is but the reflection of diffused beams of that Being who hath an infinite fullness of brightness and glory. God's beauty is infinitely more valuable than that of all other beings upon both those accounts mentioned, viz. the *degree* of his virtue and the greatness of the being possessed of this virtue. And God has sufficiently exhibited himself, in his being, his infinite greatness and excellency: and has given us faculties, whereby we are capable of plainly discovering immense superiority to all other beings in these respects. Therefore he that has true virtue, consisting in benevolence to Being in general, and in that complacence in virtue, or moral beauty, and benevolence to virtuous being, must necessarily have a supreme love to God, both of benevolence and complacence. And all true virtue must radically and essentially, and as it were summarily, consist in this. Because God is not only infinitely greater and more excellent than all other being, but he is the head of the universal system of existence; the foundation and fountain of all being and all beauty; from whom all is perfectly derived, and on whom all is most absolutely and perfectly dependent; *of whom*, and *through whom*, and *to whom* is all being and all perfection; and whose being and beauty is as it were the sum and comprehension of all existence and excellence: much more than the sun is the fountain and summary comprehension of all the light and brightness of the day. . . .

There seems to be an inconsistence in some writers on morality, in this respect, that they don't wholly exclude a regard to the *Deity* out of their schemes of morality, but yet mention it so slightly, that they leave me room and reason to suspect they esteem it a less important and a subordinate part of true morality; and insist on benevolence to the *created system* in such a manner as would naturally lead one to suppose they look upon that as by far the most important and essential thing in their scheme. But why should this be? If true virtue consists partly in a respect to God, then doubtless it consists *chiefly* in it. If true morality requires that we should have some regard, some benevolent affection to our Creator, as well as to his creatures, then doubtless it requires the first regard to be paid to him; and that he be every way the supreme object of our benevolence. If his being above our reach, and beyond all capacity of being profited by us, don't hinder but that nevertheless he is the proper object of our love, then it don't hinder that he should be loved according to his *dignity*, or according to the degree in which he has those things wherein worthiness of regard consists, so far as we are capable of it. But this worthiness, none will deny, consists in these two things, *greatness* and moral *goodness*. And those that own a God don't deny that he infinitely exceeds all other beings in these. If the Deity is to be looked upon as within that system of beings which properly terminates our benevolence, or belonging to that whole, certainly he is to be regarded as the *head* of the system, and the *chief* part of it; if it be proper to call him a *part* who is infinitely more than all the rest, and in comparison of whom and without whom all the rest are nothing, either as to beauty or existence. And therefore certainly, unless we will be atheists, we must allow that true virtue does primarily and most essentially consist in a supreme love to God; and that where this is wanting, there can be no true virtue.

But this being a matter of the highest importance, I shall say something further to make it plain that love to God is most essential to true virtue; and that no benevolence whatsoever to other beings can be of the nature of true virtue, without it.

And therefore let it be supposed that some beings, by natural instinct or by some other means, have a determination of mind to union and benevolence to a *particular person* or *private system*,[2] which is but a small part of the universal system of being: and that this disposition or determination of mind is independent on, or not subordinate to, benevolence to *Being in general*. Such a determination, disposition, or affection of mind is not of the nature of true virtue.

This is allowed by all with regard to *self-love*, in which good will is confined to one single person only. And there are the same reasons why any other private affection or good will, though extending to a society of persons, independent of, and unsubordinate to, benevolence to the universality, should not be esteemed truly virtuous. For, notwithstanding it extends to a number of persons which taken together are more than a single person, yet the whole falls infinitely short of the universality of existence; and if put in the scales with it, has no greater proportion to it than a single person.

However, it may not be amiss more particularly to consider the reasons why *private affections*, or good will limited to a particular circle of beings, falling infinitely short of the whole existence, and not dependent upon it; nor subordinate to general benevolence, cannot be of the nature of true virtue.

1. Such a private affection, detached from general benevolence and

---

2. It may be here noted that when hereafter I use a phrase as "private system of beings," or others similar, I thereby intend any system or society of beings that contains but a small part of the great system comprehending the universality of existence. I think *that* may well be called a "private system" which is but an infinitely small part of this great whole we stand related to. I therefore also call that affection "private affection" which is limited to so narrow a circle; and that "general affection" or "benevolence" which has *Being in general* for its object.—Edwards' note.

independent on it, as the case may be, will be *against* general benevolence, or of a contrary tendency; and will set a person *against* general existence, and make him an enemy to it. As it is with *selfishness*, or when a man is governed by a regard to his own private interest, independent of regard to the public good, such a temper exposes a man to act the part of an enemy to the public. As, in every case wherein his private interest seems to clash with the public; or in all those cases wherein such things are presented to his view that suit his personal appetites or private inclinations, but are inconsistent with the good of the public. On which account a selfish, contracted, narrow spirit is generally abhorred, and is esteemed base and sordid. But if a man's affection takes in half a dozen more and his regards extend so far beyond his own single person as to take in his children and family; or if it reaches further still, to a larger circle, but falls infinitely short of the universal system, and is exclusive of Being in general; his private affection exposes him to the same thing, viz. to pursue the interest of its particular object in *opposition* to general existence: which is certainly contrary to the tendency of true virtue; yea, directly contrary to the main and most essential thing in its nature, the thing on account of which chiefly its nature and tendency is good. For the chief and most essential good that is in virtue is its favoring Being in general. Now certainly, if private affection to a limited system had in itself the essential nature of virtue, it would be impossible that it should in any circumstance whatsoever have a tendency and inclination directly *contrary* to that wherein the essence of virtue chiefly consists.

2. Private affection, if not subordinate in general affection, is not only liable, as the case *may* be, to issue in enmity to Being in general, but has a *tendency* to it, as the case certainly *is* and must necessarily be. For he that is influenced by private affection, not subordinate to regard to Being in general, sets up its particular or limited object *above* Being in general; and this most naturally tends to enmity against the latter, which is by right the great supreme, ruling, and absolutely sovereign object of our regard. Even as the setting up another prince as supreme in any kingdom, distinct from the lawful sovereign, naturally tends to enmity against the lawful sovereign. Wherever it is sufficiently published that the supreme, infinite, and all-comprehending Being requires a supreme regard to himself; and in-

sists upon it, that our respect to him should universally rule in our hearts, and every other affection be subordinate to it, and this under the pain of his displeasure (as we must suppose it is in the world of intelligent creatures, if God maintains a moral kingdom in the world), then a consciousness of our having chosen and set up another prince to rule over us, and subjected our hearts to him, and continuing in such an act, must unavoidably excite enmity and fix us in a stated opposition to the Supreme Being. This demonstrates that affection to a private society or system, independent on general benevolence, cannot be of the nature of true virtue. For this would be absurd, that it has the nature and essence of true virtue and yet at the same time has a *tendency opposite* to true virtue.

3. Not only would affection to a private system, unsubordinate to regard to Being in general, have a tendency to opposition to the supreme object of virtuous affection, as its effect and consequence, but would become *itself* an opposition to that object. Considered by itself in its nature, detached from its effects, it is an instance of great opposition to the rightful supreme object of our respect. For it exalts its private object above the other great and infinite object; and sets that up as supreme, in opposition to this. It puts down Being in general, which is infinitely superior in itself and infinitely more important, in an inferior place; yea, subjects the supreme general object to this private, infinitely inferior object: which is to treat it with great contempt and truly to act in opposition to it, and to act in opposition to the true order of things, and in opposition to that which is infinitely the supreme interest; making this supreme and infinitely important interest, as far as in us lies, to be subject to, and dependent on, an interest infinitely inferior. This is to act against it, and to act the part of an enemy to it. He that takes a subject, and exalts him above his prince, sets him as supreme instead of the prince, and treats his prince wholly as a subject, therein acts the part of an enemy to his prince.

From these things, I think, it is manifest that no affection limited to any private system, not dependent on, nor subordinate to Being in general can be of the nature of true virtue; and this, whatever the private system be, let it be more or less extensive, consisting of a greater or smaller number of individuals, so long as it contains an infinitely little part of universal existence, and so bears no proportion to the great all-comprehending system. And consequently, that no affection whatsoever to any creature, or any system of created beings, which is not dependent on, nor subordinate to a propensity or union of the heart to God, the Supreme and Infinite Being, can be of the nature of true virtue.

From hence also it is evident that the *divine virtue*, or the virtue of the divine mind, must consist primarily in *love to himself*, or in the mutual love and friendship which subsists eternally and necessarily between the several persons in the Godhead, or that infinitely strong propensity there is in these divine persons one to another. There is no need of multiplying words to prove that it must be thus, on a supposition that virtue in its most essential nature, consists in benevolent affection or propensity of heart towards Being in general; and so flowing out to particular beings, in a greater or lesser degree, according to the measure of existence and beauty which they are possessed of. It will also follow from the foregoing things that God's goodness and love to created beings is derived from and subordinate to his love to himself. . . .

With respect to the manner in which a virtuous love in *created* beings, *one to another*, is dependent on, and derived from love to *God*, this will appear by a proper consideration of what has been said; that it is sufficient to render love to any created being virtuous, if it arise from the temper of mind wherein consists a disposition to love God supremely. Because it appears from what has been already observed, all that love to *particular beings* which is the fruit of a benevolent propensity of heart to Being in general, is virtuous love. But, as has been remarked, a benevolent propensity of heart to Being in general, and a temper or disposition to love God supremely, are in effect the same thing. Therefore, if love to a created being comes from that temper or propensity of the heart, it is virtuous.

However, every particular exercise of love to a creature may not *sensibly* arise from any exercise of love to God, or an explicit consideration of any similitude, conformity, union or relation to God in the creature beloved. . . .

By these things it appears that a truly virtuous mind, being as it were under the sovereign dominion of *love to God*, does above all things seek the *glory of God*, and makes *this* his supreme, governing, and ultimate end: consisting in the expression of God's perfections in their proper effects, and in the manifestation of God's glory to created understandings, and the communications of the infinite fullness of God to the creature; in the creature's highest esteem of God, love to God, and joy in God, and in the proper exercises and expressions of these. And so far as a virtuous mind exercises true virtue in benevolence to created beings, it chiefly seeks the good of the creature, consisting in its knowledge or view of God's glory and beauty, its union with God, and conformity to him, love to him, and joy in him. And that temper or disposition of heart, that consent, union, or propensity of mind to Being in general, which appears chiefly in such exercises, is virtue, truly so called; or in other words, true grace and real holiness. And no other disposition or affection but this is of the nature of true virtue.

Corollary. Hence it appears that these *schemes* of religion or moral philosophy, which, however well in some respects they may treat of benevolence to *mankind,* and other virtues depending on it, yet have not a supreme regard to God, and love to him, laid in the *foundation* and all other virtues handled in a *connection* with this, and in a *subordination* to this, are no true schemes of philosophy, but are fundamentally and essentially defective. And whatever other benevolence or generosity towards mankind, and other virtues, or moral qualifications which go by that name, any are possessed of that are not attended with a *love to God,* which is altogether above them, and to which they are subordinate, and on which they are dependent, there is nothing of the nature of true virtue or religion in them. And it may be asserted in general that nothing is of the nature of true virtue, in which God is not the *first* and the *last;* or which, with regard to their exercises in general, have not their first foundation and source in apprehensions of God's supreme dignity and glory, and in answerable esteem and love of him, and have not respect to God as the supreme end. . . .

Chapter IV. Of Self-Love and Its Various Influence to Cause Love to Others, or the Contrary

Many assert that all love arises from self-love. In order to determine this point, it should be clearly determined what is meant by self-love.

Self-love, I think, is generally defined: a man's love of his own happiness. Which is short, and may be thought very plain: but indeed is an ambiguous definition, as the pronoun "his own" is equivocal, and liable to be taken in two very different senses. For a man's "own happiness" may either be taken universally, for all the happiness or pleasure which the mind is in any regard the subject of, or whatever is grateful and pleasing to men; or it may be taken for the pleasure a man takes in his own proper, private, and separate good. And so "self-love" may be taken two ways.

1. Self-love may be taken for the same as his loving whatsoever is grateful or pleasing to him. Which comes only to this, that self-love is a man's liking, and being suited and pleased in that which he likes, and which pleases him; or that 'tis a man's loving what he loves. For whatever a man loves, that thing is grateful and pleasing to him, whether that be his own peculiar happiness, or the happiness of others. And if this be all that they mean by self-love, no wonder they suppose that all love may be resolved into self-love. For it is undoubtedly true that whatever a man loves, his love may be resolved into his loving what he loves—if that be proper speaking. If by self-love is meant nothing else but a man's loving what is grateful or pleasing to him, and being averse to what is disagreeable, this is calling *that* "self-love" which is only a general capacity of loving, or hating; or a capacity of being either pleased or displeased: which is the same thing as a man's having a faculty of will. For if nothing could be either pleasing or displeasing, agreeable or disagreeable, to a man, then he could incline to nothing, and will nothing. But if he is capable of having inclination, will and choice, then what he inclines to, and chooses, is grateful to him; whatever that be, whether it be his own private good, the good of his neighbors, or the glory of God. And so far as it is grateful or pleasing to him, so far it is a part of his pleasure, good, or happiness.

But if this be what is meant by "self-love," there is an impropriety and absurdity even in the putting of the question, Whether all our love, or our love to each particular object of our love, don't arise from self-love? For that would be the same as to inquire, Whether the reason why our love is fixed on such and such particular objects is not that we have a capacity of loving some things? This may be a general reason why men love or hate anything at all; and therein differ from stones and trees, which love nothing and hate nothing.

But it can never be a reason why men's love is placed on such and such objects. That a man, in general, loves and is pleased with happiness, or (which is the same thing) has a capacity of enjoying happiness, cannot be the reason why such and such things become his happiness: as for instance, why the good of his neighbor, or the happiness and glory of God, is grateful and pleasing to him, and so becomes a part of his happiness.

Or if what they mean, who say that all love comes from self-love, be not that our loving such and such particular persons and things, arises from our love to happiness in general, but from a love to love our own happiness, which consists in these objects; so, the reason why we love benevolence to our friends, or neighbors, is because we love our happiness, consisting in their happiness, which we take pleasure in—still the notion is absurd. For here the effect is made the cause of that of which it is the effect: our happiness, consisting in the happiness of the person beloved, is made the cause of our love to that person. Whereas, the truth plainly is that our love to the person is the cause of our delighting, or being happy in his happiness. How comes our happiness to consist in the happiness of such as we love, but by our hearts being first united to them in affection, so that as it were, we look on them as ourselves, and so on their happiness as our own?

Men who have benevolence to others have pleasure when they see others' happiness, because seeing their happiness gratifies some inclination that was in their hearts before. They before inclined to their happiness; which was by benevolence or good will; and therefore when they see their happiness, their inclination is suited, and they are pleased. But the being of inclinations and appetites is prior to any pleasure in gratifying these appetites.

2. "Self-love," as the phrase is used in common speech, most commonly signifies a man's regard to his confined *private self*, or love to himself with respect to his *private interest*.

By "private" interest I mean that which most immediately consists in those pleasures, or pains, that are *personal*. For there is a comfort, and a grief, that some have in others' pleasures, or pains; which are in others originally, but are derived to them, or in some measure become theirs, by virtue of a benevolent union of heart with others. And there are other pleasures and pains that are originally our own, and not what we have by such a participation with others, which consist in perceptions agreeable, or contrary, to certain personal inclinations implanted in our nature; such as the sensitive appetites and aversions. Such also is the disposition or the determination of the mind to be pleased with external beauty, and with all inferior secondary beauty, consisting in uniformity, proportion, etc., whether in things external or internal, and to dislike the contrary deformity. Such also is the natural disposition in men to be pleased in a perception of their being the objects of the honor and love of others, and displeased with others' hatred and contempt.

For pleasures and uneasinesses of this kind are doubtless as much owing to an immediate determination of the mind by a fixed law of our nature as any of the pleasures or pains of external sense. And these pleasures are properly of the private and personal kind; being not by any participation of the happiness or sorrow of others, through benevolence.

'Tis evidently mere self-love that appears in this disposition. It is easy to see that a man's love to himself will make him love love to himself, and hate hatred to himself. And as God has constituted our nature, self-love is exercised in no one disposition more than in this. Men, probably, are capable of much more pleasure and pain through this determination of the mind than by any other personal inclination or aversion whatsoever. Though perhaps we don't so very often see instances of extreme suffering by this means, as by some others; yet we often see evidences of men's dreading the contempt of others more than death: and by such instances may conceive something what men would suffer, if universally hated and despised; and may reasonably infer something of the greatness of the misery that would arise under a sense of universal abhorrence, in a great view of intelligent Being in general, or in a clear view of the Deity, as incomprehensibly and immensely great, so that all other beings are as nothing and vanity—together with a sense of his immediate continual presence, and an infinite concern with him and dependence upon him— and living constantly in the midst of most clear and strong evidences and manifestations of his hatred and contempt and wrath.

But to return, these things may be sufficient to explain what I mean by private interest; in regard to which self-love, most properly so called, is immediately exercised.

And here I would observe that if we take self-love in this sense, so love to some others may truly be the effect of self-love; i.e. according to the common method and order which is maintained in the laws of nature. For no created thing has power to produce an effect any otherwise than by virtue of the laws of nature. Thus, that a man should love those that are of his party, when there are different parties contending one with another; and that are warmly engaged on his side, and promote his interest: this is the natural consequence of a private self-love. . . . [A] man's love to those that love him is no more than a certain expression or effect of self-love. No other principle is needful in order to the effect, if nothing intervenes to countervail the natural tendency of self-love. Therefore there is no more virtue in a man's thus loving his friends merely from self-love than there is in self-love itself, the principle from whence it proceeds. So, a man's being disposed to hate those that hate him, or to resent injuries done him, arises from self-love in like manner as the loving those that love us, and being thankful for kindness shown us. . . .

Another sort of affections which may be properly referred to self-love, as its source, and which might be expected to be the fruit of it, according to the general analogy of nature's laws, is affections to such as are near to us by the ties of nature; that we look upon as those whose beings we have been the occasions of, and that we have a very peculiar propriety in, and whose circumstances, even from the very beginning of their existence, do many ways lead them, as it were, necessarily to an high esteem of us, and to treat us with great dependence, submission and compliance; and whom the constitution of the world makes to be united in interest, and accordingly to act as one in innumerable affairs, with a communion in each other's affections, desires, cares, friendships, enmities, and pursuits. Which is the case of men's affection to their children. And in like manner self-love will also beget in man some degree of affections towards others with whom he has connection in any degree parallel. . . .

And as men may love persons and things from self-love, so may love to qualities and characters arise from the same source. Some represent as

though there were need of a great degree of metaphysical refining to make
it out that men approve of others from self-love, whom they hear of at a
distance, or read of in history, or see represented on the stage, from whom
they expect no profit or advantage. But perhaps it is not considered that
what we approve of in the first place is the character; and from the
character we approve the person. And is it a strange thing that men should
from self-love like a temper or character, which in its nature and tendency
falls in with the nature and tendency of self-love; and which, we know by
experience and self-evidence, without metaphysical refining, in the general tends to men's pleasure and benefit? And on the contrary, should
dislike what they see tends to men's pain and misery? Is there need of a
great degree of subtilty and abstraction to make it out that a child, which
has heard and seen much, strongly to fix an idea of the pernicious deadly
nature of the rattlesnake, should have aversion to that species or form,
from self-love; so as to have a degree of this aversion and disgust excited by
seeing even the picture of that animal? And that from the same self-love it
should be pleased and entertained with a lively figure and representation
of some pleasant fruit, which it has often tasted the sweetness of? Or, with
the image of some bird which, it has always been told, is innocent, and
whose pleasant singing it has often been entertained with?—though the
child neither fears being bitten by the picture of the snake, nor expects to
eat of the painted fruit, or to hear the figure of the bird sing. I suppose
none will think it difficult to allow that such an approbation or disgust of a
child may be accounted for from its natural delight in the pleasures of taste
and hearing, and its aversion to pain and death, through self-love, together with the habitual connection of these agreeable or terrible ideas
with the form and qualities of these objects, the ideas of which are impressed on the mind of the child by their images.

And where is the difficulty of allowing that a child or man may hate the
general character of a spiteful and malicious man, for the like reason as he
hates the general nature of a serpent; knowing, from reason, instruction
and experience, that malice in men is pernicious to mankind, as well as
spite or poison in a serpent? And if a man may from self-love disapprove
the vices of malice, envy, and others of that sort which naturally tend to the
hurt of mankind, why may he not from the same principle approve the

contrary virtues of meekness, peaceableness, benevolence, charity, generosity, justice, and the social virtues in general; which, he as easily and clearly knows, naturally tend to the good of mankind?

'Tis undoubtedly true that some have a love to these virtues from a higher principle. But yet I think it as certainly true that there is generally in mankind a sort of approbation of them which arises from self-love.

Besides what has been already said, the same thing further appears from this: that men commonly are most affected towards, and do most highly approve, those virtues which agree with their interest most, according to their various conditions in life. We see that persons of low condition are especially enamored with a condescending, accessible, affable temper in the great; not only in those whose condescension has been exercised towards themselves; but they will be peculiarly taken with such a character when they have accounts of it from others, or when they meet with it in history, or even in romance. The poor will most highly approve and commend liberality. The weaker sex, who especially need assistance and protection, will peculiarly esteem and applaud fortitude and generosity in those of the other sex they read or hear of, or have presented to them on a stage.

As I think it plain from what has been observed that men may approve, and be disposed to commend a benevolent temper from self-love, so the higher the degree of benevolence is, the more may they approve of it. Which will account for some kind of approbation, from this principle, even of love to enemies; viz. as a man's loving his enemies is an evidence of a high degree of benevolence of temper—the degree of it appearing from the obstacles it overcomes. . . .

Some vices may become in a degree odious by the influence of self-love, through an habitual connection of ideas of contempt with it; contempt being what self-love abhors. So it may often be with drunkenness, gluttony, sottishness, cowardice, sloth, niggardliness. The idea of contempt becomes associated with the idea of such vices, both because we are used to observe that these things are commonly objects of contempt, and also find that they excite contempt in ourselves. Some of them appear marks of littleness, i.e. of small abilities, and weakness of mind, and insufficiency for any considerable effects among mankind. By others, men's influence is contracted into a narrow sphere, and by such means persons become of less importance, and more insignificant among mankind. And things of little importance are naturally little accounted of. And some of these ill qualities are such as mankind find it their interest to treat with contempt, as they are very hurtful to human society.

There are no particular moral virtues whatsoever, but what in some or other of these ways, and most of them in several of these ways, come to have some kind of approbation from self-love, without the influence of a truly virtuous principle; nor any particular vices, but what by the same means meet with some disapprobation.

This kind of approbation and dislike, through the joint influence of self-love and association of ideas, is in very many vastly heightened by education; as this is the means of a strong, close, and almost irrefragable association, in innumerable instances, of ideas which have no connection any other way than by education; and of greatly strengthening that association, or connection, which persons are led into by other means: as anyone would be convinced, perhaps more effectually than in most other ways, if they had opportunity of any considerable acquaintance with American savages and their children. . . .

Personal Writings

Diary (1722)

Dec. 18, [1722]. This day made the 35th Resolution. The reason why I, in the least, question my interest in God's love and favor, is, 1. Because I cannot speak so fully to my experience of that preparatory work, of which divines speak. 2. I do not remember that I experienced regeneration, exactly in those steps, in which divines say it is generally wrought. 3. I do not feel the Christian graces sensibly enough, particularly faith. I fear they are only such hypocritical outside affections, which wicked men may feel, as well as others. They do not seem to be sufficiently inward, full, sincere, entire and hearty. They do not seem so substantial, and so wrought into my very nature, as I could wish. 4. Because I am sometimes guilty of sins of omission and commission. Lately I have doubted, whether I do not transgress in evil speaking. This day, resolved, No.

Wednesday, Jan. 2, 1722–23. Dull. I find by experience, that let me make resolutions, and do what I will, with never so many inventions, it is all nothing, and to no purpose at all, without the motions of the Spirit of God: for if the Spirit of God should be as much withdrawn from me always, as for the week past, notwithstanding all I do, I should not grow; but should languish, and miserably fade away—there is no dependence upon myself. It is to no purpose to resolve, except we depend on the grace of God; for if it were not for his mere grace, one might be a very good man one day, and a very wicked one the next. I find also by experience, that there is no guessing out the ends of providence, in particular dispensations towards me—any otherwise than as afflictions come as corrections for sin, and God intends when we meet with them, to desire us to look back on our ways, and see wherein we have done amiss, and lament that particular sin, and all our sins, before him: knowing this, also, that all things shall work together for our good; not knowing in what way, indeed, but trusting in God.

Wednesday, Jan. 9, at night. Decayed. I am sometimes apt to think, I have a great deal more of holiness than I have. I find now and then, that abominable corruption which is directly contrary to what I read of eminent Christians. I do not seem to be half so careful to improve time, to do everything quick, and in as short a time as I possibly can, nor to be perpetually engaged to think about religion, as I was yesterday and the day before, nor indeed as I have been at certain times, perhaps a twelvemonth ago. If my resolutions of that nature, from that time, had always been kept alive and awake, how much better might I have been, than I now am. How deceitful is my heart! I take up a strong resolution, but how soon does it weaken!

Thursday, Jan. 10, about noon. Reviving. 'Tis a great dishonor to Christ, in whom I hope I have an interest, to be uneasy at my worldly state and condition. When I see the prosperity of others, and that all things go easy with them; the world is smooth to them, and they are happy in many respects, and very prosperous, or are advanced to much honor, etc. to grudge and envy them, or be the least uneasy at it; to wish or long for the same prosperity, and that it would ever be so with me. Wherefore concluded always to rejoice in everyone's prosperity, and to expect for myself no happiness of that nature as long as I live; but depend upon afflictions, and betake myself entirely to another happiness.

I think I find myself much more sprightly and healthy, both in body and mind, for my self-denial in eating, drinking, and sleeping.

I think it would be advantageous every morning to consider my business and temptations; and what sins I shall be exposed to that day: and to make a resolution how to improve the day, and to avoid those sins. And so at the beginning of every week, month and year.

I never knew before what was meant by not setting our hearts upon these things. 'Tis, not to care about them, to depend upon them, to afflict ourselves much with fears of losing them, nor please ourselves with expectation of obtaining them, or hope of the continuance of them. At night made the 41st Resolution.

Saturday, Jan. 12, in the morning. I have this day solemnly renewed my
baptismal covenant and self-dedication, which I renewed when I was
received into communion of the church. I have been before God; and have
given myself, all that I am and have to God, so that I am not in any respect
my own: I can challenge no right in myself, I can challenge no right in this
understanding, this will, these affections that are in me; neither have I any
right to this body, or any of its members: no right to this tongue, these
hands, nor feet: no right to these senses, these eyes, these ears, this smell or
taste. I have given myself clear away, and have not retained anything as my
own. I have been to God this morning, and told him that I gave myself
wholly to him. I have given every power to him; so that for the future I will
challenge no right in myself, in any respect. I have expressly promised
him, and do now promise almighty God, that by his grace I will not. I have
this morning told him, that I did take him for my whole portion and
felicity, looking on nothing else as any part of my happiness, nor acting as
if it were; and his law for the constant rule of my obedience: and would
fight with all my might against the world, the flesh, and the devil, to the
end of my life. And did believe in Jesus Christ, and receive him as a prince
and a Savior; and would adhere to the faith and obedience of the gospel,
how hazardous and difficult soever the profession and practice of it may
be. That I did receive the blessed Spirit as my teacher, sanctifier and only
comforter; and cherish all his motions to enlighten, purify, confirm, comfort and assist me. This I have done. And I pray God, for the sake of
Christ, to look upon it as a self-dedication; and to receive me now as
entirely his own, and deal with me in all respects as such; whether he
afflicts me or prospers me, or whatever he pleases to do with me, who am
his. Now, henceforth I am not to act in any respect as my own. I shall act as
my own, if I ever make use of any of my powers to anything that is not to
the glory of God, and don't make the glorifying him my whole and entire
business; if I murmur in the least at afflictions; if I grieve at the prosperity
of others; if I am anyway uncharitable; if I am angry because of injuries; if I
revenge: if I do anything, purely to please myself, or if I avoid anything for
the sake of my ease: if I omit anything because it is great self-denial: if I
trust to myself: if I take any of the praise of any good that I do, or rather
God does by me; or if I am anyway proud.

This day made the 42nd and 43rd Resolutions. Whether or no, any other end ought to have any influence at all, on any of my actions or, whether any action ought to be any otherwise, in any respect, than it would be, if nothing else but religion had the least influence on my mind. Wherefore, I make the 44th Resolution.

Query: Whether any delight, or satisfaction, ought to be allowed, because any other end is obtained, beside a religious one. In the afternoon, I answer, Yes; because, if we should never suffer ourselves to rejoice, but because we have obtained a religious end, we should never rejoice at the sight of friends, we should not allow ourselves any pleasure in our food, whereby the animal spirits would be withdrawn, and good digestion hindered. But the query is to be answered thus: We never ought to allow any joy or sorrow, but what helps religion. Wherefore, I make the 45th Resolution.

The reason why I so soon grow lifeless, and unfit for the business I am about, I have found out, is only because I have been used to suffer myself to leave off, for the sake of ease, and so, I have acquired a habit of expecting ease; and therefore, when I think I have exercised myself a great while, I cannot keep myself to it any longer, because I expect to be released, as my due and right. And then, I am deceived, as if I were really tired and weary. Whereas, if I did not expect ease, and was resolved to occupy myself by business, as much as I could; I should continue with the same vigor at my business, without vacation time to rest. Thus, I have found it in reading the Scriptures; and thus, I have found it in prayer; and thus, I believe it to be in getting sermons by heart, and in other things.

At night. This week, the weekly account rose higher than ordinary. It is suggested to me, that too constant a mortification, and too vigorous application to religion, may be prejudicial to health; but nevertheless, I will plainly feel it and experience it, before I cease, on this account. It is no matter how much tired and weary I am, if my health is not impaired.

Saturday, Feb. 23. I find myself miserably negligent, and that I might do twice the business that I do, if I were set upon it. See how soon my thoughts of this matter, will be differing from what they are now. I have been indulging a horrid laziness a good while, and did not know it. I can do seven times as much in the same time now, as I can at other times, not because my faculties are in better tune; but because of the fire of diligence that I feel burning within me. If I could but always continue so, I should not meet with one quarter of the trouble. I should run the Christian race much better, and should go out of the world a much better man.

Saturday, March 2. O how much more base and vile am I, when I feel pride working in me, than when I am in a more humble disposition of mind! How much, how exceedingly much, more lovely is an humble, than a proud, disposition! I now plainly perceive it, and am really sensible of it. How immensely more pleasant is an humble delight, than a high thought of myself! How much better do I feel, when I am truly humbling myself, than when I am pleasing myself with my own perfections. O, how much pleasanter is humility than pride! O, that God would fill me with exceeding great humility, and that he would evermore keep me from all pride! The pleasures of humility are really the most refined, inward and exquisite delights in the world. How hateful is a proud man! How hateful is a worm that lifts up itself with pride! What a foolish, silly, miserable, blind, deceived, poor worm am I, when pride works! *At night.* I have lately been negligent as to reading the Scriptures. Notwithstanding my resolutions on Saturday was se'night, I have not been sedulous and diligent enough.

Wednesday, May 1, forenoon. Last night I came home, after my melancholy parting from New York.[1]

I have always, in every different state of life, I have hitherto been in, thought the troubles and difficulties of that state, to be greater than those of any other, that I proposed to be in; and when I have altered with assurance of mending myself, I have still thought the same; yea, that the difficulties of that state, are greater than those of that I left last. Lord, grant that from hence I may learn to withdraw my thoughts, affections, desires and expectations, entirely from the world, and may fix them upon the heavenly state; where there is fullness of joy; where reigns heavenly, sweet, calm and delightful love without alloy; where there are continually

1. Edwards had ministered to a Presbyterian church in New York City during 1722 and 1723.

the dearest expressions of their love: where there is the enjoyment of the persons loved, without ever parting: where those persons, who appear so lovely in this world, will really be inexpressibly more lovely, and full of love to us. How sweetly will the mutual lovers join together to sing the praises of God and the Lamb! How full will it fill us with joy to think, this enjoyment, these sweet exercises, will never cease or come to an end, but will last to all eternity.

Remember, after journeys, removes, overturnings and alterations in the state of my life, to reflect and consider, whether therein I have managed the best way possible, respecting my soul? And before such alterations, if foreseen, to resolve how to act.

Monday, July 29. When I am concerned how I shall perform anything to public acceptance, to be very careful that I have it very clear to me, that I do what is duty and prudence in the matter.[2] I sometimes find myself able to trust God, and to be pretty easy when the event is uncertain; but I find it difficult, when I am convinced beforehand, that the event will be adverse. I find that this arises, 1. From my want of faith, to believe that that particular advantage will be more to my advantage, than disadvantage: 2. From the want of a due sense of the real preferableness of that good, which will be obtained, to that which is lost. 3. From the want of a spirit of adoption.

Tuesday night, July 30. Have concluded to endeavor to work myself into duties by searching and tracing back all the real reasons why I do them not, and narrowly searching out all the subtle subterfuges of my thoughts, and answering them to the utmost of my power, that I may know what are the very first originals of my defect, as with respect to want of repentance, love to God, loathing of myself—to do this sometimes in sermons. Vid. Resolution 8. Especially, to take occasion therefrom, to bewail those sins of which I have been guilty, that are akin to them; as for instance, from pride in others, to take occasion to bewail my pride; from their malice, to take occasion to bewail the same in myself: when I am evil-spoken of, to

2. Edwards refers to his public examination for the M.A. at Yale College.

take occasion to bewail my evil speaking: and so of other sins. *Memorandum.* To receive slanders and reproaches, as glorious opportunities of doing this.

Saturday morning, Aug. 24. Have not practiced quite right about revenge; though I have not done anything directly out of revenge, yet, I have perhaps, omitted some things, that I should otherwise have done; or have altered the circumstances and manner of my actions, hoping for a secret sort of revenge thereby. I have felt a little sort of satisfaction, when I thought that such an evil would happen to them by my actions, as would make them repent what they have done. To be satisfied for their repenting, when they repent from a sense of their error, is right. But a satisfaction in their repentance, because of the evil that is brought upon them, is revenge. This is in some measure, a taking the matter out of God's hands when he was about to manage it, who is better able to plead it for me. Well, therefore, may he leave me to boggle at it. *Near sunset.* I yet find a want of dependence on God, to look unto him for success, and to have my eyes unto him for his gracious disposal of the matter: for want of a sense of God's particular influence, in ordering and directing all affairs and businesses, of whatever nature, however naturally, or fortuitously, they may seem to succeed; and for want of a sense of those great advantages, that would follow therefrom: not considering that God will grant success, or make the contrary more to my advantage; or will make the advantage accruing from the unsuccessfulness, more sensible and apparent; or will make it of less present and outward disadvantage; or will some way, so order the circumstances, as to make the unsuccessfulness more easy to bear; or several, or all of these. This want of dependence, is likewise for want of the things mentioned, July 29. Remember to examine all narrations, I can call to mind; whether they are exactly according to verity.

Monday, Sept. 23. I observe that old men seldom have any advantage of new discoveries, because they are beside a way of thinking, they have been so long used to. *Resolved,* if ever I live to years, that I will be impartial to hear the reasons of all pretended discoveries, and receive them if rational, how long so ever I have been used to another way of thinking. My time is so short, that I have not time to perfect myself in all studies: wherefore resolved, to omit and put off, all but the most important and needful studies.

Monday, Jan. 20, [1724]. I have been very much to blame, in that I have not been as full, and plain and downright, in my standing up for virtue and religion, when I have had fair occasion, before those who seemed to take no delight in such things. If such conversation would not be agreeable to them, I have in some degree minced the matter, that I might not displease, and might not speak right against the grain, more than I should have loved to have done with others, to whom it would be agreeable to speak directly for religion. I ought to be exceedingly bold with such persons, not taking in a melancholy strain, but in one confident and fearless, assured of the truth and excellence of the cause.

Saturday night, June 6. This week has been a remarkable week with me with respect to despondencies, fears, perplexities, multitudes of cares and distraction of mind; being the week I came hither to New Haven, in order to entrance upon the office of tutor of the College. I have now abundant reason to be convinced of the troublesomeness and vexation of the world, and that it never will be another kind of world.

Nov. 16, [1725]. When confined at Mr. Stiles'.[3] I think it would be of special advantage to me, with respect to my truer interest, as near as I can in my studies, to observe this rule. To let half a day's, or at most, a day's study in other things, be succeeded, by half a day's, or a day's study in divinity.

One thing wherein I have erred, as I would be complete in all social duties, is, in neglecting to write letters to friends. And I would be fore-warned of the danger of neglecting to visit my friends and relations, when we are parted.

When one suppresses thoughts that tend to divert the run of the mind's

3. In September 1725, Edwards fell ill for several months as a result of his labors as college tutor; the Rev. Isaac Stiles (1697–1760), pastor of North Haven, Connecticut, was a relative of Edwards'.

operations from religion, whether they are melancholy, or anxious, or passionate, or any others; there is this good effect of it, that it keeps the mind in its freedom. Those thoughts are stopped in the beginning, that would have set the mind a-going in that stream.

There are a great many exercises, that for the present, seem not to help, but rather impede, religious meditation and affections, the fruit of which is reaped afterwards, and is of far greater worth than what is lost; for thereby the mind is only for the present diverted; but what is attained is, upon occasion, of use for the whole lifetime.

Sept. 26, 1726. 'Tis just about three years, that I have been for the most part in a low, sunk estate and condition, miserably senseless to what I used to be, about spiritual things. 'Twas three years ago, the week before commencement; just about the same time this year, I began to be somewhat as I used to be.

Resolutions (1722)

Being sensible that I am unable to do anything without God's help, I do humbly entreat him by his grace to enable me to keep these Resolutions, so far as they are agreeable to his will, for Christ's sake.

Remember to read over these Resolutions once a week.

1. Resolved, that I will do whatsoever I think to be most to God's glory, and my own good, profit and pleasure, in the whole of my duration, without any consideration of the time, whether now, or never so many myriads of ages hence. Resolved to do whatever I think to be my duty, and most for the good and advantage of mankind in general. Resolved to do this, whatever difficulties I meet with, how many and how great soever.

2. Resolved, to be continually endeavoring to find out some new invention and contrivance to promote the forementioned things.

3. Resolved, if ever I shall fall and grow dull, so as to neglect to keep any part of these Resolutions, to repent of all I can remember, when I come to myself again.

4. Resolved, never to do any manner of thing, whether in soul or body, less or more, but what tends to the glory of God; nor be, nor suffer it, if I can avoid it.

5. Resolved, never to lose one moment of time; but improve it the most profitable way I possibly can.

6. Resolved, to live with all my might, while I do live.

7. Resolved, never to do anything, which I should be afraid to do, if it were the last hour of my life.

8. Resolved, to act, in all respects, both speaking and doing, as if nobody had been so vile as I, and as if I had committed the same sins, or had the same infirmities or failings as others; and that I will let the knowledge of their failings promote nothing but shame in myself, and prove only an occasion of my confessing my own sins and misery to God. . . .

9. Resolved, to think much on all occasions of my own dying, and of the common circumstances which attend death.

10. Resolved, when I feel pain, to think of the pains of martyrdom, and of hell.

11. Resolved, when I think of any theorem in divinity to be solved, immediately to do what I can towards solving it, if circumstances don't hinder.

12. Resolved, if I take delight in it as a gratification of pride, or vanity, or on any such account, immediately to throw it by.

13. Resolved, to be endeavoring to find out fit objects of charity and liberality.

14. Resolved, never to do anything out of revenge.

15. Resolved, never to suffer the least motions of anger to irrational beings.

16. Resolved, never to speak evil of anyone, so that it shall tend to his dishonor, more or less, upon no account except for some real good.

17. Resolved, that I will live so as I shall wish I had done when I come to die.

18. Resolved, to live so at all times, as I think is best in my devout frames, and when I have clearest notions of things of the gospel, and another world.

19. Resolved, never to do anything, which I should be afraid to do, if I

expected it would not be above an hour, before I should hear the last trump.

20. Resolved, to maintain the strictest temperance in eating and drinking.

21. Resolved, never to do anything, which if I should see in another, I should count a just occasion to despise him for, or to think any way the more meanly of him.

22. Resolved, to endeavor to obtain for myself as much happiness, in the other world, as I possibly can, with all the power, might, vigor, and vehemence, yea violence, I am capable of, or can bring myself to exert, in any way that can be thought of.

23. Resolved, frequently to take some deliberate action, which seems most unlikely to be done, for the glory of God, and trace it back to the original intention, designs and ends of it; and if I find it not to be for God's glory, to repute it as a breach of the 4th Resolution.

24. Resolved, whenever I do any conspicuously evil action, to trace it back, till I come to the original cause; and then both carefully endeavor to do so no more, and to fight and pray with all my might against the original of it.

25. Resolved, to examine carefully, and constantly, what that one thing in me is, which causes me in the least to doubt of the love of God; and to direct all my forces against it.

26. Resolved, to cast away such things, as I find do abate my assurance.

27. Resolved, never willfully to omit anything, except the omission be for the glory of God; and frequently to examine my omissions.

28. Resolved, to study the Scriptures so steadily, constantly and frequently, as that I may find, and plainly perceive myself to grow in the knowledge of the same.

29. Resolved, never to count that a prayer, nor to let that pass as a prayer, nor that as a petition of a prayer, which is so made, that I cannot hope that God will answer it; nor that as a confession, which I cannot hope God will accept.

30. Resolved, to strive to my utmost every week to be brought higher in religion, and to a higher exercise of grace, than I was the week before.

31. Resolved, never to say anything at all against anybody, but when it is

perfectly agreeable to the highest degree of Christian honor, and of love to mankind, agreeable to the lowest humility, and sense of my own faults and failings, and agreeable to the golden rule; often, when I have said anything against anyone, to bring it to, and try it strictly by the test of this Resolution.

32. Resolved, to be strictly and firmly faithful to my trust, that that in Prov. 20:6, "A faithful man who can find?" may not be partly fulfilled in me.

33. Resolved, always to do what I can towards making, maintaining, establishing and preserving peace, when it can be without over-balancing detriment in other respects. *Dec. 26, 1722.*

34. Resolved, in narrations never to speak anything but the pure and simple verity.

35. Resolved, whenever I so much question whether I have done my duty, as that my quiet and calm is thereby disturbed, to set it down, and also how the question was resolved. *Dec. 18, 1722.*

36. Resolved, never to speak evil of any, except I have some particular good call for it. *Dec. 19, 1722.*

37. Resolved, to inquire every night, as I am going to bed, wherein I have been negligent, what sin I have committed, and wherein I have denied myself: also at the end of every week, month and year. *Dec. 22 and 26, 1722.*

38. Resolved, never to speak anything that is ridiculous, sportive, or matter of laughter on the Lord's day. *Sabbath evening, Dec. 23, 1722.*

39. Resolved, never to do anything that I so much question the lawfulness of, as that I intend, at the same time, to consider and examine afterwards, whether it be lawful or no: except I as much question the lawfulness of the omission.

40. Resolved, to inquire every night, before I go to bed, whether I have acted in the best way I possibly could, with respect to eating and drinking. *Jan. 7, 1723.*

41. Resolved, to ask myself at the end of every day, week, month and year, wherein I could possibly in any respect have done better. *Jan. 11, 1723.*

42. Resolved, frequently to renew the dedication of myself to God, which was made at my baptism; which I solemnly renewed, when I was

received into the communion of the church; and which I have solemnly re-made this twelfth day of January, 1722–23.

43. Resolved, never henceforward, till I die, to act as if I were any way my own, but entirely and altogether God's, agreeable to what is to be found in *Saturday, January 12. Jan. 12, 1723.*

44. Resolved, that no other end but religion, shall have any influence at all on any of my actions; and that no action shall be, in the least circumstance, any otherwise than the religious end will carry it. *Jan. 12, 1723.*

45. Resolved, never to allow any pleasure or grief, joy or sorrow, nor any affection at all, nor any degree of affection, nor any circumstance relating to it, but what helps religion. *Jan. 12 and 13, 1723.*

46. Resolved, never to allow the least measure of any fretting uneasiness at my father or mother. Resolved to suffer no effects of it, so much as in the least alteration of speech, or motion of my eye: and to be especially careful of it, with respect to any of our family.

47. Resolved, to endeavor to my utmost to deny whatever is not most agreeable to a good, and universally sweet and benevolent, quiet, peaceable, contented, easy, compassionate, generous, humble, meek, modest, submissive, obliging, diligent and industrious, charitable, even, patient, moderate, forgiving, sincere temper; and to do at all times what such a temper would lead me to. Examine strictly every week, whether I have done so. *Sabbath morning, May 5, 1723.*

48. Resolved, constantly, with the utmost niceness and diligence, and the strictest scrutiny, to be looking into the state of my soul, that I may know whether I have truly an interest in Christ or no; that when I come to die, I may not have any negligence respecting this to repent of. *May 26, 1723.*

49. Resolved, that this never shall be, if I can help it.

50. Resolved, I will act so as I think I shall judge would have been best, and most prudent, when I come into the future world. *July 5, 1723.*

51. Resolved, that I will act so, in every respect, as I think I shall wish I had done, if I should at last be damned. *July 8, 1723.*

52. I frequently hear persons in old age say how they would live, if they were to live their lives over again: Resolved, that I will live just so as I can think I shall wish I had done, supposing I live to old age. *July 8, 1723.*

53. Resolved, to improve every opportunity, when I am in the best and happiest frame of mind, to cast and venture my soul on the Lord Jesus Christ, to trust and confide in him, and consecrate myself wholly to him; that from this I may have assurance of my safety, knowing that I confide in my Redeemer. *July 8, 1723.*

54. Whenever I hear anything spoken in conversation of any person, if I think it would be praiseworthy in me, Resolved to endeavor to imitate it. *July 8, 1723.*

55. Resolved, to endeavor to my utmost to act as I can think I should do, if I had already seen the happiness of heaven, and hell torments. *July 8, 1723.*

56. Resolved, never to give over, nor in the least to slacken my fight with my corruptions, however unsuccessful I may be.

57. Resolved, when I fear misfortunes and adversities, to examine whether I have done my duty, and resolve to do it; and let it be just as providence orders it, I will as far as I can, be concerned about nothing but my duty and my sin. *June 9,* and *July 13, 1723.*

58. Resolved, not only to refrain from an air of dislike, fretfulness, and anger in conversation, but to exhibit an air of love, cheerfulness and benignity. *May 27,* and *July 13, 1723.*

59. Resolved, when I am most conscious of provocations to ill nature and anger, that I will strive most to feel and act good-naturedly; yea, at such times, to manifest good nature, though I think that in other respects it would be disadvantageous, and so as would be imprudent at other times. *May 12, July 11,* and *July 13.*

60. Resolved, whenever my feelings begin to appear in the least out of order, when I am conscious of the least uneasiness within, or the least irregularity without, I will then subject myself to the strictest examination. *July 4,* and *13, 1723.*

61. Resolved, that I will not give way to that listlessness which I find unbends and relaxes my mind from being fully and fixedly set on religion, whatever excuse I may have for it—that what my listlessness inclines me to do, is best to be done, etc. *May 21,* and *July 13, 1723.*

62. Resolved, never to do anything but duty; and then according to Eph. 6:6–8, do it willingly and cheerfully as unto the Lord, and not to

man; "knowing that whatever good thing any man doth, the same shall he receive of the Lord." *June 25,* and *July 13, 1723.*

63. On the supposition, that there never was to be but one individual in the world, at any one time, who was properly a complete Christian, in all respects of a right stamp, having Christianity always shining in its true luster, and appearing excellent and lovely, from whatever part and under whatever character viewed: Resolved, to act just as I would do, if I strove with all my might to be that one, who should live in my time. *Jan. 14,* and *July 13, 1723.*

64. Resolved, when I find those "groanings which cannot be uttered" [Rom. 8:26], of which the Apostle speaks, and those "breakings of soul for the longing it hath," of which the Psalmist speaks, Psalm 119:20, that I will promote them to the utmost of my power, and that I will not be weary of earnestly endeavoring to vent my desires, nor of the repetitions of such earnestness. *July 23,* and *August 10, 1723.*

65. Resolved, very much to exercise myself in this all my life long, viz. with the greatest openness I am capable of, to declare my ways to God, and lay open my soul to him: all my sins, temptations, difficulties, sorrows, fears, hopes, desires, and every thing, and every circumstance; according to Dr. Manton's 27th Sermon on the 119th Psalm.[4] *July 26,* and *Aug. 10, 1723.*

66. Resolved, that I will endeavor always to keep a benign aspect, and air of acting and speaking in all places, and in all companies, except it should so happen that duty requires otherwise.

67. Resolved, after afflictions, to inquire, what I am the better for them, what good I have got by them, and what I might have got by them.

68. Resolved, to confess frankly to myself all that which I find in myself, either infirmity or sin; and, if it be what concerns religion, also to confess the whole case to God, and implore needed help. *July 23,* and *August 10, 1723.*

69. Resolved, always to do that, which I shall wish I had done when I see others do it. *Aug. 11, 1723.*

4. Thomas Manton, *One Hundred and Ninety Sermons on the Hundred and Nineteenth Psalm* (London, 1681). Manton (1620–77), an English Non-conformist, was a highly respected preacher and biblical commentator.

70. Let there be something of benevolence, in all that I speak. *Aug. 17, 1723.*

Apostrophe to Sarah Pierpont (c. 1723)

They say there is a young lady in [New Haven] who is beloved of that almighty Being, who made and rules the world, and that there are certain seasons in which this great Being, in some way or other invisible, comes to her and fills her mind with exceeding sweet delight, and that she hardly cares for anything, except to meditate on him—that she expects after a while to be received up where he is, to be raised up out of the world and caught up into heaven; being assured that he loves her too well to let her remain at a distance from him always. There she is to dwell with him, and to be ravished with his love and delight forever. Therefore, if you present all the world before her, with the richest of its treasures, she disregards it and cares not for it, and is unmindful of any pain or affliction. She has a strange sweetness in her mind, and singular purity in her affections; is most just and conscientious in all her actions; and you could not persuade her to do anything wrong or sinful, if you would give her all the world, lest she should offend this great Being. She is of a wonderful sweetness, calmness and universal benevolence of mind; especially after those seasons in which this great God has manifested himself to her mind. She will sometimes go about from place to place, singing sweetly; and seems to be always full of joy and pleasure; and no one knows for what. She loves to be alone, and to wander in the fields and on the mountains, and seems to have someone invisible always conversing with her.

Personal Narrative (c. 1739)

I had a variety of concerns and exercises about my soul from my childhood; but had two more remarkable seasons of awakening, before I met with that change, by which I was brought to those new dispositions, and that new sense of things, that I have since had. The first time was when I was a boy, some years before I went to college, at a time of remarkable awakening in my father's congregation. I was then very much affected for many months, and concerned about the things of religion, and my soul's salvation; and was abundant in duties. I used to pray five times a day in secret, and to spend much time in religious talk with other boys; and used to meet with them to pray together. I experienced I know not what kind of delight in religion. My mind was much engaged in it, and had much self-righteous pleasure; and it was my delight to abound in religious duties. I, with some of my schoolmates joined together, and built a booth in a swamp, in a very secret and retired place, for a place of prayer. And besides, I had particular secret places of my own in the woods, where I used to retire by myself; and used to be from time to time much affected. My affections seemed to be lively and easily moved, and I seemed to be in my element, when engaged in religious duties. And I am ready to think, many are deceived with such affections, and such a kind of delight, as I then had in religion, and mistake it for grace.

But in process of time, my convictions and affections wore off; and I entirely lost all those affections and delights, and left off secret prayer, at least as to any constant performance of it; and returned like a dog to his vomit, and went on in ways of sin.

Indeed, I was at some times very uneasy, especially towards the latter part of the time of my being at college. Till it pleased God, in my last year at college, at a time when I was in the midst of many uneasy thoughts about the state of my soul, to seize me with a pleurisy; in which he brought me nigh to the grave, and shook me over the pit of hell.

But yet, it was not long after my recovery, before I fell again into my old ways of sin. But God would not suffer me to go on with any quietness; but I had great and violent inward struggles: till after many conflicts with wicked inclinations, and repeated resolutions, and bonds that I laid myself under by a kind of vows to God, I was brought wholly to break off all former wicked ways, and all ways of known outward sin; and to apply myself to seek my salvation, and practice the duties of religion: but without that kind of affection and delight, that I had formerly experienced. My concern now wrought more by inward struggles and conflicts, and self-reflections. I made seeking my salvation the main business of my life. But yet it seems to me, I sought after a miserable manner: which has made me sometimes since to question, whether ever it issued in that which was saving; being ready to doubt, whether such miserable seeking was ever succeeded. But yet I was brought to seek salvation, in a manner that I never was before. I felt a spirit to part with all things in the world, for an interest in Christ. My concern continued and prevailed, with many exercising things and inward struggles; but yet it never seemed to be proper to express my concern that I had, by the name of terror.

From my childhood up, my mind had been wont to be full of objections against the doctrine of God's sovereignty, in choosing whom he would to eternal life, and rejecting whom he pleased; leaving them eternally to perish, and be everlastingly tormented in hell. It used to appear like a horrible doctrine to me. But I remember the time very well, when I seemed to be convinced, and fully satisfied, as to this sovereignty of God, and his justice in thus eternally disposing of men, according to his sovereign pleasure. But never could give an account, how, or by what means, I was thus convinced; not in the least imagining, in the time of it, nor a long time after, that there was any extraordinary influence of God's Spirit in it: but only that now I saw further, and my reason apprehended the justice and reasonableness of it. However, my mind rested in it; and it put an end to all those cavils and objections, that I had till then abode with me, all the preceding part of my life. And there has been a wonderful alteration in my mind, with respect to the doctrine of God's sovereignty, from that day to this; so that I scarce ever have found so much as the rising of an objection against God's sovereignty, in the most absolute sense, in showing mercy on whom he will show mercy, and hardening and eternally damning whom he will. God's absolute sovereignty, and justice, with respect to salvation and damnation, is what my mind seems to rest assured of, as much as of anything that I see with my eyes; at least it is so at times. But I have oftentimes since that first conviction, had quite another kind of sense of God's sovereignty, than I had then. I have often since, not only had a conviction, but a *delightful* conviction. The doctrine of God's sovereignty has very often appeared, an exceeding pleasant, bright and sweet doctrine to me: and absolute sovereignty is what I love to ascribe to God. But my first conviction was not with this.

The first that I remember that ever I found anything of that sort of inward, sweet delight in God and divine things, that I have lived much in since, was on reading those words, I Tim. 1:17. "Now unto the King eternal, immortal, invisible, the only wise God, be honor and glory forever and ever, Amen." As I read the words, there came into my soul, and was as it were diffused through it, a sense of the glory of the Divine Being; a new sense, quite different from anything I ever experienced before. Never any words of Scripture seemed to me as these words did. I thought with myself, how excellent a Being that was; and how happy I should be, if I might enjoy that God, and be wrapped up to God in heaven, and be as it were swallowed up in him. I kept saying, and as it were singing over these words of Scripture to myself; and went to prayer, to pray to God that I might enjoy him; and prayed in a manner quite different from what I used to do; with a new sort of affection. But it never came into my thought, that there was anything spiritual, or of a saving nature in this.

From about that time, I began to have a new kind of apprehensions and ideas of Christ, and the work of redemption, and the glorious way of salvation by him. I had an inward, sweet sense of these things, that at times came into my heart; and my soul was led away in pleasant views and contemplations of them. And my mind was greatly engaged, to spend my time in reading and meditating on Christ; and the beauty and excellency of his person, and the lovely way of salvation, by free grace in him. I found no books so delightful to me, as those that treated of these subjects. Those words, Cant. 2:1, used to be abundantly with me: "I am the rose of Sharon, the lily of the valleys." The words seemed to me, sweetly to represent, the loveliness and beauty of Jesus Christ. And the whole Book of Canticles used to be pleasant to me; and I used to be much in reading it, about that time. And found, from time to time, an inward sweetness, that used, as it were, to carry me away in my contemplations; in what I know not how to express otherwise, than by a calm, sweet abstraction of soul from all the concerns of this world; and a kind of vision, or fixed ideas and imaginations, of being alone in the mountains, or some solitary wilderness, far from all mankind, sweetly conversing with Christ, and wrapped and swallowed up in God. The sense I had of divine things, would often of a sudden as it were, kindle up a sweet burning in my heart; an ardor of my soul, that I know not how to express.

Not long after I first began to experience these things, I gave an account to my father, of some things that had passed in my mind. I was pretty much affected by the discourse we had together. And when the discourse was ended, I walked abroad alone, in a solitary place in my father's pasture, for contemplation. And as I was walking there, and looked up on the sky and clouds; there came into my mind, a sweet sense of the glorious majesty and grace of God, that I know not how to express. I seemed to see them both in a sweet conjunction: majesty and meekness joined together: it was a sweet and gentle, and holy majesty; and also a majestic meekness; an awful sweetness; a high, and great, and holy gentleness.

After this my sense of divine things gradually increased, and became more and more lively, and had more of that inward sweetness. The appearance of everything was altered: there seemed to be, as it were, a calm, sweet cast, or appearance of divine glory, in almost everything. God's excellency, his wisdom, his purity and love, seemed to appear in everything; in the sun, moon and stars; in the clouds, and blue sky; in the grass, flowers, trees; in the water, and all nature; which used greatly to fix my mind. I often used to sit and view the moon, for a long time; and so in the daytime, spent much time in viewing the clouds and sky, to behold the sweet glory of God in these things: in the meantime, singing forth with a low voice, my contemplations of the Creator and Redeemer. And scarce anything, among all the works of nature, was so sweet to me as thunder and lightning. Formerly, nothing had been so terrible to me. I used to be a person uncommonly terrified with thunder: and it used to strike me with terror, when I saw a thunderstorm rising. But now, on the contrary, it rejoiced me. I felt God at the first appearance of a thunderstorm. And used to take the opportunity at such times, to fix myself to view the clouds, and see the lightnings play, and hear the majestic and awful voice of God's thunder: which oftentimes was exceeding entertaining, leading me to sweet contemplations of my great and glorious God. And while I viewed, used to spend my time, as it always seemed natural to me, to sing or chant forth my meditations; to speak my thoughts in soliloquies, and speak with a singing voice.

I felt then a great satisfaction as to my good estate. But that did not content me. I had vehement longings of soul after God and Christ, and after more holiness; wherewith my heart seemed to be full, and ready to

Conversion @
20

break: which often brought to my mind, the words of the Psalmist, Ps. 119:28, "My soul breaketh for the longing it hath." I often felt a mourning and lamenting in my heart, that I had not turned to God sooner, that I might have had more time to grow in grace. My mind was greatly fixed on divine things; I was almost perpetually in the contemplation of them. Spent most of my time in thinking of divine things, year after year. And used to spend abundance of my time, in walking alone in the woods, and solitary places, for meditation, soliloquy and prayer, and converse with God. And it was always my manner, at such times, to sing forth my contemplations. And was almost constantly in ejaculatory prayer, wherever I was. Prayer seemed to be natural to me; as the breath, by which the inward burnings of my heart had vent.

The delights which I now felt in things of religion, were of an exceeding different kind, from those forementioned, that I had when I was a boy. They were totally of another kind; and what I then had no more notion or idea of, than one born blind has of pleasant and beautiful colors. They were of a more inward, pure, soul-animating and refreshing nature. Those former delights, never reached the heart; and did not arise from any sight of the divine excellency of the things of God; or any taste of the soul-satisfying, and life-giving good, there is in them.

My sense of divine things seemed gradually to increase, till I went to preach at New York; which was about a year and a half after they began. While I was there, I felt them, very sensibly, in a much higher degree, than I had done before. My longings after God and holiness, were much increased. Pure and humble, holy and heavenly Christianity, appeared exceeding amiable to me. I felt in me a burning desire to be in everything a complete Christian; and conformed to the blessed image of Christ: and that I might live in all things, according to the pure, sweet and blessed rules of the gospel. I had an eager thirsting after progress in these things. My longings after it, put me upon pursuing and pressing after them. It was my continual strife day and night, and constant inquiry, how I should be more holy, and live more holily, and more becoming a child of God, and disciple of Christ. I sought an increase of grace and holiness, and that I might live an holy life, with vastly more earnestness, than ever I sought grace, before I had it. I used to be continually examining myself, and studying and contriving for likely ways and means, how I should live holily, with far greater diligence and earnestness, than ever I pursued anything in my life: but with too great a dependence on my own strength; which afterwards proved a great damage to me. My experience had not then taught me, as it has done since, my extreme feebleness and impotence, every manner of way; and the innumerable and bottomless depths of secret corruption and deceit, that there was in my heart. However, I went on with my eager pursuit after more holiness; and sweet conformity to Christ.

The heaven I desired was a heaven of holiness; to be with God, and to spend my eternity in divine love, and holy communion with Christ. My mind was very much taken up with contemplations on heaven, and the enjoyments of those there; and living there in perfect holiness, humility and love. And it used at that time to appear a great part of the happiness of heaven, that there the saints could express their love to Christ. It appeared to me a great clog and hindrance and burden to me, that what I felt within, I could not express to God, and give vent to, as I desired. The inward ardor of my soul, seemed to be hindered and pent up, and could not freely flame out as it would. I used often to think, how in heaven, this sweet principle should freely and fully vent and express itself. Heaven appeared to me exceeding delightful as a world of love. It appeared to me, that all happiness consisted in living in pure, humble, heavenly, divine love.

I remember the thoughts I used then to have of holiness. I remember I then said sometimes to myself, I do certainly know that I love holiness, such as the gospel prescribes. It appeared to me, there was nothing in it but what was ravishingly lovely. It appeared to me, to be the highest beauty and amiableness, above all other beauties: that it was a *divine* beauty; far purer than anything here upon earth; and that everything else, was like mire, filth and defilement, in comparison of it.

Holiness, as I then wrote down some of my contemplations on it, appeared to me to be of a sweet, pleasant, charming, serene, calm nature. It seemed to me, it brought an inexpressible purity, brightness, peacefulness and ravishment to the soul: and that it made the soul like a field or garden of God, with all manner of pleasant flowers; that is all pleasant, delightful and undisturbed; enjoying a sweet calm, and the gently vivifying beams of the sun. The soul of a true Christian, as I then wrote my meditations, appeared like such a little white flower, as we see in the spring of the year; low and humble on the ground, opening its bosom, to receive the pleasant beams of the sun's glory; rejoicing as it were, in a calm rapture; diffusing around a sweet fragrancy; standing peacefully and lovingly, in the midst of other flowers round about; all in like manner opening their bosoms, to drink in the light of the sun.

There was no part of creature-holiness, that I then, and at other times, had so great a sense of the loveliness of, as humility, brokenness of heart and poverty of spirit: and there was nothing that I had such a spirit to long for. My heart as it were panted after this, to lie low before God, and in the dust; that I might be nothing, and that God might be all; that I might become as a little child.

While I was there at New York, I sometimes was much affected with reflections on my past life, considering how late it was, before I began to be truly religious; and how wickedly I had lived till then: and once so as to weep abundantly, and for a considerable time together.

On January 12, 1722–23, I made a solemn dedication of myself to God, and wrote it down; giving up myself, and all that I had to God; to be for the future in no respect my own; to act as one that had no right to himself, in any respect. And solemnly vowed to take God for my whole portion and felicity; looking on nothing else as any part of my happiness, nor acting as if it were: and his law for the constant rule of my obedience: engaging to fight with all my might, against the world, the flesh and the devil, to the end of my life. But have reason to be infinitely humbled, when I consider, how much I have failed of answering my obligation.

I had then abundance of sweet religious conversation in the family where I lived, with Mr. John Smith, and his pious mother. My heart was knit in affection to those, in whom were appearances of true piety; and I could bear the thoughts of no other companions, but such as were holy, and the disciples of the blessed Jesus.

I had great longings for the advancement of Christ's kingdom in the world. My secret prayer used to be in great part taken up in praying for it. If I heard the least hint of any thing that happened in any part of the world, that appeared to me, in some respect or other, to have a favorable aspect on the interest of Christ's kingdom, my soul eagerly catched at it; and it would much animate and refresh me. I used to be earnest to read public newsletters, mainly for that end; to see if I could not find some news favorable to the interest of religion in the world.

I very frequently used to retire into a solitary place, on the banks of Hudson's River, at some distance from the city, for contemplation on divine things, and secret converse with God; and had many sweet hours there. Sometimes Mr. Smith and I walked there together, to converse of the things of God; and our conversation used much to turn on the advancement of Christ's kingdom in the world, and the glorious things that God would accomplish for his church in the latter days.

I had then, and at other times, the greatest delight in the holy Scriptures, of any book whatsoever. Oftentimes in reading it, every word seemed to touch my heart. I felt an harmony between something in my heart, and those sweet and powerful words. I seemed often to see so much light, exhibited by every sentence, and such a refreshing ravishing food communicated, that I could not get along in reading. Used oftentimes to dwell long on one sentence, to see the wonders contained in it; and yet almost every sentence seemed to be full of wonders.

I came away from New York in the month of April 1723, and had a most bitter parting with Madam Smith and her son. My heart seemed to sink within me, at leaving the family and city, where I had enjoyed so many sweet and pleasant days. I went from New York to Wethersfield by water. As I sailed away, I kept sight of the city as long as I could; and when I was out of sight of it, it would affect me much to look that way, with a kind of melancholy mixed with sweetness. However, that night after this sorrowful parting, I was greatly comforted in God at Westchester, where we went ashore to lodge: and had a pleasant time of it all the voyage to Saybrook. It was sweet to me to think of meeting dear Christians in heaven, where we should never part more. At Saybrook we went ashore to lodge on Saturday, and there kept sabbath; where I had a sweet and refreshing season, walking alone in the fields.

After I came home to Windsor, remained much in a like frame of my mind, as I had been in at New York; but only sometimes felt my heart ready to sink, with the thoughts of my friends at New York. And my refuge and support was in contemplations on the heavenly state; as I find in my Diary of May 1, 1723. It was my comfort to think of that state, where there is fullness of joy; where reigns heavenly, sweet, calm and delightful love, without alloy; where there are continually the dearest expressions of this love; where is the enjoyment of the persons loved, without ever parting; where these persons that appear so lovely in this world, will really be inexpressibly more lovely, and full of love to us. And how sweetly will the mutual lovers join together to sing the praises of God and the Lamb! How full will it fill us with joy, to think, that this enjoyment, these sweet exercises will never cease or come to an end; but will last to all eternity!

Continued much in the same frame in the general, that I had been in at New York, till I went to New Haven, to live there as tutor of the College; having one special season of uncommon sweetness: particularly once at Bolton, in a journey from Boston, walking out alone in the fields. After I went to New Haven, I sunk in religion; my mind being diverted from my eager and violent pursuits after holiness, by some affairs that greatly perplexed and distracted my mind.

In September 1725, was taken ill at New Haven; and endeavoring to go home to Windsor, was so ill at the North Village, that I could go no further: where I lay sick for about a quarter of a year. And in this sickness, God was pleased to visit me again with the sweet influences of his Spirit. My mind was greatly engaged there on divine, pleasant contemplations, and longings of soul. I observed that those who watched with me, would often be looking out for the morning, and seemed to wish for it. Which brought to my mind those words of the Psalmist, which my soul with sweetness made its own language. "My soul waiteth for the Lord more than they that watch for the morning: I say, more than they that watch for the morning" [Ps. 130:6]. And when the light of the morning came, and the beams of the sun came in at the windows, it refreshed my soul from one morning to another. It seemed to me to be some image of the sweet light of God's glory.

I remember, about that time, I used greatly to long for the conversion of some that I was concerned with. It seemed to me, I could gladly honor them, and with delight be a servant to them, and lie at their feet, if they were but truly holy.

But some time after this, I was again greatly diverted in my mind, with some temporal concerns, that exceedingly took up my thoughts, greatly to the wounding of my soul: and went on through various exercises, that it would be tedious to relate, that gave me much more experience of my own heart, than ever I had before.

Since I came to [Northampton], I have often had sweet complacency in God in views of his glorious perfections, and the excellency of Jesus Christ. God has appeared to me, a glorious and lovely Being, chiefly on the account of his holiness. The holiness of God has always appeared to me the most lovely of all his attributes. The doctrines of God's absolute sovereignty, and free grace, in showing mercy to whom he would show mercy; and man's absolute dependence on the operations of God's Holy Spirit, have very often appeared to me as sweet and glorious doctrines. These doctrines have been much my delight. God's sovereignty has ever appeared to me, as great part of his glory. It has often been sweet to me to go to God, and adore him as a sovereign God, and ask sovereign mercy of him.

I have loved the doctrines of the gospel: they have been to my soul like green pastures. The gospel has seemed to me to be the richest treasure; the treasure that I have most desired, and longed that it might dwell richly in me. The way of salvation by Christ, has appeared in a general way, glorious and excellent, and most pleasant and beautiful. It has often seemed to me, that it would in a great measure spoil heaven, to receive it in any other way. That text has often been affecting and delightful to me, Is. 32:2, "A man shall be an hiding place from the wind, and a covert from the tempest; as rivers of water in a dry place, as the shadow of a great rock in a weary land."

It has often appeared sweet to me, to be united to Christ; to have him for my head, and to be a member of his body: and also to have Christ for my teacher and prophet. I very often think with sweetness and longings and pantings of soul, of being a little child, taking hold of Christ, to be led by him through the wilderness of this world. That text, Matt. 18, at the beginning, has often been sweet to me: "Except ye be converted, and become as little children, ye shall not enter into the kingdom of heaven." I love to think of coming to Christ, to receive salvation of him, poor in spirit, and quite empty of self; humbly exalting him alone; cut entirely off from my own root, and to grow into, and out of Christ: to have God in Christ to be all in all; and to live by faith on the Son of God, a life of humble, unfeigned confidence in him. That Scripture has often been sweet to me, Ps. 115:1, "Not unto us, O Lord, not unto us, but unto thy name give glory, for thy mercy, and for thy truth's sake." And those words of Christ, Luke 10:21, "In that hour Jesus rejoiced in spirit, and said, I thank thee, O Father, Lord of heaven and earth, that thou hast hid these things from the wise and prudent, and hast revealed them unto babes: even so, Father; for so it seemed good in thy sight." That sovereignty of God that Christ rejoiced in, seemed to me to be worthy to be rejoiced in; and that rejoicing of Christ, seemed to me to show the excellency of Christ, and the Spirit that he was of.

Sometimes only mentioning a single word, causes my heart to burn within me: or only seeing the name of Christ, or the name of some attribute of God. And God has appeared glorious to me, on account of the Trinity. It has made me have exalting thoughts of God, that he subsists in three persons; Father, Son, and Holy Ghost.

The sweetest joys of delights I have experienced, have not been those that have arisen from a hope of my own good estate; but in a direct view of the glorious things of the gospel. When I enjoy this sweetness, it seems to carry me above the thoughts of my own safe estate. It seems at such times a loss that I cannot bear, to take off my eye from the glorious, pleasant object I behold without me, to turn my eye in upon myself, and my own good estate.

My heart has been much on the advancement of Christ's kingdom in the world. The histories of the past advancement of Christ's kingdom, have been sweet to me. When I have read histories of past ages, the pleasantest thing in all my reading has been, to read of the kingdom of Christ being promoted. And when I have expected in my reading, to come to any such thing, I have lotted upon it all the way as I read. And my mind has been much entertained and delighted, with the Scripture promises and prophecies, of the future glorious advancement of Christ's kingdom on earth.

I have sometimes had a sense of the excellent fullness of Christ, and his meetness and suitableness as a Savior; whereby he has appeared to me, far above all, the chief of ten thousands. And his blood and atonement has appeared sweet, and his righteousness sweet; which is always accompanied with an ardency of spirit, and inward strugglings and breathings and groanings, that cannot be uttered, to be emptied of myself, and swallowed up in Christ.

Once, as I rid out into the woods for my health, anno 1737; and having lit from my horse in a retired place, as my manner commonly has been, to walk for divine contemplation and prayer; I had a view, that for me was extraordinary, of the glory of the Son of God; as mediator between God and man; and his wonderful, great, full, pure and sweet grace and love, and meek and gentle condescension. This grace, that appeared to me so calm and sweet, appeared great above the heavens. The person of Christ appeared ineffably excellent, with an excellency great enough to swallow up all thought and conception. Which continued, as near as I can judge, about an hour; which kept me, the bigger part of the time, in a flood of tears, and weeping aloud. I felt withal, an ardency of soul to be, what I know not otherwise how to express, than to be emptied and annihilated; to lie in the dust, and to be full of Christ alone; to love him with a holy and pure love; to trust in him; to live upon him; to serve and follow him, and to be totally wrapped up in the fullness of Christ; and to be perfectly sanctified and made pure, with a divine and heavenly purity. I have several other times, and views very much of the same nature, and that have had the same effects.

I have many times had a sense of the glory of the third person in the Trinity, in his office of sanctifier; in his holy operations communicating divine light and life to the soul. God in the communications of his Holy Spirit, has appeared as an infinite fountain of divine glory and sweetness; being full and sufficient to fill and satisfy the soul: pouring forth itself in sweet communications, like the sun in its glory, sweetly and pleasantly diffusing light and Life.

I have sometimes had an affecting sense of the excellency of the Word of God, as a Word of life; as the light of life; a sweet, excellent, life-giving Word: accompanied with a thirsting after that Word, that it might dwell richly in my heart.

I have often since I lived in this town, had very affecting views of my own sinfulness and vileness; very frequently so as to hold me in a kind of loud weeping, sometimes for a considerable time together: so that I have often been forced to shut myself up. I have had a vastly greater sense of my own wickedness, and the badness of my heart, since my conversion, than ever I had before. It has often appeared to me, that if God should mark iniquity against me, I should appear the very worst of all mankind; of all that have been since the beginning of the world to this time: and that I should have by far the lowest place in hell. When others that have come to talk with me about their soul concerns, have expressed the sense they have had of their own wickedness, by saying that it seemed to them, that they were as bad as the devil himself; I thought their expressions seemed exceeding faint and feeble, to represent my wickedness. I thought I should wonder, that they should content themselves with such expressions as these, if I had any reason to imagine, that their sin bore any proportion to mine. It seemed to me, I should wonder at myself, if I should express *my* wickedness in such feeble terms as they did.

My wickedness, as I am in myself, has long appeared to me perfectly ineffable, and infinitely swallowing up all thought and imagination; like an infinite deluge, or infinite mountains over my head. I know not how to express better, what my sins appear to me to be, than by heaping infinite upon infinite, and multiplying infinite by infinite. I go about very often, for this many years, with these expressions in my mind, and in my mouth, "Infinite upon Infinite. Infinite upon Infinite!" When I look into my heart, and take a view of my wickedness, it looks like an abyss infinitely deeper than hell. And it appears to me, that were it not for free grace, exalted and raised up to the infinite height of all the fullness and glory of the great Jehovah, and the arm of his power and grace stretched forth, in all the majesty of his power, and in all the glory of his sovereignty; I should appear sunk down in my sins infinitely below hell itself, far beyond sight of everything, but the piercing eye of God's grace, that can pierce even down to such a depth, and to the bottom of such an abyss.

And yet, I ben't in the least inclined to think, that I have a greater conviction of sin than ordinary. It seems to me, my conviction of sin is exceeding small, and faint. It appears to me enough to amaze me, that I have no more sense of my sin. I know certainly, that I have very little sense of my sinfulness. That my sins appear to me so great, don't seem to me to be, because I have so much more conviction of sin than other Christians, but because I am so much worse, and have so much more wickedness to be convinced of. When I have had these turns of weeping and crying for my sins, I thought I knew in the time of it, that my repentance was nothing to my sin.

I have greatly longed of late, for a broken heart, and to lie low before God. And when I ask for humility of God, I can't bear the thoughts of being no more humble, than other Christians. It seems to me, that though their degrees of humility may be suitable for them; yet it would be a vile self-exaltation in me, not to be the lowest in humility of all mankind. Others speak of their longing to be humbled to the dust. Though that may be a proper expression for them, I always think for myself, that I ought to be humbled down below hell. 'Tis an expression that it has long been natural for me to use in prayer to God. I ought to lie infinitely low before God.

It is affecting to me to think, how ignorant I was, when I was a young Christian, of the bottomless, infinite depths of wickedness, pride, hypocrisy and deceit left in my heart.

I have vastly a greater sense, of my universal, exceeding dependence on God's grace and strength, and mere good pleasure, of late, than I used formerly to have; and have experienced more of an abhorrence of my own righteousness. The thought of any comfort or joy, arising in me, on any consideration, or reflection on my own amiableness, or any of my performances or experiences, or any goodness of heart or life, is nauseous and detestable to me. And yet I am greatly afflicted with a proud and self-righteous spirit; much more sensibly, than I used to be formerly. I see that serpent rising and putting forth its head, continually, everywhere, all around me.

Though it seems to me, that in some respects I was a far better Christian, for two or three years after my first conversion, than I am now; and lived in a more constant delight and pleasure: yet of late years, I have had a more full and constant sense of the absolute sovereignty of God, and a delight in that sovereignty; and have had more of a sense of the glory of

Christ, as a mediator, as revealed in the gospel. On one Saturday night in particular, had a particular discovery of the excellency of the gospel of Christ, above all other doctrines; so that I could not but say to myself; "This is my chosen light, my chosen doctrine": and of Christ, "This is my chosen prophet." It appeared to me to be sweet beyond all expression, to follow Christ, and to be taught and enlightened and instructed by him; to learn of him, and live to him.

Another Saturday night, January 1738-39, had such a scene, how sweet and blessed a thing it was, to walk in the way of duty, to do that which was right and meet to be done, and agreeable to the holy mind of God; that it caused me to break forth into a kind of a loud weeping, which held me some time; so that I was forced to shut myself up, and fasten the doors. I could not but as it were cry out, "How happy are they which do that which is right in the sight of God! They are blesses indeed, they are the happy ones!" I had at the same time, a very affecting sense, how meet and suitable it was that God should govern the world, and order all things according to his own pleasure, and I rejoiced in it, that God reigned, and that his will was done.

Receipt for Slave Venus (1731)

KNOW ALL MEN by these presents That I Richard Perkins of Newport in the County of Newport & Colony of Rhode Island &c Marriner For & in Consideration of the Sum of Eighty pounds of lawful Current money of said Colony To me in hand well & truly paid at & before the ensealing & delivery hereof by Jonathan Edwards of Northampton in the County of Hampshire & Province of the Massachusetts Bay in New England Clerk, The receipt whereof I do hereby acknowledge and thereof & of every part and parcel thereof do exonerate aquit & Discharge the said Jonathan Edwards his heirs Exec^{rs} Adm^{rs} & Assigns by these presents HAVE bargained sold & delivered. And I the said Richard Perkins do hereby bargain sell & deliver unto the said Jonathan Edwards a Negro Girle named Venus ages Fourteen years or thereabout, TO HAVE AND TO HOLD the said Negro girl named Venus unto the said Jonathan Edwards his heirs Exec^{rs} & Assigns and to his & their own proper Use & behoof for Ever.

AND I the said Richard Perkins do hereby for my Self my heirs Exec^rs &
Adm^rs covenant promise & agree to & with the said Jonathan Edwards
his heirs Exec^rs Adm^rs & Assigns by these presents That I the said
Richard Perkins at the ensealing & delivery hereof have in my own Name
good Right, full Power & lawfull Authority to bargain sell & deliver the
said Negro Girl named Venus unto the [said Jonathan Edwards] in manner & form aforesaid. And shall & will warrant & defend the said Negro
Girle named Venus unto the said Jonathan Edwards his heirs Exec^rs
Adm^rs & Assigns against the lawfull Challenge & Demand of all manner
of Persons whatsoever Claiming or to claim by from or under me or otherwise howsoever. IN WITNESS whereof I the said Richard Perkins have
hereunto set my hand & Seal the Seventh day of June in the Fourth Year
of the Reign of our Soveraign Lord George the Second by the grace of
God of Great Britain France & Ireland King Defender of the Faith &c
Anno Dm 1731.

Richd Perkins

Sealed & Delivered
in the presence of us
    John Cranston
    Jas. Martin

Letters

To Timothy Edwards

Yale College, March 1, 1721

Honored Sir,

It was not with a little joy, and satisfaction that I received your letter of the 21st of February, by Mr. Grant,[1] and with a great deal of thankfulness from the bottom of my heart for your wholesome advice, and counsel, and the abundance of father-like tenderness therein expressed. As concerning the complaint of the scholars about their commons; the manner of it I believe was no less surprising to me, than to you. It was on this wise: every undergraduate, one and all that had anything to do with college commons, all on a sudden, before Mr. Cutler,[2] or (I believe) anybody knew that they were discontented, entered into a bond of 15s never to have any more commons of the steward, whereupon they all forewarned him never to provide more for them, telling him if he did they would not pay him for it. Mr. Brown[3] notwithstanding ordered commons to be provided, and set upon the table as it used to be, and accordingly it was, but there was nobody to eat it: Mr. Cutler as soon as he was apprised of this cabal sent on the same day for Mr. Andrew, and Mr. Russel,[4] who came on the next, and with the Rector ordered all to appear before them; where the Rector manifested himself exceedingly vexed and displeased, at the act, which so affrighted the scholars that they unanimously agreed to come into commons again. I believe the scholars that were in this agreement have so lost Mr. Cutler's favor that they scarce ever will regain it. Stiles[5] (to my grief and I believe much more to his) was one that set his hand to this bond; he

1. Mr. John Grant, a resident of East Windsor and a member of Timothy Edwards' church.

2. Rev. Timothy Cutler (1684–1765), Rector of Yale College.

3. Daniel Brown (1698–1723), one of the tutors of the College.

4. Rev. Samuel Andrew (1675–1738), pastor of Milford, Connecticut; and Rev. Samuel Russel (1693–1746), pastor of Branford, Connecticut. Both were founders and trustees of Yale College.

5. Isaac Stiles (1697–1760), one of Timothy Edwards' pupils, who would later be the pastor of North Haven, Connecticut.

did it by the strong instigations of others who persuaded him to it; neither had he a minute's time to consider before his hand was down: as soon as I understood him to be one of them, I told him that I thought he had done exceeding unadvisedly, and told him also what I thought the ill consequences of it would be, and quickly made him sorry that he did not take advice in the matter. I am apt to think that this thing will be the greatest obstacle of any to Stiles' being Butler. I must needs say for my own part, that although the commons at sometimes have not been sufficient as to quality, yet I think there has been very little occasion for such an insurrection as this. Although these disturbances were so speedily quashed, yet they are succeeded by much worse, and greater, and I believe greater than ever were in the college before; they are occasioned by the discovery of some monstrous impieties, and acts of immorality lately committed in the college, particularly stealing of hens, geese, turkeys, pigs, meat, wood, etc., unseasonable night-walking, breaking people's windows, playing at cards, cursing, swearing, and damning, and using all manner of ill language, which never were at such a pitch in the college as they now are. The Rector has called a meeting of the trustees on this occasion; they are expected here today; 'tis thought the upshot will be the expulsion of some, and the public admonition of others: through the goodness of God I am perfectly free of all their janglings. My condition at the college at present is every way comfortable: I live in very good amity and agreement with my chambermate. There has no new quarrels broke out betwixt me and any of the scholars, though they still persist in their former combination; but I am not without hopes that it will be abolished by this meeting of the trustees. I have not as yet wrote to uncle Mix,[6] because I heard he was coming down. But he delaying his coming I shall do it speedily. I am at present in perfect health, and it is a time of health throughout the college and town. I am about taking the remainder of my lignum vitæ. I am much reformed with respect to visiting of friends, and intend to do more at it for the future than in time past. I think I shall not have occasion for the coat you mentioned in your letter till I come home. I received a letter from my

6. Rev. Stephen Mix (1672–1738), the pastor of Wethersfield, Connecticut, who, like Timothy Edwards, had married a daughter of Solomon Stoddard; his son Elisha Mix had been Edwards' roommate.

sister Mary the week before last and have heard of her welfare this week by a man that came directly from thence. I pray you in your next letter to send me your advice whether or no I had best come home in May, or tarry till June.

Please to give my humble duty to my mother, hearty love to sisters and Mercy, and still to be mindful before the throne of grace of me, who am,

> Honored sir,
> your most dutiful son,
> Jonathan E.

Stiles presents his duty to yourself with my mother and service to my sisters.

To George Whitefield

Northampton in New England, Feb. 12, 1739/40

Reverend Sir,

My request to you is, that in your intended journey through New England the next summer, you would be pleased to visit Northampton. I hope it is not wholly from curiosity that I desire to see and hear you in this place; but I apprehend, from what I have heard, that you are one that has the blessing of heaven attending you wherever you go: and I have a great desire, if it may be the will of God, that such a blessing as attends your person & labors may descend on this town, and may enter mine own house, and that I may receive it in my own soul. Indeed I am fearful whether you will not be disappointed in New England, and will have less success here than in other places: we who have dwelt in a land that has been distinguished with light, and have long enjoyed the gospel, and have been glutted with it, and have despised it, are I fear more hardened than most of those places where you have preached hitherto. But yet I hope in that power and mercy of God that has appeared so triumphant in the success of your labors in other places, that he will send a blessing with you even to us, though we are unworthy of it. I hope, if God preserves my life, to see something of that salvation of God in New England which he has now begun, in a benighted, wicked and miserable world and age and in the most guilty of all nations. It has been with refreshment of soul that I have heard of one raised up in the Church of England to revive the mysterious, spiritual, despised and exploded doctrines of the gospel, and full of a spirit of zeal for the promotion of real vital piety, whose labors have been attended with such success. Blessed be God that hath done it! who is with you, and helps you, and makes the weapons of your warfare mighty. We see that God is faithful, and never will forget the promises that he has made to his church; and that he will not suffer the smoking flax to be quenched, even when the floods seem to be overwhelming it; but will revive the flame again, even in the darkest times. I hope this is the dawning of a day of God's mighty power and glorious grace to the world of mankind. May you go on reverend sir! and may God be with you more and more abundantly, that the work of God may be carried on by a blessing on your labors still, with that swift progress that it has been hitherto, and rise to a greater height, and extend further and further, with an irresistible power bearing down all opposition! And may the gates of hell never be able to prevail against you! and may God send forth more laborers into his harvest of a like spirit, until the kingdom of Satan shall shake, and his proud empire fall throughout the earth, and the kingdom of Christ, that glorious kingdom of light, holiness, peace and love, shall be established from one end of the earth unto the other!

Give my love to Mr. Seward:[7] I hope to see him here with you. I believe I may venture to say that what has been heard of your labors and success has not been taken notice of more in any place in New England than here, or received with fuller credit. I hope therefore if we have opportunity, we shall hear you with greater attention. The way from New York to Boston through Northampton is but little further than the nearest that is; and I think leads through as populous a part of the country as any. I desire that you and Mr. Seward would come directly to my house. I shall account it a great favor and smile of providence to have opportunity to entertain such guests under my roof, and to have some acquaintance with such persons.

I fear it is too much for me to desire a particular remembrance in your prayers, when I consider how many thousands do doubtless desire it, who

7. William Seward, Whitefield's associate and publicist.

can't all be particularly mentioned; and I am far from thinking myself worthy to be distinguished. But pray, sir, let your heart be lifted up to God for me among others, that God would bestow much of that blessed Spirit on me that he has bestowed on you, and make me also an instrument of his glory.

> I am, reverend sir,
> unworthy to be called your
> fellow laborer,
> Jonathan Edwards

To Moses Lyman

Northampton, May 10, 1742

My Dear Friend,[8]

I am fully satisfied by the account your father has given me, that you have lately gone out of the way of your duty, and done that which did not belong to you, in exhorting a public congregation. I know you to be a person of good judgment and discretion; and therefore can with the greater confidence put it to you to consider with yourself, what you can reasonably judge would be the consequence, if I, and all other ministers, should approve and publicly justify such things, as laymen's taking it upon them to exhort after this manner? If one may, why mayn't another? And if there be no certain limits or bounds, but everyone that inclines may have liberty, alas! what should we soon come to? If God had not seen it necessary that such things should have certain limits and bounds, he never would have appointed a certain particular order of men to that work and office, to be set apart to it, in so solemn a manner, in the name of God. The head of the church is wiser than we, and knew how to regulate things in his church.

'Tis no argument that such things are right, that they do a great deal of good for the present, and within a narrow sphere; when at the same time, if we look on them in the utmost extent of their consequences and in the

8. Moses Lyman was the son of Capt. Moses and Sarah Lyman of Northampton; he moved to Goshen, Connecticut, in 1739, where he became a deacon of the local church, and died in 1768.

long run of events, they do ten times as much hurt as good. Appearing events are not our rule, but the law and the testimony. We ought to be vigilant and circumspect, and look on every side, and as far as we can, to the further end of things.

God may if he pleases in his sovereign providence, turn that which is very wrong to do a great deal of good for the present, for he does what he pleases. I hope you will consider the matter and for the future avoid doing thus. You ought to do what good you can, by private, brotherly, humble admonitions and counsels: but 'tis too much for you to exhort public congregations, or solemnly to set yourself, by a set speech, to counsel a roomful of people, unless it be children or those that are much your inferior, or to speak to any in an authoritative way. Such things have done a vast deal of mischief in the country, and have hindered the work of God exceedingly. Mr. Tennent[9] has lately wrote a letter to one of the ministers of New England, earnestly to dissuade from such things. Your temptations are exceeding great; you had need to have the prudence and humility of ten men. If you are kept humble and prudent, you may be a great blessing on that part of the land; otherwise you may do as much hurt in a few weeks as you can do good in seven years. You might be under great advantage by your prudence to prevent those irregularities and disorders in your parts that prevail, and greatly hinder the work of God in other parts of the country: but by such things as these you will weaken your own hands, and fill the country with nothing but vain and fruitless and pernicious disputes. Persons, when very full of a great sense of things, are greatly exposed: for then they long to do something, and to do something extraordinary; and then is the devil's time to run them upon their heads, if they ben't extraordinary circumspect, and self-diffident.

I hope these lines will be taken in good part from your assured friend,

Jonathan Edwards

P.S. Give my love to your dear wife. I long to see you both, whom I love as a couple of the dear children of God united, as I trust, in happy bands.

9. Rev. Gilbert Tennent (1703–64), the famous Presbyterian revivalist, then minister of New Brunswick, New Jersey.

To Joseph Bellamy

Northampton, Jan. 15, 1746/47

Dear Sir,

I received your letter by Mr. Strong[10] this day. Mr. Searl[11] was here at my house presently after, and I gave your questions to him, and told him the bearer intended quickly to return.

(As to the affair of sheep, I am much obliged to you for the pains you have taken. I believe you have acted the part of a trusty friend therein. I suppose it is known by this time, whether the man that went to Newtown has succeeded. If he has, and the sheep are bought, we shall rest in what you have done; but if not, and you shall have found no opportunity till this letter reaches you, it is so late in the year, that I desire you would keep the money till shearing time is over, and then buy; when I suppose they may be bought much cheaper than now. But I would pray you to send us word by the first opportunity, that if we are not like to have any sheep this year, we may seasonably be looking out, and laying in for wool elsewhere, for the supply of the family. In the spring, if you can give us any encouragement, I should be glad to lay out £60 more for sheep in those parts, as soon as shearing time is over, besides the £30 you have in your hands. But only, if you buy so many sheep for us, it might be perhaps expedient on some accounts, for the present, not to let it be known who the sheep are for.)

As to the books you speak of, Mastricht[12] is sometimes in one volume, a very thick, large quarto; sometimes in two quarto volumes. I believe it could not be had new under eight or ten pounds. Turretine[13] is in three volumes in quarto, and would probably be about the same price. They are both excellent. Turretine is on polemical divinity; on the Five Points, and all other controversial points; and is much larger in these than Mastricht; and is better for one that desires only to be thoroughly versed in controver-

10. Possibly Job Strong of Northampton.

11. John Searl (1721–87), a former pupil of Edwards', who graduated from Yale College in 1745; he would be ordained at Sharon, Connecticut, in 1749.

12. Peter van Mastricht (1630–1706), a Dutch Reformed theologian, wrote *Theoretica-Practica Theologia* (Rhenum, 1699).

13. Francis Turretin (1623–87), a Protestant scholastic based in Geneva, wrote *Institutio Theologia Elenctica* (Geneva, 1688).

sies. But take Mastricht for divinity in general, doctrine, practice and controversy; or as an universal system of divinity; and it is much better than Turretine, or any other book in the world, excepting the Bible, in my opinion. I have thoughts of sending, myself, this year to England, for a few books; and have written to Mr. Quincy, a merchant in Boston, about it, to desire his advice and assistance, as to the course to be taken to obtain 'em. If I employ him to send for me, I shall be willing to serve you (as I desire you to serve me about the sheep). I am willing to take your money, and put it with my own, and put your books into my catalog and have the books all come as mine: or shall be willing to serve you, if I can in any respect, by writing to my correspondents in Scotland.

I have been reading Whitby,[14] which has engaged me pretty thoroughly in the study of the Arminian controversy; and I have writ considerably upon it in my private papers. I must entreat you, if possible, to borrow for me Dr. Stebbing, on the Spirit.[15] I had rather pay something for the use of it than not have some considerable opportunity with it. I am got so deep into their controversy, that I am not willing to dismiss it, till I know the utmost of their matters.

I have very lately received a packet from Scotland, with several copies of a memorial, for the continuing and propagating an agreement for joint prayer, for the general revival of religion; three of which I here send you, desiring you to dispose of two of 'em where they will be most serviceable. For my part, I heartily wish it was fallen in with by all Christians from the rising to the setting sun.

I have returned you Mr. Dickinson's book, but must pray you, let me have further opportunity with Dr. Johnson's.[16] If you could inquire of

14. Daniel Whitby (1638–1726), a minister in the Church of England and Arminian apologist. Edwards refers to his *Discourse Concerning I. The True Import of the Words Election and Reprobation . . . II. The Extent of Christ's Redemption. III. The Grace of God . . . IV. The Liberty of the Will . . . V. The Perseverance or Defectability of the Saints* (London, 1710).

15. Henry Stebbing (d. 1763), a minister in the Church of England who espoused Arminianism, wrote the *Treatise Concerning the Operations of the Holy Spirit* (London, 1719).

16. Jonathan Dickinson (1688–1747), a Presbyterian minister at Elizabethtown, New Jersey, and renowned defender of orthodox Calvinism, published *Vindication of God's Sovereign Free Grace* in Boston in 1746; Samuel Johnson (1696–1772), author of *Letter from Aristocles to Authades Concerning the Sovereignty and the Promises of God* (Boston, 1745), was at the time of this letter a missionary for the Church of England at Stratford, Connecticut, and would later become the president of King's College in New York.

Dr. Johnson, or Mr. Beach[17] or some other, and find out what is the best book on the Arminian side, for the defense of their notion of free will; and whether there be any better and more full than Whitby, I should be glad; provided you have convenient opportunity. I don't know but I shall publish something after a while on that subject.

Dear sir, we have so many affairs to confer upon, that concern us both, that I would propose you should come this way again in February or March. You han't a great family to tie you at home, as I have. But if you can't come I must desire you to write fully and largely on all the foregoing particulars of this letter. Herein you will oblige, your cordial and affectionate friend and brother,

Jonathan Edwards

P.S. It now comes to my mind that I heard that Dr. Pynchon of Longmeadow[18] has Turretine, and that he lately offered to change them away for other books; so that in all probability you may there have those books at a moderate price.

To Sarah Pierpont Edwards

Northampton, June 22, 1748

My Dear Companion,

I wrote you a few lines the last sabbath day by Ensign Dwight,[19] which I hope you will receive. By this I would inform you that Betty[20] seems really to be on the mending hand; I can't but think she [is] truly better, both as to her health and her sores, since she has been at Mrs. Phelps'. The first two or three days, before she was well acquainted, she was very unquiet; but now more quiet than she used to be at home. This is lecture-day morning, and your two eldest daughters[21] went to bed last night, both

17. Rev. John Beach (1700–82), who successively pastored the Congregational and then the Episcopalian churches of Newtown, Connecticut, from 1732 to 1782.

18. Joseph Pynchon, who practiced medicine.

19. Timothy Dwight, Jr. (d. 1776), who eventually achieved the rank of major, was a Northampton merchant who married Edwards' daughter Mary in 1750.

20. Elizabeth Edwards, b. May 6, 1747; d. Jan. 1, 1762.

sick; and rose beat out, and having the headache. We got Hannah Root to help them yesterday in the afternoon, [and] expect her again today. How Sarah [and] Esther do today I can't tell, for they are not up. We have been without you almost as long as we know how to be; but yet are willing you should obey the calls of providence with regard to Col. Stoddard.[22]

If you have money to spare, and it isn't too late, I should be glad if you would buy us some cheese in Boston, and [send it] with other things if it can be safely.

Give my humble service to Mr. Bromfield and Madam and proper salutations to other friends.

I am your most affectionate companion,
Jonathan Edwards

To Thomas Foxcroft

Northampton, May 24, 1749

Rev. and Honored Sir,

I have herewith sent an answer to three other objections against the doctrine maintained in my discourse now in the press; which objections I find by further consideration and conversation, there is a necessity should be answered. I have also sent a short preface, and an abstract of your letter to me on this subject. I have taken such things from the letter as I desire may be published. If they are published as something that I add to my own book, as an abstract of a letter which I received from you (in the form wherein I have here sent it), it may be best to be as an appendix: but if it be published as something that you add in your own name, I should think it would be better to be in a preface. I should choose the latter, viz. that you should add these things in a preface in your own name: but I must leave it

---

21. Sarah Edwards, b. Aug. 25, 1728, m. Elihu Parsons, June 11, 1750; Esther Edwards, b. Feb. 13, 1732, m. Rev. Aaron Burr, June 29, 1752.

22. John Stoddard, the son of Solomon Stoddard, was a wealthy and influential inhabitant of Northampton and Edwards' chief ally and adviser up until his death, on June 15, 1748. Sarah Edwards was there to tend him during his last illness.

with your judgment. I should be glad that something may be observed concerning the opinion of the late and present divines in England and Scotland. Some things I have observed, that lead me to suppose that their opinion is generally agreeable to Mr. Baxter's.

In my narrative of the work of God wrought here 14 years ago, which was sent to Dr. Watts and Dr. Guyse,[23] I observed something of the manner of our church, to admit members without a profession of conversion. They, in some of their letters written to Dr. Colman, appeared much offended at it. I have a sermon of Dr. Guyse, preached at the ordination of Mr. Gibbons in London, wherein he plainly manifests his mind with regard to the qualifications of the members of a Christian church. And I have seen a practical discourse of Mr. Willison's of Dundee, wherein he is much in warning graceless persons not to presume to approach the Lord's Table. But you have vastly greater opportunities of full information concerning the present principles and practice in England and Scotland, than I. And an account of this would be more likely to have influence on some, than an account of what was in the last and preceding centuries.

You speak in your last letter, as though Mr. Stoddard's opinion was far from being the prevailing opinion in your parts. If it be so, I should be glad if this also might be inserted; for people in general here are not sensible but that their opinion is become the established opinion almost all over New England. You say, you believe the generality of the churches and elderly ministers, your way hold to the first principles of New England in this matter: if you mean not only with respect to qualifications for the Lord's Supper, but also baptism, 'tis what I was by no means aware of, and quite otherwise than I supposed. I did suppose it to be the universal, and long-established custom of the country to admit to baptism on lower terms than to the Lord's Supper; excepting those churches where Mr. Stoddard's principles were established; and particularly that it was the custom to admit parents who desired baptism for their children into the church, in a *state of education*, on their *owning the covenant*, as it is called:

23. *A Faithful Narrative of the Surprising Work of God*, to which Isaac Watts and John Guyse, two eminent English dissenting clergymen, wrote a commendatory preface.

which they do, not as professing or pretending to saving faith and repentance, or regenerating grace. I should be glad to be more particularly informed as to that matter. And if it be otherwise than I have conceived, I think it had best by all means be published in the book; for 'tis undoubtedly very diverse from what is universally received to be fact in these parts.

The greatest difficulty of all relating to my principles is here, respecting baptism. I am not sure but that my people, in length of time, and with great difficulty, might be brought to yield the point as to the qualifications for the Lord's Supper (though that is very uncertain); but with respect to the other sacrament, there is scarce any hope of it. And this will be very likely to overthrow me, not only with regard to my usefulness in the work of the ministry here, but everywhere; if the case *be*, as I supposed it *was* in the country. The ministers in New Jersey and Pennsylvania are many of them strict with regard to qualifications for the Lord's Supper; but I understand they are not so with regard to baptism; but do admit all, on owning the covenant, not under the notion of a profession of true godliness.

If I should be wholly cast out of my ministry, I should be in many respects in a poor case: I shall not be likely to be serviceable to my generation, or get a subsistence, in a business of a different nature. I am by nature very unfit for secular business; and especially am now unfit, after I have been so long in the work of the ministry. I am now comfortably settled, have as large a salary settled upon me as most have out of Boston and have the largest, and most chargeable family of any minister, perhaps within an hundred miles of me.

I have many enemies abroad in the country, who hate me for my stingy principles, enthusiasm, rigid proceedings, etc. that now are expecting full triumph over me. I need the prayers of my fathers and brethren who are friendly to me, that I may have wisdom given me by my great Master, and that I may be enabled to conduct with a steady faithfulness to him, under all trials, and whatever may be the issue of this affair. I seem as it were to be casting myself off from a precipice; and have no other way, but to go on, as it were blindfold, i.e. shutting my eyes to everything else but the evidences of the mind and will of God, and the path of duty; which I would observe with the utmost care.

This western part of New England is exceeding full of noise about this affair; and few are indifferent. Some of the ministers in Connecticut, that have been chief favorers and promoters of the late work of God, have a spirit of opposing zeal excited on this occasion (from whom I should have least expected it), and appear strangely ready to entertain groundless surmises, and receive false reports and misrepresentations concerning me, which the country is very full of.

As to three objections to which I have now sent answers, I think the *first* of them may properly be placed the first of all the objections. As to the placing of the other two, I must leave it to your discretion, who have the book before you, and see the order of the objections, and can better judge where they will most properly come in, than I, who don't fully remember their order.

If you should see Rector Williams[24] at Boston, I hope you will endeavor to dissuade him from writing against me, as he has given out. Not that I am afraid of the strength of any fair arguing against the doctrine I maintain; but such are my peculiarly disadvantageous circumstances, that he doubtless has it in the power of his hands to do me a great deal of hurt, let his arguments be never so weak; yea, if they should be far worse than nothing in the esteem of observing and discerning readers, yet its only being said that Rector Williams has written an answer to me, will do me great hurt with my people. It would be a very likely way to discourage Mr. Williams from writing, if he could be made to believe that it would not be for his honor; and particularly if he could be artfully led to think that my books would go to Great Britain, to England and Scotland; and that his opposing me in this matter would be offensive to learned men there, and not for his honor in that part of the world.

I should be glad if his writing might be prevented, not only for the reason already mentioned, but also on this account, that it would save me a long and perhaps almost endless labor of replying. For though I have been with great reluctance brought to begin to write, yet since divine provi-

24. Rev. Elisha Williams (1694–1755), Edwards' uncle and former tutor, who was the Rector of Yale College from 1726 to 1739 and a powerful political figure in Massachusetts.

dence has compelled me, and I have put my hand to the plow, I shall look upon it [as] my duty to pursue the matter to the end; and to write as long as I see there is any need of writing in order to defend this important doctrine, and God gives me ability and opportunity.

If you observe any expressions in my manuscript not respectful enough to my grandfather, I would pray you to inform me of it. I would in no degree be guilty of the sin of Canaan, in his disrespect of his grandfather.

I desire you to inform Messrs. Kneeland and Green,[25] that Capt. Church and Mr. Potwine of Hartford, when I lately saw 'em together there, desired me, if there should be occasion for it, to inform my undertaker, that they would jointly take off an hundred of the books, and send him the money: and Mr. John Brainerd of New Jersey has engaged to take 50; and Mr. Bellamy of Bethlehem in Connecticut, has engaged to take 50 more, provided the undertaker will wait for the money till the Fall of the year.

I thank you for the pains you have taken to forward the printing of this book, and your readiness to take pains to get subscriptions, and to take care of and correct the impression. Under these obligations, and in hope of your future friendliness to me, and prayers for me under my present difficulties, I subscribe myself, honored sir, your respectful and most obliged,

> Brother and servant,
> Jonathan Edwards

To Esther Edwards Burr

Stockbridge, March 28, 1753

Dear Child,

We are glad to hear that you are in any respect better, but concerned at your remaining great weakness. I am glad to see some of the contents of your letter to your mother; and particularly that you have been enabled to

25. Edwards' publishers in Boston.

make a free-will offering of yourself to God's service, and that you have experienced some inward divine consolations under your affliction, by the extreme weakness and distressing pains, you have been the subject of. For these you ought to be thankful, and also for that unwearied kindness and tender care of your companion,[26] which you speak of. I would not have you think that any strange thing has happened to you in this affliction: 'tis according to the course of things in this world, that after the world's smiles, some great affliction soon comes. God has now given you early and seasonable warning, not at all to depend on worldly prosperity. Therefore I would advise, if it pleases God to restore you, to let upon no happiness here. Labor while you live, to serve God and do what good you can, and endeavor to improve every dispensation to God's glory and your own spiritual good, and be content to do and bear all that God calls you to in this wilderness, and never expect to find this world anything better than a wilderness. Lay your account to travel through it in weariness, painfulness and trouble, and wait for your rest and your prosperity till hereafter, where they that die in the Lord rest from their labors, and enter into the joy of the Lord. You are like to spend the rest of your life (if you should get over this illness) at a great distance from your parents; but care not much for that. If you lived near us, yet our breath and yours would soon go forth, and we should return to our dust, whither we are all hastening. 'Tis of infinitely more importance to have the presence of an heavenly Father, and to make progress towards an heavenly home. Let us all take care that we may meet there at last.

As to means for your health, we have procured one rattlesnake, which is all we could get. It is a medicine that has been very serviceable to you heretofore, and I would have you try it still. If your stomach is very weak and will bear but little, you must take it in smaller quantities. We have sent you some ginseng. I should think it best for you to make trial of that various ways: try stewing it in water, and take it in strength and quantity as you find suits your stomach best. You may also try steeping it in wine, in

26. Rev. Aaron Burr (d. 1757), pastor of the Newark, New Jersey, Presbyterian Church and president of the College of New Jersey. He and Esther Edwards had married in 1752.

good Madeira or claret; or if these wines are too harsh, then in some good white wine. And whether you stew or steep it, you had best to slice it very thin, or bruise it in an iron mortar. And for a cordial take some spices steeped in some generous wine that suits your taste, and stomach. And above all the rest, use riding in pleasant weather: and when you can bear it, riding on horseback; but never so as to fatigue you. And be very careful to avoid taking cold. And I should think it best pretty much to throw by doctors, and be your own physician, hearkening to them that are used to your constitution.

I desire that Mr. Burr and you would be frequent in counseling Timmy[27] as to his soul concerns.

Commending you to God, before whom we daily remember you in our prayers, I am,

> Your affectionate father,
> Jonathan Edwards

P.S. Your mother would have you use a conserve of raisins; a pound of good sugar to a pound of raisins, after they are stoned. Mix with it, nutmegs, mace, cinnamon, cloves, ground in a spice mill, with some orange-pill; one nutmeg to half a pound of conserve, and the other spices in the same quantity.

Take a little as suits your stomach, in the morning, and an hour before dinner, and in the afternoon. The same spices and orange-pill to be put into your spiced wine. But when you take this, you must omit taking the wine. The only danger we apprehend in these things is that possibly the heat of 'em may raise a fever; therefore you must observe the operation of them as to that: and when you drink your spiced wine you may mix some water with it to abate the heat of it. Your mother has also an inclination that you should sometimes try a tea made of the leaves of Robin's Plantain, if it be known at Newark by that name; she says she has found it very strengthening and comfortable to her in her weakness.

The family all unites in their love to you.

27. Edwards' eldest son, Timothy Edwards (1738–1813), who was then attending the College of New Jersey.

To Thomas Prince

Stockbridge, May 10, 1754

Rev. and Honored Sir,

I thank you for your favor of April 17, which came safe to hand the last week, with Mr. Hollis' money;[28] which was brought from Northampton by my son.

I find by the contents of your letter that there is need of your having laid before you a particular account of many things relating to the past and present state of Mr. Hollis' school, that you may have some tolerable idea of the circumstances of the affair.

Mr. Hollis has maintained a school in this place in all about nine years, three years before Capt. Kellogg[29] was improved and six years before one Mohawk was taken into the school on Mr. Hollis' account. After the school was set up and had been continued for some time, consisting only of Stockbridge boys, the Stockbridge Indians, excited by Mr. Sergeant,[30] gave of their own land, a farm of two hundred acres, of an excellent soil, within half a mile of the meetinghouse, for the use of the boarding school, with a special view to the benefit of their children; for the school had then always consisted of such only; and it was long before any of the Mohawks looked this way. The farm is very conveniently situated, being a peninsula, encompassed on three sides by the river; and is of great value. The Indians, besides giving this farm, helped to clear some of it, and were at the trouble and cost of building a bridge over the river to accommodate the school. Afterwards an house was built for the school on this farm; and about £500 laid out upon it; which had been charitably contributed in Stockbridge and other places; besides £500 more given by the Commissioners: and all this before the Mohawks so much as talked of coming hither.

When the Mohawks first came down in the fall of the year 1750, Capt. Kellogg did not take any of 'em on Mr. Hollis' account: but not having heard from Mr. Hollis a long time, and not knowing but he was dead, he dismissed all Mr. Hollis' scholars (Stockbridge boys) and in their room

---

28. Isaac Hollis was an English benefactor of the Stockbridge mission.
29. Capt. Martin Kellogg, a resident of Stockbridge and the master of the Indian school.
30. Rev. John Sergeant (1710–49), ordained in 1735 as the first missionary of Stockbridge.

took Mohawk boys, to look after; not on Mr. Hollis' account, but on the account of the country, and was paid by the Province. When the Mohawks first came, Capt. Kellogg was mightily taken, and was very full of his promises to them what great things should be done for them and their children, how well they should be fed and clothed and instructed, and looked after in all respects; raising their expectations very high. Which promises the Indians remembered, and often put us in mind of 'em afterwards.

Capt. Kellogg went on with the Mohawks at the charge of the Province till the next summer, 1751; when, Mr. Hollis having been informed of the Mohawks' coming, Capt. Kellogg received a letter from him, wherein he writes as supposing his school still in being consisting of 12 boys, agreeable to his former orders which related only to Stockbridge boys, and he now ordered him to add 12 boys more to the number: far from ordering him to dismiss his 12 Stockbridge boys; but his letter plainly implying the contrary. On which Capt. Kellogg, now having no boys at all on Mr. Hollis' account, goes about to get his 24 boys; and to make up the number, he took up some Mohawks and some Stockbridge boys; but the greater part Mohawks; for by this time the Stockbridge Indians were heartily sick of Capt. Kellogg's managements, and but few of their boys could be obtained by him: so that he could not make up his full number of 24 as yet.

By this time, there began to appear an uneasiness among the Stockbridge Indians; that whereas they had given the farm, built the bridge, etc. to accommodate the school, with a special view to the benefit of their own children, their boys had the fall before been turned away, and Mohawks taken into the house and upon the farm in their stead. And we had several meetings with 'em on this affair, before they could be quieted with respect to it. Finally, they were made easy with this, that there was no design of excluding their children, or taking away the land from them; but that special regard should be had to their children still, according to their intention in the sequestration of the farm; and that the Mohawks were like to improve their land but a little while, the design being that they should be removed to the Hop-Lands.

In the month of August of that summer, 1751, was here in Stockbridge, a grand conference of the Committee of the General Court with the sachems of the Mohawks; who came down from their own country with a great train of about 100 young and old, being invited hither to confer about the affair of the Mohawks settling in the country, and putting their children to school here. In the conference, the Mohawks objected that the promises of the English concerning their care for the instruction of their children in times past had not been fulfilled. They mentioned a treaty which they had had with this Province many years ago, wherein the English had promised to send them a missionary to preach to 'em, and a schoolmaster or masters to instruct their children; and produced a silver box with the Province seal in it, which they said was given 'em to confirm these promises; which yet had never been fulfilled. Moreover they said, that when some of their people came down hither the preceding fall, they were promised that their children should be handsomely clothed, and in other respects well looked after; whereas, they found their children naked, and nasty, and in a worse condition than they were in in their own country; and that they observed a great neglect and woeful confusion in the manner of their instruction, quite diverse from what they had observed in English schools. . . .

What stories some of my enemies might tell the Indians concerning my designs, to make 'em cry, I can't tell: I know it has been the manner of some to take almost an unbounded liberty in stories they have told the Indians to disaffect 'em to me: and I have good reason to think there are some in the town would do their utmost to alienate the Indians from me, and to discourage the Mohawks from letting their children come under my care.

Besides what I said to the Mohawks at the forementioned conference, I afterwards, at every opportunity, renewed my offers of taking their children; and offered for the present to take 'em to my own house, and look after 'em as my own children. Yea, and have actually taken one of them to live at my house before the others went away. And because the parents were none of 'em willing to leave their children unless they could live here themselves, I have laid out myself to get some land for 'em to improve, and also to get it plowed for 'em; and to that end have been at the trouble of a great deal of consultation with the English and the Stockbridge Indians.

The representation made in the letter you speak of is of a piece with what is daily done here. There are some here that industriously spread abroad such representations, and say that the school was in flourishing circumstances till it came into my hands, and that I immediately threw up the school after I had taken it, and that I had broken up the Mohawk affair, etc., etc.

They have been this several years murdering the Mohawk affair themselves with cruel hands; and now just as it is expiring, they lay to me the mischief which they have most apparently done themselves, and are indefatigably endeavoring to possess everybody with an agreeable opinion. And I have no reason to expect anything else of them, as long as they stay here, but that they will with all imaginable industry and craftiness, not to say guile and deceitfulness, seek by all means, to clog, embarrass, and ruin my affairs. And from the representations which are sent to Boston, we may easily conjecture what representations will be sent to Mr. Hollis. But I would entreat you, sir, for the future, in justice to me, to pay no regard to the representations of my known and open enemies. And I desire, sir, that you would show the person or persons to whom the letter you mention was written about my grieving the Mohawks, what I have here written concerning that matter, and the testimonies about it which I herewith send.

But to resume my narrative: though the Mohawks seemed to be so much fixed in their resolution of all leaving the place, yet some of 'em, on further consideration, came and offered to deliver their children to me, as soon as they should return from sugaring: which offer I readily accepted, and told 'em they should come and live at my house till I could get a good master to come and board 'em and look after 'em. After this, the mother of two of the children that were offered came to me again with her eldest son (one of those fellows I mentioned before as disaffected and probably joining in the horrid designs of some of the young Indians of the Stockbridge Tribe) and told me that this, her son, would not consent to her leaving any of her children. I then renewedly used arguments to persuade her. The woman seemed to have a great mind her children should stay, and seemed to argue the matter much with her son; but he would by no means consent. But finally she promised she would return some time in the summer, and bring back her children, and put 'em under my care: and so left some of her things at my house as a pledge of it.

Now there was left but one Mohawk boy; whom I have taken to my own house. Besides the Mohawks, there were a number of Stockbridge boys which had belonged to Mr. Hollis' school; which therefore, if I tied myself exactly to Mr. Hollis' instructions, I should have *collected together*. But I knew most of 'em were wholly unfit to answer his design, never having been at all cultivated under Capt. Kellogg's care, but rather had grown more rough and wild than when he first took them, and were now past their forming age, and would be likely to corrupt and spoil the rest of the scholars. There were two of 'em that were not past a capacity of cultivation. These therefore I took. And instead of those others (some of which had a mind to come in), I took three new ones that were young, such as I thought likely and promising. I thought if I pretended to keep the school in being, I could not take less than six. So that the school now consists of one Mohawk, and five Stockbridge boys. The Mohawk is at my house. The others live all at the house of Mr. Joseph Woodbridge; a very desirable family; the man one of the best sort of men that I am acquainted with, the most faithful and thorough in business, and of the most generous Christian and public spirit. The boys at present go to school to Mr. Timothy Woodbridge, whom I have desired to take extraordinary pains with them, till I can get another master for 'em.

This sir, is what I have done: and I will now give you the reasons of my conduct. It was apparent that it was absolutely necessary that the school should be kept in being. To let it sink for the present under a notion of reviving it again sometime hereafter, would be the way to have it sink finally, especially as to the Mohawks. To have let fall the school wholly, because new Mohawk boys are not to be obtained, in hopes of getting half a dozen Mohawk boys hereafter to begin the school with them, would have been to have proceeded on a vain and unreasonable expectation. They have been so often disappointed with respect to the state of the school, and so continually and long deceived with fair promises of a better state of it, that 'tis now apparent that, not the hearing of the ear, but the sight of the eye only, will convince 'em. There is not the least hope of ever regaining Mohawk children to the school any other way than this, viz. by giving them to see, not only that the school is upheld, but that 'tis well settled, and indeed in good circumstances, and established under a far more happy regulation than it used to be: and this they must see for some time, before their prejudices will be removed. If they see this indeed brought to effect, that the school is established, and continues in good circumstances, then perhaps, by Mr. Hawley's help, in length of time, a number, yea, a considerable number of Mohawk boys might be obtained. But how should they see this if the school has no being? And when the Mohawks at present refuse to leave their children, how shall we give the school a being, that the Mohawks may see it, and see its flourishing state, in order to our gaining their children, otherwise than by our constituting the school at present of such children as can be had? And it was of vast importance that the school, now it is come into new hands, should be soon amended and settled under a happy regulation. For if the Indians, after they have seen it so long in such miserable, broken circumstances, and have had their patience and hopes so worn out by multiplied disappointments, should see it continuing in its broken state still, now it is got into quite other hands, it will tend to their utterly despairing of ever seeing it otherwise; and the not taking speedy care that it might be otherwise, would be to give the finishing stroke to that important affair that was before just expiring. . . .

I should not have thought, sir, that I had run any venture in proceeding as I have done, had it not been for your letter. But I am here alone entrusted with this business, and could do no otherwise than according to my own best discretion, with the advice of my friends that are here, who see the state of things and have known Mr. Hollis' and Mr. Sergeant's manner from the beginning; who thought it no venture to do as I have done: they say Mr. Sergeant, who undoubtedly was a very honest, faithful man, ever went on those principles to attend Mr. Hollis' instructions as far as the state of things (which he knew and which it was impossible for Mr. Hollis to know) would allow. But to proceed so as not to defeat Mr. Hollis' main design, for fear of departing from his instructions in some punctilios, and that Mr. Sergeant took a far greater liberty than I have done in this respect, and was never blamed for it by Mr. Hollis.

But we in our great caution, lest we should not be punctual to Mr. Hollis' instructions, are knocking on the head the thing which he mainly has his heart upon, and taking a course to spend his money to little purpose, in comparison of what might be, if we acted as we see the state of things absolutely requires.

I know not what I shall do. I have been endeavoring to persuade the Mohawks to let me have their children with such arguments, that probably the school would soon be under much better regulations than it used to be. But if they see it long in an unsettled state, I shall soon be ranked with others that heretofore have deluded 'em with such promises, and shall have no more credit with them. But now I must wait for new instructions from Mr. Hollis; and you see, sir, how long it has been in times past before we could have any new instructions from him. For five or six years past, his letters have not arrived but about once in two years. And we find it is commonly two or three months before we can have a return from Boston. I can't but think Mr. Hollis will be grieved when he comes to understand the state of things; and will be ready to blame us for needless and excessive caution, when he comes to understand the bad consequences of it.

This affair comes into my hands under the most difficult, perplexed circumstance imaginable, just as all was falling into ruin, etc. You was pleased sir, in your former letter kindly to warn me against triumphing on the receipt of Mr. Hollis' letter—I took the caution well. But really, at present, I have much greater temptation to be heartily sorry, that I have any concern in a matter embarrassed with so many discouraging, perplexing circumstances, than to triumph in it. . . .

And pray for me sir, that I may have the divine assistance in the difficult affairs which lie so heavy on my feeble shoulders. I am, honored sir,

> Your most respectful son and servant,
> Jonathan Edwards

To the Trustees of the College of New Jersey

Stockbridge, Oct. 19, 1757

Reverend and Honored Gentlemen,

I was not a little surprised, on receiving the unexpected notice of your having made choice of me to succeed the late President Burr,[31] as the head of Nassau Hall. I am much in doubt whether I am called to undertake the business, which you have done me the unmerited honor to choose me for. If some regard may be had to my outward comfort, I might mention the many inconveniencies and great detriment, which must be sustained, by my removing with my numerous family, so far from all the estate I have in the world (without any prospect of disposing of it, under present circumstances, without losing it, in great part), now when we have scarcely got over the trouble and damage sustained by our removal from Northampton, and have but just begun to have our affairs in a comfortable situation, for a subsistence in this place; and the expense I must immediately be at to put myself into circumstances tolerably comporting with the needful support of the honors of the office I am invited to; which will not well consist with my ability.

But this is not my main objection: the chief difficulty in my mind, in the way of accepting this important and arduous office, are these two: first my own defects, unfitting me for such an undertaking, many of which are generally known; besides others, which my own heart is conscious to. I have a constitution in many respects peculiar unhappy, attended with flaccid solids, vapid, sizy and scarce fluids, and a low tide of spirits; often occasioning a kind of childish weakness and contemptibleness of speech, presence and demeanor; with a disagreeable dullness and stiffness, much unfitting me for conversation, but more especially for the government of a college. This poorness of constitution makes me shrink at the thoughts of taking upon me, in the decline of life, such a new and great business, attended with such a multiplicity of cares, and requiring such a degree of activity, alertness and spirit of government; especially as succeeding one, so remarkably well qualified in these respects, giving occasion to everyone

31. Rev. Aaron Burr, Edwards' son-in-law, who died September 27, 1757.

to remark the wide difference. I am also deficient in some parts of learning, particularly in algebra, and the higher parts of mathematics, and in the Greek classics; my Greek learning having been chiefly in the New Testament. The other thing is this; that my engaging in this business, will not well consist, with those views, and that course of employ in my study, which have long engaged, and swallowed up my mind, and been the chief entertainment and delight of my life.

And here, honored sirs (emboldened by the testimony, I have now received of your unmerited esteem, to rely on your candor), I will with freedom open myself to you.

My method of study, from my first beginning the work of the ministry, has been very much by writing; applying myself in this way, to improve every important hint; pursuing the clue to my utmost, when anything in reading, meditation or conversation, has been suggested to my mind, that seemed to promise light, in any weighty point—thus penning what appeared to me my best thoughts, on innumerable subjects, for my own benefit. The longer I prosecuted my studies in this method, the more habitual it became, and the more pleasant and profitable I found it. The further I traveled in this way, the more and wider the field opened, which has occasioned my laying out many things, in my mind, to do in this manner, if God should spare my life, which my heart hath been much upon: particularly many things against most of the prevailing errors of the present day, which I cannot with any patience see maintained (to the utter subverting of the gospel of Christ) with so high a hand, and so long continued a triumph, with so little control, when it appears so evident to me, that there is truly no foundation for any of this glorying and insult. I have already published something on one of the main points in dispute between the Arminians and Calvinists:[32] and have it in view, God willing (as I have already signified to the public), in like manner to consider all the other controverted points, and have done much towards a preparation for it. But besides these, I have had on my mind and heart (which I long ago began, not with any view to publication) a great work, which I call *A History of the Work of Redemption*, a body of divinity in an entire new

32. *Freedom of the Will*, published in 1754.

method, being thrown into the form of an history, considering the affair of Christian theology, as the whole of it, in each part, stands in reference to the great work of redemption by Jesus Christ; which I suppose is to be the grand design, of all God's designs, and the *summum* and *ultimum* of all the divine operations and decrees; particularly considering all parts of the grand scheme in their historical order. The order of their existence, or their being brought forth to view, in the course of divine dispensations, or the wonderful series of successive acts and events; beginning from eternity and descending from thence to the great work and successive dispensations of the infinitely wise God in time, considering the chief events coming to pass in the church of God, and revolutions in the world of mankind, affecting the state of the church and the affair of redemption, which we have account of in history or prophecy; till at last we come to the general resurrection, last judgment, and consummation of all things; when it shall be said, "It is done. I am Alpha and Omega, the beginning and the end" [Rev. 21:6]. Concluding my work, with the consideration of that perfect state of things, which shall be finally settled, to last for eternity. This history will be carried on with regard to all three worlds, heaven, earth and hell: considering the connected, successive events and alterations, in each so far as the Scriptures give any light; introducing all parts of divinity in that order which is most scriptural and most natural: which is a method which appears to me the most beautiful and entertaining, wherein every divine doctrine, will appear to greatest advantage in the brightest light, in the most striking manner, showing the admirable contexture and harmony of the whole.

I have also for my own profit and entertainment, done much towards another great work, which I call *The Harmony of the Old and New Testaments* in three parts. The first considering the prophecies of the Messiah, his redemption and kingdom; the evidences of their references to the Messiah, etc. comparing them all one with another, demonstrating their agreement and true scope and sense; also considering all the various particulars wherein these prophecies have their exact fulfillment; showing the universal, precise, and admirable correspondence between predictions and events. The second part: considering the types of the Old Testament, showing the evidence of their being intended as representations of the

great things of the gospel of Christ: and the agreement of the type with
the antitype. The third and great part, considering the harmony of the
Old and New Testaments, as to doctrine and precept. In the course of this
work, I find there will be occasion for an explanation of a very great part of
the holy Scripture; which may, in such a view be explained in a method,
which to me seems the most entertaining and profitable, best tending to
lead the mind to a view of the true spirit, design, life and soul of the
Scriptures, as well as to their proper use and improvement.

I have also many other things in hand, in some of which I have made
great progress, which I will not trouble you with an account of. Some of
these things, if divine providence favor, I should be willing to attempt a
publication of. So far as I myself am able to judge of what talents I have,
for benefiting my fellow creatures by word, I think I can write better than I
can speak.

My heart is so much in these studies, that I cannot find it in my heart to
be willing to put myself into an incapacity to pursue them any more, in the
future part of my life, to such a degree as I must, if I undertake to go
through the same course of employ, in the office of a president, that Mr.
Burr did, instructing in all the languages, and taking the whole care of the
instruction of one of the classes in all parts of learning, besides his other
labors. If I should see light to determine me to accept the place offered me,
I should be willing to take upon me the work of a president, so far as it
consists in the general inspection of the whole Society and subservient to
the school, as to their order and methods of study and instruction, assisting myself in immediate instruction in the arts and sciences (as discretion
should direct and occasion serve, and the state of things require), especially the senior class: and added to all, should be willing to do the whole
work of a professor of divinity, in public and private lectures, proposing
questions to be answered, and some to be discussed in writing and free
conversation, in meetings of graduates and others, appointed in proper
seasons for these ends. It would be now out of my way, to spend time, in a
constant teaching of the languages; unless it be the Hebrew tongue, which
I should be willing to improve myself in, by instructing others.

On the whole, I am much at a loss, with respect to the way of my duty in
this important affair: I am in doubt, whether if I should engage in it, I

should not do what both you and I should be sorry for afterwards. Nevertheless, I think the greatness of the affair, and the regard due to so worthy and venerable a body, as that of the Trustees of Nassau Hall, requires my taking the matter into serious consideration: and unless you should appear to be discouraged, by the things which I have now represented, as to any further expectation from me, shall proceed to ask advice, of such as I esteem most wise, friendly and faithful; if after the mind of the commissioners in Boston is known, it appears that they consent to leave me at liberty, with respect to the business they have employed me in here. . . .

[Jonathan Edwards]

Index